Essentials

Autodesk® CFD 2017

July 2016

AUTODESK.
Authorized Publisher

Contents

Introduction

Welcome to the *Autodesk® CFD 2017 Essentials* student guide, for use in Authorized Training Center (ATC®) locations, corporate training settings, and other classroom settings.

Although this student guide is designed for instructor-led courses, you can also use it for self-paced learning.

This introduction covers the following topics:

- Course Description
- Prerequisites
- Using This Student Guide
- Downloading and Installing the Exercise Files
- Feedback
- Free Autodesk Software for Students and Educators

This student guide is complementary to the software documentation. For detailed explanations of features and functionality, refer to the Help in the software.

Course Description

The *Autodesk® CFD 2017 Essentials* student guide instructs students in the use of the Autodesk® CFD software. The software provides computational fluid dynamics and thermal simulation tools to predict product performance, optimize designs, and validate product behavior before manufacturing. Through a hands-on, practice-intensive curriculum, students acquire the knowledge required to work in the Autodesk CFD environment to setup and conduct thermal and flow analyses on part and assembly models. Exercises are provided that cover electronic cooling, flow control, and AEC type models.

This guide covers the following topics:

- Open and navigate the Autodesk CFD environment to conduct flow and thermal analyses on part and assembly models.
- Use the Model Assessment Toolkit to investigate the suitability of model geometry for analysis and use Autodesk® SimStudio Tools to make required changes to the CAD geometry.
- Create internal and external fluid volumes.
- Setup analyses by applying appropriate materials, boundary conditions, and mesh settings.
- Refine mesh to obtain a proper solution.
- Apply appropriate solver settings to run your analyses and converge to an acceptable solution.
- Use the visualization tools to compare summary images, summary values, and summary plots of your analyses to compare design and scenario results of an Autodesk CFD analysis.
- Conduct a final validation of your solution by running through a validation checklist.

Prerequisites

This student guide assumes that a student has some Flow and Thermal analysis knowledge and can interpret results. The main goal of this student guide is to teach a user that is new to the Autodesk® CFD software how to navigate the interface to successfully analyze a model.

This student guide was written using the 20160317 build of the Autodesk® CFD 2017 software. The software user-interface and workflow may vary if newer versions of the software are being used. The exercises were completed using the advanced solver license. Instructions are provided to complete this class with a basic solver license.

Using This Student Guide

The lessons are generally independent of each other. It is recommended that you complete the lessons in the student guide in the order that they are presented, unless you are familiar with the concepts and functionality described in those lessons.

Each chapter contains:

- **Lessons** - Usually two or more lessons in each chapter.
- **Exercises** - Practical, real-world examples for you to practice using the functionality you have just learned. Each exercise contains step-by-step procedures and graphics to help you complete the exercise successfully.
    - If a chapter's secondary exercise is dependent on a prior exercise, a prepared class file is provided for you. It will have all of the previous exercises' steps completed for you.
    - Depending on the analysis and computer resources, it can take some time to run.

Downloading and Installing the Exercise Files

The Exercise Files page in this student guide contains a link and instructions on how to download and install all of the data required to complete the exercises.

Feedback

Autodesk understands the importance of offering you the best learning experience possible. If you have comments, suggestions, or general inquiries about Autodesk Learning, please contact us at learningtools@autodesk.com.

As a result of the feedback we receive from you, we hope to validate and append to our current research on how to create a better learning experience for our customers.

Free Autodesk Software for Students and Educators

The Autodesk Education Community is an online resource with more than five million members that enables educators and students to download for free the same software used by professionals worldwide (see website for terms and conditions). You can also access additional tools and materials to help you design, visualize, and simulate ideas. Connect with other learners to stay current with the latest industry trends and get the most out of your designs.

Get started today. Register at the Autodesk Education Community (www.autodesk.com/joinedu) and download one of the many available Autodesk software applications.

Note: Free products are subject to the terms and conditions of the end-user license and services agreement that accompanies the software. The software is for personal use for education purposes only and is not intended for classroom or lab use.

Exercise Files

To download the exercise files for this student guide, use the following steps:

1. Type the URL shown in the following image into the address bar of your Internet browser. The URL must be typed **exactly as shown**. If you are using an ASCENT ebook, you can click on the link to download the file.

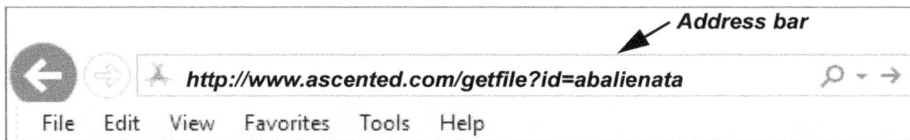

Address bar

http://www.ascented.com/getfile?id=abalienata

File   Edit   View   Favorites   Tools   Help

2. Press <Enter> to download the .ZIP file that contains the Exercise Files.

3. Once the download is complete, unzip the file to a local folder. The unzipped file contains an .EXE file.

4. Double-click on the .EXE file and follow the instructions to automatically install the Exercise Files on the C:\ drive of your computer.

   Do not change the location in which the Exercise Files folder is installed. Doing so can cause errors when completing the exercises in this student guide.

http://www.ascented.com/getfile?id=abalienata

Getting Started

A Computational Fluid Dynamics (CFD) simulation is a computerized method for predicting how a model reacts to fluid and thermal dynamics once it is manufactured/built and working in a real-world environment. Autodesk® CFD plays a key role in the design and development of a product and provides tools that enable you to study CFD to improve designs. Autodesk CFD enables users to integrate analysis directly as a stage in the modeling workflow. This chapter introduces digital prototyping, the basics of CFD simulation, and explains how Autodesk CFD can be used to analyze your models and to make educated decisions on whether this anticipated reaction meets design requirements.

Objectives

After completing this chapter, you will be able to:

- Describe how to use the Autodesk CFD in the design of products in a digital prototyping workflow.
- Describe the Design Study Bar nodes available in an Autodesk CFD simulation.
- Navigate the model in the graphics window using the ViewCube, Navigation Bar, and Navigation panel controls.
- Hide/Unhide geometry in the model, as required, to permit easy interaction with the model.
- List the file formats generated when you run an Autodesk CFD Design Study simulation.
- Describe the general steps in the Autodesk CFD workflow.
- Describe the best use of the Autodesk CFD software in the overall design cycle.

Lesson: Introduction to CFD

Overview

This lesson provides an overview of digital prototyping and explains how to use the Autodesk CFD software in the testing and validation stage of a product's development. Additionally, it provides an overview of Computational Fluid Dynamics (CFD) and explains how using Autodesk CFD can predict a design's performance before it is ever built. The inclusion of CFD in the design workflow enables designers to anticipate how the model will react and to make educated decisions on whether this anticipated reaction meets design requirements.

Objectives

After completing this lesson, you will be able to:

- Describe how to use the Autodesk CFD in the design of products in a digital prototyping workflow.

Introduction to Digital Prototyping

Digital prototyping enables you to explore your design ideas before they are even built. Traditional design environments provide individual tools that are used to develop each phase in a design independently. Using the intelligent, model-based approach of digital prototyping, integrated tools are used throughout the design process. You can explore design ideas, gather design data from all phases of the process into a single digital model, validate it against product requirements, and reference all of the data as you build deliverables for release. The process enables team members to collaborate across disciplines, with the aim of getting better products to market faster. From concept through design, manufacturing, marketing and beyond, the digital prototyping software solutions provided by Autodesk streamline the product development process from start to finish.

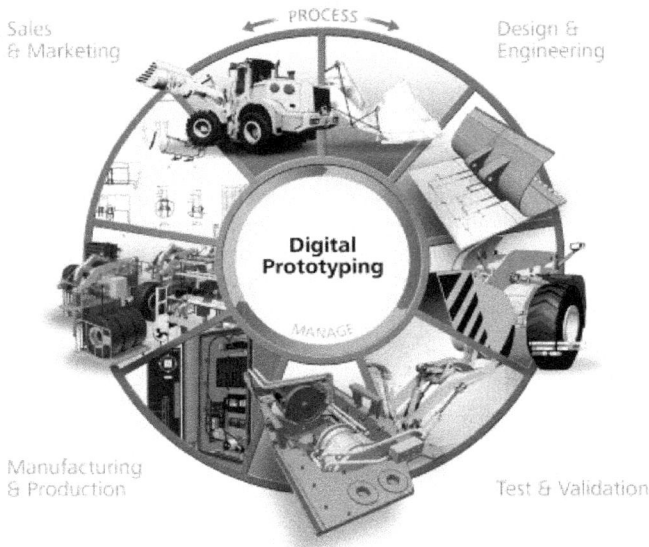

Computational Fluid Dynamics (CFD)

The Test and Validation phase is a key phase in the digital prototyping cycle and can involve the use of CFD tools among others. Fluids affect the performance of just about every widget, device, and structure. CFD is an important part of the design process and benefits areas such as energy efficiency, risk reduction, and spark innovation. The overall goals for the use of Autodesk CFD tools enable you to:

- Explore design options early in the design cycle, inspiring questions and critical thinking that leads to innovative design.
- Reduce energy consumption and improve efficiency.
- Reduce risk by catching and solving various issues before they become serious problems.
- Validate designs to predict performance before creating and testing expensive prototypes.

Autodesk CFD Solutions

With the purchase/installation of your CFD software solution, you are provided with the following:

- Design study environment - This provides access to the software user interface.
- Solver License - There are three tiers of solver licenses available: Autodesk® CFD (Basic), Autodesk® CFD Advanced, and Autodesk® CFD Motion; each of which unlocks different solver functionality.
- The Autodesk® SimStudio Tools is an application installed by default with the CFD software options. It can be used as a tool in the workflow to create CAD surface and solid models as well as to simplify or repair existing CAD models. Regardless of the original source of the CAD data, this tool can be used and the file can be transferred back to CFD for analysis.

This student guide concentrates on the basic functionality and workflow when using CFD. Autodesk SimStudio Tools will be discussed briefly, focusing on how it can be used in the design workflow.

Why use Computational Fluid Dynamics (CFD)

Computational Fluid Dynamics (CFD) is a computerized method for predicting how a product reacts to real-world fluid flow and heat transfer. Fluid flow is the study of how liquids and gases move in and around solid objects. Heat Transfer is the study of how things get hot or cold, and why. With CFD analysis, you can understand the flow and heat transfer throughout your design process and make educated design decisions. The following are just a few common applications in which CFD analyses are frequently used.

- Wind resistance of a car or motorcycle

- Pressure drop through a valve

- Component temperatures in an electronics enclosure

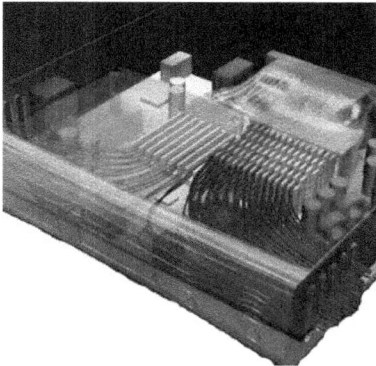

- Comfort of people in a crowded meeting hall

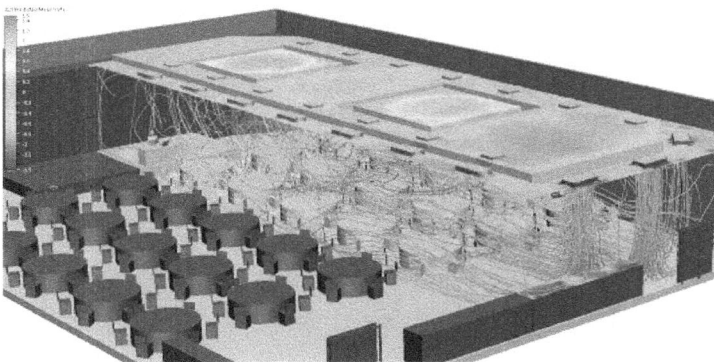

Theory Behind CFD

The partial differential equations governing fluid flow and heat transfer include the continuity equations, the Navier-Stokes equations, and the energy equations. These equations are incredibly complex (shown in the following image) and very difficult to solve. This complexity has led to a software revolution that uses computers to predict the behavior of liquids and gases and how they work with the designed products. Autodesk CFD solves the following equations for you.

- Continuity Equations

$$\frac{\partial \rho}{\partial t} + \frac{\partial \rho u}{\partial x} + \frac{\partial \rho v}{\partial y} + \frac{\partial \rho w}{\partial z} = 0$$

- Navier-Stokes or Momentum Equations

  X-Momentum Equation:

  $$\rho \frac{\partial u}{\partial t} + \rho u \frac{\partial u}{\partial x} + \rho v \frac{\partial u}{\partial y} + \rho w \frac{\partial u}{\partial z}$$

  $$= \rho g_x - \frac{\partial p}{\partial x} + \frac{\partial}{\partial x}\left[2\mu \frac{\partial u}{\partial x}\right] + \frac{\partial}{\partial y}\left[\mu\left(\frac{\partial u}{\partial y} + \frac{\partial v}{\partial x}\right)\right] + \frac{\partial}{\partial z}\left[\mu\left(\frac{\partial u}{\partial z} + \frac{\partial w}{\partial x}\right)\right] + S_\omega + S_{DR}$$

  Y-Momentum Equation:

  $$\rho \frac{\partial v}{\partial t} + \rho u \frac{\partial v}{\partial x} + \rho v \frac{\partial v}{\partial y} + \rho w \frac{\partial v}{\partial z}$$

  $$= \rho g_y - \frac{\partial p}{\partial y} + \frac{\partial}{\partial x}\left[\mu\left(\frac{\partial u}{\partial y} + \frac{\partial v}{\partial x}\right)\right] + \frac{\partial}{\partial y}\left[2\mu \frac{\partial v}{\partial y}\right] + \frac{\partial}{\partial z}\left[\mu\left(\frac{\partial v}{\partial z} + \frac{\partial w}{\partial y}\right)\right] + S_\omega + S_{DR}$$

  Z-Momentum Equation:

  $$\rho \frac{\partial w}{\partial t} + \rho u \frac{\partial w}{\partial x} + \rho v \frac{\partial w}{\partial y} + \rho w \frac{\partial w}{\partial z}$$

  $$= \rho g_z - \frac{\partial p}{\partial z} + \frac{\partial}{\partial x}\left[\mu\left(\frac{\partial u}{\partial z} + \frac{\partial w}{\partial x}\right)\right] + \frac{\partial}{\partial y}\left[\mu\left(\frac{\partial v}{\partial z} + \frac{\partial w}{\partial y}\right)\right] + \frac{\partial}{\partial z}\left[2\mu \frac{\partial w}{\partial z}\right] + S_\omega + S_{DR}$$

- Energy Equation (incompressible and subsonic compressible flow, written in terms of static temperature)

  $$\rho C_p \frac{\partial T}{\partial t} + \rho C_p u \frac{\partial T}{\partial x} + \rho C_p v \frac{\partial T}{\partial y} + \rho C_p w \frac{\partial T}{\partial z} = \frac{\partial}{\partial x}\left[k\frac{\partial T}{\partial x}\right] + \frac{\partial}{\partial y}\left[k\frac{\partial T}{\partial y}\right] + \frac{\partial}{\partial z}\left[k\frac{\partial T}{\partial z}\right] + q_V$$

- Energy Equation (multi-phase flows, such as steam/water, written in terms of enthalpy)

  $$\rho \frac{\partial h}{\partial t} + \rho u \frac{\partial h}{\partial x} + \rho v \frac{\partial h}{\partial y} + \rho w \frac{\partial h}{\partial z} = \frac{\partial}{\partial x}\left[k\frac{\partial T}{\partial x}\right] + \frac{\partial}{\partial y}\left[k\frac{\partial T}{\partial y}\right] + \frac{\partial}{\partial z}\left[k\frac{\partial T}{\partial z}\right] + q_V$$

- Energy equation (compressible flow, written in terms of total temperature) - where Φ is the dissipation function. Note that Einstein tensor notation is used for the total energy equation for conciseness. The last three terms are only present for compressible flows.

  $$\rho C_p \left(\frac{\partial T_0}{\partial t}\right) + \rho C_p V_i\left(\frac{\partial T_0}{\partial X_i}\right) = \frac{\partial}{\partial X_i}\left[k\frac{\partial T_0}{\partial X_i}\right] + q_V$$

  $$+ \mu V_i\left[\frac{\partial^2 V_i}{\partial X_j \partial X_j} + \frac{\partial}{\partial X_i}\frac{\partial V_j}{\partial X_j}\right] + \frac{1}{2C_P}\frac{\partial}{\partial X_j}\left[k\frac{\partial}{\partial X_j}(V_j V_j)\right] + \Phi$$

The variables in these equations are defined as follows:

Variable	Description
Cp	constant pressure specific heat
gx, gy, gz	gravitational acceleration in x, y, z directions
h	enthalpy
k	thermal conductivity
p	pressure
qV	volumetric heat source
T	temperature
t	time
u	velocity component in x-direction
v	velocity component in y-direction
w	velocity component in z-direction
μ	viscosity
ρ	density

Lesson: Getting Started in Autodesk CFD

The layout of the ribbon, tabs, and panels in the Autodesk CFD software is similar to other Autodesk software products. In this lesson, you will learn how to use the Design Study Bar, which is the key component of the interface. This tree-based tool is used for defining and managing all aspects of the Autodesk CFD process. You will also learn to navigate your model, control its appearance, and use the Autodesk CFD interface to initiate commands.

Objectives

After completing this lesson, you will be able to:

- Describe the Design Study Bar nodes available in an Autodesk CFD simulation.
- Navigate the model in the graphics window using the ViewCube, Navigation Bar, and Navigation panel controls.
- Hide/Unhide geometry in the model, as required, to permit easy interaction with the model.
- List the file formats generated when you run an Autodesk CFD Design Study simulation.

Autodesk CFD User Interface

There are several key areas in the Autodesk CFD software that are used to create new design studies, setup the properties for a scenario, manipulate the model, and review the output. Many of the Autodesk CFD software tools can be located in multiple areas, for example in both the ribbon and the shortcut menu. As you become more familiar with the software, you will start using workflows that best suit your needs. The key areas of the software are described below:

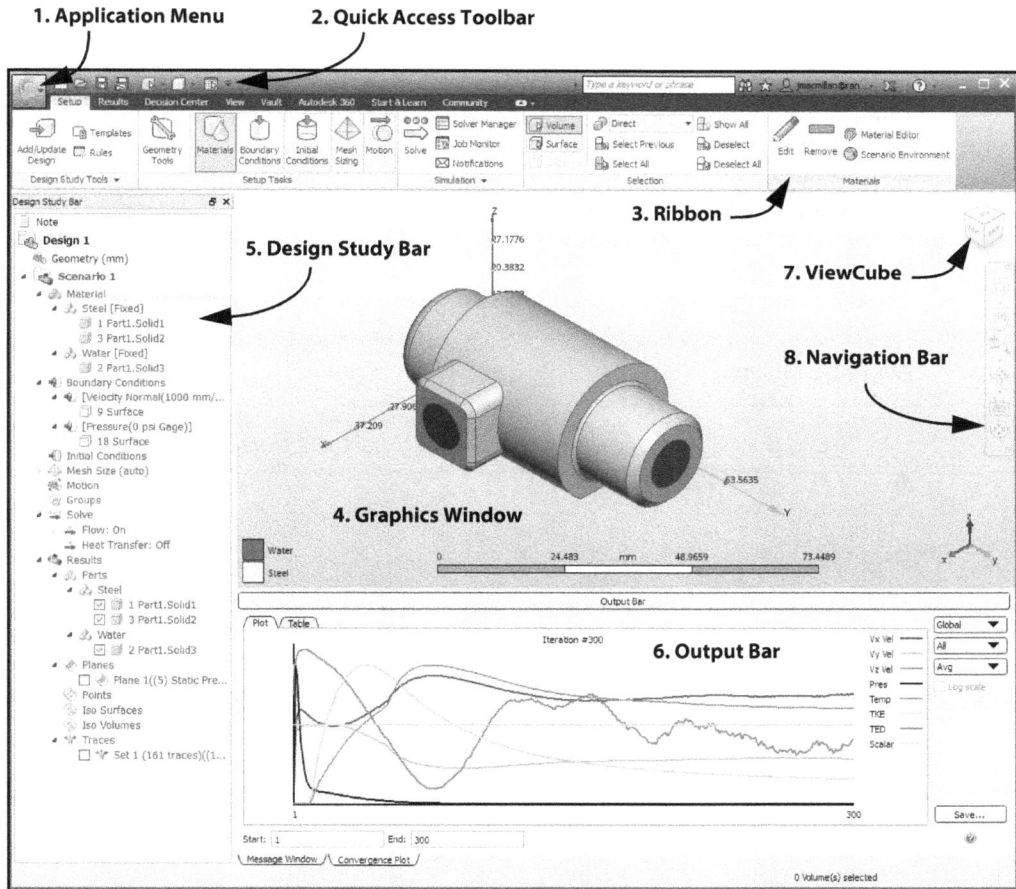

Application Menu (1)

The Application Menu provides access to commonly accessed tools. To access its commands, click

in the top left corner of the Autodesk CFD software. The commands available in this menu include: file actions (New, Open, Save, and Save As), Export commands, as well as access to Vault and

the Print command. In this menu, Options provides access to the User Interface Preferences dialog box which enables you to customize the global settings.

Quick Access Toolbar (2)

At the top of the application window, the Quick Access Toolbar displays frequently used commands from the ribbon and the Application Menu.

- A default set of commands have been included in the Quick Access Toolbar. To enable/disable these defaults, click ▼ at the end of the Quick Access Toolbar and select the commands to be included.
- You can add an unlimited number of buttons to the Quick Access Toolbar by selecting the command on its tab, right-clicking, and selecting Add to Quick Access Toolbar. New buttons are added to the right of the default commands.
- You can add separators between the buttons to subdivide the commands. To add a separator, right-click on the Quick Access Toolbar in the location where the separator is required, and select Add Separator. Separators can be removed by right-clicking on them and selecting Remove from Quick Access Toolbar.
- You can position the Quick Access Toolbar either above or below the ribbon. To move its position, click ▼ at the end of the Quick Access Toolbar and select either Show Below the Ribbon or Show Above the Ribbon.

> Only commands on the ribbon can be added to the Quick Access Toolbar. Commands that extend past the maximum length of the toolbar display as flyouts.

Ribbon (3)

The ribbon is the area at the top of the software window that displays task-based tools and controls. Similar to many Autodesk software products, the Autodesk CFD ribbon contains multiple tabs and panels. The panels contain all the commands required to setup, run, and visualize the results of a simulation. To activate a command on the ribbon, simply navigate to the tab and panel and select the command.

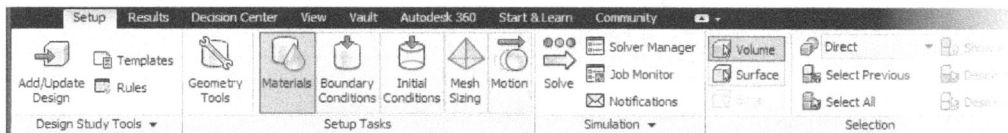

- In general, the tabs and panels in the Autodesk CFD ribbon are listed in the same order as the general workflow that is used to conduct a simulation (left to right).
- When some commands are activated, context-sensitive panels might be added to the ribbon. This means that they are only displayed when required. For example, when defining the materials, only the panels that pertain to defining materials display. When the boundary conditions are being defined, the material panels are removed from the display.

- Expandable panels, indicated with the ▼ icon in the panel name, contain additional options that, by default, are not available in the main panel. Select the panel heading to access these options.

- Every command on a toolbar includes a tooltip, which describes the function the button activates. Hovering the cursor over a button displays a brief instruction on how to use this feature.

You can customize the ribbon depending on your needs in the following ways:

- To specify which tabs and panels will display, right-click on the ribbon, and on the shortcut menu, click or clear the names of the tabs or panels. Only certain tabs and panels can be removed.

- You can change the order of the tabs by clicking the tab you want to move, dragging it to the required position, and releasing.

- You can change the order of the panels by clicking the panel you want to move, dragging it to the required position, and releasing.

- You can control the amount of space the ribbon takes in the application window. There are two buttons to the right of the tabs on the ribbon, that enable you to choose the ribbon toggle and ribbon minimize states. Click ⬚ to cycle between the minimized ribbon states. Once fully compressed, click ⬚ to resume the full ribbon display state. The minimize ribbon states enable you to minimize to tabs only, minimize to panel titles only, and minimize to panel buttons only. The ⬚ drop-down enables you to control which of the states can be accessed while cycling.

> 💡 Throughout this student guide, the tabs, panels and commands will be discussed in more depth.

Graphics Window (4)

The Graphics Window is the area of the interface where the model is viewed. All interaction with the model is done here.

> 💡 To change the background color in the Autodesk CFD Graphics window, on the View Tab, in the Appearance panel, click ⬚ (Background). Use the Background Color dialog box to select and assign the new color.

Design Study Bar (5)

The Design Study Bar is a fully interactive tree-based tool for defining and managing all aspects of the Autodesk CFD process. The Design Study Bar follows a hierarchical structure that organizes the simulation process into three fundamental levels--Design Study, Design, and Scenario. You use the Design Study Bar to manage all aspects of the design study including renaming, copying (cloning), and deleting scenarios and designs. It is not recommend to perform these tasks through the file system.

Each design study contains at least one design (specific CAD geometry) and each design contains at least one Scenario, which is a collection of materials, boundary conditions, and mesh settings, along with the associated analysis results. When active, designs are listed in bold black letters and scenarios are shown in bold blue letters. The setup assignments and results are listed in thin blue letters in each scenario.

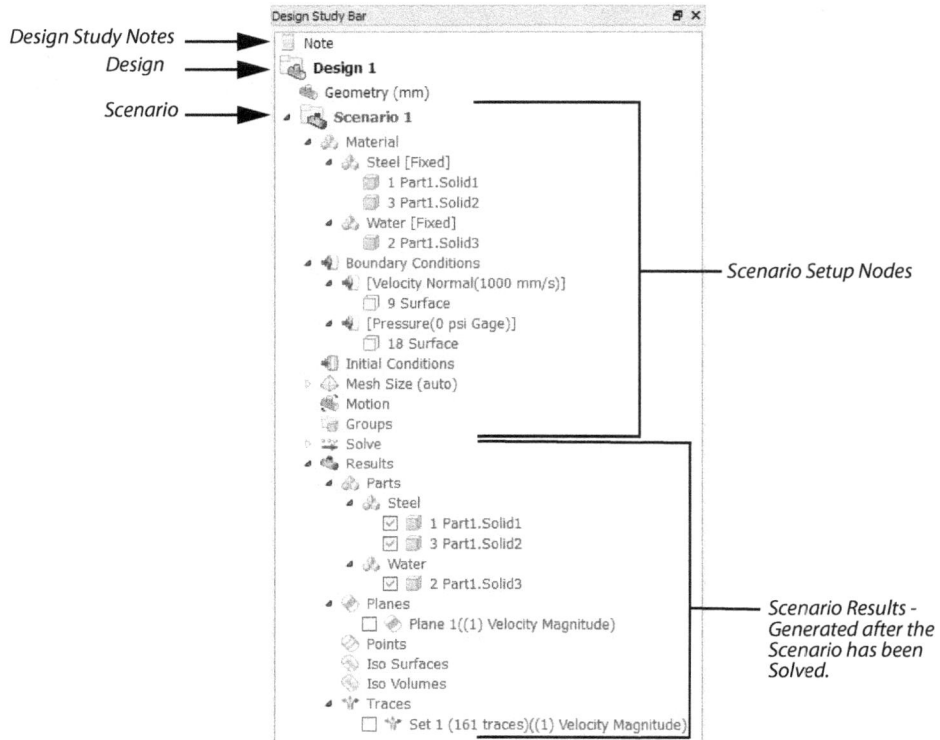

Keeping accurate records about each scenario is very important, especially when comparing a large number of designs and scenarios. Recording specific conditions, as well as any adjustments and important findings, is key to repeatability and organization of a large project. Consider using the Note file (Rich-Text editor) that is available with every Design Study to record this information.

To open the Note file:

- Double-click on the Note branch at the top of the Design Study Bar.
- Right-click on the Note branch at the top of the Design Study Bar and click Edit.

Design

A design is a unique geometric model, and is referenced by one or more scenarios. At a minimum, there is one design in every design study. By right-clicking the Design node in the Design Study Bar, you can access a context menu that enables you to do the following:

- Activate a design if multiple designs exist in the design study.
- Rename the Design.
- Copy a design (Clone) so that its settings can be reused for a new design.
- Create a new scenario in the design.
- Delete an existing design from the design study. This is only possible if there are multiple designs in the study.
- Save the design as a template so that the current settings are retained for reuse.
- Apply a template to a design.

Geometry

The geometry studied in a design is assigned either when a new Design Study is created or if a new design is created in the overall Design Study. There are three essential functions that can be performed using the Geometry branch in the Design, which can be accessed by right-clicking the Geometry branch in the Design Study Bar. They enable you to do the following:

- Set the analysis length units.
- Create an internal or external volume using the geometry tools.
- Set the coordinate system for 2D models.

> These geometry tools will be discussed throughout this student guide, when applicable.

Scenario

A scenario is an individual analysis. Every scenario that references a design is based on the same geometry model, but can have different settings (boundary conditions, materials, etc.). At a minimum, every design contains one scenario. All of the nodes in a Scenario define the settings that are assigned to the geometry and that will be tested in the simulation. By right-clicking the Scenario node in the Design Study Bar, you can access a context menu that enables you to do the following:

- Activate a scenario if multiple scenarios exist in the design study.
- Rename the scenario.
- Copy a scenario (Clone) so that its settings can be reused for a scenario.
- Delete an existing scenario from the Design. This is only possible if there are multiple scenarios.
- Generate the mesh for the scenario.
- Solve the design scenario.

Once a scenario is solved, the Results node displays in the Scenario. If a setting is changed after a scenario is solved, the results are no longer current with the model setup. The out of date icons display on the Scenario ( ) and Results ( ) branches, indicating that the simulation should be rerun.

> The specific nodes that exist in a Scenario will be discussed throughout this student guide as you learn how to apply each setup task.

Output Bar (6)

The Output bar is the primary communication area of Autodesk CFD. Status messages and errors are written to the Message window during several critical stages of the simulation process, (model loading, during simulation, and at simulation completion).

In addition to the Message Window, the Output bar is used to display the following:

- Simulation progress in the Convergence Plot
- Summary Values
- Summary Images

> The Output Bar will be discussed in more depth later in this student guide.

ViewCube (7)

The ViewCube is used to reorient the current view of a model. You can reorient the view of a model with the ViewCube tool by clicking predefined areas on the ViewCube to assign preset views, click and drag on the ViewCube to freely change the view angle of the model, and define and restore the Home view.

- The ViewCube tool has twenty-six defined areas to click and change the current view of a model. The twenty-six defined areas are categorized into three groups: corner, edge, and face. Of the twenty-six defined areas, six represent standard orthogonal views of a model: top, bottom, front, back, left, and right. Orthogonal views are set by clicking one of the faces on the ViewCube tool. The other twenty defined areas are used to access angled views of a model. Clicking one of the corners on the ViewCube tool reorients the current view of the model to a three-quarter view, based on a viewpoint defined by three sides of the model. Clicking one of the edges reorients the view of the model to a half view based on two sides of the model.

> When the cursor is over one of the clickable areas of the ViewCube tool, the clickable face, corner, or edge highlights and the cursor changes to an arrow with a small cube to indicate that it is over the ViewCube tool. A tooltip also displays. The tooltip describes the action that you can perform based on the location of the cursor over the ViewCube tool.

- You can also click and drag the ViewCube tool to reorient the view of a model to a custom view other than one of the twenty-six predefined parts. As you drag, the cursor changes to indicate that you are reorienting the current view of the model. If you drag the ViewCube tool close to one of the preset orientations, and it is set to snap to the closest view, the ViewCube tool rotates to the closest preset orientation.

> The outline of the ViewCube tool helps you identify the form of orientation it is in: standard or fixed. When the ViewCube tool is in standard orientation (i.e., not orientated to one of the twenty-six predefined parts) its outline displays as dashed. The ViewCube tool is outlined in a solid continuous line when it is constrained to one of the predefined views.

- When you view a model from one of the face views, two roll arrow buttons display near the ViewCube tool. Use the roll arrows to rotate the current view 90 degrees clockwise or counterclockwise around the center of the view.
- When the ViewCube tool is active while viewing a model from one of the face views, four orthogonal triangles display near the ViewCube tool. You use these triangles to switch to one of the adjacent face views.
- Clicking in the top right corner of the ViewCube reorients the Scene View to its default orientation and zoom level.

Additional ViewCube options can be accessed by clicking in the bottom left corner of the ViewCube. These options enable you to define the view setting, the Home and Front orientations, as well as access its properties.

The display of the ViewCube can be set in the View tab by enabling/disabling the Show View Cube option in the User Interface drop-down list.

Navigation Bar (8)

The Navigation bar is a user interface element that enables you to access both unified and product-specific navigation tools. Unified navigation tools (such as Autodesk® ViewCube® and SteeringWheels®) are those that can be found across many Autodesk products. Product-specific navigation tools are unique to a product. The navigation bar floats over and along one of the sides of the graphics window.

You can control the display of the Navigation bar on the View tab, in the User Interface drop-down list in the Window panel, by selecting/deselecting the Show Navigation Bar option. The options in the Navigation Bar are described as follows:

Icon	Name	Description
	Full Navigation Wheel	The Navigation wheel contains common 3D navigation tools used for both viewing models. There are two sizes of wheels, full and mini. You can expand the current command in the Navigation Bar to gain access to and enable an alternate navigation wheel. Although the display of the two wheels vary, the commands on each are similar. You can zoom in or out, pan or orbit around a the model, rewind between views, or center around a selected point.
	Pan	Drag in any direction to move the camera correspondingly. Hold <Shift> and the middle mouse button to temporarily switch to Orbit (rotate).
	Zoom	Drag up or down to move the camera in and out along the axis of the focal point.
	Zoom (Window)	Click and drag a box over an area on the scene to zoom into the bounding area.
	Zoom (Displayed)	Zoom in to the displayed items in the graphics window.
	Zoom (Fit All)	Fit the complete model into the graphics window.
	Orbit	Orbit (rotate) the camera around the focal point; drag in any direction to orbit correspondingly. Orbit mode resets the world up vector. Press the middle mouse button to temporarily change to Pan.
	Orbit (Constrained)	Spin the model as if it is sitting on a turntable.
	Look At	Looks at a particular face in the scene. The camera orients so that the selected face is centered and parallel with the screen.
	Focus	Focus an item to the center of the scene window. Select, then click on an item to center it.

The Navigate panel in the View tab provides an alternative method for accessing the pan, zoom, spin, and orienting tools. The only command that is not available in the Navigation Bar or in the ViewCube is the ⌐⌐⌐ (Previous) command. This command provides a quick and convenient way to return to the model's last view orientation.

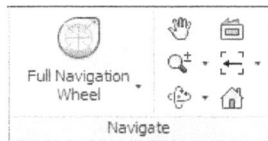

Full Navigation Wheel

Navigate

Additional Interface Tools

The Autodesk CFD interface also includes dialog boxes, shortcut context menus, and the mini-toolbar. These are used when working with the software.

- Dialog boxes, similar to the Solve dialog box shown in the following image, display when defining the simulation. In general, they look similar and enable you to define options.

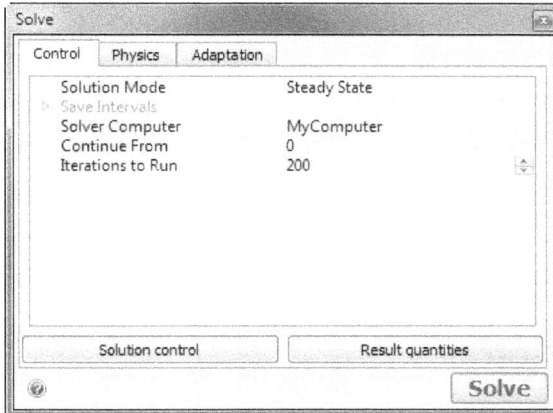

- When right-clicking on the model or in the graphics window, a context-sensitive menu displays. This menu only provides the applicable options for the current task.

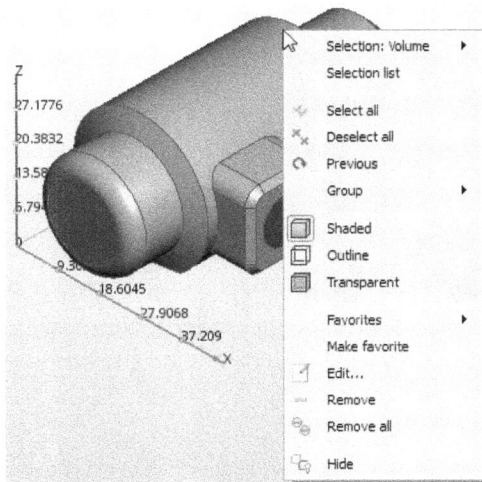

- When left-clicking on the model, the mini-toolbar displays. You can select the icons in the mini-toolbar to activate commands. Hover the cursor over the icons to display a tooltip to help identify the command.

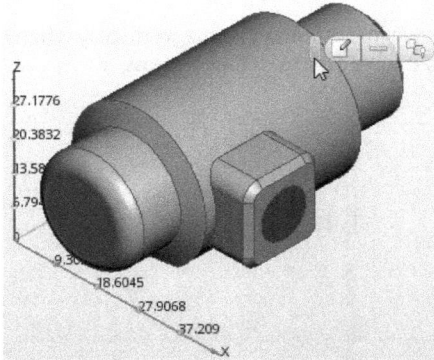

Model Display Manipulation

The Hide tool is a commonly used tool in Autodesk CFD. It is used to hide an exterior part to access the internal geometry that will be analyzed in a CFD simulation.

To hide geometry, use one of the following methods:

- Hover the cursor over the geometry to be hidden, hold <Ctrl> and the middle mouse button.

- Hover over the geometry to be hidden, left click, and select [icon] (Hide) in the mini-toolbar.
- Right-click on the geometry to be hidden and select Hide in the context menu.

To show hidden geometry, use one of the following methods:

- Move the cursor away from the model in the graphics window, hold <Ctrl> and press the middle mouse button again.

- Left-click in the graphics window and select [icon] (Show All) in the mini-toolbar.
- Right-click in the graphics window and select Show All in the context menu.

Alternatively, you can hold <Ctrl> and scroll using the middle mouse button. Scrolling towards you hides each successive part and scrolling away shows each part.

The Autodesk CFD navigation can be set to function similar to many common CAD tools. To change to an alternate navigation mode, in the Start & Learn tab, select ▦ (Options) and select the Navigation tab in the User Interface Preferences dialog box. Using the Navigation mode drop-down list, select an alternate software tool, as shown in the following image.

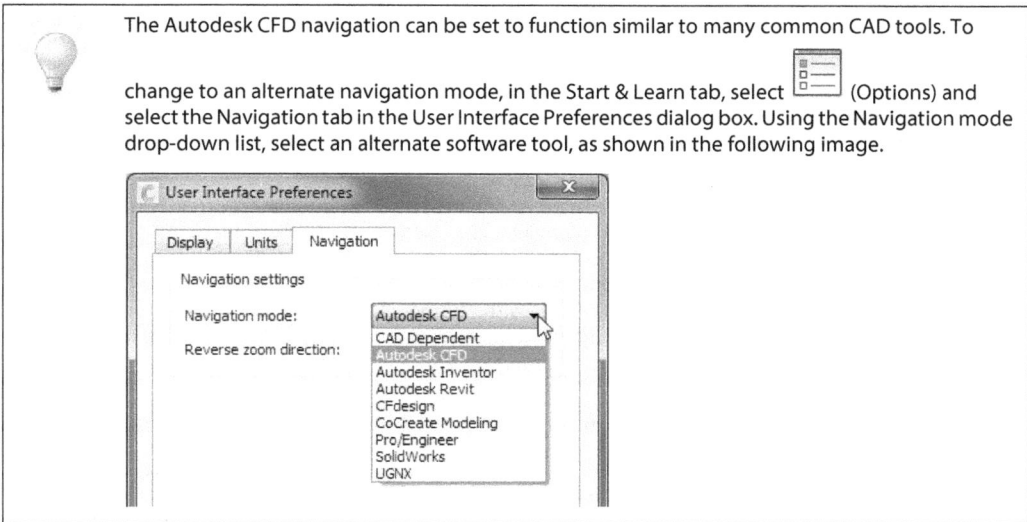

Autodesk CFD File Formats

A predefined folder structure is created when a model is simulated using Autodesk CFD. The model that is opened and used in a design can be from various CAD products (e.g., Inventor parts/assemblies, Catia, Creo Parametric (PRO/E), SOLIDWORKS, .SAT, .STEP, ,IGS, etc.). Once selected and used in a Design Study, the following folders are created.

◢ 📁 Geometry Folder
  ◢ 📁 Design Study Folder
    ◢ 📁 Design Folder
      ◢ 📁 Scenarios Folder
          📁 Logs Folder

- The *Geometry* folder contains the geometry files and an automatically generated support file for each design study when the analysis has been run. This folder is not created by Autodesk CFD, and its name is defined by the user.
- The *Design Study* folder contains files specific to the design study and a subfolder for each design.
- The *Design* folder contains files specific to the design and a subfolder for each scenario.
- The *Scenario* folder contains the files specific to the scenario and subfolders for log files.
- The *Logs* folder contains log files for each scenario. These are often useful for troubleshooting problems, thus technical support may request them for additional information.

All folders except the geometry folder are named after their respective design study, design, or scenario. The following shows and overview of the files formats most commonly used with Autodesk CFD.

File Extension	Description	Location
.	CAD model	
*_support.cfz	Support file - This is a compact version of the share file that only includes parameters (no mesh or results data). Ideal for sending to Autodesk CFD Technical Support. This is created when the study is solved. If opened, it generates a new folder structure with _support appended to the folder name. This folder structure will not contain results.	*Geometry* folder
*.cfdst	Design Study file	*Design Study* folder
design_studies.info	Text file containing the names of the designs and scenarios in the design study.	*Design Study* folder
preview.jpg	Thumbnail image of the Design Study file.	*Design Study* folder
*.bld	Text file that lists all settings for all scenarios in the design study. Primarily used in conjunction with the Design Study Builder, a tool for automating the creation of design studies.	*Design Study* folder
.vtfx	Summary Image files that are created for the results. These are used in the Decision Center for comparing results.	*Design Study* folder
*.cfz	Share file - The Share file is a reduced-size version of the Design Study file, and is useful for archiving and sending to others. This is not automatically created. Click Save File Share in the Quick Access Toolbar.	*Design Study* folder (or user-defined)
*.cfdes	Design file	*Design* folder
*.cfdsc	Scenario file	*Scenario* folder

Lesson: Autodesk CFD Workflow

In this lesson, you will gain an overall understanding of the workflow that should be used for Autodesk CFD. This is a key step in learning how this software tool can be best utilized in your design workflow.

Objectives

After completing this lesson, you will be able to:

- Describe the general steps in the Autodesk CFD workflow.

Autodesk CFD Workflow

Autodesk CFD should be used throughout the design process from concept, through to design, and validation in order to gain insight and to make good design decisions. Just like in design, a workflow should be followed in the Autodesk CFD software. In Autodesk CFD, this workflow can be further broken down into individual phases that have their own specific workflow. The following details the stages and the recommended general workflow.

> When working in the Autodesk CFD software, the panels in the ribbon generally progress you through the steps required to complete an analysis (left to right). Additionally, the same panel names are repeated as nodes in the design study bar (top to bottom)

Phase 1: Create the CAD Model for use in Autodesk CFD.

In this phase, you are preparing the model for study in Autodesk CFD.

1. Create the CAD model to be simulated. This can be a concept design or a fully functioning model. The flow part that represents the internal volume of the model can be created in the CAD tool or using tools in the Autodesk CFD software.

   - Models can brought in from various Autodesk design software tools or a file can be imported from other CAD software packages.

2. Create a new Design Study. This involves assigning a name for the study and browsing to and selecting a CAD model.

   - A new design study can also be created by using an Add-in to Launch CFD from common CAD platforms.

Phase 2: Model Setup.

This phase typically requires the definition of several parameters that define the environment in which the final design will be used in the real-world. This includes defining materials, boundary conditions, and mesh settings, among others.

3. Verify the units of the design. Modify them, if required.

4. Assign the Material properties for the fluids and solids, as required.

5. Assign Boundary Conditions for the model.

   - Boundary Conditions accurately describe the flow at the openings and heat transfer wherever heat enters or leaves the system. Boundary conditions define the inputs of the simulation model.

6. Assign the Initial Conditions for the model.

   - Initial Conditions are enforced at the beginning of the analysis only. They are primarily used for transient analyses.

   - The use of initial conditions is an advanced topic and is not covered in this student guide.

7.   Mesh the model.

- Meshing breaks up the geometry into small pieces called elements. The corner of each element is a node. Calculations are performed at the nodes. These elements and nodes make up the mesh. In three dimensional models, most elements are tetrahedrals: a four sided, triangular-faced element. In two dimensional models, most elements are triangles.

Phase 3: Run the Simulation and Visualize the Results.

The Solve dialog box provides parameters to define how the simulation should be run. There are a number of tools that can be used to visualize and quantify results, some of which can even be used while the model is running.

8.   Setup and run the simulation.

- Autodesk CFD uses an iterative calculation process. This means that the solver computes a solution in many small steps (iterations). Throughout these steps, the solution evolves. After some number of iterations, the solution no longer changes and is considered "converged."
- In general, the run times for CFD simulations are generally longer than structural analyses.

9.   Visualize the results of the simulation.

- The results can be viewed directly in the graphics window or you can use the Decision Center.

Phase 4: Compare.

By cloning designs and scenarios, rerunning the solver, and visualizing all scenarios side-by-side in the Decision Center, this stage of the workflow is key in enabling you to predict how a product reacts to real-world fluid flow and heat transfer situations.

10.   Create alternate variations in the study.

- Clone a Design or Scenario, make changes to their design parameters, and rerun the solver.

11.   Explore different design concepts using the Decision Center to compare results and make informed design decisions.

> It is highly recommended to validate the Autodesk CFD simulation results. For more information, refer to *Chapter 8.*

> The Autodesk CFD Motion Module provides the ability to analyze the interaction between solid objects in motion and the surrounding fluid. The effect of the motion on the fluid medium as well as the flow-induced forces on the object can both be analyzed efficiently and quickly. There are seven motion types: Linear, Angular, Combined Linear/Angular, Combined Orbital/Rotational, Nutating, Sliding Vane, and Free Motion.
>
> This module is not discussed in this student guide. However, in terms of the overall workflow, Motion parameters would be defined in *Phase 2: Model Setup.*

Lesson: When to use Autodesk CFD

In the previous lesson, you learned the overall workflow on how the Autodesk CFD software is used to predict and analyze a design's reaction to fluid and thermal dynamics. This lesson furthers that discussion to understanding when you should incorporate the use of the Autodesk CFD software in the overall design cycle. Autodesk CFD is not simply a validation tool. It is a valuable Design tool that should be used throughout the design cycle.

Objectives

After completing this lesson, you will be able to:

- Describe the best use of the Autodesk CFD software in the overall design cycle.

When to use Autodesk CFD

As previously mentioned when discussing the Autodesk CFD workflow, this tool should be used throughout the design process from concept, through to design, and validation in order to gain insight and to make good design decisions. It should not simply be used as an end of cycle validation tool as it can provide valuable insight throughout the design process.

Design Study Concept

A single Design and Scenario for that Design is generally the first step in an Autodesk CFD simulation. In many cases, you will want to compare several Design alternatives that may vary model geometry, as well as vary the parameters defined in the Scenarios of a current study. Autodesk CFD makes it easy to transfer settings from one model to another and run variations in the same design study or to duplicate and slightly modify scenarios for the same model.

Cloning in Autodesk CFD

The Clone command is used to duplicate either a Design or Scenarios in a Design, to compare design alternatives. Cloning is the foundation for leveraging the settings of an existing design study when creating a new design or alternate scenarios. Once cloned, you can edit the existing properties to make changes.

When cloning a Design, consider the following:

- Cloning a Design also clones all scenarios in the design.
- A design can be cloned before or after scenarios have been run, but not while one is running.
- When you clone a design, you have the option to select which scenarios will be cloned and included in the new design. You can also select if you want to clone the mesh and results as well as the geometry and settings.
- It is possible to continue running a cloned scenario from a saved iteration.

When cloning a Scenario, consider the following:

- A scenario cannot be cloned while running.
- If a scenario has been run before being cloned, no results can be visualized in the cloned scenario. However, the cloned scenario will contain the mesh.
- A cloned scenario can be continued from a saved iteration in the Solve dialog box.

The following image details the directory structure of a Design Study after both a Design and Scenarios in the Design were cloned. Consider the following:

- Design 1 and Scenario 1 were the defaults in the study. *Design1.cfdes* and *Scenario 1.cfdsc* are the files in their respective directories that define how each were setup.

- Scenario 2 was cloned using Scenario 1 as a reference. Changes were made to its parameters and the details are stored in *Scenario 2.cfdsc*.

- Design 2 is a clone of Design 1. When created, only Scenario 1 was cloned into Design 2. After cloning, the model used in Design 1 was replaced with one that had a slight geometry change. *Design2.cfdes* and *Scenario 1.cfdsc* (stored under the Design 2 folder) are the files that define how each were setup.

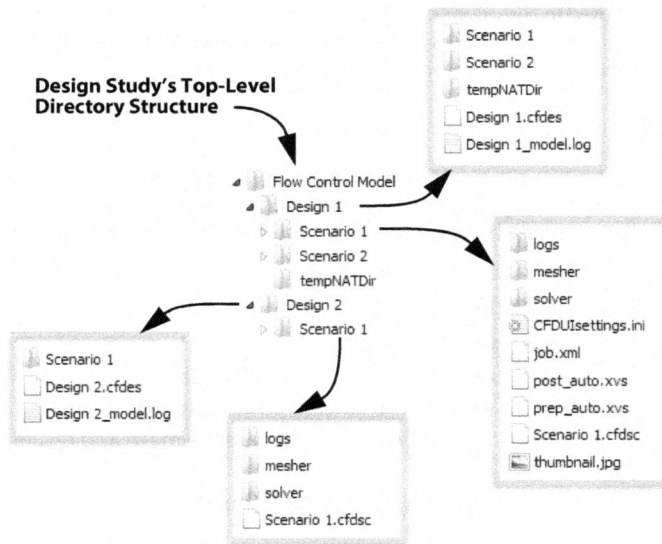

It is highly recommended to use descriptive names when cloning either Design or Scenarios. Use names that will help you identify what is being varied or studied.

Results Comparison in Decision Center

The Decision Center is the environment for comparing design alternatives. It can help you identify the design that satisfies your design objectives by performing the following tasks:

- Extract specific results values
- Compare results from multiple scenarios

Visualization objects such as Results Parts, Results Planes, Result Points, and XY-plots form the basis of the Decision Center. You can create an object on one Scenario and designate it as a "Summary" object, and the Decision Center computes the results for every scenario in the Study.

To open the Decision Center, click the Decision Center tab.

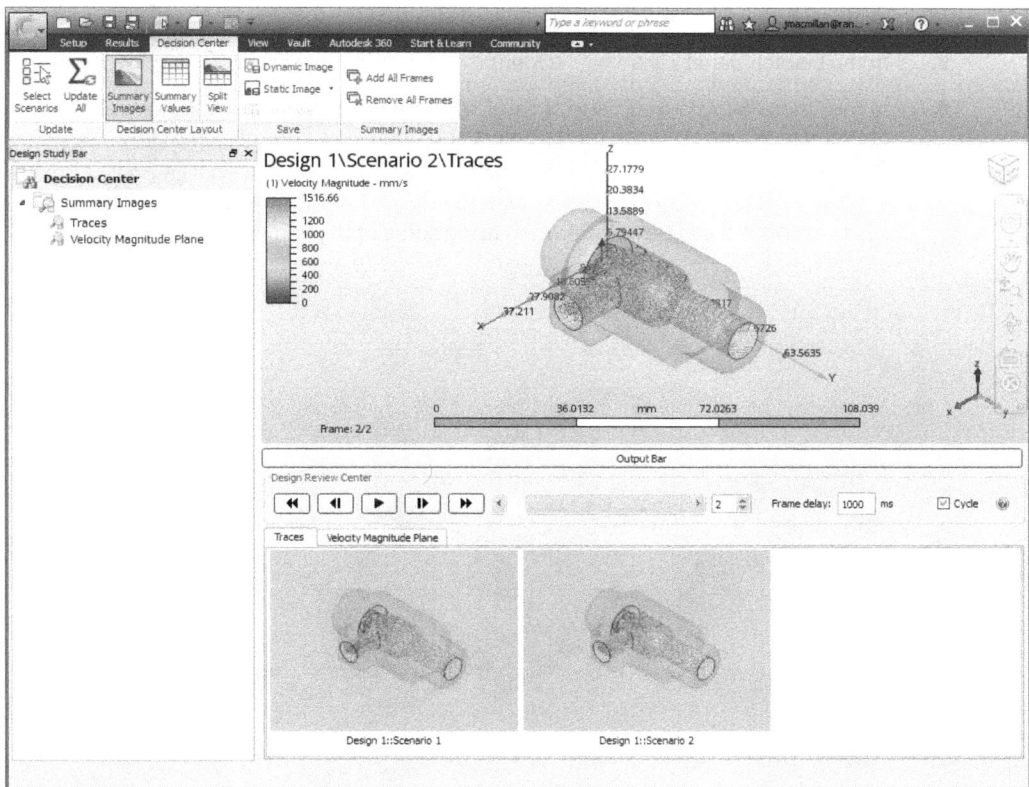

Exercise: Flow through a Hydraulic Valve

In this exercise, you will open an existing simulation that will show the flow through a hydraulic valve. The working fluid is water and the valve is about half open. The objectives in this exercise are to:

- Use the Autodesk CFD interface to review a simulation.
- Visualize the flow through the valve.

Open the Model in the Autodesk CFD Environment.

1. Launch Autodesk CFD, if not already running.

2. Select the Start & Learn tab on the ribbon, if not already active.

3. In the Launch panel, click ⬚ (Open).

4. In the Open dialog box, browse to the *C:\Autodesk CFD 2017 Essentials Exercise Files\Getting Started\Flow Control Model* folder. Select and open *Flow Control Model.cfdst*. The model displays as shown in the following image.

    - The triad and scale that display with the model help identify the size, scale, and units for the model. It can be helpful when using some of the commands in Autodesk CFD.

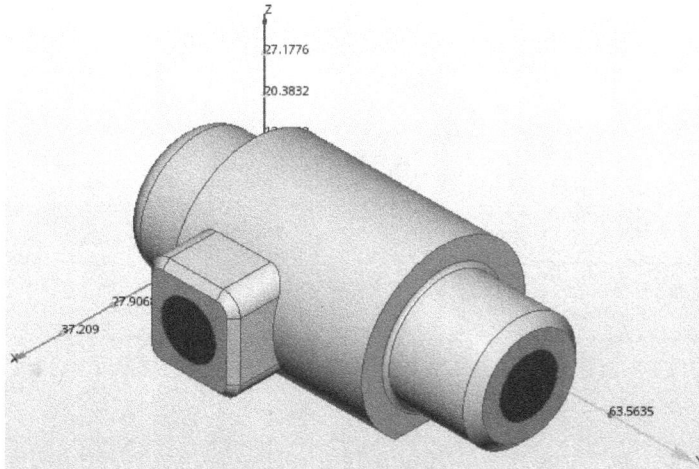

5. The Design Study Bar displays as shown in the following image. Note the following:

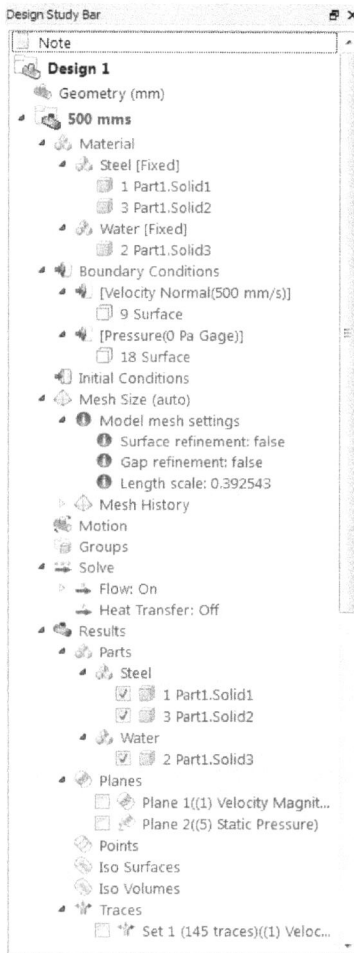

- Design 1 is the name of the study. You can right-click this branch to access options that enable you to rename, clone, create new scenarios, etc.

- The Geometry branch specifies the unit system, which is mm in this example. Additional customization options of the design model can be accessed through this branch. These will be discussed later in the student guide.

- There is currently a single scenario setup in this design study named 500 mms. It represents a single simulation. The nodes in this branch define the specifics of the simulation. Every scenario in a Design is based on the same geometry model, but can have different settings (boundary conditions, materials, etc.). Alternatively, multiple Designs that reference different models can also be included in a study.

6. Expand the Material node and Steel and Water sub-nodes of the Design Study Bar, if not already expanded.

- Note that there are three parts listed in the model. The three parts were modeled in a CAD software product. The third part represents the empty interior volume that the fluid will flow through.

- Each part has been assigned a material.
  - The Valve (Part1.Solid1) and Poppet (Part1. Solid2) are assigned as Steel.
  - The Flow Volume (Part1.Solid3) is assigned as Water.

7. In the Setup tab, in the Setup Tasks panel, ensure that (Materials) is the active Setup Task, as indicated with blue highlighting of the icon. This icon activates material assignment as the current task for setting up the model. Once active, the Materials context panel displays.

8. In the Design Study Bar, review the three parts and verify that they have been assigned a material. Review the bottom left-hand corner of the graphics window to view the color assignment of these parts.

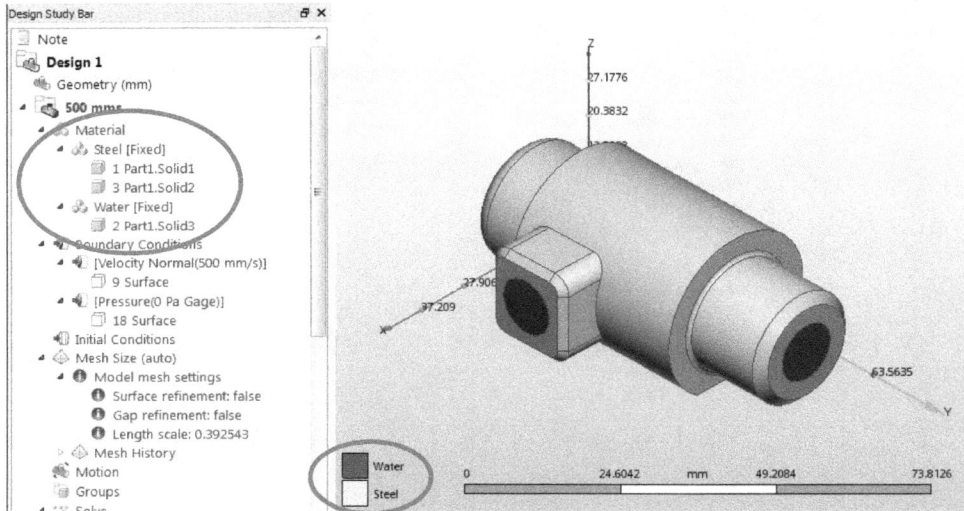

Control the display of parts in the study.

The Hide tool is a commonly used tool in Autodesk CFD. It is used to hide an exterior part to access the internal geometry that will be analyzed in a CFD simulation.

1. To hide the exterior of the valve, hover over it, hold <Ctrl> and press the middle mouse button.

    Alternatively, hover over the geometry, left click, and select ⬚ (Hide) in the mini-toolbar. The model should display as shown in the following image. This model represents the Flow Volume and it displays in blue. The legend indicates that the material for this part is Water.

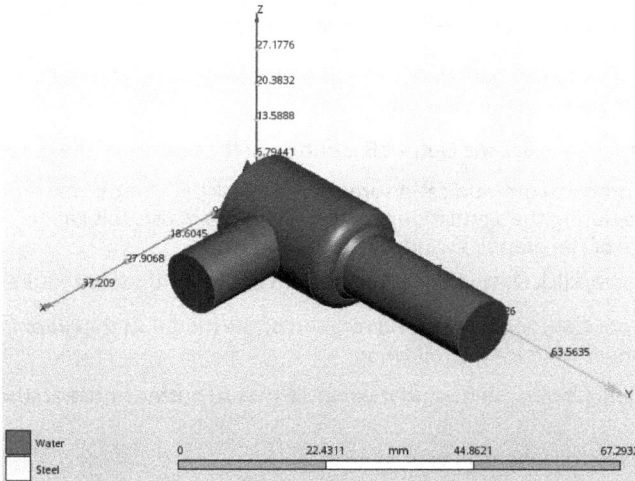

2. Hover the cursor over the model again, hold <Ctrl> and press the middle mouse button. The model should display as shown in the following image. This model represents the Poppet and it displays in gray. The legend indicates that the material for this part is Steel.

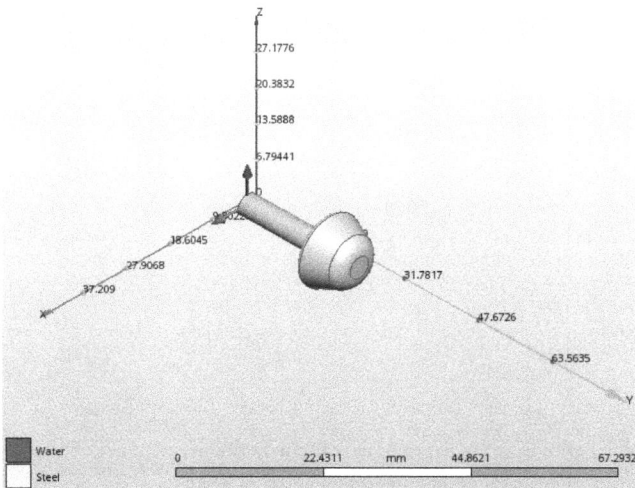

3. To display all the parts, move the mouse away from the model, hold <Ctrl>, and press the middle mouse button again.

- Alternatively, right-click in the graphics window and select ⊞ (Show All) in the context menu or left-click and select ⊞ (Show All) in the mini-toolbar.
- You can also hold <Ctrl> and scroll the middle mouse button. Scrolling towards you hides each successive part while scrolling away shows each part.

4. Select the arrow adjacent to the Material node in the Design Study Bar to compress it.

Navigate the model and practice using the interface.

In this task, you will learn how to navigate the model using the ViewCube, Navigation Bar, and the commands in the Navigate panel, in the View tab.

1. To collapse the Output Bar, click the Output Bar button at the bottom of the graphics window.

- This area is the primary communication area of Autodesk CFD. Status messages and errors are written here during the simulation process. When not in use, this can be minimized to increase the size of the graphics window.
- To expand the area, click Output Bar at the bottom of the window, as required.

2. To manipulate the position, zoom level, and rotation of the model, in the graphics window using the mouse wheel, practice the following:

- To rotate the model, hold <Shift> and the middle mouse button and drag the mouse to rotate.
- To zoom, roll the scroll wheel on your mouse.
- To pan (move), press and hold the middle mouse button and drag the mouse.

Use these tools to reorient the model as shown in the following image.

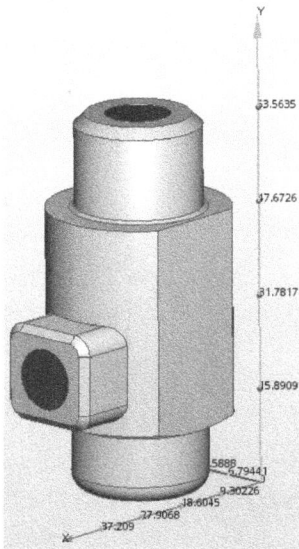

3. To manipulate the orientation of the model using the ViewCube, practice the following methods. The ViewCube is located in the top right-hand corner of the graphics window.

   ▪ To rotate the model, press and hold the left mouse button over the ViewCube in the top right-hand corner of the graphics window and drag the mouse to rotate.

   Press and hold the left mouse button over the ViewCube and drag to orient.

   ▪ To orient the model to a specific orientation, select a face, edge, or corner on the ViewCube.

   Select a face on the ViewCube to orient to a planar face.

   ▪ Use the arrows that display around the ViewCube to rotate the view in 90° increments.

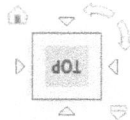

   Hover the cursor over the ViewCube and select the arrows to rotate or flip to adjacenet sides.

4. Select 🏠 on the ViewCube to return to the model's default Home view.

5. Select the corner of the cube to reorient the model as shown in the following image.

   Hover the cursor over the ViewCube and select the highlighted corner.

   The model should reorient as shown in the following image. Use this orientation to continue in the exercise.

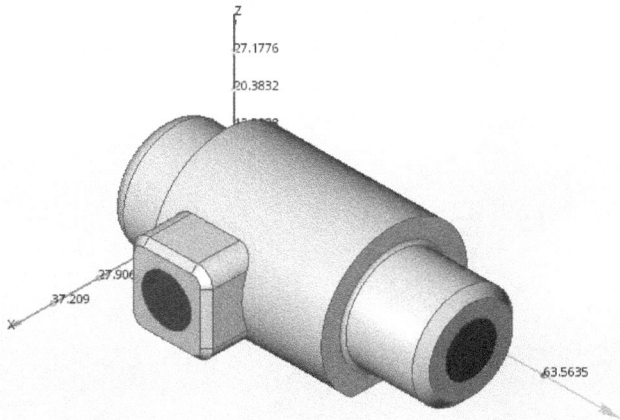

6.   Locate the Navigation Bar in the graphics window. By default, this is located below the ViewCube. Its commands are consistent with those in many Autodesk software products. Hover the cursor over the commands to display a tooltip describing their function. These commands are similar to those that can be used with your mouse and the ViewCube.

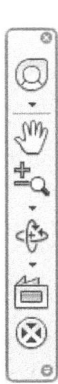

- Practice rotating( ), panning ( ), and zooming ( ) the model in the graphics window using the Navigation Bar commands.

- Select (Look At) in the Navigation Bar and select a face directly on the model. This command enables you to orient the model so that select faces are displayed parallel to the screen. This is not available through the ViewCube controls where only faces perpendicular to the coordinate system can be selected.

- Select (Full Navigation Wheel) in the Navigation Bar. This provides quick access to all the navigation tools from the cursor. You can select an option and manipulate the model without having to use the ViewCube or Navigation Bar.

- Select (Center) in the Navigation Bar and select a new location on the model. Try rotating using either of the methods discussed and note how the center has changed to the selected point.

- Select on the ViewCube. This resets the center of the model back to the origin, and the zoom level and orientation of the model back to its default Home view.

7.   Select the View tab in the ribbon. The Navigate panel provides an alternate for accessing the pan, zoom, spin, and orienting tools that were accessed on the Navigation Bar in the graphics window.

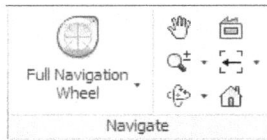

- In the Navigate panel, click (Previous) to return to the last view orientation of the model. This command is not available on the Navigation Bar or ViewCube.

8.   Use any of the techniques discussed to orient the model as shown in the following image.

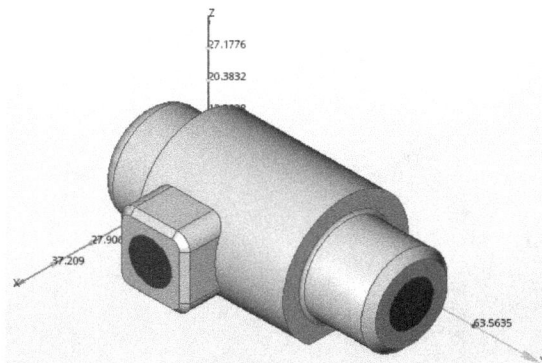

Review the Boundary Conditions for the simulations.

Defining the Boundary Conditions for a simulation enables you to describe how the model will be used in its real-world operating conditions. For this simulation, a constant velocity was assigned to the inlet of the valve. In many valve simulations, either the flow rate or the pressure drop is known. Either condition can be used, as required, instead of a specified velocity. (Do not apply more than one flow condition to the same inlet.) Additionally, an ambient pressure condition was assigned to the valve outlet. This is the typical way to model where flow leaves the device.

1. In the Setup tab, in the Setup Tasks panel, click ⬆ (Boundary Conditions) to activate this stage of the model setup. The Boundary Conditions context panel displays.

2. Ensure that all parts are visible in the model by pressing and holding <Ctrl> and clicking the middle mouse anywhere away from the model in the graphics window.

3. In the Design Study Bar and in the graphics window, note the following:

   - Now that the Boundary Condition setup task is active, the colors on the model are no longer visible.

   - In the Design Study Bar, confirm that the value for the condition on the inlet is 500 mm/s. The stripe on the inlet face (black) should correspond to the boundary conditions type in the legend.

   - In the Design Study Bar, confirm that the value for the condition on the outlet is 0 Pa. This defines a static gage pressure of 0, which simulates the flow outlet. The stripe on the outlet face (gold) should correspond to the boundary conditions type in the legend.

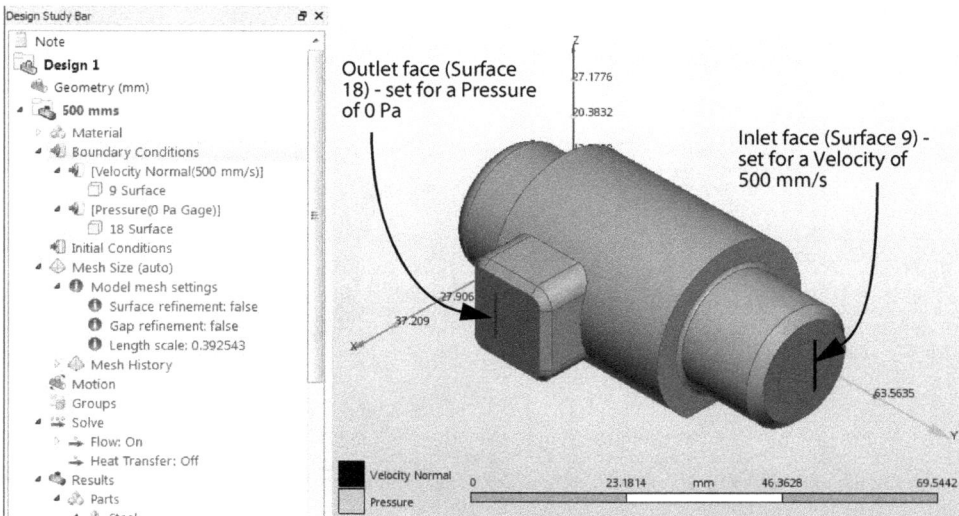

4. Select the arrow adjacent to the Boundary Conditions node to compress it. This helps simplify the display of the Design Study Bar.

5. Note that there is no expand/compress icon adjacent to the Initial Conditions node. This is because no Initial Condition was defined for this simulation. The node will remain regardless of whether an Initial Condition was set or not.

Review the Mesh that was assigned for the simulation.

In this task, you will review the default mesh that was used for the simulation. No further changes will be made to the mesh as this time. Later in this student guide, you will learn more specifics about the tools that can be used to modify the mesh.

1. In the Setup tab, in the Setup Tasks panel, click ◇ (Mesh Sizing) to activate this stage of the model setup. The Mesh Sizing context panels displays.

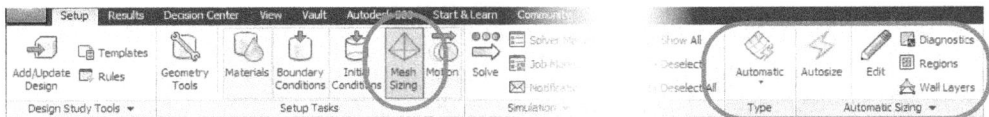

2. In the Design Study Bar and in the graphics window, note the following:
   - Now that the Mesh Sizing setup task is active, the colors and boundary conditions on the model are no longer visible.
   - In the Design Study Bar, review the Mesh Size node. The word "auto" after the node name indicates that the mesh was automatically generated based on the Autosize settings.
   - You should see blue dots along every edge of the model. These dots provide a simple preview of the mesh distribution. You will learn more about meshing later in this student guide.

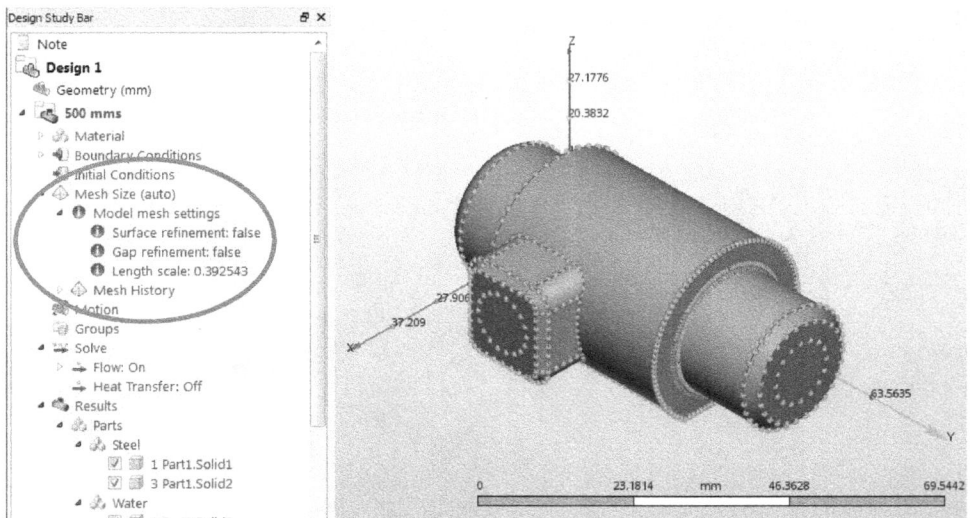

3. Compress the Mesh Size node.

Visualize the results for the simulation.

The simulation for this study has already been run. In this task, you will graphically display the results of the simulation and view the flow through the valve. You will visualize the flow using a Plane and Traces result view. Planes are great for showing a two-dimensional slice through the model, but the best information often comes in three dimensions so particle traces are used for a more complete view of the flow. Additional result views will be discussed later in this student guide.

1. The Results tab automatically activates once the simulation is run. Since an existing study that has results was opened, the tab must be selected. Select the Results tab. The Results Tasks panel displays the various results that can be used to study the simulation.

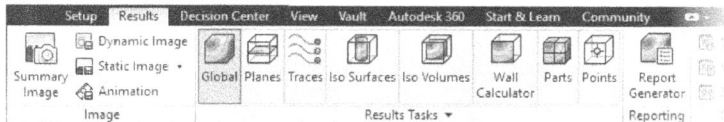

2. In this Design Study, three result sets were created and will be reviewed. Note the following:

    ▪ The model display has changed so that the part models are transparent. This was done to help visualize the results. This process will be taught later in this student guide.

    ▪ There have been two planes and traces sets created for you that will be used to display the velocity magnitude and static pressure results.

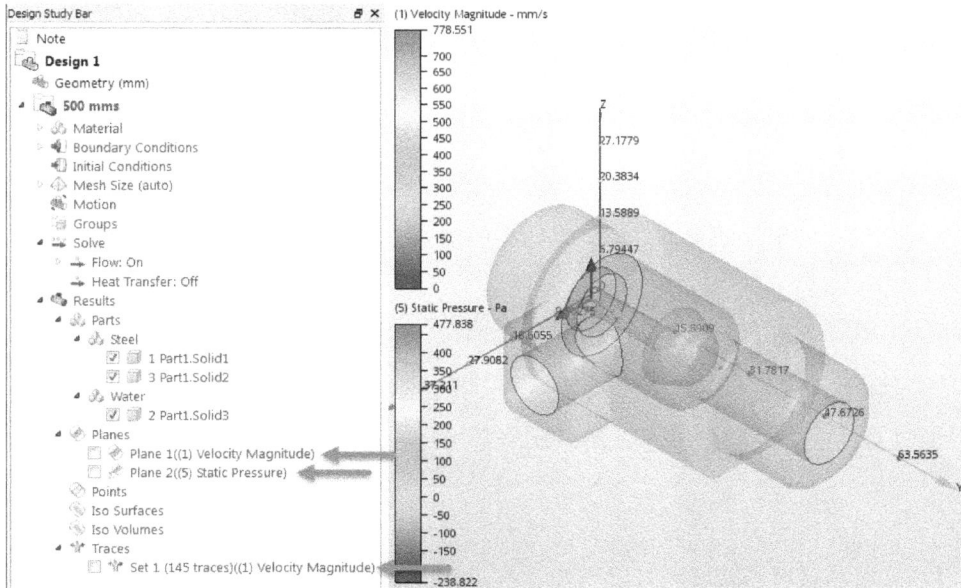

3. In the Design Study Bar, in the Results>Parts>Steel node, clear the selection of the Part1.Solid1 and Part1. Solid2 parts, as shown in the following image. This clears them from the display to help visualize the results.

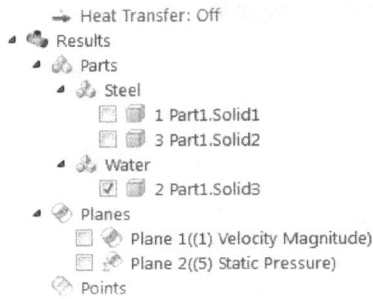

4. In the Design Study Bar, in the Results>Planes node, select Plane 1. This toggles on the display of this result so that you can review it.

5. Use the ViewCube to reorient the plane as shown in the following image.

6. Toggle on the display of the two parts again to see the Plane result with the components showing. Review the image and note the following:

    ▪ The orange regions near the top of the poppet mean that the flow is accelerating through the gap.

    ▪ Recirculating regions of flow are observed near the top of the poppet on both sides of this view, as well as just below the poppet and at the base of the poppet.

    ▪ As the flow turns toward the outlet, it accelerates off the inside corner.

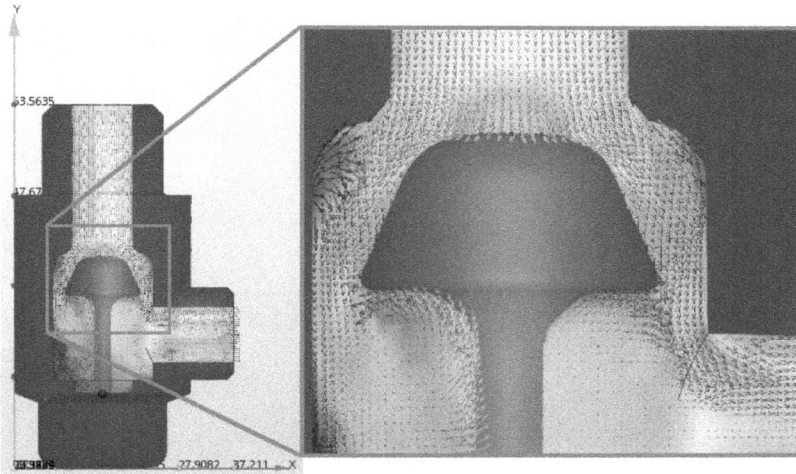

7. To see the pressure drop through the valve, right-click on the plane in the graphics window and click Plane result>Static Pressure.

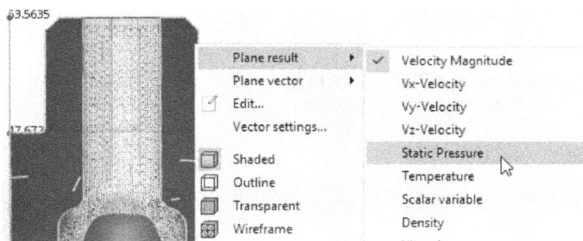

8. Review the following image and note the following:

   - This is a plot of the static gage pressure. Recall that the outlet boundary condition was set to 0 Pa, so everything in this plot is relative to that value.
   - This plot shows the pressure drop through the valve. Because the pressure is 0 at the outlet, the pressure at the inlet is the overall pressure drop. Note that the pressure dips pretty low as it turns the inside corner near the outlet. However, it is not so low that cavitation is an issue.

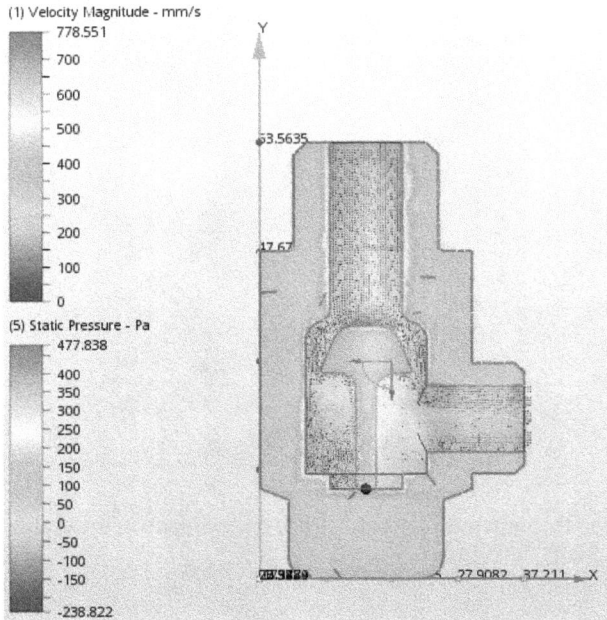

9. In the Design Study Bar, in the Results>Planes node, clear the selection of Plane 1 to toggle off its results display.

10. In the Results>Traces node, select Set 1.

11. Reorient the model to the 3D view that has been shown throughout the exercise.

12. Review the following image and note the following:

- This view helps understand how the flow moves through the valve. The traces are colored by velocity magnitude, so you can see how the flow accelerates as the water enters the outlet pipe.

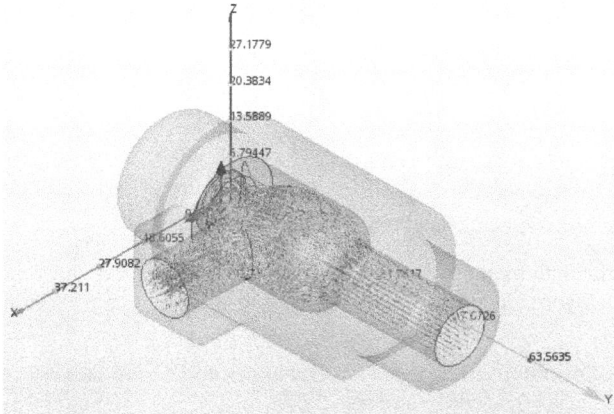

13. In the Design Study Bar, in the Results>Traces node, clear the selection of Set 1 to toggle off its results display.

14. Return to the Setup tab. Note that the models display is no longer transparent. This was set as part of the Result.

Review the Decision Center.

The Decision Center is the Autodesk CFD environment used to compare design alternatives. You can use it to extract specific results values or compare results from multiple scenarios and designs. In this task, you will review the image files that were created for you from the velocity Magnitude Plane result and the Trace result.

1. Click the Decision Center tab to open the Decision Center.

2. Select Traces in the Summary Images list of the Decision Center's Design Study Bar to review it. This is the same image as the one that was reviewed using the Results tab.

3. Select Velocity Magnitude Plane in the Summary Images list. This is the same image as the one that was reviewed using the Results tab. These images were created for you, from the Results tab.

4. Return to the Setup tab.

Clone the simulation, make a change, and compare results.

In this task, you will create a copy (clone) of the scenario that was created for you. Using the cloned scenario, you will make a change to the setup parameters, solve the simulation, and then compare the results in the Decision Center.

1. At the top of the Design Study Bar, right-click on 500 mms and select Clone. In the Clone Scenario dialog box, complete the following:

   - Enter **1500 mms** as the new name.
   - Select Include mesh and results.
   - Click OK.

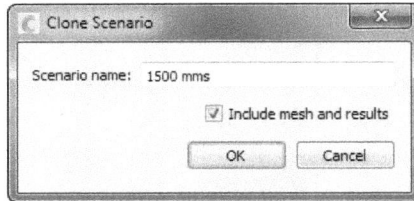

2. 1500 mms becomes the active scenario in the Design Study Bar. It is highlighted bold and it displays in blue. The 500 mms scenario is compressed and it displays in gray, indicating that it is not active.

3. Expand the Boundary Conditions node if not already expanded. Right-click on the Velocity Normal (500mm/s) boundary condition and select Edit.

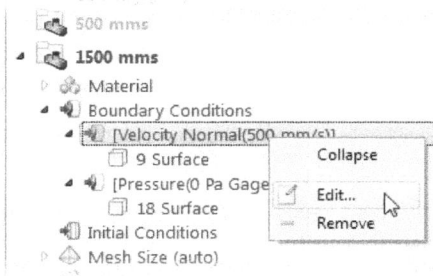

4. In the Boundary Conditions dialog box, select the Velocity Magnitude property value and enter 1500. Click Apply. This changes the velocity of the water entering the valve, which provides an alternate scenario.

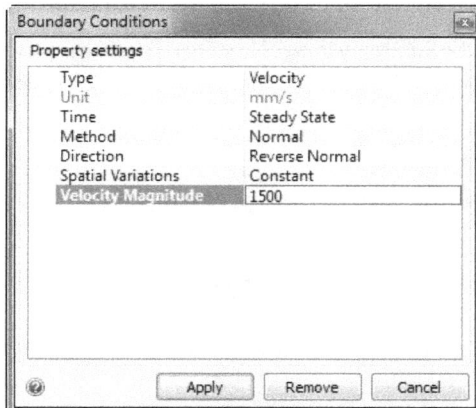

5. In the Setup tab, Simulation panel, click ⟶ (Solve). Complete the following in the Solve dialog box:

- Maintain the Interactions to Run property value as 200.
- Ensure that the Continue From property value is set to 0.
- Click Solve.
- If you are prompted to delete results, click Yes. This is just a warning that results will be replaced. Since there are currently no results in this Scenario, nothing will be deleted.

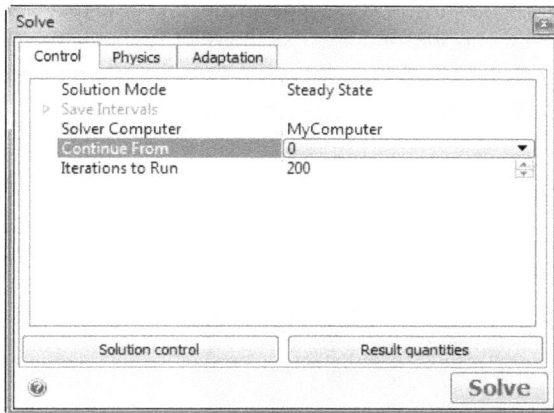

6. The Output Bar updates showing the Plot of the iterations being done to conduct the simulation. The plot results will be discussed in more detail later in this student guide.

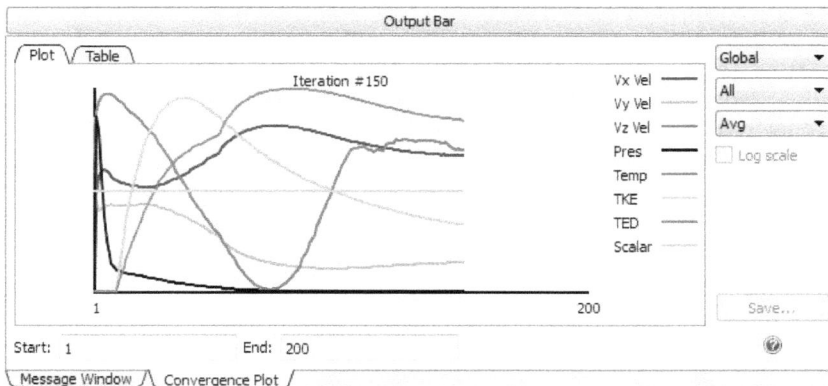

Once the 200 iterations have been completed, the Message Window tab displays indicating that the Analysis completed successfully.

Note: The simulation will take a few minutes to solve all 200 iterations. The performance of the computer hardware affects this solve time.

7. Select the Decision Center tab.

8. Note that the Summary Images are appearing out of date, as indicated by the ⚠ icon in the Design Study Bar.

9. Right-click on the Summary Images node and select Update all images. The images are no longer out of date. Additionally, images of the results for Scenario 2 are created so that you can compare the Traces and Velocity Magnitude Plane.

10. In the Decision Center's Design Study Bar, select Traces. Use the playback controls to move between the two images to compare them. Review the images and note that the trace curves show similar flow patterns, with only the magnitude of the velocity changing.

Design 1\500 mms\Traces

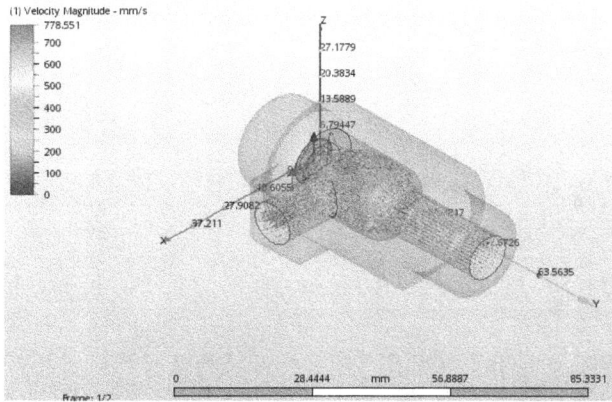

Design 1\1500 mms\Traces

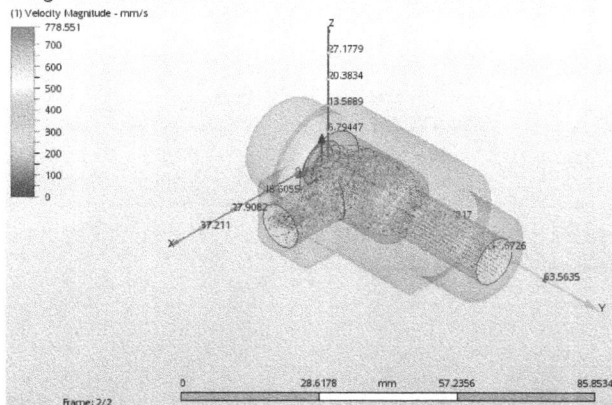

11. In the Decision Center's Design Study Bar, select Velocity Magnitude Plane. Use the playback controls to move between the two images to compare them. Review the images and note that the recirculation is reduced on one side of the poppet.

Design 1\500 mms\Velocity Magnitude Plane

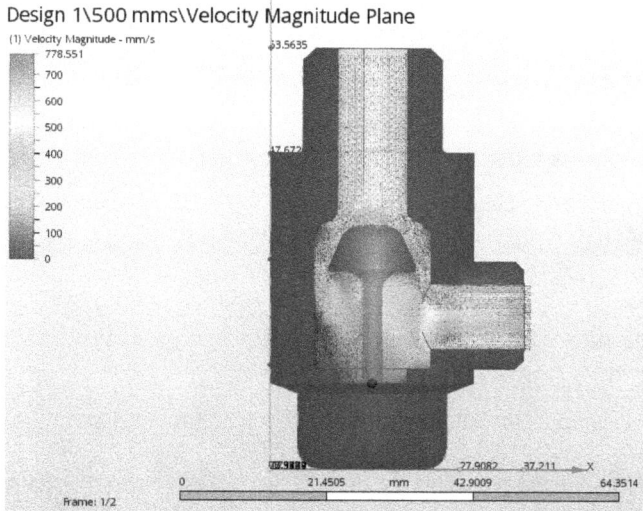

Design 1\1500 mms\Velocity Magnitude Plane

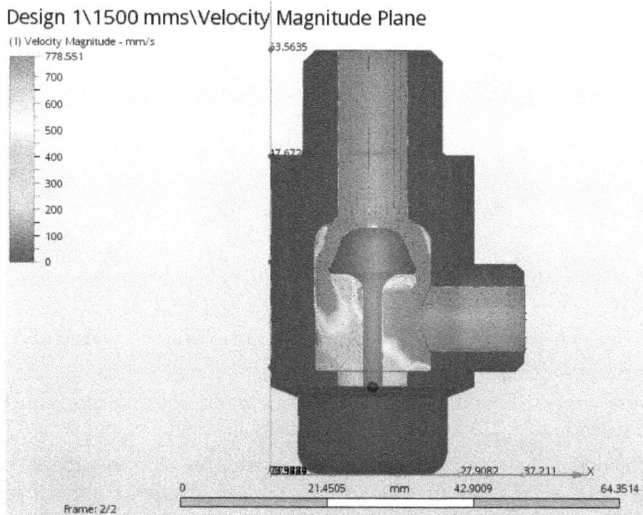

12. In the Decision Center's Design Study Bar, select the Summary Values node. Note that the Summary Images are also out of date, as indicated by the ⚠ icon. Right-click on the Summary Values node and select Update summary values. Note that the increase in velocity has resulted in an increase in pressure, as indicated in the Planes tab.

Result Quantity	Design 1 500 mms	Design 1 1500 mms	Reference	Units
Plane 2				
Pressure	345.537	2153.37	N/A	Pa ▾

13. In the Quick Access toolbar, click 🖫 (Save) to save the study.

Note: Design Studies cannot be closed directly in Autodesk CFD. To close, you can exit the software, open a existing design study, or create a new one.

14. Leave the software open. In the next chapter, you will create a new design study.

Review the Files that are Created from an Autodesk CFD Simulation.

In this task, you will navigate to the working folder for the Design Study. You will review the files created when the simulation was setup and run using Autodesk CFD.

1. Open Windows Explorer and navigate to the *C:\Autodesk CFD 2017 Essentials Exercise Files\ Getting Started* folder. Note the files and folders that were created:

Name	Date modified	Type	Size
Flow Control Model	6/13/2016 11:09 AM	File folder	
Flow Control Model_support.cfz	6/13/2016 11:09 AM	CFD 2017	336 KB
Flow-Control-Valve-model.sat	1/16/2014 3:14 PM	SAT File	91 KB

- *Flow-Control-Valve-model.sat* - Model geometry that was imported into Autodesk CFD for simulation.
- *Flow Control Model_support.cfz* - This is a support file. It is a compact version of the design file that only includes parameters (no mesh or results data) and is ideal for sending to Autodesk CFD Technical Support. This is created when the study is solved.
- *Flow Control Model* folder - Folder generated when the Design Study is created.

Name	Date modified	Type	Size
Design 1	6/13/2016 11:05 AM	File folder	
design_studies.info	6/13/2016 11:11 AM	INFO File	1 KB
Flow Control Model.bld	6/13/2016 11:17 AM	BLD File	20 KB
Flow Control Model.cfdst	5/9/2016 7:54 PM	CFD 2017	29 KB
preview.jpg	6/13/2016 11:17 AM	JPEG image	72 KB
Traces_sdi.vtfx	6/13/2016 11:12 AM	CFD_VIEWER...	1,856 KB
Velocity Magnitude Plane_sdi.vtfx	6/13/2016 11:12 AM	CFD_VIEWER...	1,054 KB

- *Design 1* folder - Folder generated when the Design Study is created and contains all the details for this Design.
- *design_studies.info* - Text file that contains the names of the designs and scenarios in the design study.
- *Flow Control Model.bld* - Text file that lists all settings for all scenarios in the design study. Primarily used in conjunction with the Design Study Builder, a tool for automating the creation of design studies.
- *Flow Control Model.cfdst* - The CFD Design Study file that was created. This is the file that you select when opening an existing study.
- *preview.jpg* - Preview image of the study, consisting of the last image in the graphics window when the study was saved.

- *Traces_sdi.vtfx* - The Summary Image file that will be used in the Decision Center for comparing Trace results from multiple scenarios. Recall that you captured the image for one scenario and Autodesk CFD automatically captured the same image for the other scenario.

- *Velocity Magnitude Plane_sdi.vtfx* - The Summary Image file that will be used in the Decision Center for comparing velocity results on a cut plane from multiple scenarios.

- *Design 1* folder - Folder that contains all the setup data for each Scenario in the Design, as well as temporary and log files.

  - *Design 1.cfdes* - File that contains the details of the Design setup.

Name	Date modified	Type	Size
500 mms	6/13/2016 11:09 AM	File folder	
1500 mms	6/13/2016 11:09 AM	File folder	
Design 1.cfdes	6/13/2016 10:34 AM	CFDES File	309 KB
Design 1_model.log	6/13/2016 10:46 AM	Text Document	1 KB

Geometry

In many situations, the CAD geometry must be modified before the simulation can be run. In some cases, problematic entities such as sliver surfaces or extra edges can significantly complicate meshing. In others, the simulation model requires additional parts to simulate the flow. These can be either inside a cavity or a flow volume that completely surrounds the original model. Although CAD systems can create very complex geometry, that same complexity can slow down analyses. In this chapter, you will investigate some of the tools available for simplifying your models.

Objectives

After completing this chapter, you will be able to:

- Understand the need for flow volumes.
- Identify the various geometry tools in Autodesk® CFD and know when to apply them.
- Recognize the impact the geometry tools have on simplification of the CFD mesh, and how that can improve analysis speed and results.
- Understand when to use the Model Assessment Toolkit.
- Use the two methods to launch the Model Assessment Toolkit.
- Understand the six different geometry issues reported on by the Model Assessment Toolkit.
- Understand the concept of Surface Wrapping.
- Describe the workflow required to apply Surface Wrapping to your model.
- Describe the uses of the Autodesk® SimStudio Tools.
- Describe the interaction between SimStudio Tools and Autodesk CFD.
- Use SimStudio Tools to modify model geometry.
- Describe the use of Devices for model simplification.

Lesson: Geometry Requirements and Tools

Overview

In many situations, the CAD geometry must be modified before the simulation can be run. Entities such as sliver surfaces or extra edges, which add complexity to the model, can greatly complicate meshing. In other situations, the simulation model requires additional geometry to simulate the flow. The additional geometry might be an inside cavity or an external volume that encompasses the model.

Objectives

After completing this lesson, you will be able to:

- Understand the need for flow volumes.
- Identify the various geometry tools in Autodesk CFD and know when to apply them.
- Recognize the impact the geometry tools have on simplification of the CFD mesh, and how that can improve analysis speed and results.

Geometry Foundations

There are several important points to consider when looking at geometry that will be used in Autodesk CFD:

- For flow analysis, a fluid volume will be required.
- Solid volumes or parts are only required for thermal studies.
- Where possible, leverage geometric simplifications to improve calculation speed.

For the purposes of Autodesk CFD, the following terms are used:

- CAD parts or bodies are referred to as Volumes.
- CAD surfaces and edges are referred to as surfaces and edges respectively.

Consider the CAD model shown in the following image.

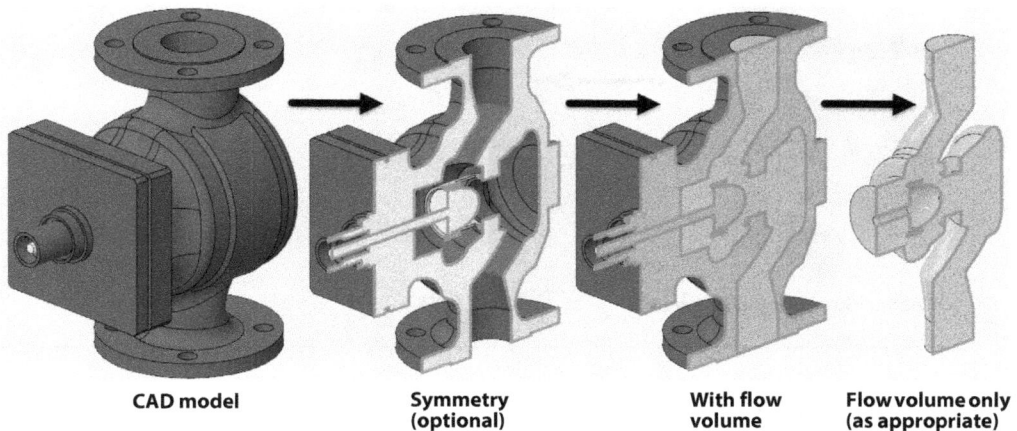

| CAD model | Symmetry (optional) | With flow volume | Flow volume only (as appropriate) |

The CAD model itself would be useful for conducting a thermal analysis, but is not appropriate for conducting a flow analysis. To conduct a flow analysis, you need to establish a fluid volume using the internal cavity of the model. With the addition of a fluid volume, you can look at flow and thermal effects in the model. However, if you were purely concerned with the flow solution, you could bring in just a fluid volume, negating the solids themselves for any thermal impact. This model happens to be Symmetric, so you could leverage symmetry to improve your simulation size and runtime.

Flow Geometry

Geometry for a fluid flow analysis is different than that used for structural analysis. Flow geometry can be broken into two broad categories: internal and external.

Examples of internal flows include:

- Flow in pipes
- Flow in valves
- Flow in electronic enclosures

Examples of external flows include:

- Flow over a car
- Flow over an airplane wing
- Flow around an electronic device exposed to the environment

Internal Flows

For internal flows, a core must be created from the existing surrounding geometry. The outer walls of the volume are omitted, unless they are to be used as part of a heat transfer calculation, and the interior volume of the valve is modeled, as shown in the following sectioned view.

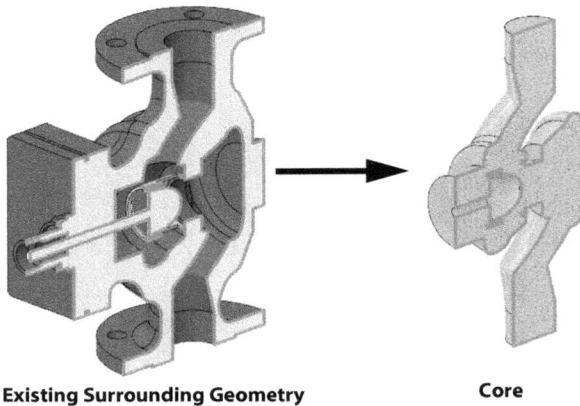

Existing Surrounding Geometry   **Core**

In a structural analysis, you would not be concerned with the void in the model and the walls of the valve would be meshed for analysis.

An analogy for the internal flow volume is a pipe filled with water that is allowed to freeze. If the pipe walls were removed, all that would remain is the solid volume of ice. This volume is where the fluid exists, and is the geometry that would be created and meshed for a CFD analysis of flow through that pipe.

The flow volume can be created directly in the CAD tool or by using the Autodesk CFD Void Fill Geometry Tool. Autodesk CFD automatically creates parts to fill fully-bounded, air-tight voids. Therefore, the use of CFD is the preferred workflow for creating the volume.

External Flows

For external flow situations, the general practice is to make the object stationary, and the flow is moved over it at the equal and opposite velocity of the physical object. When the CAD models are created, the volume that surrounds the device is rarely included as part of the production CAD model. However, if you want to analyze the external flow, it is required to add a surrounding volume to the model that encompasses the area of the model that is to be subject to the airflow. The flow volume can be modeled directly in the CAD tool or with the Autodesk CFD External Volume Geometry Tool. If modeled in the CAD tool, the shape of the external air volume can be modeled as a sphere or dome. The Autodesk CFD geometry creation tool is limited to the creation of only a rectangular shape.

- In the following example, the flow over electronic components are to be analyzed so a volume that fully encloses these components is required. To create this external volume, the Autodesk CFD Geometry Tools were used.

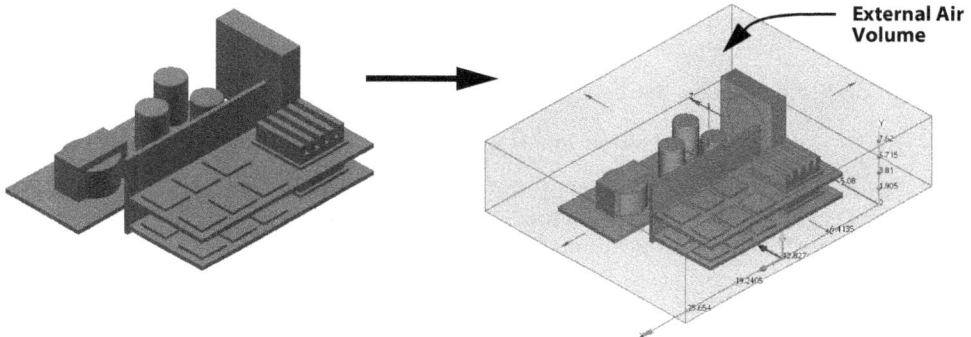

External Air Volume

- In the following example, an LED light and surrounding enclosure are modeled in CAD. To account for convective heat transfer, you must define an air volume around the model. The external volume shown was modeled in CAD to create a solid 3D cylindrical volume.

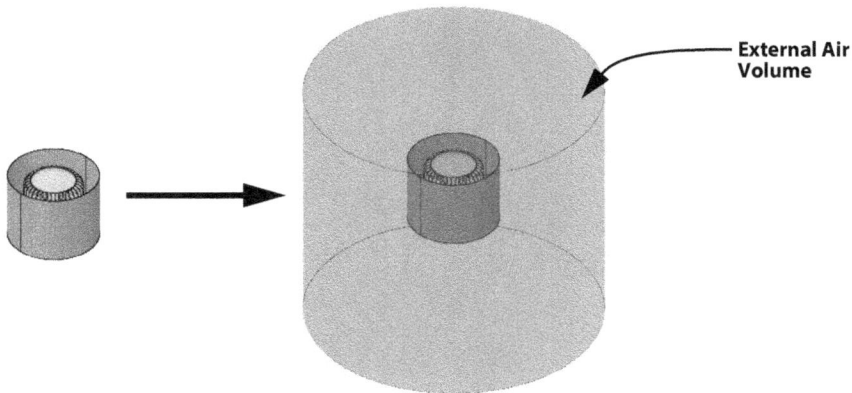

External Air Volume

Using Geometry Tools

When you first create a Design Study in Autodesk CFD, the Geometry Tools dialog box opens. Geometry Tools provide a way to modify the CAD model from the perspective of the mesher. This doesn't actually change the geometry.

- **Edge Merging**: Connect edges that share a vertex with an inflection less than a specified tolerance.

- **Small Object Removal**: Remove very small surfaces and edges that are typically too small to see, but can greatly affect meshing.

- **Void Fill Creation**: Fill an internal cavity with a meshable volume to simulate the flow.

- **External Volume Creation**: Immerse the model in a flow volume to simulate external flow.

To access the Geometry Tools, select the Setup tab, and in the Setup Tasks panel, select Geometry Tools. Alternatively, right-click on the Geometry branch of the Design Study bar and click Edit. The Geometry Tools also automatically display when creating a new study.

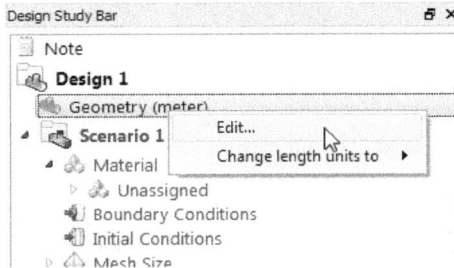

The tabs are arranged in the recommended order of use: Edge Merging --> Small Object Removal --> Void Fill --> External Volume

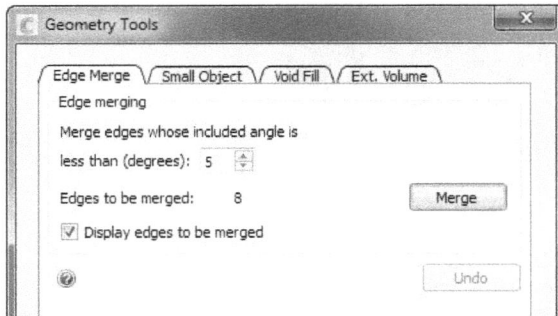

> The use of the geometry tools should be carefully considered. If used indiscriminately, they can cause additional issues with the model. Carefully observing which edges or small objects are going to be removed is a requirement.

Edge Merging

In many cases, the solid CAD geometry can have edges that meet at a common vertex. These edges can result in an overly complex model, so Edge Merging unifies edges, especially small ones. The merging of edges reduces overall mesh density, and therefore the analysis time.

Edges that can be merged are marked with an arrow and the number of edges to be merged is shown in the Geometry Tools dialog box, as shown in the following image.

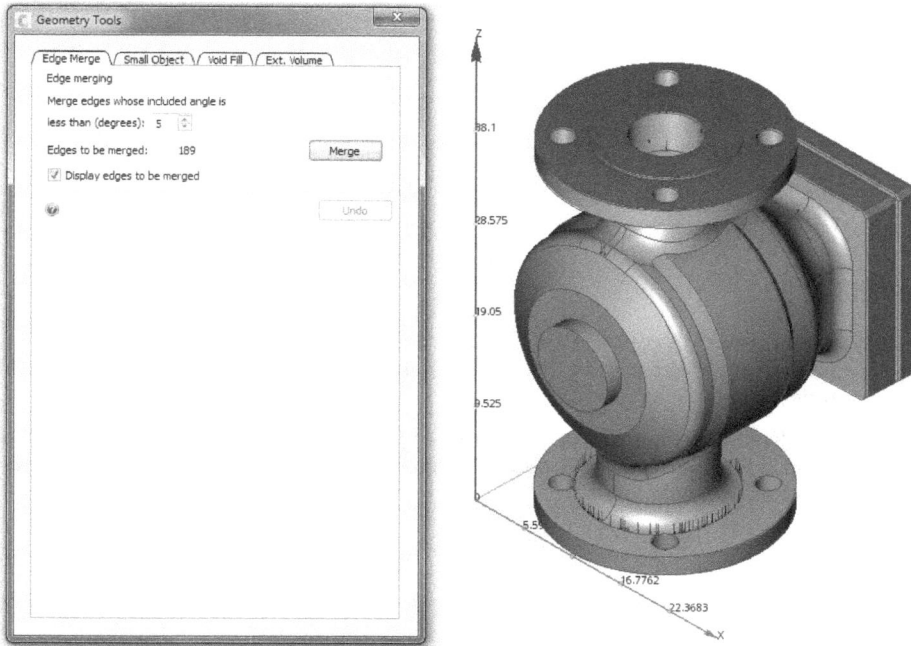

Small Object Removal

The Small Object Removal tool will remove very small edges or surfaces that are either too small to be seen or that have minimal impact on design, but that can result in an excessive mesh density. For example, in the left-hand image below, a very small sliver surface is shown in the middle of the top surface. This loop results in a very high mesh density, that will increase analysis time. The right-hand image shows the much less dense mesh that results from removing the sliver surfaces.

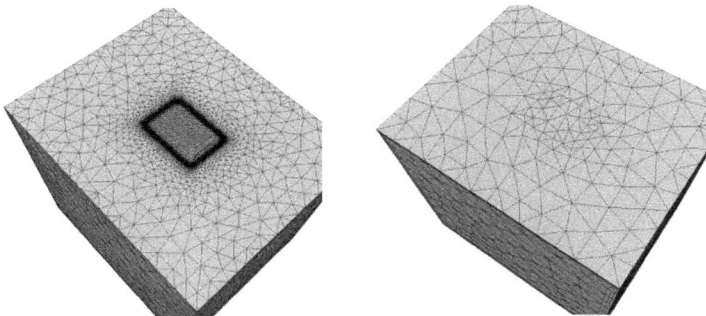

To access Small Object Removal, select the Small Object tab as shown in the following image.

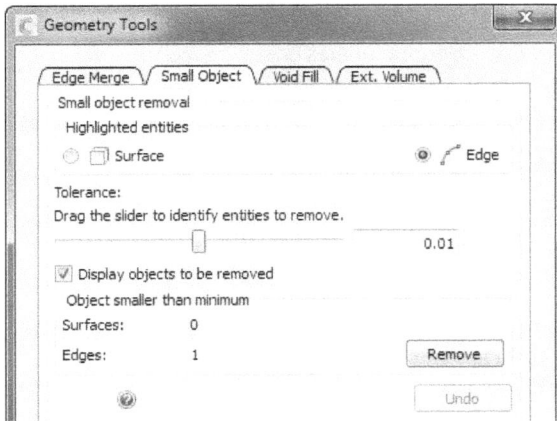

Void Fill

Typically, solid geometry is contained in the CAD model, but the fluid volume is not. The fluid region is usually defined within and around the solids, but in most cases is not explicitly constructed as part of the geometric model.

CAD models will typically have openings where the working fluid (air, water, and so on) will enter and leave, as shown in the following valve model. This model is not suitable for a flow analysis in its current state because there is no fluid part.

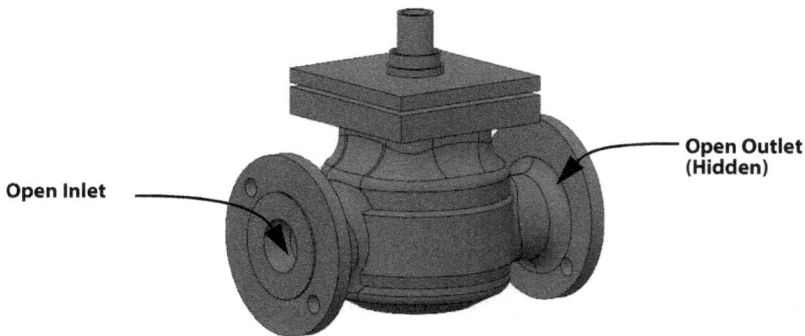

To access Void Filling, select the Void Fill tab in the Geometry Tools dialog box. The Void Fill tool provides the ability to create capping surfaces that will form a closed internal void. The surfaces and volumes created are geometry that can have boundary conditions, materials, etc. applied to them, and are meshed as part of the simulation model.

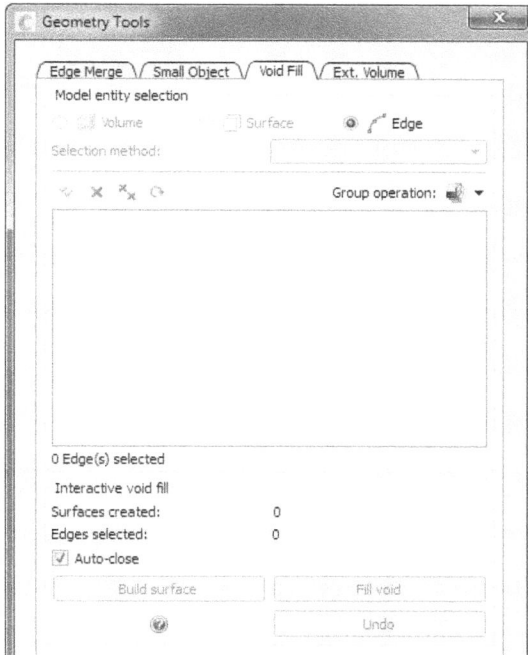

To fill a void and create a capping surface, select an edge(s) that form(s) a closed opening. If the Auto-close option is selected, the system will select adjacent edges to create a complete boundary. If Auto-close is not selected, you can manually select enough edges to enclose the opening. The surface created must be planar and cannot overlap or cut through existing geometry. Regions created with the Void Fill tool are added to the Parts branch and are named Volume. They are part of the simulation model and can be meshed.

In the following example, edges in the left-hand image were selected to fill a void. The capped surface is shown on the right.

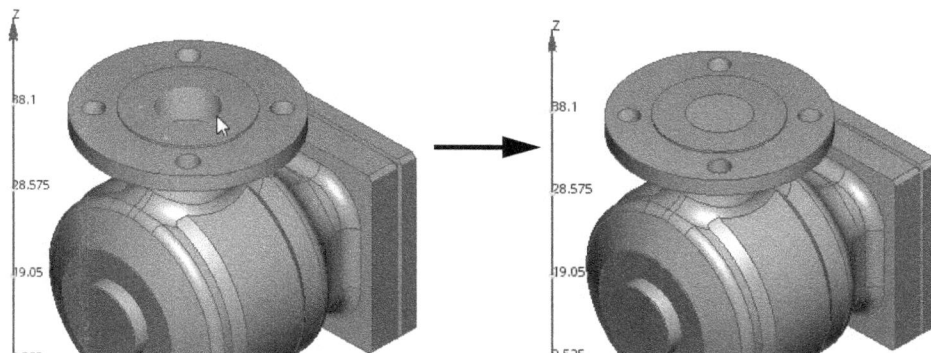

External Volume

Many models are immersed in a fluid (e.g., air or water), so a key factor in the design of these models is how the fluid flows around the device. The External Volume tool enables you to quickly and easily establish the surrounding fluid volume directly on the simulation model in Autodesk CFD. Using this tool means that you do not have to create the volume in the CAD geometry.

To access External Volume creation, select the Ext. Volume tab in the Geometry Tools dialog box.

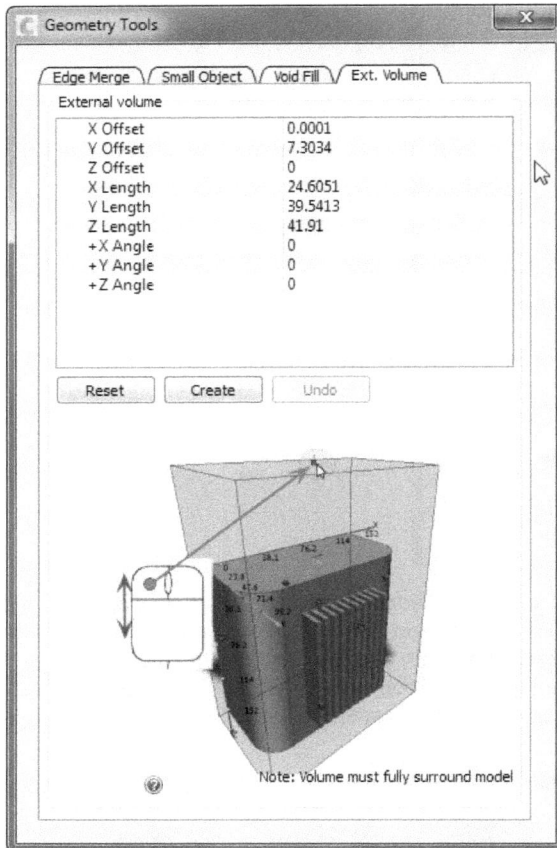

Drag the arrows on the volume to increase or decrease the default volume size. Alternatively, you can use the entry fields in the dialog box. This tool is only able to create the volume around the entire model. If the volume is to lie on a specific face that is for example, attached to other geometry, the volume must be created in the CAD model.

Lesson: Model Assessment Toolkit

Overview

Your CAD model should be evaluated for possible issues to ensure successful import and meshing in Autodesk CFD. Before you import a model, you can use the Model Assessment Toolkit (MAT) to evaluate your model for six different types of geometry issues. You can iterate between your CAD system and the MAT until your model is ready for use in CFD.

Objectives

After completing this lesson, you will be able to:

- Understand when to use the Model Assessment Toolkit.
- Use the two methods to launch the Model Assessment Toolkit.
- Understand the six different geometry issues reported on by the Model Assessment Toolkit.

Why use the Model Assessment Toolkit (MAT)

In an effort to reduce the occurrences of mesh failures and unpredictable simulation results due to poorly formed geometry, Autodesk has added the MAT into the CFD product.

The general workflow for analyzing a model is to establish your fluid volume in the CAD model, import that model into CFD, set up materials and boundary conditions, mesh the fluid volumes, then run the simulation. The quality of the fluid volumes or geometry you create with your CAD model will dictate how successful the overall process is.

The MAT provides tools to ensure that the geometry results in quality fluid volumes before running a time consuming analysis. For example, if the fluid contains unusually small volumes, the mesher could fail or the model could end up with areas of high mesh concentration.

Launching MAT

You can launch the MAT directly from your CAD system. For example, if you are working in Autodesk® Inventor®, select the Simulation tab and click Active Model Assessment Tool to launch and open your model in the MAT. The Autodesk CFD 2017 panel for Autodesk Inventor is shown in the following image. Other CAD systems have similar commands.

You can also enter the MAT when importing geometry directly into CFD. This is done by selecting the Model Diagnostic option from the drop-down list, as shown in the following image, when setting up a new study.

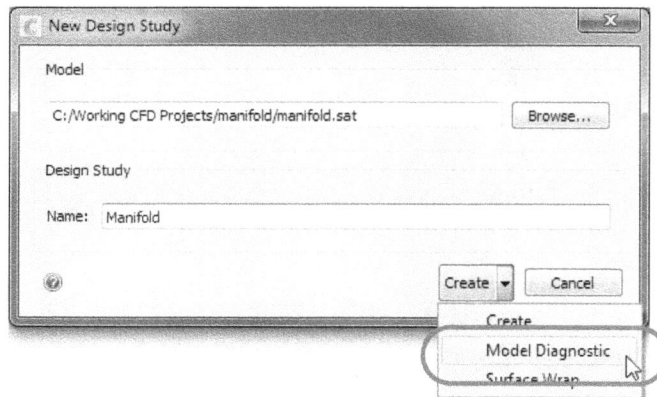

The MAT Environment

The MAT is an add-in for the CFD application. When the MAT is active, the Model Assessment tab is available in the ribbon.

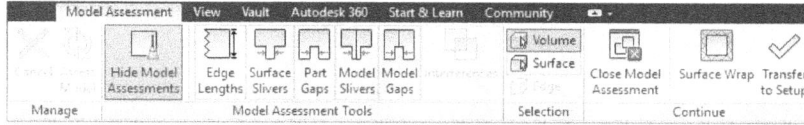

Manage the Analysis

Your CAD model opens in the MAT and it steps through the various analyses. The Model Assessment window in the MAT shows the progress of each analysis that is listed in the Assess Model tab. Green checkmarks indicate that the analyses are complete. You can cancel the ongoing and queued analyses by clicking Cancel in the Model Assessment window or in the Manage panel. Canceling can be done up until all analyses are complete. If you do cancel before all analyses are complete, you can click Assess Model to restart. Note that all analyses are performed again, including those that were already run.

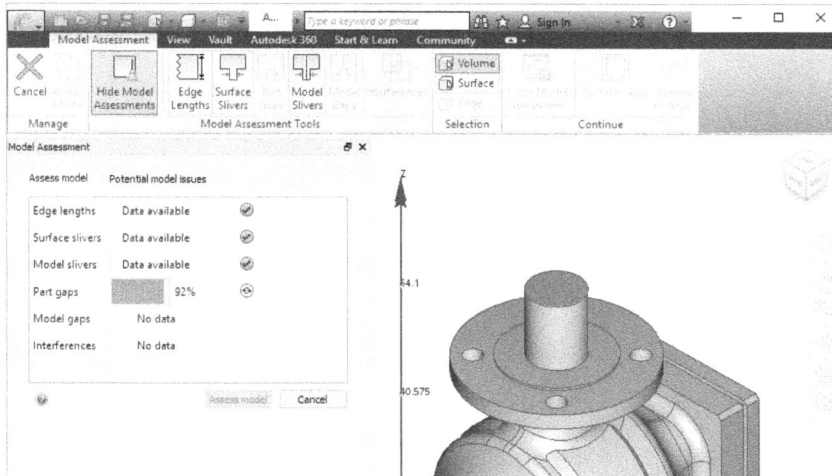

Model Assessment Tools

You can access the assessment tools using either of the following methods. Note that the analysis does not have to be complete to select any of the available tools.

- Select the appropriate tool in the Model Assessment Tools panel on the ribbon.
- Selecting appropriate tool in the Model Assessment Tools drop-down list in the Potential model issues tab.

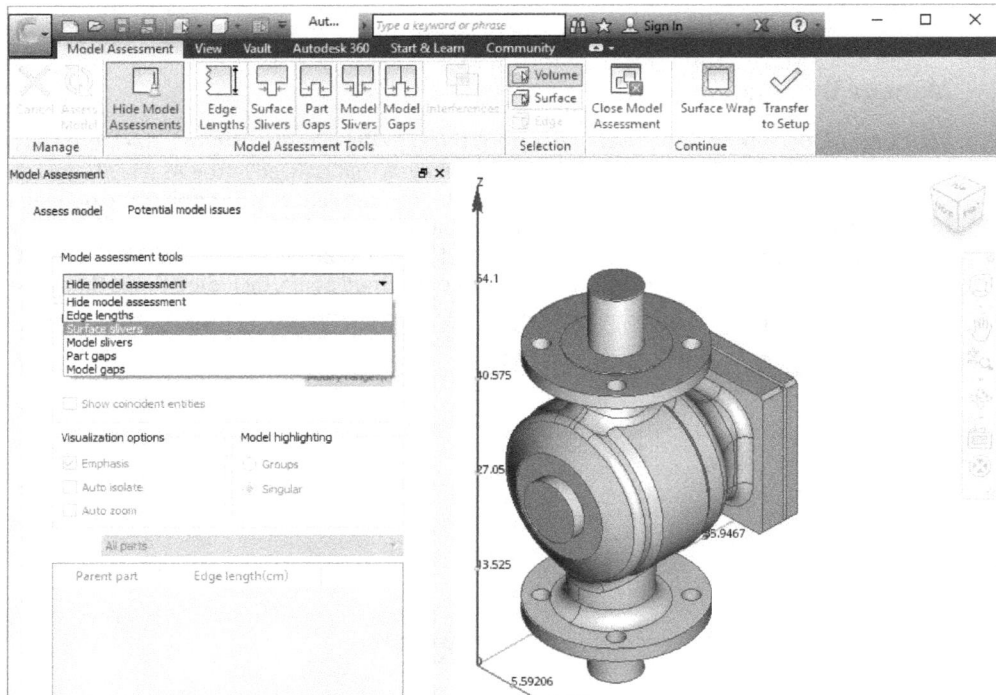

Use the Edge Lengths, Surface Slivers and Part Gaps assessment tools to assess your model for part issues. The Model Slivers, Model Gaps, and Interferences assessment tools are used to assess the model for assembly issues. The following image shows the user interface when the Model Gaps tool is active, but the settings and controls are similar for each of the tools.

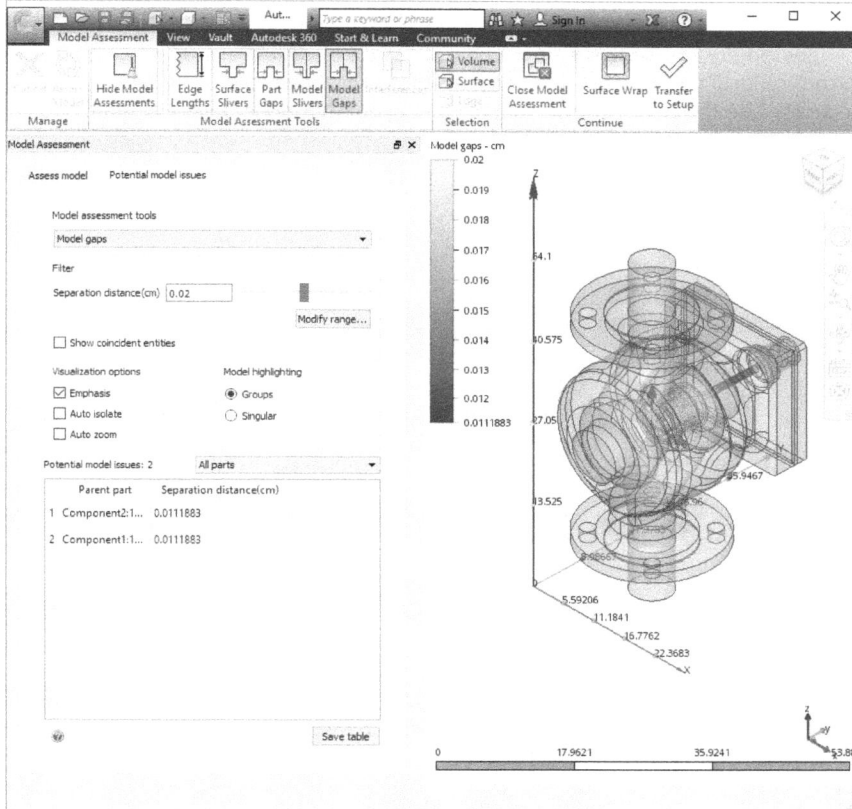

The following sections are available for all assessment tools:

- **Filter** - The filter settings are used to isolate objects that potentially have issues. The slider bar is used to vary the maximum object size, where any object smaller than the slider bar value is included as a potential issue. You can also type a value into the slider size box, or use the Modify range option to specify the object's size range to be assessed. As changes are made to the filter settings, the number of Potential model issues will vary.

- **Visualization options** - These settings are used to customize how the model displays as you click on the parent parts in the issues table. You can multi-select table entries, if appropriate.

- **Model highlighting** - Using the Singular option, the parts selected in the issue table will highlight on the model. Alternatively, you can select Groups to highlight the associated group of parts.

- **Potential model issues** - The Potential model issues list displays the number of issues found using the current filter settings. Use the drop-down to display issues associated with a specific part. Select individual or multiple table entries to study them in the graphics window.

Assessment Tools

Each assessment tool looks at different aspect of the model.

Edge Lengths

Small part edges require fine mesh seeding, which can significantly increase mesh counts. Small edges can also introduce local discontinuity in the mesh length scales, which can negatively impact the solution accuracy. Use the Edge Lengths tool to assess your model for potential small edge issues.

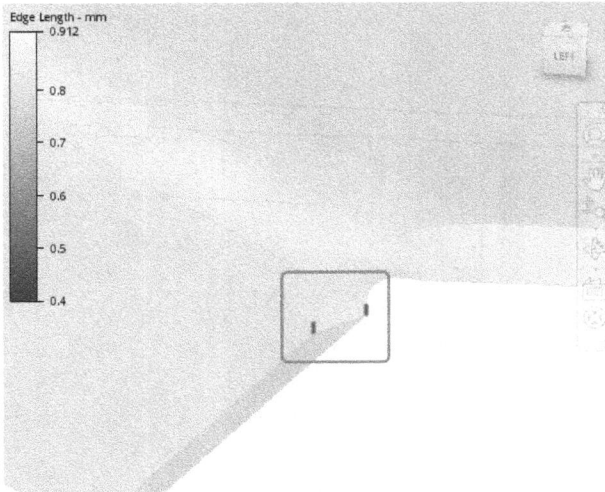

Surface Slivers

Similar to short edges, small surfaces on parts can result in mesh length scale issues. Use the Surface Slivers tool to assess your model for small surfaces that cause issues with the CFD mesher.

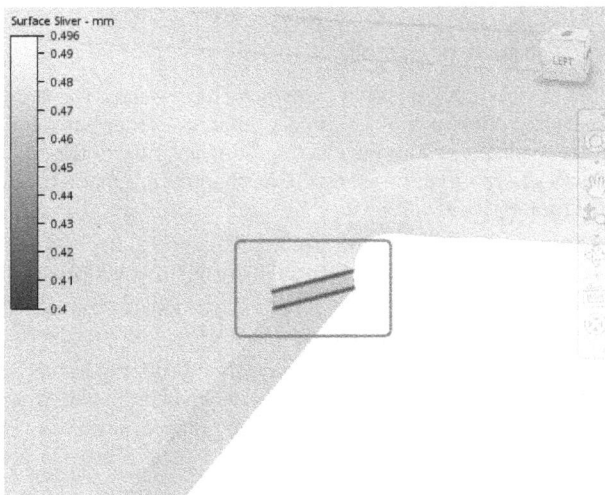

Part Gaps

The Part Gaps tool assesses your model for small gaps that may create issues with CFD mesher. Small gaps create issues as a fluid volume will have to squeeze into that gap, often causing meshing failures.

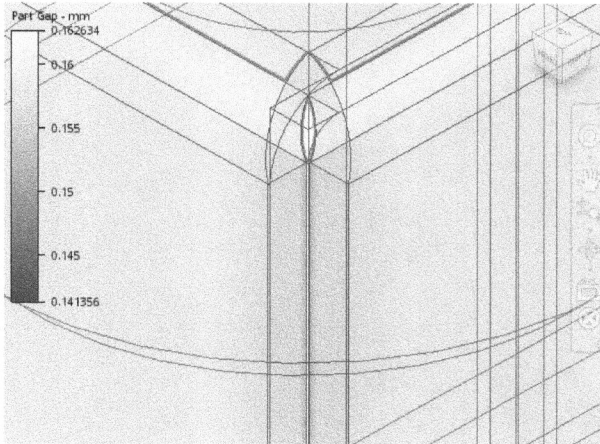

Model Slivers

Assembled components can generate small sliver surfaces where the components come in contact. Sliver surfaces require fine mesh seeding, which can significantly increase mesh counts and also introduce local discontinuity in the mesh length scales. For example, in the following image, a small offset exists between the edges of the heat sinks and chips. This offset is likely due to incorrectly applied assembly constraints; however, transferring this model into CFD without correcting the issue results in the creation of a large surface with a small sliver.

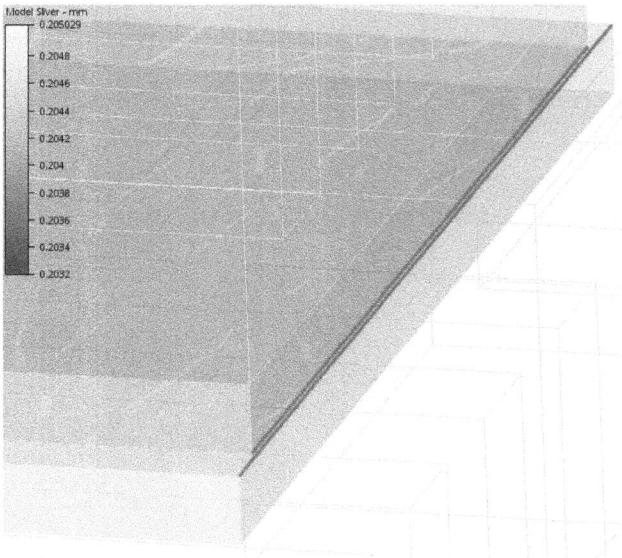

Model Gaps

Small gaps between assembly parts can also result in mesh length scale issues. The Model Gaps tool identifies these small gaps, which can create meshing difficulties.

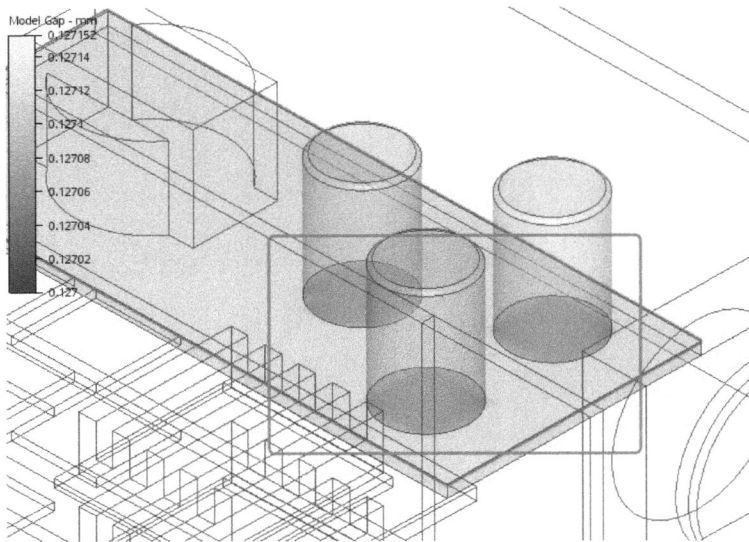

Interferences

Interferences between parts will create additional volumes when brought into Autodesk CFD. This is because a boolean operation is initiated during the importing process, which generates these volumes. Very small interferences can create small edges and sliver surfaces. However, larger interferences can be used to your benefit (not in Creo or Catia). For example, when making an external fluid volume it is not required to make a perfect cut out of the model. You can completely interfere the parts.

Exiting MAT

The MAT is simply used to identify potential issues. Once identified, return to the source CAD system to edit the geometry to repair the problems. Once changes are made, it is recommended that you rerun the assessment using MAT again. Working with MAT and your CAD system is an iterative process.

Once the CAD model is ready for simulation in CFD, click ✓ (Transfer to Setup) or ◻ (Surface Wrap).

Lesson: Surface Wrapping

Autodesk® Surface Wrap is used to surface wrap a model, add an external volume, and generate a mesh for transfer into Autodesk CFD.

Objectives

After completing this lesson, you will be able to:

- Understand the concept of Surface Wrapping.
- Describe the workflow required to apply Surface Wrapping to your model.

Surface Wrapping

For external flow analyses or wind tunnel type models such as vehicles, airplanes and so on, you can use Autodesk Surface Wrap. Autodesk Surface Wrap will surface wrap the model, add an external volume, and generate a quality mesh for transfer into Autodesk CFD. Extremely complex models, such as the models shown in the following image, can require extensive CAD cleanup in order to generate a mesh. However, Autodesk Surface Wrap simplifies the process.

To access Surface Wrap, use either of the following methods:

- Begin the creation of a new design study, select the model you want to import, and select the Surface Wrap option.

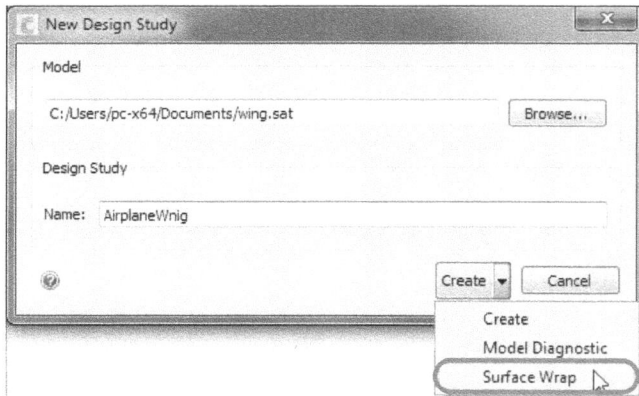

- In the Model Assessment Toolkit tab, in the Continue panel, click ⬜ (Surface Wrap).

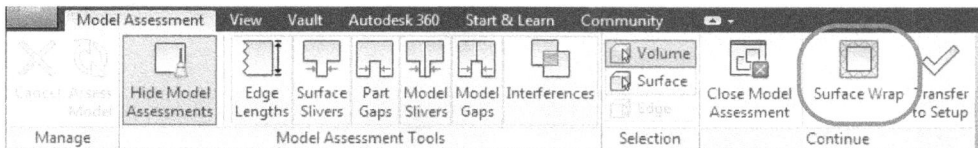

The Surface Wrap tab displays as shown in the following image.

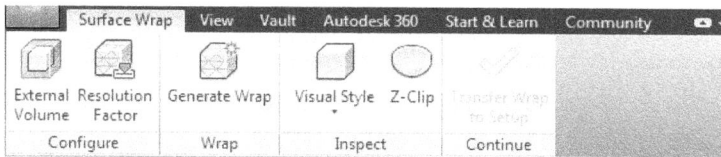

Use the following procedure to apply the surface wrap workflow:

1. In the Surface Wrap tab, in the Configure panel, click ⬜ (External Volume) to create the external volume surrounding the model. This simulates placing the model in a wind tunnel.

    ▪ Size the volume using the appropriate dialog box options or drag the arrows on the bounding box, then click Close.

    ▪ Unlike the external volume that can be created using the Geometry Tools functionality, this external volume can be aligned with a model's edge. This enables it to be to used to analyze portions of a model that attach to other geometry.

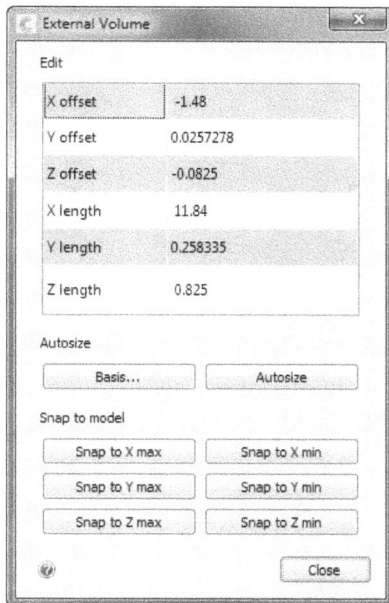

2. In the Configure panel, click ⬛ (Resolution Factor) to set the appropriate level of detail for the surface mesh. Note the following:

    ▪ High values give you a mesh that closely represents the physical model.

    ▪ Lower values result in a faster, but coarser mesh.

3. In the Wrap panel, click ⬚ (Generate Wrap) to create the surface mesh.

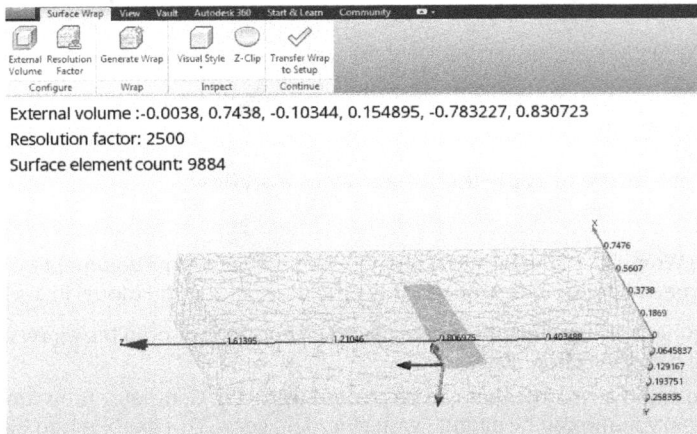

External volume :-0.0038, 0.7438, -0.10344, 0.154895, -0.783227, 0.830723
Resolution factor: 2500
Surface element count: 9884

4. In the Continue panel, click ✓ (Transfer Wrap to Setup) to transfer your mesh to Autodesk CFD where you can complete the model setup and analysis.

Lesson: SimStudio Tools Overview

Autodesk SimStudio Tools is used to prepare geometry for your simulation applications, including Autodesk CFD. Once a model is complete, the geometry is exported to a file or pushed to Autodesk CFD.

Objectives

After completing this lesson, you will be able to:

- Describe the uses of SimStudio Tools.
- Describe the interaction between SimStudio Tools and Autodesk CFD.
- Use SimStudio Tools to modify model geometry.

SimStudio Tools Overview

Autodesk SimStudio Tools is used to prepare geometry for your simulation applications, including Autodesk CFD. Once your model is complete, you can export the geometry to a standard CAD file, or push it to Autodesk CFD.

User Interface

The main areas of the SimStudio Tools user interface are the following:

1. Main graphics window
2. Workspace toolbar
3. Model browser
4. Marking menu
5. Navigation bar
6. Display settings
7. ViewCube

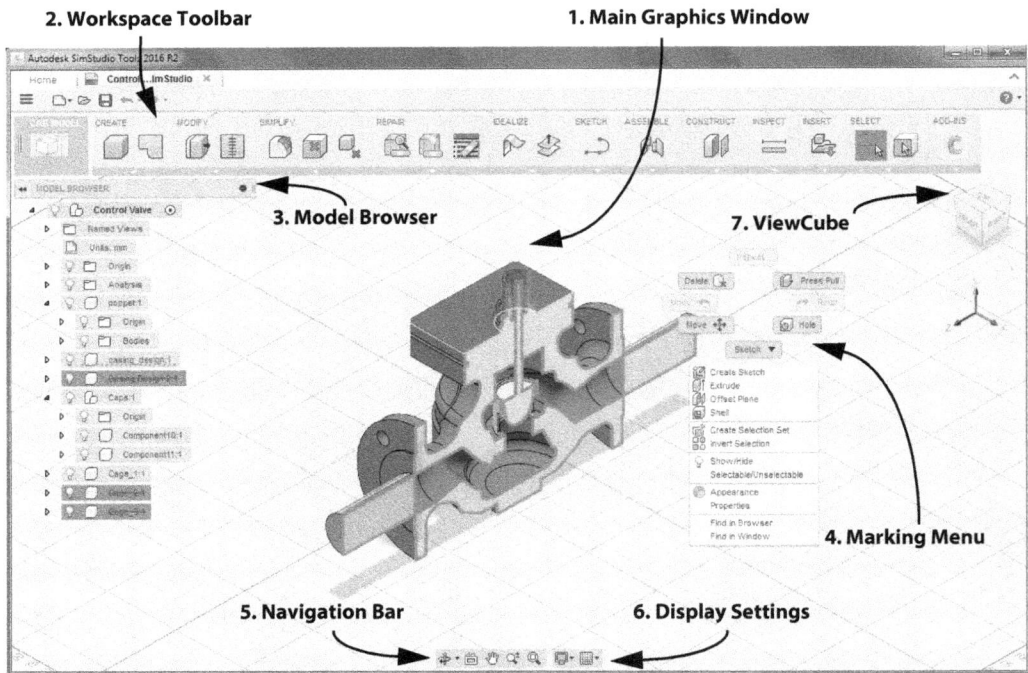

Main Graphics Window (1)

This is the area in which you will view the model, make selections on the model, and spin and zoom the display.

Workspace Toolbar (2)

The toolbar contains the commands required to work with your model. It is organized in panels that group similar commands together. On the toolbar, click the drop-down arrows to view hidden commands in the panels. Hover the cursor over a command to view an associated tooltip for that command.

Model Browser (3)

The MODEL BROWSER lists the elements that make up the model. These include reference entities, components, bodies and so on, that comprise your model.

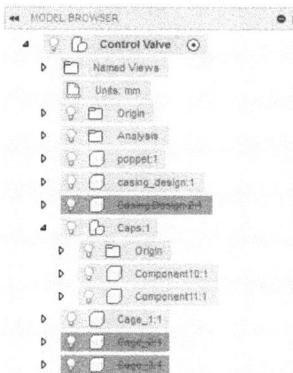

You can expand and collapse the browser nodes to clean up the display or focus on a specific element. Right-clicking on any node in the browser provides quick access to available commands.

Marking Menu (4)

If you right-click the graphics window, the marking menu displays, providing access to available commands. The marking menu and command list are context-sensitive in that the displayed commands will differ depending on what objects are currently selected.

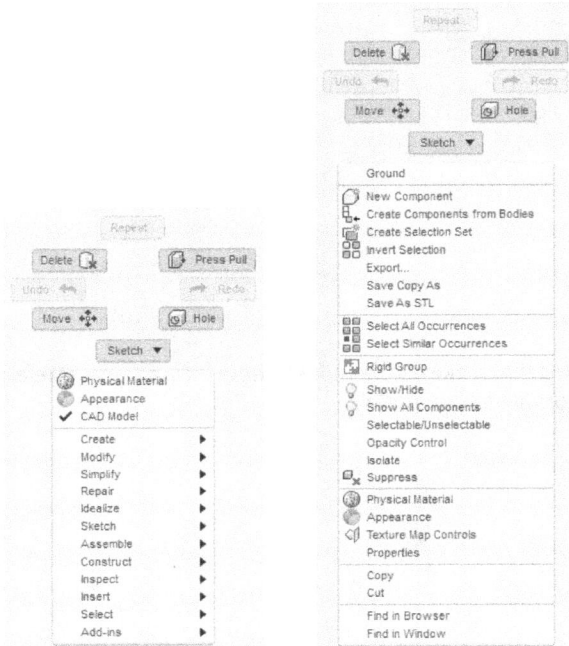

No Object Selected   **Component Selected**

Navigation Bar (5)

The Navigation bar, located at the bottom of the SimStudio Tools window, provides quick access to several viewing options. These are described in the following table.

Icon	Name	Description
	Constrained Orbit	Spin the model as if it is sitting on a turntable.
	Free Orbit	Orbit (rotate) the camera around the focal point; drag in any direction to orbit correspondingly. Orbit mode resets the world up vector. Press the middle mouse button to temporarily change to Pan.
	Look At	Looks at a particular face in the scene. The camera orients so that the selected face is centered and parallel with the screen.
	Pan	Drag in any direction to move the camera correspondingly. Hold <Shift> and the middle mouse button to temporarily switch to Orbit (rotate).

Icon	Name	Description
Q±	Zoom	Drag up or down to move the camera in and out along the axis of the focal point.
Q	Fit	Reset the view to fully fit in the graphics window, without reorienting.

Display Settings (6)

The Display Settings bar, located at the bottom of the SimStudio Tools window, provides quick access to multiple display options, as outlined in the following table:

Icon	Name	Description
▼	Display Settings	Access display settings such as Visual Style, Environments, Effects and so on.
▼	Grid and Snaps	Access options for toggling the Layout grid on and off, snapping to the grid, and so on.

ViewCube (7)

The ViewCube works in SimStudio Tools in the same way that it works in Autodesk CFD, and it is used to reorient the current view of a model, or quickly return to the Home orientation.

Solid Modeling in SimStudio Tools

Unlike history based modeling tools such as Autodesk Inventor, SimStudio Tools is a direct modeler. This means that a model is a collection of features and geometry where no history of feature creation is maintained. With direct modeling, you can change geometry without editing the feature.

You can create standard modeling features like extrudes, fillets, and ribs. Several boolean options such as Join, Cut, Intersect, and New Component are also available. Most features become independent geometry after they are created, so you can only edit a few features, like holes and patterns.

Each component is comprised of a solid body and multiple solid bodies can be included to represent an assembly.

Creating Geometry in SimStudio Tools

You can create both solid and surface geometry using SimStudio Tools. The tools for creating geometry are found by expanding the Create panel.

Select the option you want to use and create the geometry. The process is similar to most CAD packages. For example, to create a cylinder, consider the following workflow:

1. Expand the Create panel and select Cylinder. Select a planar surface, face or datum plane to sketch on as shown in the following image.

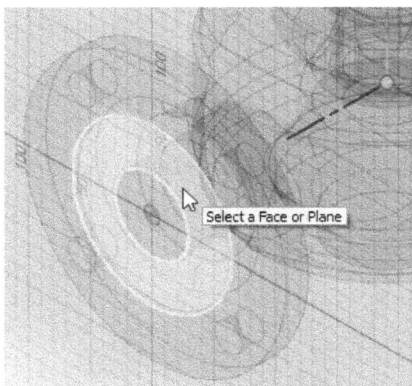

---

2. Select the center point for the circle and a second point to set the diameter of the circle. Alternatively, you can enter a diameter value in the input field and press <Enter>.

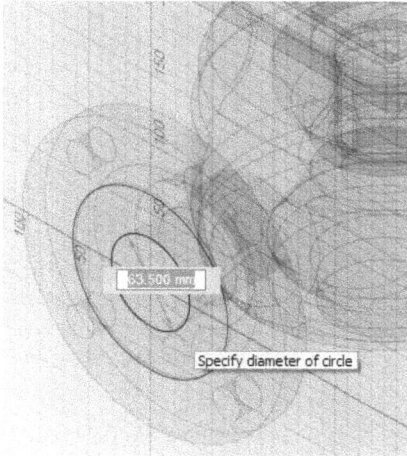

3. Select a point on the sketch to access the CYLINDER dialog box. If you had simply selected the diameter in the previous step, the dialog box would have immediately opened.

4. Use the Cylinder dialog box (as shown in the following image) to enter a Height value. Alternatively, you can also enter a new Diameter value.

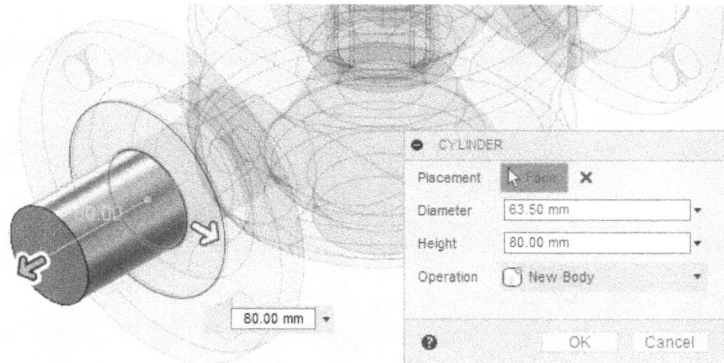

5. Click OK to create the geometry.

Simplification

Although CAD systems are capable of capturing incredible levels of detail, that same detail can create issues with mesh creation and unnecessary complexity in a CFD analysis. Features that are very small with respect to the overall analysis are most likely negligible. For example, typical modeled geometry such as serial numbers and rounds can be omitted from the simulation.

To help reduce computation time and reduce meshing issues, SimStudio Tools has several options for simplifying model geometry.

Suppress Objects

You can reduce the complexity of your model by suppressing objects prior to using the geometry in the Autodesk CFD software. Typically, object suppression can be used for objects that have negligible or no impact on the analysis. For example, in a very complex PCB assembly, some of the very small and complex components will have little effect on a heat transfer analysis and can be suppressed.

- To suppress objects, select the objects and use (Suppress) in the Simplify panel.

- To resume the objects, click (Unsuppress).

Objects that are suppressed display in the MODEL BROWSER with a dark box with a strikeout through the name, as shown in the following image.

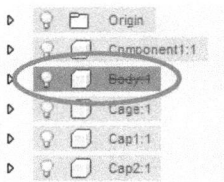

Remove Features and Faces

You can also reduce complexity by removing features and faces in your model.

- To remove faces, select the objects and use ![icon](Remove Faces) (Remove Faces) in the Simplify panel. This will remove the selected surface and any adjacent surfaces also need to be removed to heal the model.

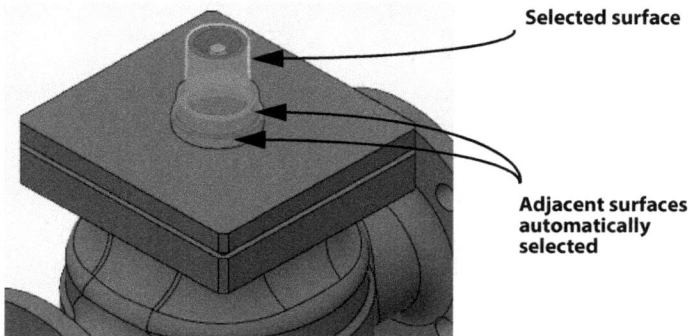

Selected surface

Adjacent surfaces automatically selected

- To remove features, select the objects and use ⬚ (Remove Features) in the Simplify panel. This will remove features that are of the type(s) and size set in the REMOVE FEATURES dialog box, as shown in the following image.

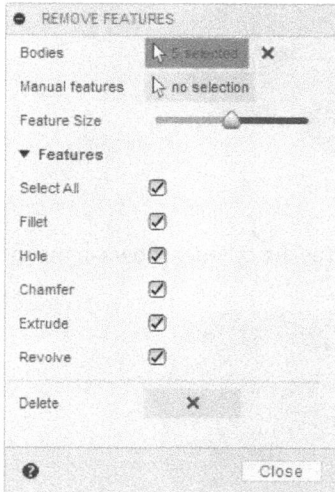

REMOVE FEATURES

Bodies	5 selected	✕
Manual features	no selection	
Feature Size	◯	

▼ Features

Select All	☑
Fillet	☑
Hole	☑
Chamfer	☑
Extrude	☑
Revolve	☑

| Delete | ✕ |

❓   Close

Each feature type is highlighted in a different color in the model. Select Manual features to remove specific features from selection, or to select specific features that are outside of the size threshold.

Flow Volume

You can create a flow volume using SimStudio Tools. This is done by capping any openings in the model using a patch surface or by creating solid features. To create a flow volume, complete the following:

1. Expand the Create panel and click ⬚ (Patch) to open the PATCH dialog box, as shown in the following image.

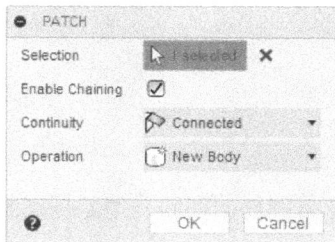

PATCH

Selection	1 selected	✕
Enable Chaining	☑
Continuity	Connected	▼
Operation	New Body	▼

❓   OK   Cancel

2. Select an edge that fully bounds an opening. SimStudio Tools caps the opening with a surface, as shown in the following image.

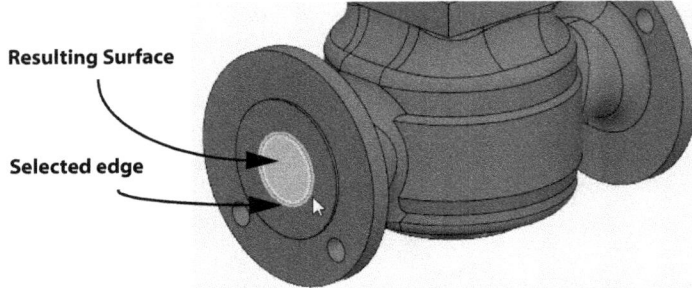

Resulting Surface

Selected edge

- Alternatively, you can create solid geometry such as the cylinder shown in the following image, to cover any openings.

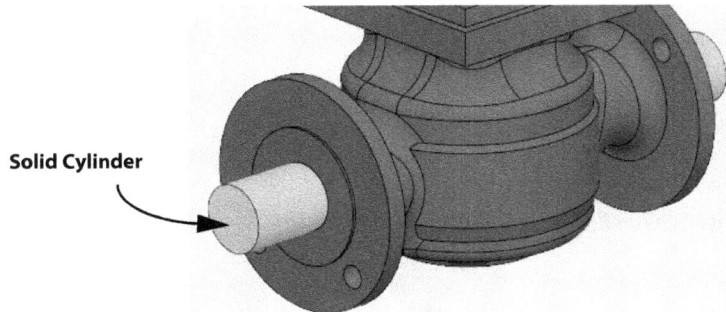

Solid Cylinder

3. Once all openings are capped to provide a water tight cavity, expand the Create panel and select Fluid Volume. The FLUID VOLUME dialog box opens as shown in the following image.

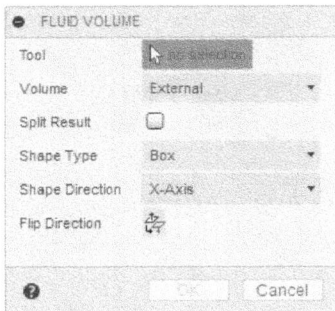

4. In the Volume drop-down list, select Internal to create an Internal volume. The default option is to create an External volume.

5. To define the volume, click and drag a rectangle around the affected geometry, as shown in the following image.

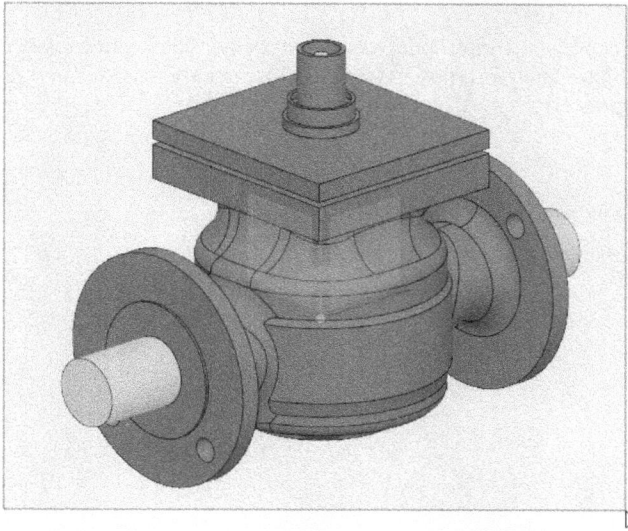

6. In the FLUID VOLUME dialog box, click OK. The flow volume is created, as shown in the sectioned view in the following image.

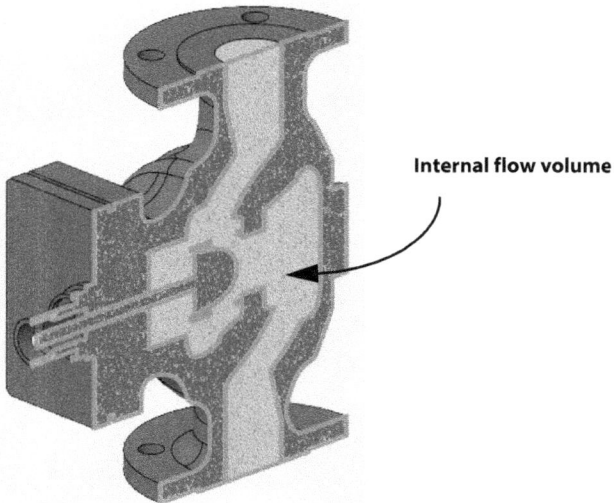

Internal flow volume

> Alternatively, the Boundary Fill option in the CREATE panel can also be used to create the flow volume. This is done by selecting references solids, surfaces, work planes as tools to form volumes.

Lesson: Using Devices to Simplify Geometry

There are situations in which the analysis model has a lot of detail that might cause the model to require more mesh and longer analysis times. In some of these situations, you can replace detail with predefined devices to improve both mesh count and simulation time.

Objectives

After completing this lesson, you will be able to:

- Describe the use of Devices for model simplification.

Using Devices

One of the most critical concepts in CFD is to simplify geometry where possible and practical, to reduce analysis time and resources, without compromising the quality of analysis results.

Autodesk CFD has a library of built in devices. Devices are a powerful way to use geometrically simple objects to represent complex parts or assemblies. They affect the flow in the same manner as the physical component, but at a fraction of the mesh size and complexity. The result is a faster and more efficient analysis process.

Devices are assigned as Materials that have the same properties of the associated device. This topic, along with materials, will be covered in more detail in the next chapter, however, an overview is provided here while model geometry is discussed.

Consider the model shown in the following image. In this model, the inlet filter can be replaced with a distributed resistance device and the blade geometry replaced with a centrifugal blower/pump device.

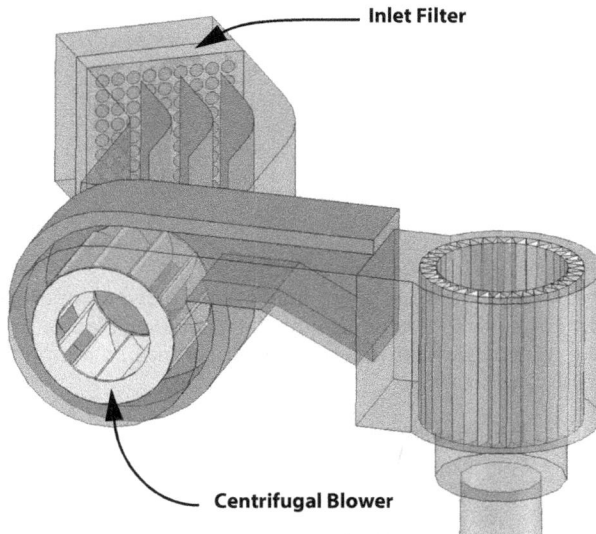

Distributed Resistance

Distributed resistances are used to represent flow obstructions in models. Consider the following example:

- The CAD model contains a sheet with perforated holes, as shown in the left-hand image. The presence of these holes can be useful if you are studying the detailed velocities of each orifice and how that velocity profile changes. However, in a larger system where this will be one component, this will introduce a pressure loss in the system.

- By replacing the detailed cad model with a distributed resistance, shown in the left-hand image, the model is simplified. The distributed resistance averages out some of the detail on the velocity profiles, predicts a similar pressure drop to that of the detailed model, and will allow the analysis to run much more efficiently.

Solid Material CAD Model　　　　　　　　　　　**Resistance Material**

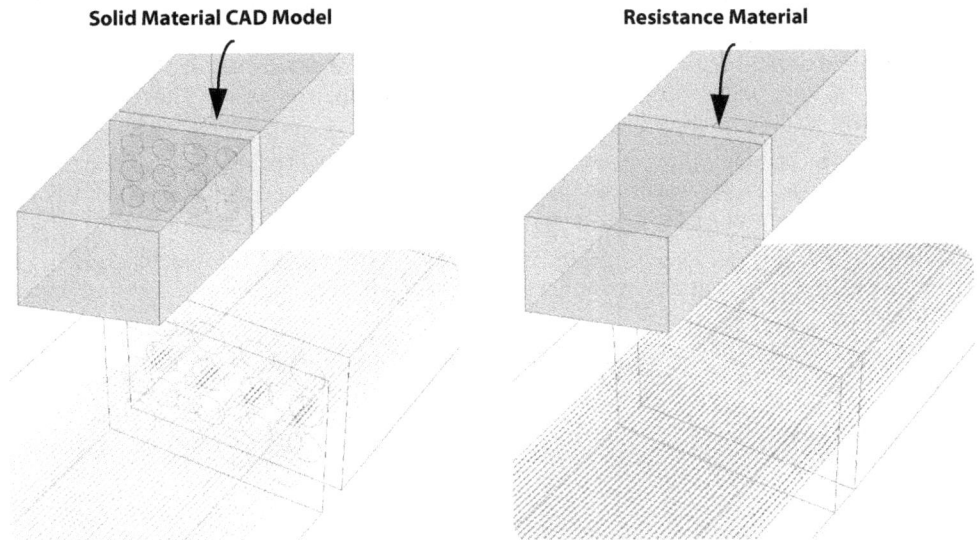

Centrifugal Blower

Centrifugal Blowers have similar simplifications as resistances. Running the blower's detailed geometry involves a transient model, to deal with the movement of the spinning blades. This would give a very detailed flow solution, but would also mean notably longer run times, as the software tries to take the transient model to a steady state solution.

Centrifugal Blower CAD Model　　　　　**Simplified Blower Material**

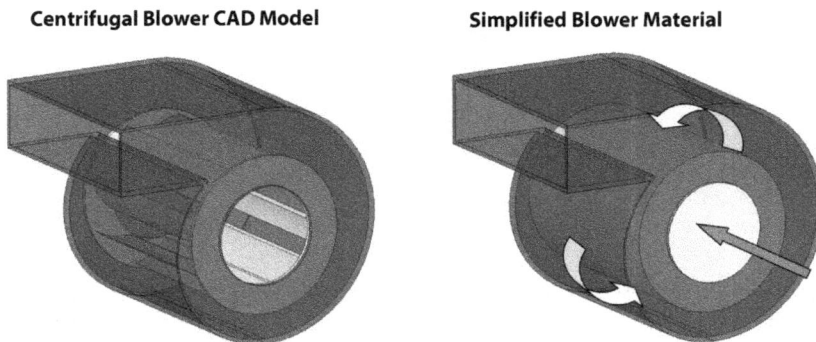

With the blower device, you can provide performance information such as the RPM and the flowrate and keep this as a quicker steady-state running model.

Exercise: Internal Flow Geometry

In this exercise, you will begin by opening a a CAD model in Autodesk SimStudio Tools and use it to review the geometry. You will then launch Autodesk CFD directly from Autodesk SimStudio Tools so that changes can be easily communicated between the two products. To complete the exercise, you will learn how Autodesk CFD can automatically create an internal flow volume. The objectives in this exercise are to:

- Use Autodesk SimStudio Tools to review a model.
- Use Autodesk SimStudio Tools to launch Autodesk CFD and create a Design Study.
- Investigate the model in Autodesk CFD.
- Use Autodesk SimStudio Tools to modify the model and update it in Autodesk CFD to allow for the automatic creation of a flow volume.

Open the Model in the Autodesk SimStudio Tools Environment.

1. Launch Autodesk SimStudio Tools, if not already running.

2. In the Home tab, click (Open).

3. In the Open dialog box, browse to the *C:\Autodesk CFD 2017 Essentials Exercise Files\Gometry\ControlValve Model* folder. Select and open *ControlValve.SimStudio*. The model displays as shown in the following image.

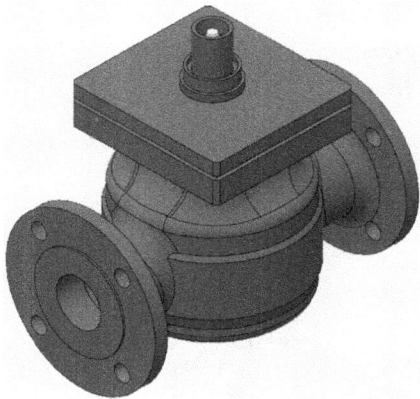

4. If your model displays a shadow, toggle off the ground plane, as shown in the following image.

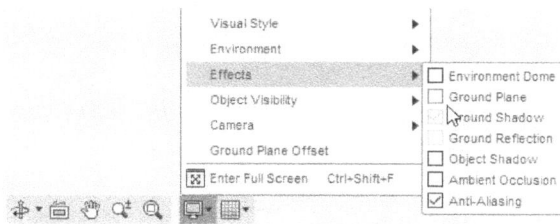

5. The MODEL BROWSER displays as shown in the following image.

  ▪ The model browser is a listing of the elements of the SimStudio file.

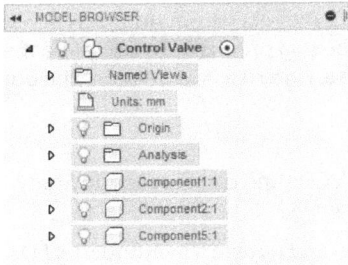

6. In the MODEL BROWSER, expand the Named Views node, if not already expanded.

  ▪ Select the TOP and RIGHT named views to reorient the model.

  ▪ Select ⌂ on the ViewCube to return to the model's default Home view. Alternatively, you can select Home in the Named Views list.

  ▪ Select faces on the ViewCube to reorient the model.

  ▪ Before continuing return to the model's Home view.

  ▪ Compress the Named Views Node.

  ▪ Hold <Shift> and the middle mouse button to spin the model.

    • Right-click on the Named Views node and select New Named View.

    • Select Named View and enter **My Custom View** as the name.

  ▪ Return to the model's default Home view.

  ▪ Compress the Named Views node.

7. In the MODEL BROWSER, expand the Origin node, if not already expanded, to view the default coordinate system, axes, and planes.

  ▪ Move the cursor over each element in the Origin node and note that the elements highlight in the model as shown in the following image.

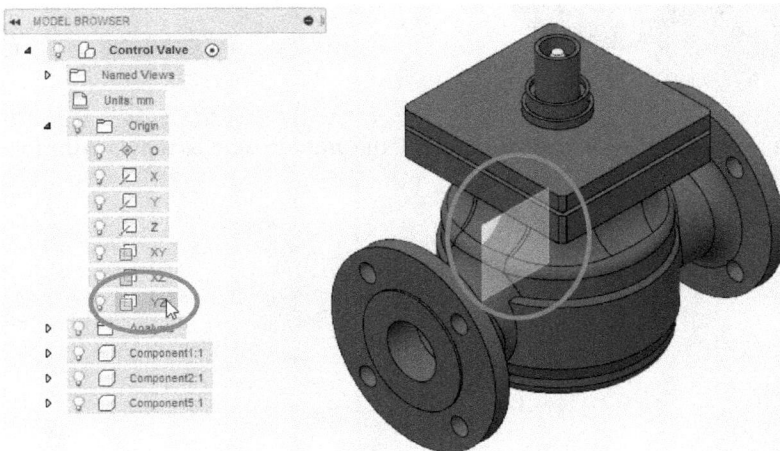

8. By default, the display of the Origin node is toggled off, as indicated by the 💡 icon. The datum entities are only displayed when the cursor is placed over them. To control their individual display, enable persistent display.

- Click 💡 next to the Origin node, which will make the datum display persistent for the coordinate system, axes, and planes.

- Click 💡 next to XY and XZ to remove them from display.

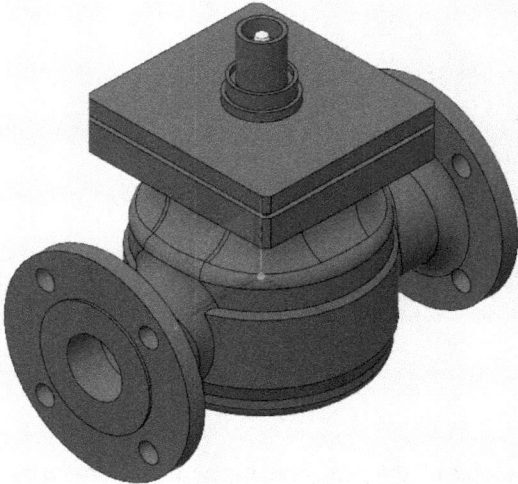

9. Create a cross-section to show the interior of the model, using the plane you just displayed.

- Expand the INSPECT panel and select Section Analysis.
- Select plane YZ on the screen or in the MODEL BROWSER.
- In the SECTION ANALYSIS dialog box, click OK. The model updates as shown in the following image. The empty interior volume is clearly displayed.

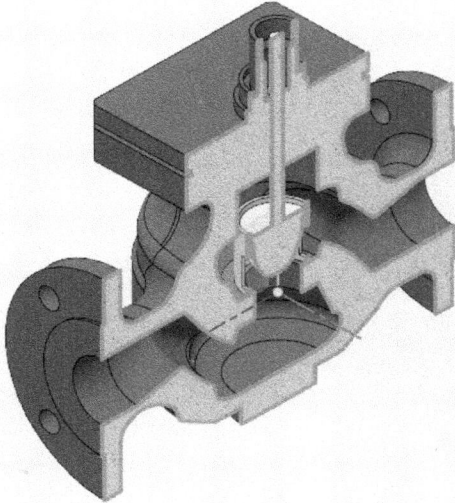

- Click 💡 next to Origin to toggle off the persistent display and compress the Origin node.

10. In the MODEL BROWSER, expand the Analysis node and note that Section1 was added there, as shown in the following image.

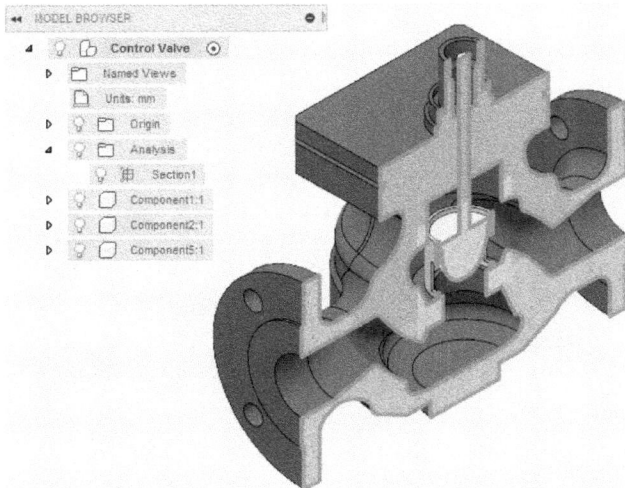

- Select 💡 next to Section1 to toggle off its display.
- Compress the Analysis node.

Launch Autodesk CFD from Autodesk SimStudio Tools and create a design study.

In this task, you will use SimStudio Tools to launch Autodesk CFD and create a design study. Using this approach, you will be able to later edit the model in SimStudio Tools and update it in the design study.

1. Expand the ADD-INS panel in the ribbon and select Simulate in CFD.

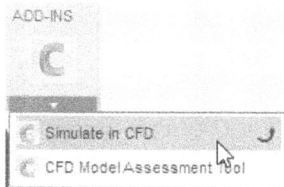

2. In the Design Study Manager dialog box, in the New design study tab, enter **Control Valve Geometry** for the Study name and click Launch.

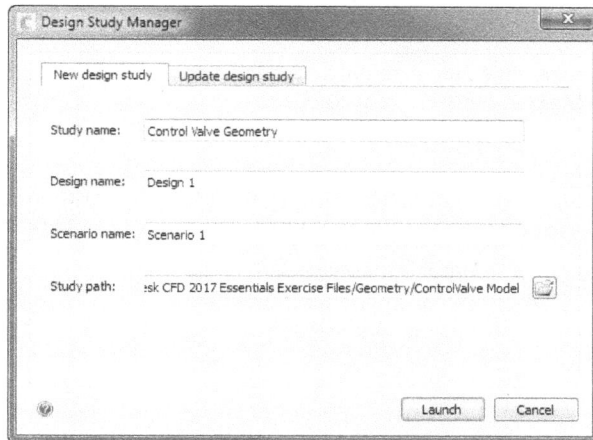

3. The Geometry tools dialog box opens and highlights the edges with an included angle less than 5 degrees. There are 189 such edges, as shown in the following image.

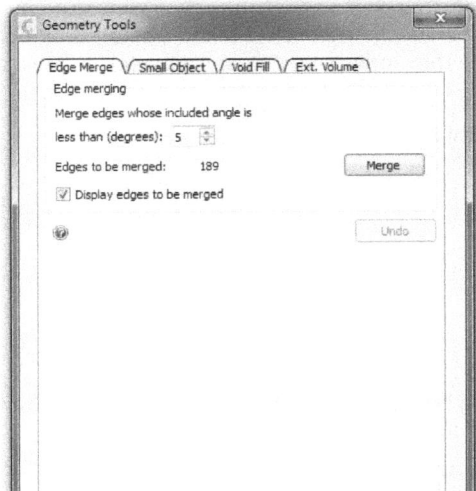

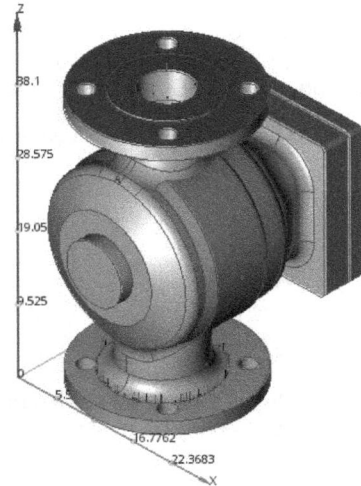

4. The majority of the edges identified are external edges. Since the focus is only on the internal flow for this valve, close the Geometry Tools dialog box.

Investigate the model geometry.

In this task, you will review the geometry that was imported into Autodesk CFD, then use the Geometry Tools to enable automatic internal flow volume creation.

1. Place the cursor over the model, hold <Ctrl> and press the middle mouse button to remove the casing from display. The two internal components, the cage and poppet, display. There is no geometry in the model to which a fluid material can be assigned.

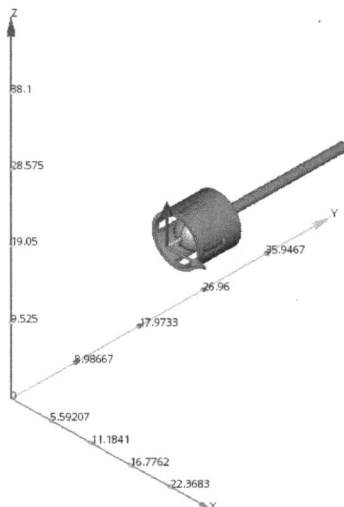

2. Hold <Ctrl> and roll the scroll wheel up once to return the casing component to display.

- The valve inlet and outlet are open, so there is no enclosed volume for the system to automatically define as the flow volume.

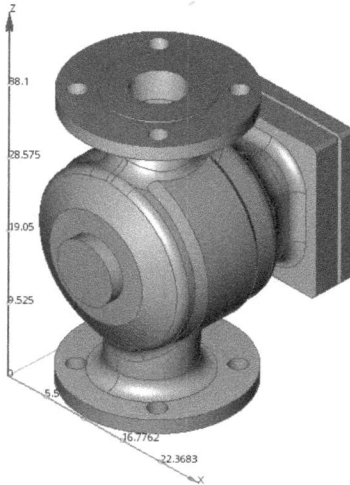

3. In the Setup tab, click (Geometry Tools) to open the Geometry Tools dialog box.

- Select the Void Fill tab.
- Enable the Auto-close option at the bottom of the tab.
- Select the edge shown in the following image. Only a segment of the edge will be initially highlighted, but because Auto-close was enabled, the entire closed set of edges are selected.

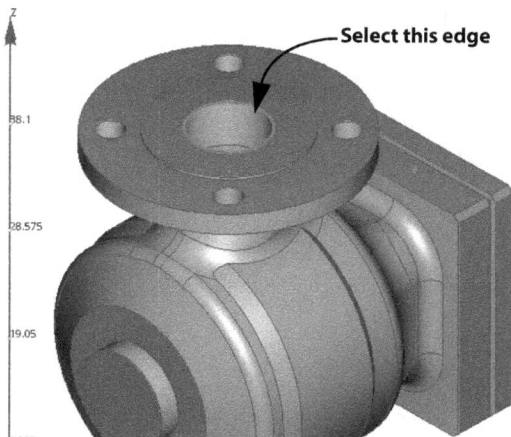

- Click Build surface. A surface is created to fill the area.

4. Hold <Shift> and the middle-mouse button to rotate the model to view the bottom of the model. With the geometry Tools dialog box still open, select the edge shown in the following image. With Auto-close still enabled, the entire closed set of edges are selected.

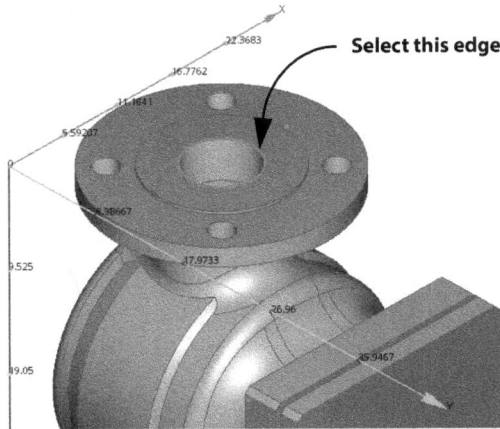

Select this edge

- Click Build surface. A second surface is created to fill this area.
- Now that both inlet and outlet are covered, click Fill void.
- Close the Geometry Tools dialog box.

5. Select ⬚ on the ViewCube to return to the model's default Home view.

6. Place the cursor over the model, hold <Ctrl> and press the middle mouse button to remove the casing from display. The system has now created an internal volume, as shown in the following image.

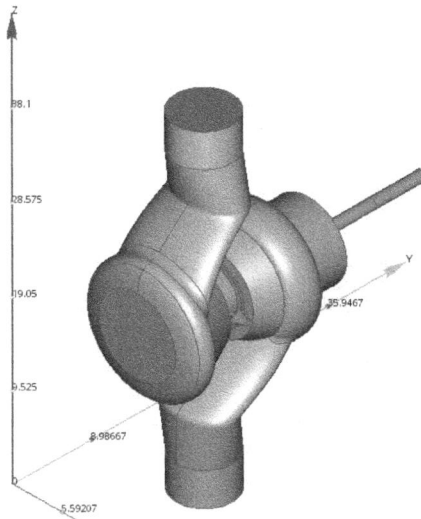

- This volume can be assigned a fluid material for use in an analysis. These steps will be covered in the next chapter.

7. Hold <Ctrl> and roll the scroll wheel up once to return the casing component to display.

- The creation of the surfaces to cap the volume is not generally considered to be the best practice. The method quickly establishes the internal flow volume, but it also means that when flow boundary conditions are applied, they may be applied too close to the area being analyzed, thus yielding unreliable results.

Return to the Autodesk SimStudio Tools application and cap the openings in the model.

As a best practice, you want to ensure boundary conditions are applied far enough away from the area you want to analyze so as to accurately reflect the flow. It is common to create caps in the CAD model that extend beyond the model geometry. In this task, you will use Autodesk SimStudio Tools to cap the model, then update the design study. Note that although Autodesk SimStudio Tools is being used, this general process applies to any compatible CAD system.

Tip: Using caps and having CFD generate the fluid volume is the preferred best method, as it will improve associativity after making design changes.

1. Click (Geometry Tools) to open the Geometry Tools dialog box.

- Click Undo.
- Click Yes in the Warning dialog box.
- The capping surfaces and internal flow volume are removed from the model.
- Close the Geometry Tools dialog box.

2. Select the Autodesk SimStudio Tools window.

3. In the MODEL BROWSER, right-click on Control Valve and select New Component, as shown in the following image.

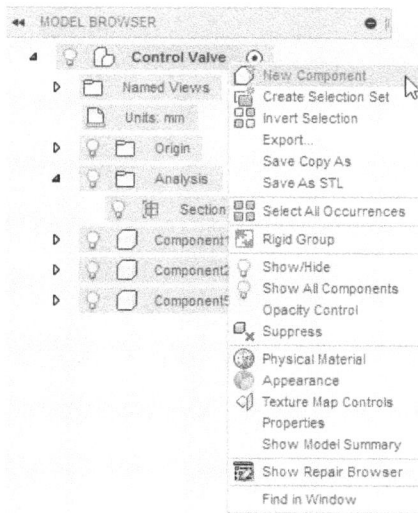

4.   Hover the cursor over Component6:1 and click the white dot to activate the component. This
     deactivates all of the other components so that you can create geometry in the new one.

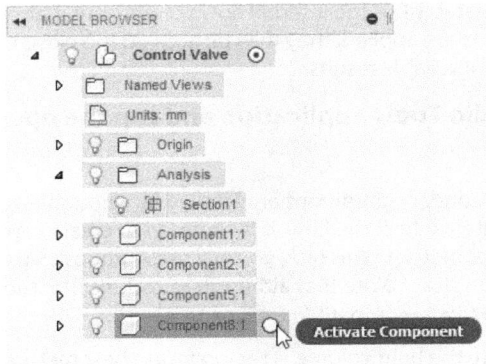

5.   Expand the CREATE panel in the ribbon and click Cylinder. Select the surface shown in the
     following image as the sketching plane.

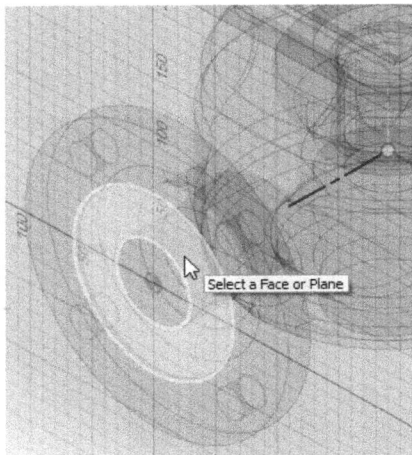

6. Click the center of the cross-hairs to locate the center of the cylinder, then click the edge of the opening. Note that the system will automatically snap the cursor to these locations.

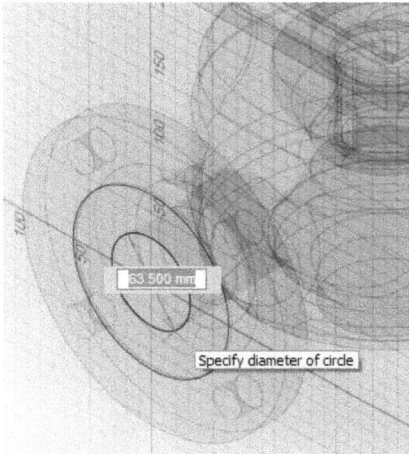

7. Drag the depth to 80 mm, as shown in the following image. Click OK in the CYLINDER dialog box.

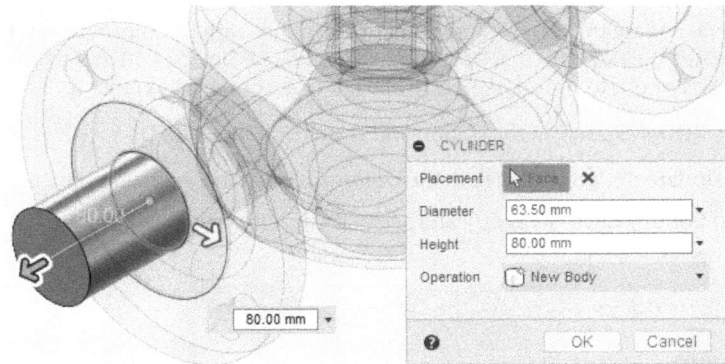

8. In the MODEL BROWSER, hover the cursor over the Control Valve node and select the white circle to activate it.

9. Right-click on Control Valve and select New Component.

10. Hover the cursor over Component7:1 and select the white circle to activate it.

11. Repeat step 4-6 to add a cylindrical cap on the other end of the valve.

12. Activate the Control Valve and select on the ViewCube to return to the model's default Home view. Click on the screen to deselect the model. The model displays as shown in the following image.

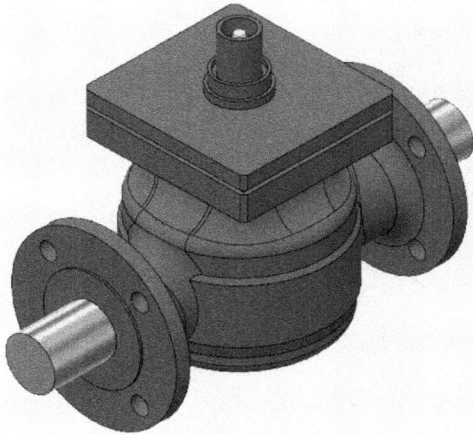

Update the Design Study.

In this task, you will update the design study, and observe that with the capped ends, the system automatically creates the flow volume. Note that you could use SimStudio Tools to create the flow volume, but you will return to Autodesk CFD to allow it to automatically create it.

1. Expand the ADD-INS panel in the ribbon and select Simulate in CFD.

2. Select the Update design study tab in the Design Study Manager dialog box.

- Expand Control Valve Geometry and select Design 1.
- Select update design.

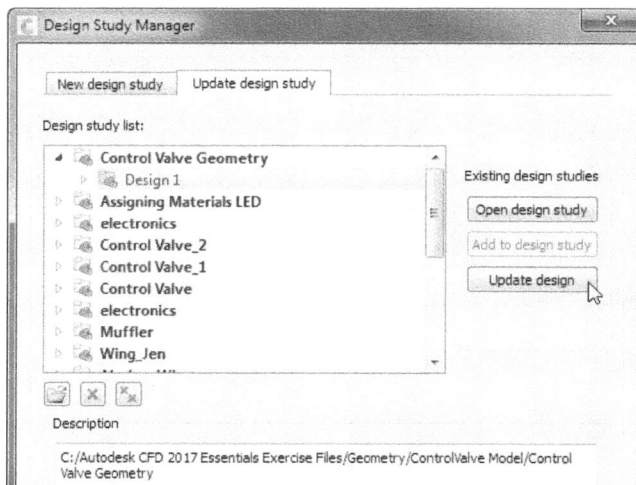

3.   Return to the Autodesk CFD window.

4.   Place the cursor over the model, hold <Ctrl> and press the middle mouse button to remove the casing from display. The system has automatically created the internal flow volume, as shown in the following image.

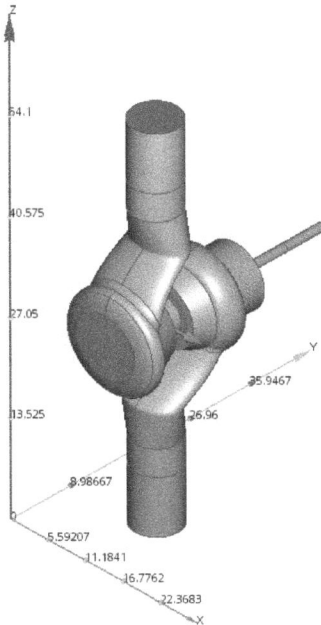

- This volume, along with the two capping volumes, can be assigned a fluid material for use in an analysis. These steps will be covered in the next chapter.

5.   In the Quick Access toolbar, click ⊟ (Save) to save the study.

6.   Close the Autodesk CFD application.

7.   Save and close the open simulation in the SimStudio Tools application.

Exercise: Using The Model Assessment Toolkit

In this exercise, you will investigate an alternate design for the control valve model. In this model, and issue causes problems with the automatic internal volume creation. You will use the Model Assessment Toolkit (MAT) to identify the issue, and Autodesk SimStudio Tools to correct it so that Autodesk CFD can automatically create an internal flow volume. The objectives in this exercise are to:

- Create a design study and determine if a flow volume is created.
- Use the MAT to review the model for possible issues.
- Use SimStudio Tools to correct any issues and review again in the MAT.

Create a Design Study and verify whether a volume is created.

This model is slightly different than the previous exercise. A design change was made that changed the diameter of the valve stem.

1. Launch Autodesk CFD, if not already running.

2. In the Home tab, click ⬜ (New). If an existing study was already open, click Yes to save the study and begin the creation of a new one.

3. In the New Design Study dialog box, browse to the *C:\Autodesk CFD 2017 Essentials Exercise Files\Gometry\MAT Model* folder. Select and open *ControlValve_MAT.sat*.

4. Type **Design1** in the Name field and click Create.

5. Close the Geometry Tools dialog box. As with the previous exercise, the edges identified for merging are on the exterior of the model, and therefore have no impact on the internal flow. The model displays as shown in the following image.

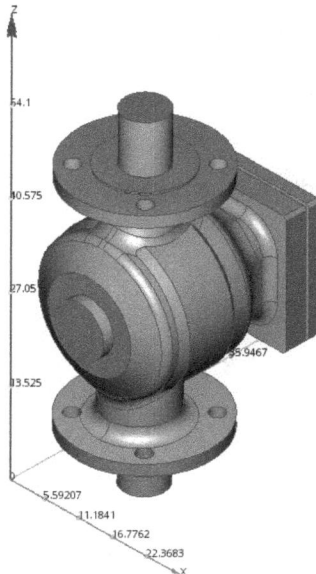

6. Place the cursor over the model, hold <Ctrl> and press the middle mouse button to remove the casing from display.

- As you saw in the previous exercise, when a model is brought into Autodesk CFD and there is an enclosed empty volume, the system automatically creates a solid volume to fill the space.
- In this model, that did not occur, so there must be an issue with the geometry. There must be an opening that has not been accounted for.

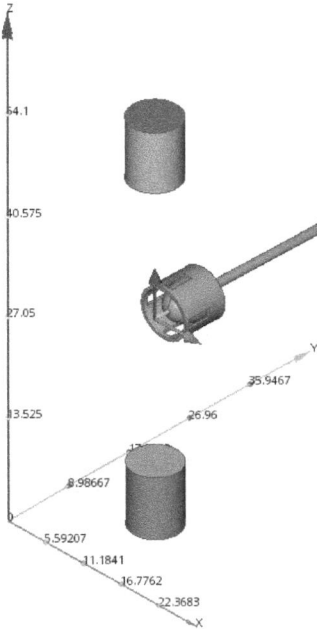

Launch Autodesk SimStudio Tools and review the model in the Model Assessment Toolkit.

In this task, you will use Autodesk SimStudio to launch the Model Assessment Toolkit and review any possible issues.

1. Launch Autodesk SimStudio Tools, if not already running.

2. In the Home tab, click 📂 (Open).

3. In the Open dialog box, browse to the *C:\Autodesk CFD 2017 Essentials Exercise Files\Gometry\ MAT Model* folder. Select and open *ControlValve_MAT.SimStudio*.

4. Expand the ADD-INS panel in the ribbon and select CFD Model Assessment Tool.

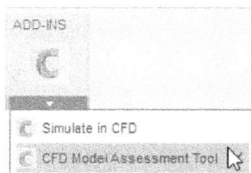

5. The Model Assessment Toolkit opens and assesses the model for the various checks shown in the following image.

   - The green checkmarks indicate that there may be issues with the geometry.
   - The yellow exclamation mark indicates that no issues were detected. As shown in the following image, no Interferences were detected between components.

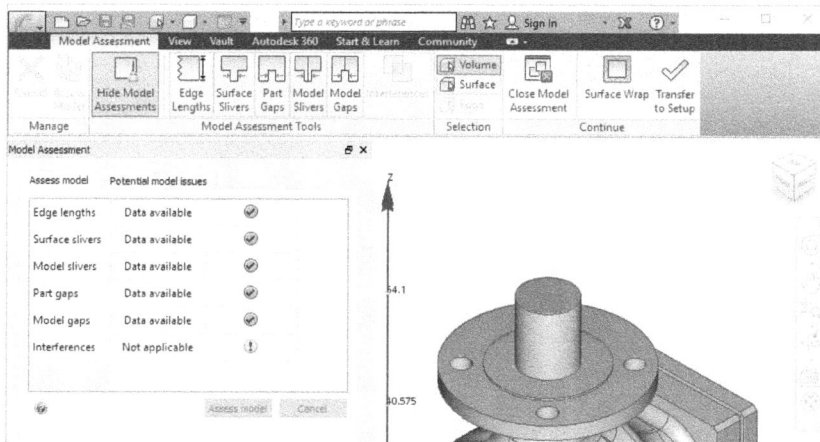

6. In the Model Assessment tab, in the Model Assessment Tools panel, click ⬚⬚ (Model Gaps).

   ▪ The MAT highlights the valve stem in purple, indicating that there as a gap between it and the surrounding geometry.

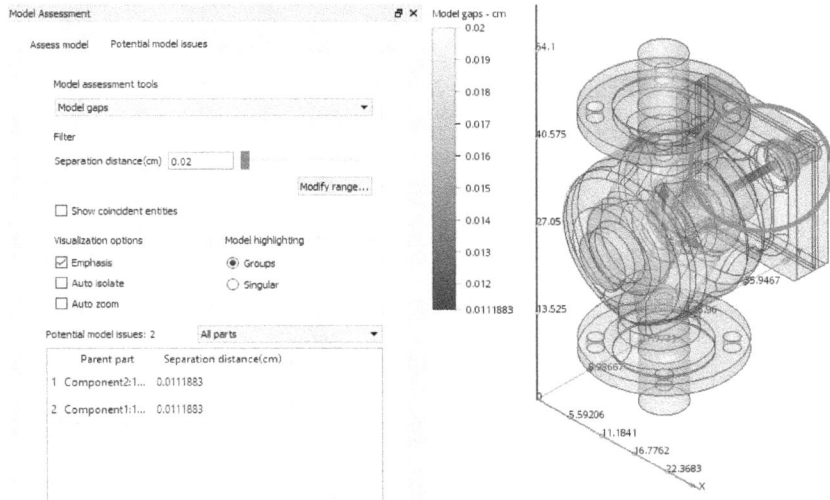

7. Click Auto zoom in the Visualization options area of the Model Assessment panel to enable the option.

8. Select Component 1:1 in the Potential model issues list and note that the system automatically zooms in on the geometry.

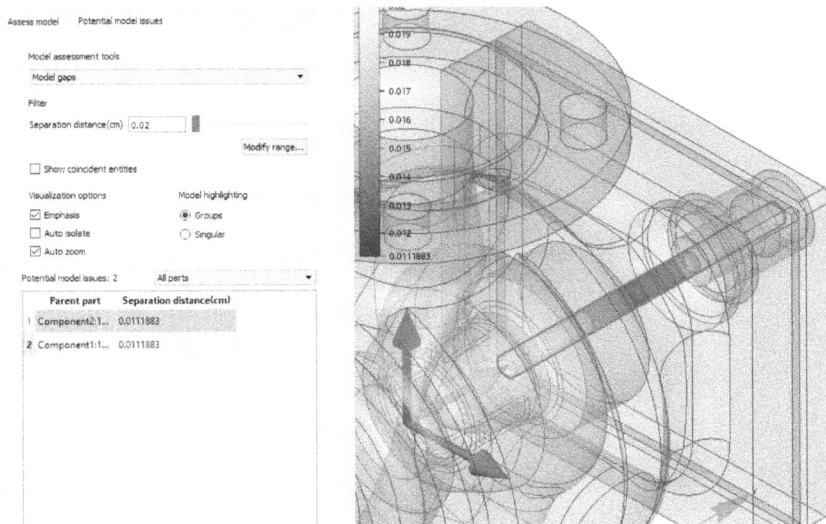

Return to Autodesk SimStudio Tools and edit the geometry.

There is a gap that is keeping the system from establishing a completely closed volume. The Model Assessment Toolkit only shows where issues are in the model and has no tools for actually editing the geometry. In this task, you will edit the valve stem so that it matches the hole it passes through, thereby closing the opening.

1. In the Model Assessment tab, in the Continue panel, click (Close Model Assessment) and click Yes when prompted to close.

2. Return to the Autodesk SimStudio Tools window.

3. In the MODEL BROWSER, click next to Component1:1 to toggle off its display.

    Spin the model to the approximate orientation shown in the following image.

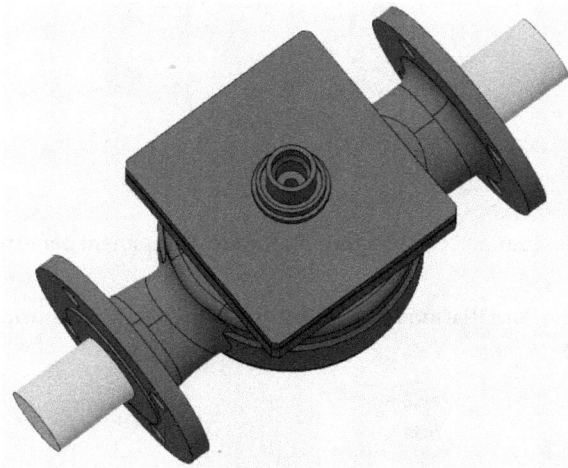

4. Expand the INSPECT panel and select Measure so you can measure the radius of the hole in the casing.

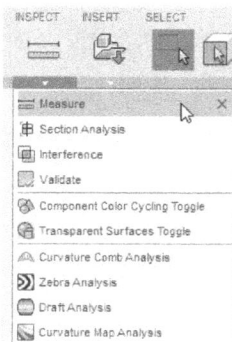

5. Select the hole and note that the radius is 5.912, as shown in the following image. Close the MEASURE dialog box and now check the radius of the valve stem.

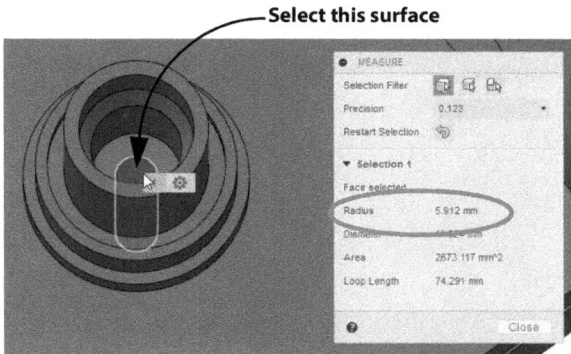

Select this surface

6. In the MODEL BROWSER, click 🔆 next to Component1:1 to toggle on its display.

7. Select 🏠 on the ViewCube to return to the model's default Home view.

8. Click 🔆 next to Component2:1 to toggle off its display, so you can easily see the valve stem. The model updates as shown in the following image.

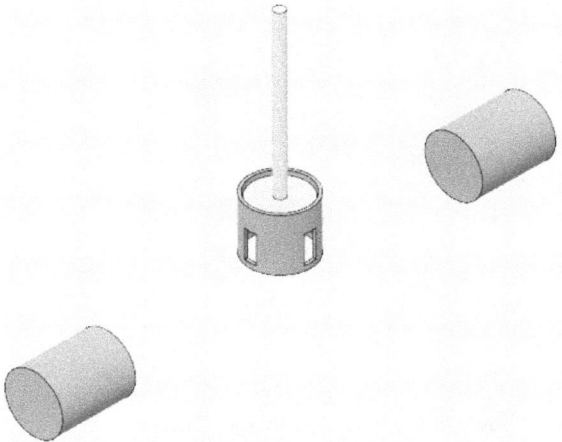

9. Expand the INSPECT panel and select Measure.

10. Select the valve stem and note that the radius is 5.8, as shown in the following image.

- Since the radius of the valve stem is smaller than the hole in the valve body, there is a gap that keeps the assembly from being water-tight. You must fix this to enable the system to automatically create the flow volume.
- Close the MEASURE dialog box.

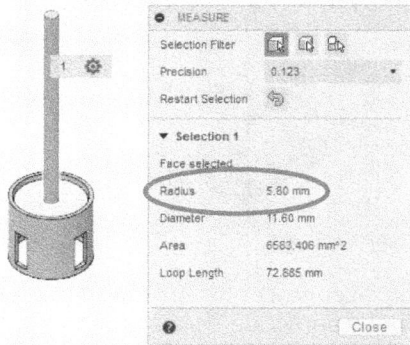

11. Edit the shaft radius to match the hole, thereby sealing the gap. Select the shaft, right-click, and select Press Pull as shown in the following image.

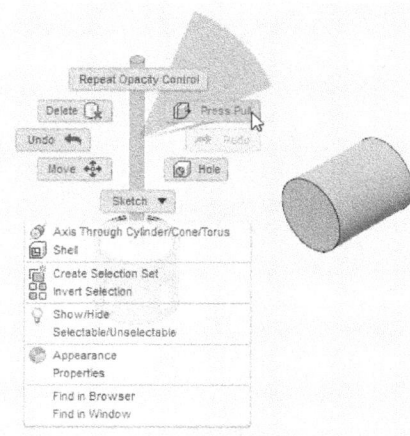

12. Edit the distance to 5.912, as shown in the following image. Click OK.

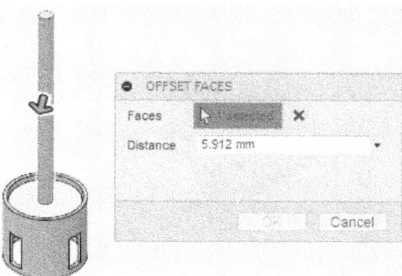

13.   In the MODEL BROWSER, click 💡 next to Component2:1 to toggle on its display.

Return to the MAT application and verify that the edit has removed the gap.

In this task, you will review the model in the MAT application and look at the Model Gap results to verify that the previous issue has been resolved.

1.   Expand the ADD-INS panel in the ribbon and select CFD Model Assessment Tool.

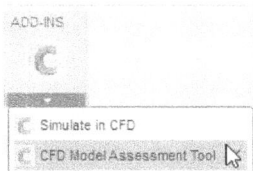

2.   In the Model Assessment tab, in the Model Assessment Tools panel, click ⊟⊟ (Model Gaps).

- Note that the purple highlighting has been removed, indicating that the gap that previously existed has been corrected.

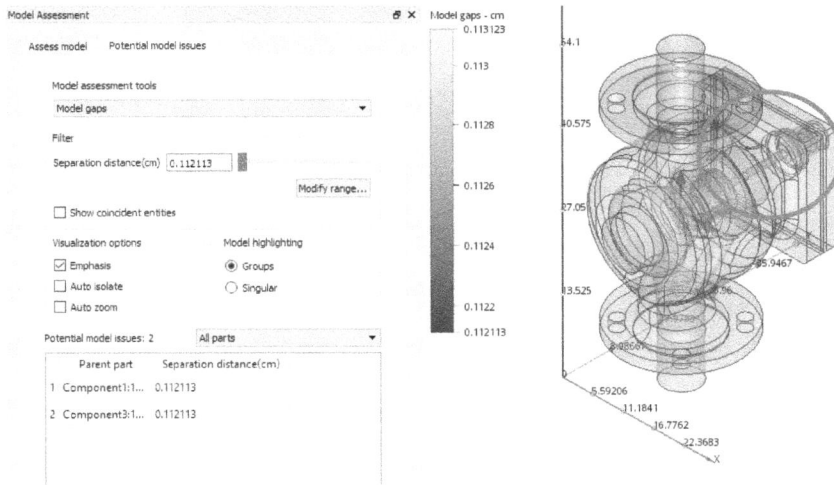

3.   In the Model Assessment tab, in the Continue panel, click 🗗⊠ (Close Model Assessment) and click Yes when prompted to close.

Update the Design Study.

In this task, you will update the design study and observe that with the edited geometry, the system automatically creates the flow volume.

1. In Autodesk SimStudio Tools, expand the ADD-INS panel in the ribbon and select Simulate in CFD.

2. In the Design Study Manager dialog box, select the Update design study tab.

   - Expand Design1 and select Design 1.
   - Select Update design.

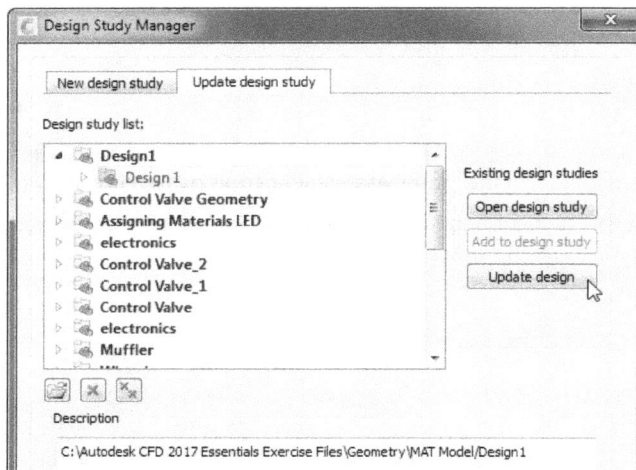

3. Return to the Autodesk CFD window.

4. Place the cursor over the model, hold <Ctrl> and press the middle mouse button to remove the casing from display. The system has created the internal flow volume, as shown in the following image.

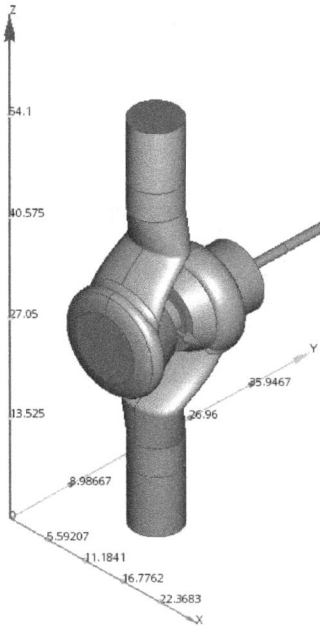

- The gap that existed with the valve stem kept the system from creating a closed volume and therefore the flow volume could not be automatically created.

5. In the Quick Access toolbar, click ▣ (Save) to save the study.

6. Close the Autodesk CFD application.

7. Save and close the open simulation in the SimStudio Tools application.

Exercise: Creating an External Flow Volume

Much like internal flow, you must also have a volume to define external flow. In this exercise, you will create an external volume around the outside of an LED light. Without a surrounding air volume, you would not be able to model heat transfer through convection. You will create an external volume first using the tools available in Autodesk CFD, and then using SimStudio Tools. The objectives in this exercise are to:

- Use Autodesk CFD to create an external volume.
- Use SimStudio Tools to create an external volume.

Create a Design Study and verify whether a volume is created.

1. Launch Autodesk SimStudio Tools, if not already running.

2. In the Home tab, click [Open icon] (Open).

3. In the Open dialog box, browse to the *C:\Autodesk CFD 2017 Essentials Exercise Files\Gometry\ LED Model* folder. Select and open *LED_External_Volume.SimStudio*.

4. The model opens as shown in the following image. Review the components in the model.

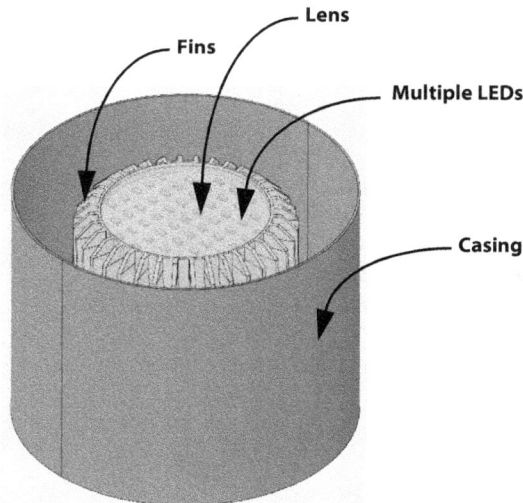

5. Expand the ADD-INS panel in the ribbon and select Simulate in CFD.

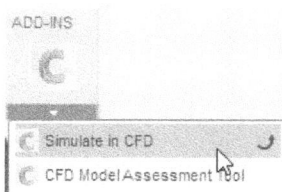

6. In the Design Study Manager, ensure that the Study name is LED_External_Volume and click Launch.

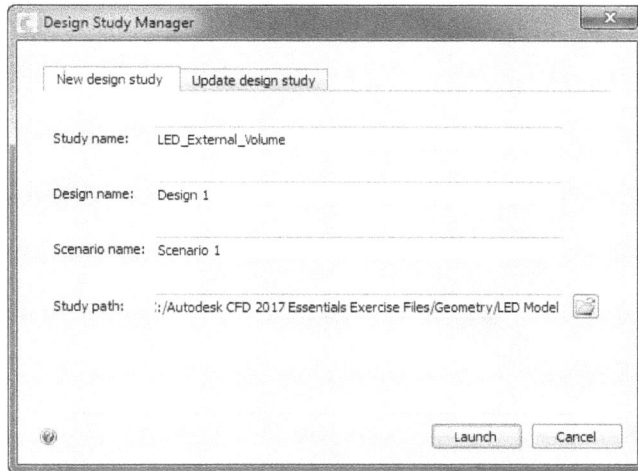

7. In the Geometry Tools dialog box in the Autodesk CFD window, select the Ext. Volume tab.

- The Autodesk CFD software creates a volume that encompasses the geometry, as shown in the following image.

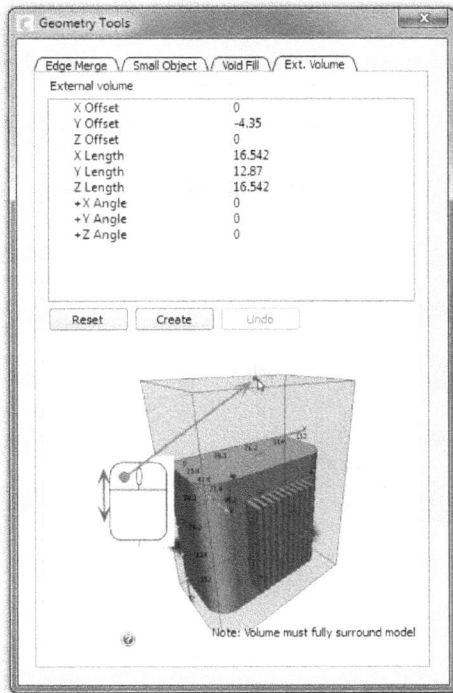

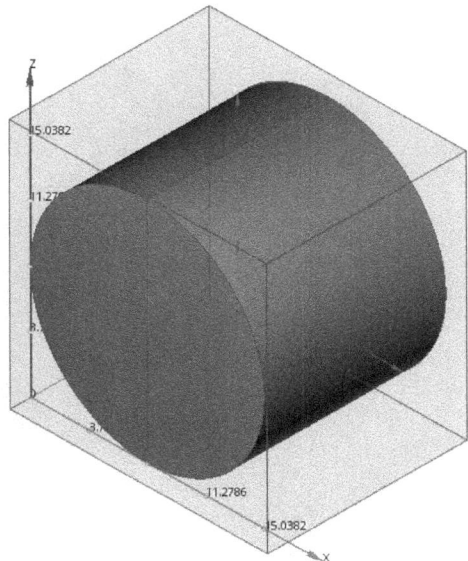

8. Use the arrows that display on each wall of the bounding box to drag the walls of the external volume similar to the size shown in the following image.

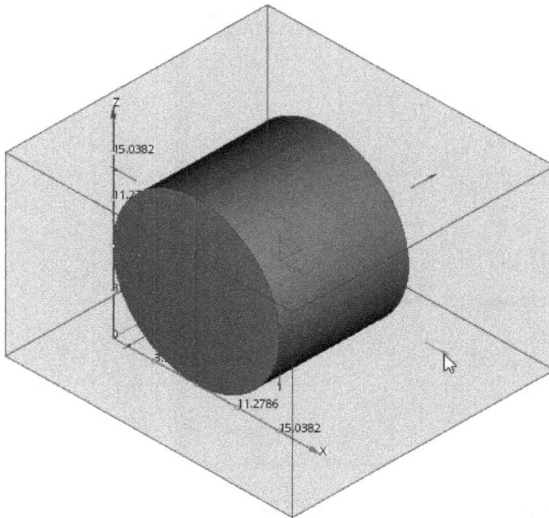

9. Click Create to create the volume.

- This technique enables you to quickly create the external volume, but limits the shape that can be used to represent the volume.
- At this point, you could assign the air material to the volume. This topic is covered in more detail in the next chapter.

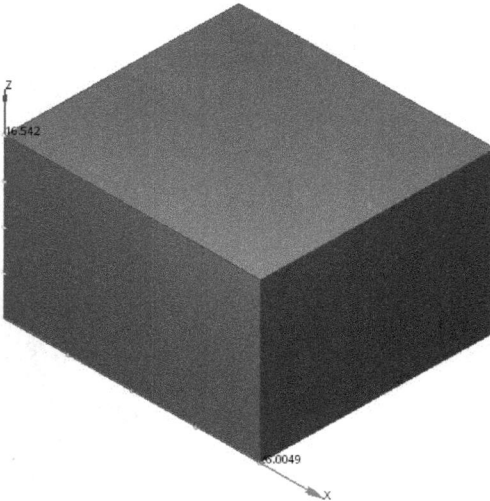

Create a volume in SimStudio Tools.

In this task, you will use Autodesk SimStudio Tools to create an external volume that more closely matches the model geometry.

1. In the Geometry Tools dialog box, click Undo to remove the volume you just created.

    ▪ Click Yes when prompted to proceed.

2. Close the Geometry Tools dialog box and return to the SimStudio Tools window.

    ▪ Do not close the Autodesk CFD window.

3. In the MODEL BROWSER, in the Autodesk SimStudio Tools window, expand Origin.

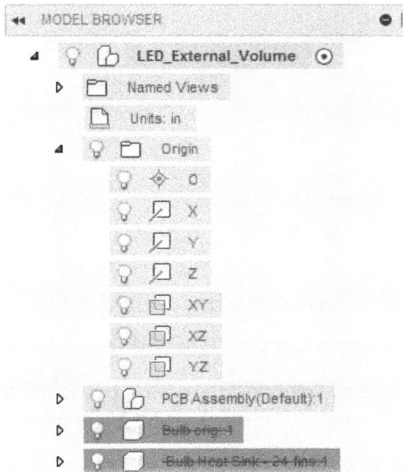

4. Expand the CONSTRUCT panel and select Offset Plane.

5. In the MODEL BROWSER, select the XZ plane.

6. Edit the offset to **6.00**, as shown in the following image, and click OK.

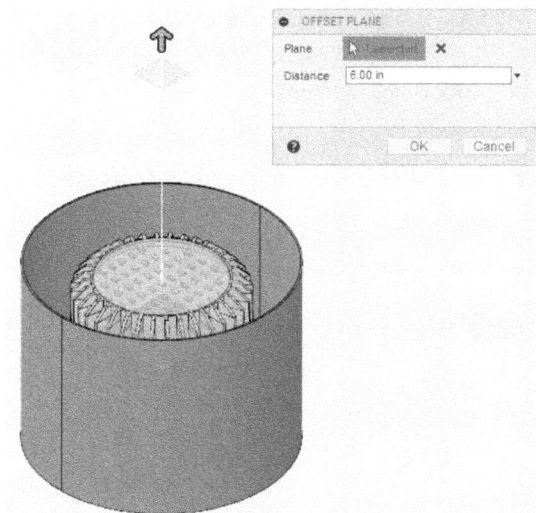

7. Expand the CREATE panel and select Cylinder.

8. In the graphics window, select the plane you just created as the sketch plane.

- Alternatively, in the MODEL BROWSER, expand Construction and select Plane2.

9. Sketch the circle shown in the following image by selecting the center point and a location for the diameter. The actual diameter does not matter, as you will edit it in the next step.

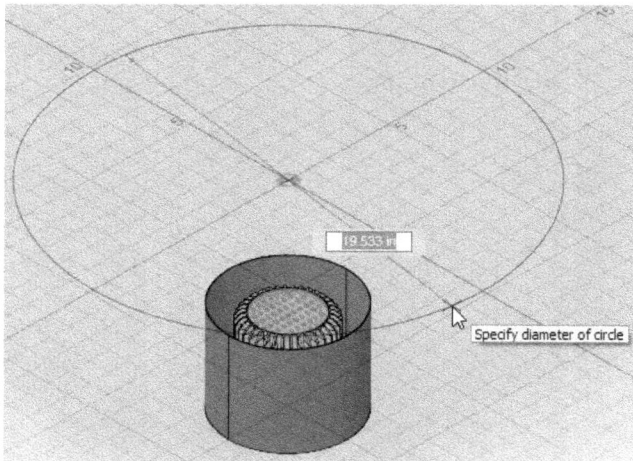

10. In the CYLINDER dialog box, set the following:

- Diameter: **19.25**
- Height: **-17.25** (the negative value changes the direction in which the cylinder is created).
- Operation: New Body

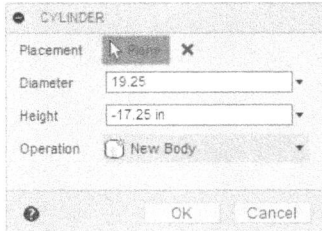

11. Click OK to complete the cylinder.

Apply an appearance to the air volume.

In this task, you will use a predefined appearance to change how the air volume displays in the model.

1. Right-click on the model and select Modify>Appearance, as shown in the following image.

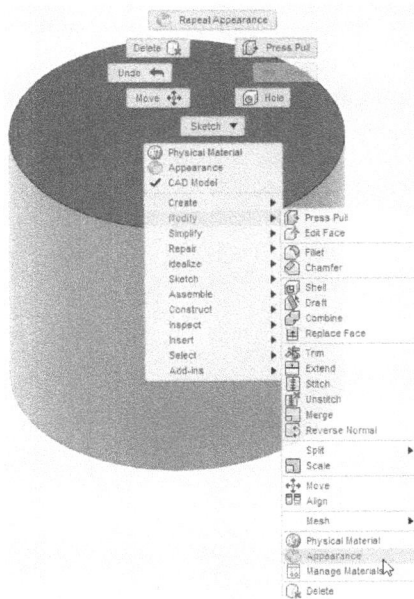

2. In the APPEARANCE dialog box, select the Air appearance shown in the following image and drag it onto the model.

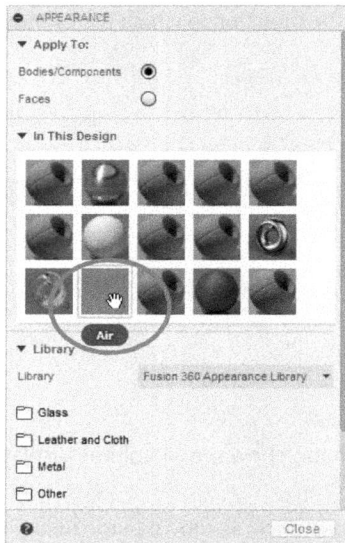

3. In the APPEARANCE dialog box, click Close. The model displays as shown in the following image.

   - The air volume displays as an outline surrounding the model.
   - Note that setting the appearance is purely visual. This is not the same as applying a material, which will be covered in the next chapter.

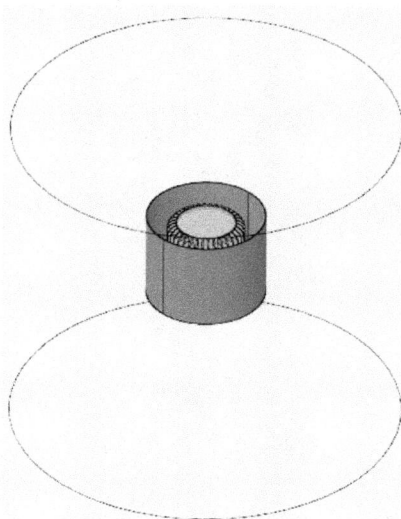

Update the Design Study.

In this task, you will update the design study, and observe that the air volume has been added.

1. Expand the ADD-INS panel in the ribbon and select Simulate in CFD.
2. In the Design Study Manager dialog box, select the Update design study tab.
    - Expand LED_External_Volume and select Design 1.
    - Select Update design.
3. Return to the Autodesk CFD window.
4. The volume is created around the LED light and housing, as shown in the following image.
    - Note that the appearance set in SimStudio Tools is not carried forward to Autodesk CFD.
    - The Air material can now be applied to the volume, which will be covered in the next chapter.

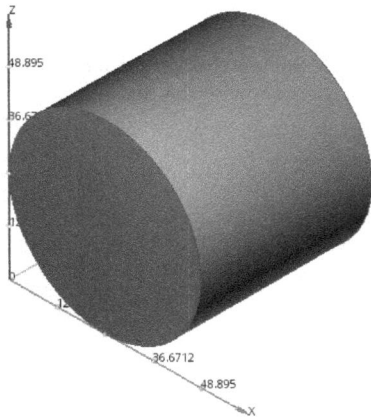

5. In the Quick Access toolbar, click 🔲 (Save) to save the study.
6. Close the Autodesk CFD application.
7. Save and close the open simulation in the SimStudio Tools application.

Exercise: Correcting Geometry Issues

In this exercise, you will use SimStudio Tools to open a modified version of the LED light model. You will use the Model Assessment Tool (MAT) to investigate the model. The MAT will uncover several issues such as interferences, gaps, and small surfaces, which you will correct in SimStudio Tools. The objectives in this exercise are to:

- Use the MAT to investigate a model.
- Use SimStudio Tools to repair issues with the model to prepare it for analysis.

Open a model in SimStudio Tools and review the geometry.

1. Launch Autodesk SimStudio Tools, if not already running.

2. In the Home tab, click ![folder icon] (Open).

3. In the Open dialog box, browse to the *C:\Autodesk CFD 2017 Essentials Exercise Files\Geometry\GeometryIssues* folder. Select and open *GeometryIssues.SimStudio*.

4. The model opens as shown in the following image. Review the components in the model. Note that upon visual inspection, there are no obvious errors with the geometry.

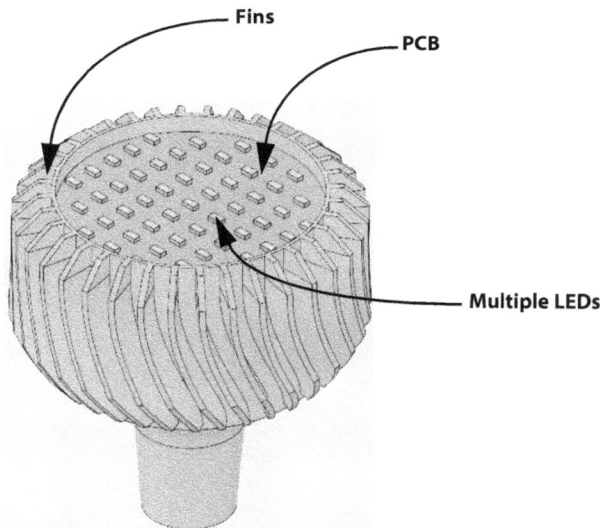

Create a design study in Autodesk CFD and prepare the model for analysis.

1. Expand the ADD-INS panel in the ribbon and select Simulate in CFD.

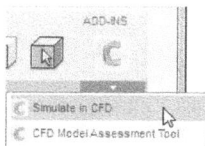

2. In the Design Study Manager, accept the default Study name of GeometryIssues and click Launch.

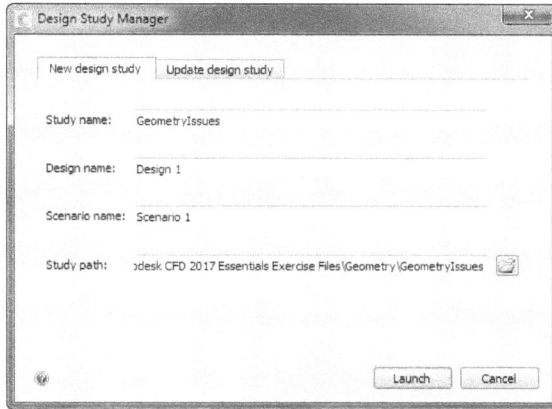

3. Close the Geometry Tools dialog box.

4. Orient the model similar to that shown in the following image.

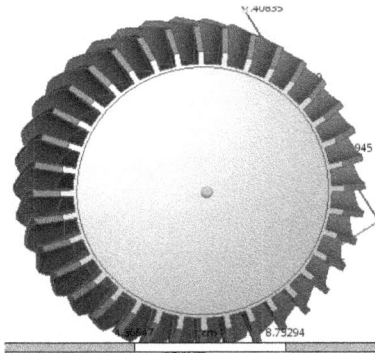

5. Hover the cursor over the flat surface of the PCB, hold <Ctrl> and press the middle mouse button until the LEDs are visible, as shown in the following image.

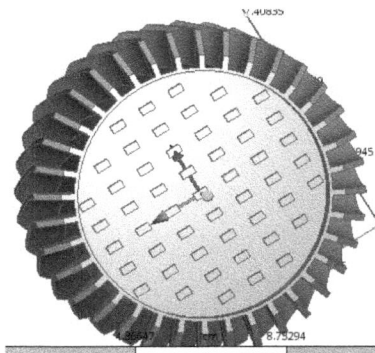

6. In the Design Study Bar, expand the Material node.

   - Hold <Ctrl>.
   - Select 1 LED, 2 LED and 5 LED, then right-click and select Edit, as shown in the following image.

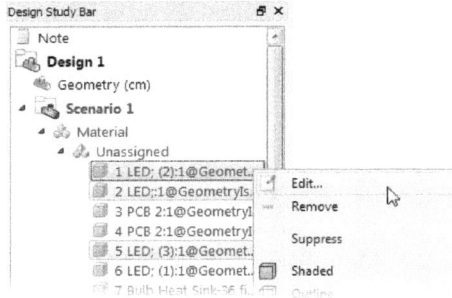

7. In the Materials dialog box, in the Type drop-down list, select LED Device.

   - Ensure that the Name is set to Cree XLamp XP-G, as shown in the following image.
   - Click Apply to assign the material.

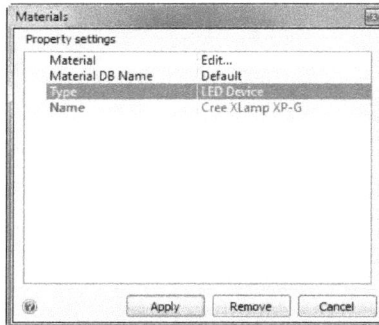

8. In the Design Study Bar, in the Material>Unassigned node.

   - Select 3 PCB 2, then right-click and select Edit, as shown in the following image.

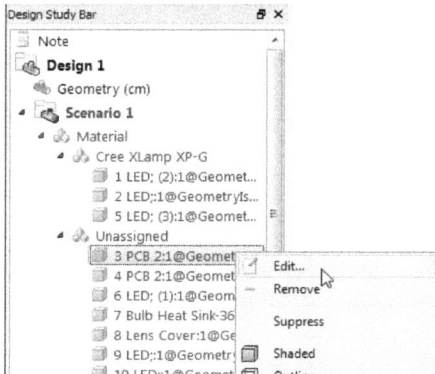

9. In the Materials dialog box, in the Type drop-down list, select Printed Circuit Boards.

    ▪ Ensure that the Name is set to Default_PCB, as shown in the following image.
    ▪ Click Apply to assign the material.

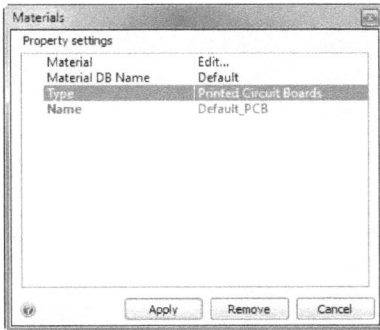

10. Repeat the previous steps to assign the Default_PCB printed circuit board to the 4 PCB 2 component. The Design Study Bar should display as shown in the following image.

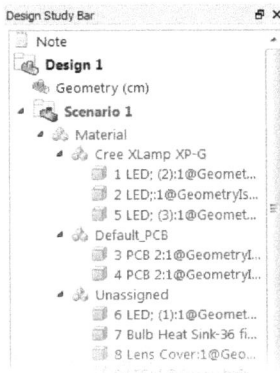

11. In the Design Study Bar, in the Material node, select 6 LED, right-click and select Edit.

12. In the Materials dialog box, in the Type drop-down list, select LED Device and ensure that the Name is set to Cree XLamp XP-G.

13. Click Apply and note that a warning dialog box opens, indicating that the setting cannot be applied to a non-cuboid volume, as shown in the following image.

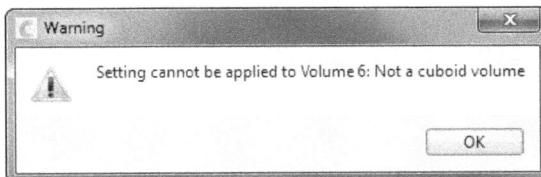

This is the first indication that there is a problem. To apply an LED Device, the object must be a cuboid, so there is something incorrect with the geometry.

14. Click OK to close the Warning dialog box and Cancel to close the Materials dialog box. Note that the LED in question is the one in the center, as shown in the following image.

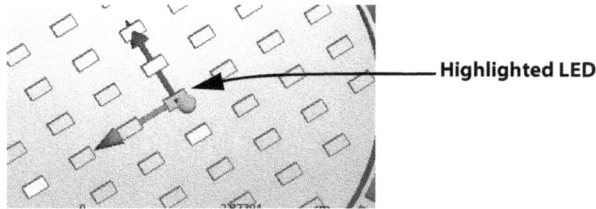

Highlighted LED

15. You should assign materials to every component before continuing your setup. However, to expedite this exercise, you will continue in order to identify other geometry errors. Click

 (Boundary Conditions).

- A warning dialog box opens, indicating that an LED is not mounted to a PCB material.
- This can be an indication of a gap between components.
- Click Close in the Compact Thermal Model dialog box.

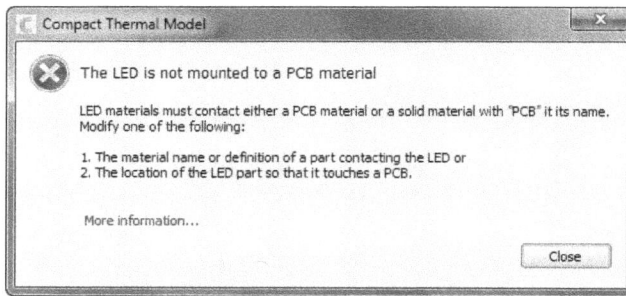

As you can see, this model is not ready for analysis. As a new user of Autodesk CFD, or even as an experienced user receiving models that you are unfamiliar with, you should always run your model through the MAT to ensure that the geometry is free of errors before attempting to set it up for analysis.

Return to SimStudio Tools and launch the MAT to investigate the issues with the model.

In this task, you will use MAT to investigate issues in the model to determine where the problems are with the geometry.

1. Activate the SimStudio Tools window.

2. Expand the ADD-INS panel in the ribbon and select CFD Model Assessment Tool.

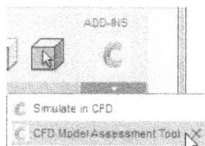

---

3. The Model Assessment Tool opens as shown in the following image. Note that it may take a few moments to complete the assessment.

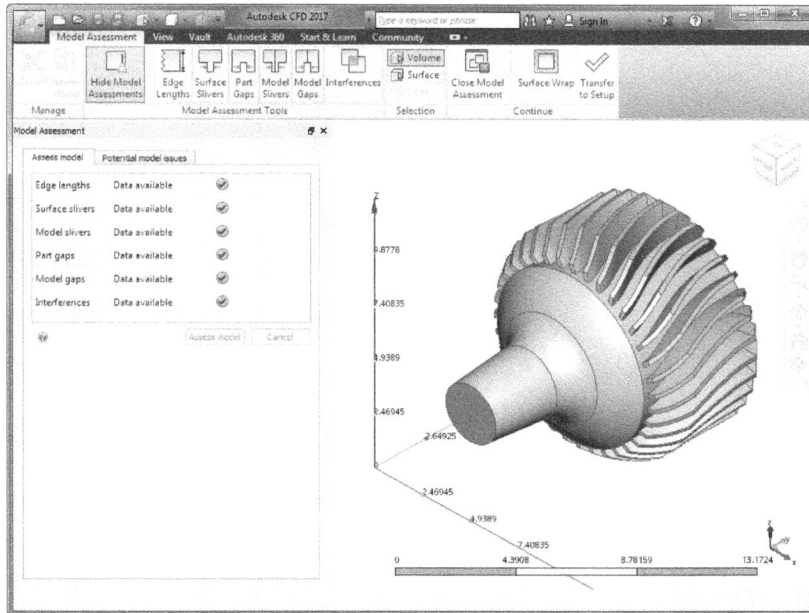

4. In the Model Assessment browser, click the Potential model issues tab.

- In the Model assessment tools drop-down list, select Edge Lengths. This is the first in the list of model assessment tools.
- The Model Assessment browser updates as shown in the following image.

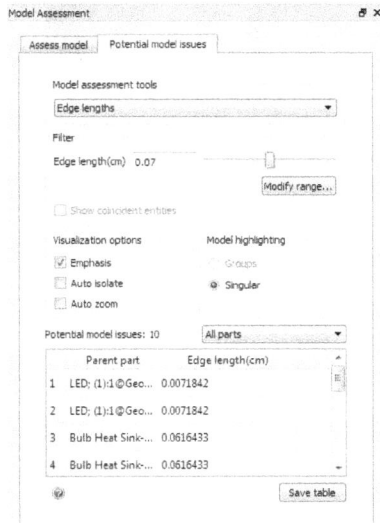

5. You know from the previous task that there is an issue with the LED geometry. The focus in this exercise will only be on the LEDs.

    ▪ Enable the Auto zoom option.

    ▪ Select the first LED listed in the Parent part column, as shown in the following image.

    ▪ Review the highlighted edge. It appears there is a chamfer on this LED, which makes it non-cuboid in shape and therefore unsuitable for applying the LED Device.

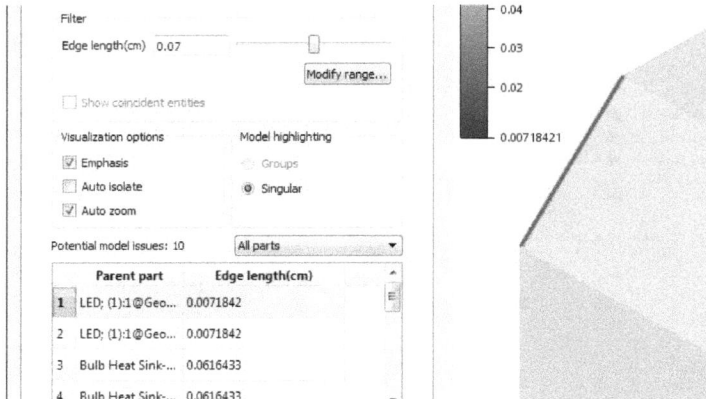

If you select the next LED entry, the edge at the other end of the chamfer will highlight.

6. In the Potential model issues tab, in the Model assessment tools drop-down list, select Surface slivers. This is an alternative method to reviewing the next assessment tool in the list. The focus in this tool will also only be on the LEDs.

    ▪ Select the first LED entry and the surface of the suspected chamfer highlights, confirming that this LED has an extra feature.

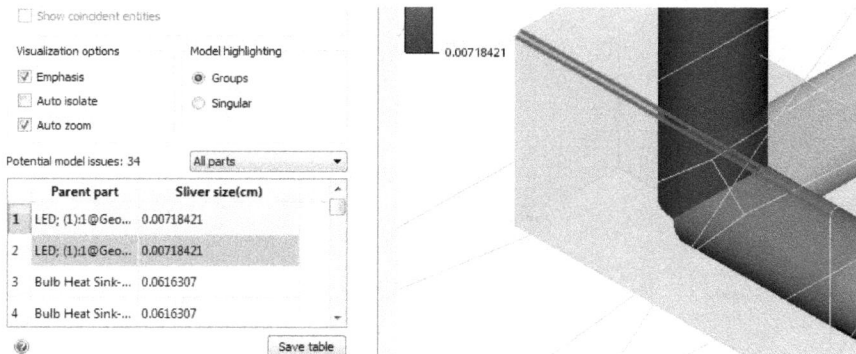

7. From the previous investigation, it is suspected that a gap exists between at least one LED and the PCB board. In the Potential model issues tab, in the Model assessment tools drop-down list, select Model gaps.

   ▪ Select the first LED entry and the surface of the suspected chamfer highlights.
   ▪ When this chamfer is corrected, this gap should no longer be an issue.

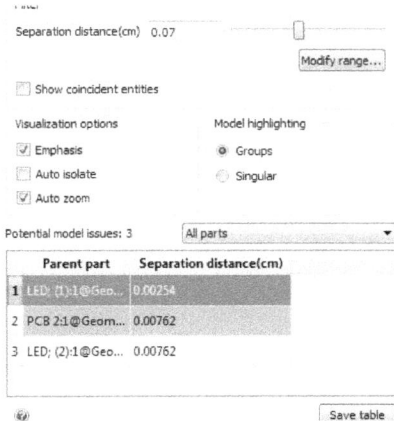

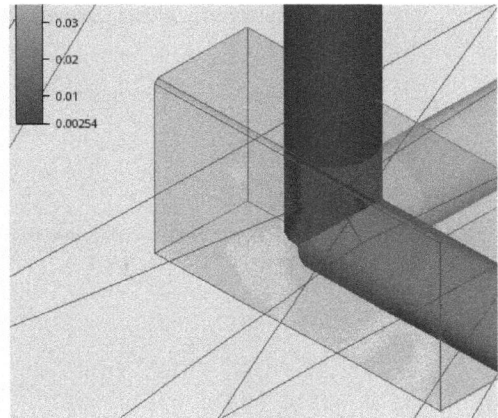

8. Select the second LED entry and a different LED highlights.

   ▪ Zoom out slightly so you can see its location.
   ▪ It is the LED located adjacent to the LED with the chamfer, in the positive Z direction.
   ▪ A gap exists between this LED and the PCB, which is why you previously received an error message indicating that the LED was not mounted to PCB material.

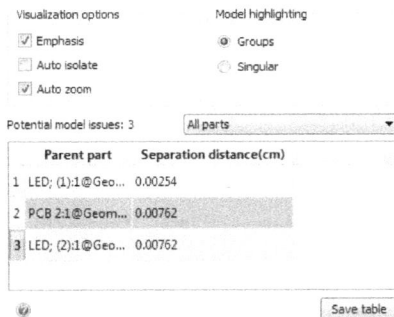

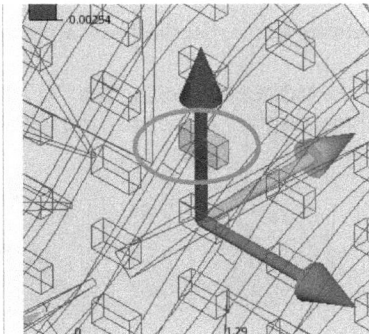

9. Finally, check the model to see if there are any interferences. In the Potential model issues tab, in the Model assessment tools drop-down list, select Interferences.

- Select the entry in the Potential model issues list.
- Zoom out slightly so you can see its location.
- It is the LED located adjacent to the LED with the chamfer, in the negative Z direction.
- An interference exists between this LED and the PCB, which needs to be corrected.

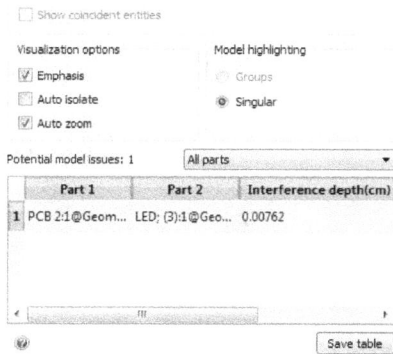

10. In the Continue panel, click 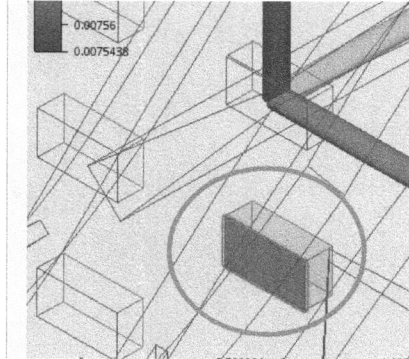 (Close Model Toolkit) and click Yes when prompted to confirm the closure.

Repair the chamfer issue.

In this task, you will use Remove Feature to repair the issue with the chamfer.

1. Activate the SimStudio Tools window.

2. In the MODEL BROWSER, click 💡 adjacent to Bulb Heat Sink -36 fins:1 to hide its display. The model displays as shown in the following image.

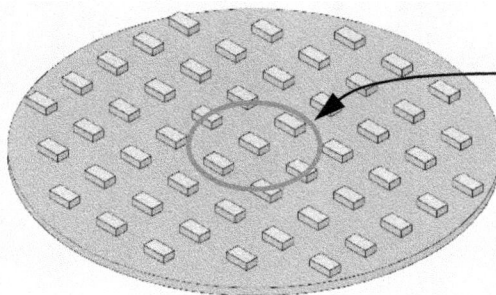

Overall, these three LEDs need to be repaired. The center LED contains the chamfer geometry.

3. Orient the model similar to that shown in the following image. Use the axis and ViewCube as a visual reference.

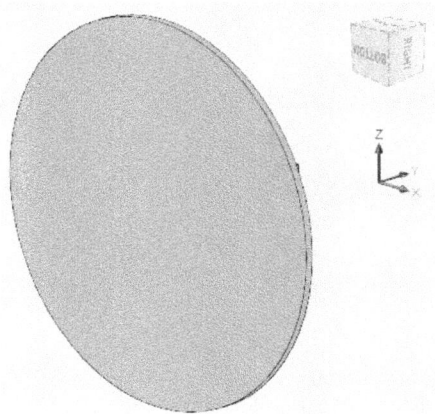

4. In the Navigation Bar, expand ▣▾ and select Visual Style>Wireframe with Hidden Edges.

5. Zoom in on the center LED and note the chamfered edge as shown in the following image. Without using the MAT tools, this chamfer would be particularly difficult to find because it is on the edge of the LCD that is attached to the PCB.

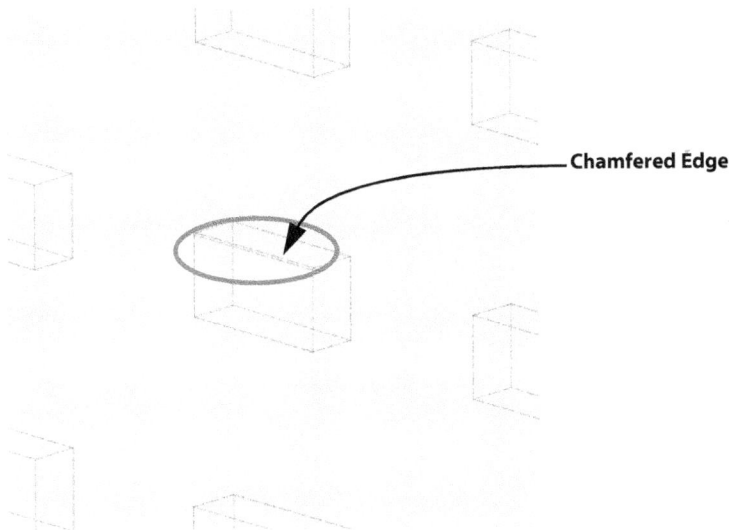

Chamfered Edge

6. In the MODEL BROWSER, select PCB Assembly (Default):1, right-click, and select Suppress, so you can easily select the LED. Alternatively, in the Simplify panel, click 🗖✖ (Suppress).

7. In the toolbar, click (Remove Features) and the REMOVE FEATURES panel opens as shown in the following image. Note that the REMOVE FEATURES panel may be compressed. Click the double-arrows to expand it.

8. Remove the checkbox next to Select All and click Chamfer. Select the LED and note that the Chamfer highlights, as shown in the following image.

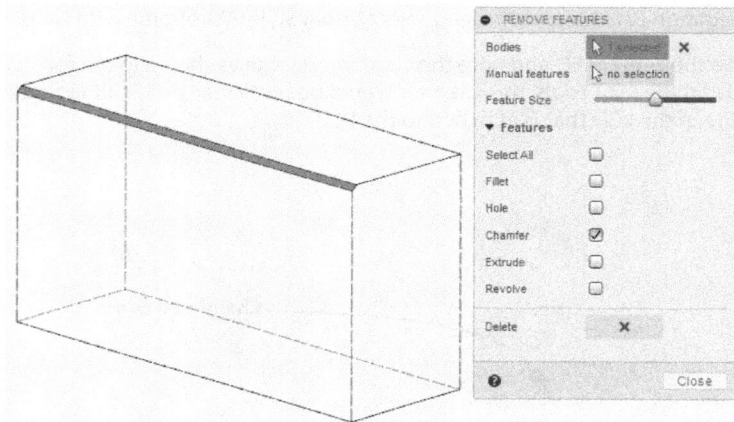

9. In the REMOVE FEATURES panel, click ✕ (Delete) and Close. The chamfer is removed.

10. In the MODEL BROWSER, select PCB Assembly (Default):1, right-click, and select Unsuppress so it is available for selection.

11. Zoom out to see all of the LEDs and orient the model similar to that shown in the following image.

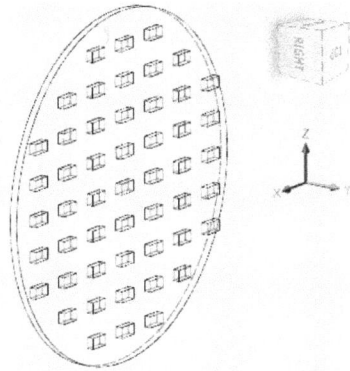

Repair the gap between another LED and the PCB.

In this task, you will use Press Pull to repair the issue with the LED that does not contact the PCB.

1. In the Select panel, click ![icon] (Select Body Priority) and select the LED shown in the following image.

- Recall that a gap was identified between this LED (first LED in the positive Z direction from the center) and the PCB.

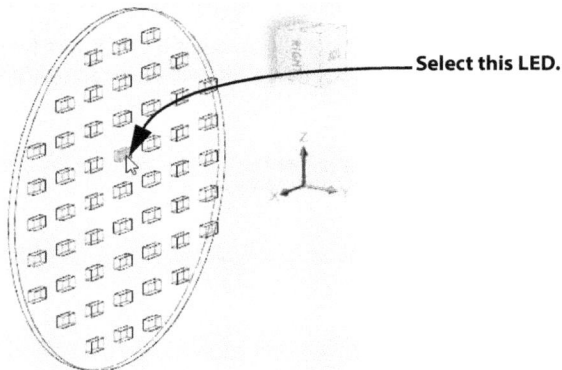

Select this LED.

2. Hold <Ctrl> and select the PCB board. Right-click and select Isolate, as shown in the following image.

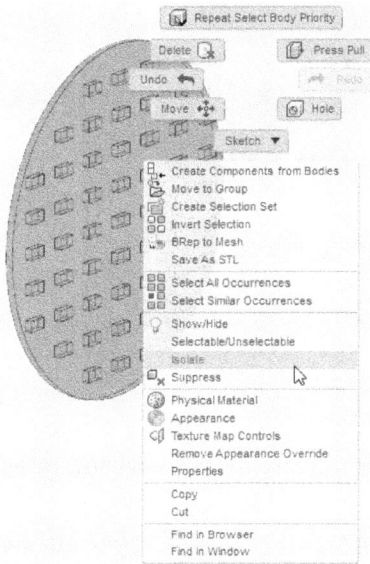

3. Only the single LED and the PCB board should be displayed. In the View Cube, click RIGHT and zoom in to display the model, as shown in the following image.

- Note the gap between the PCB and the LED.
- You can use Press Pull to extend the face of the LED to meet the PCB, and SimStudio Tools has the ability to measure the distance on the fly, as you will see in an upcoming step.

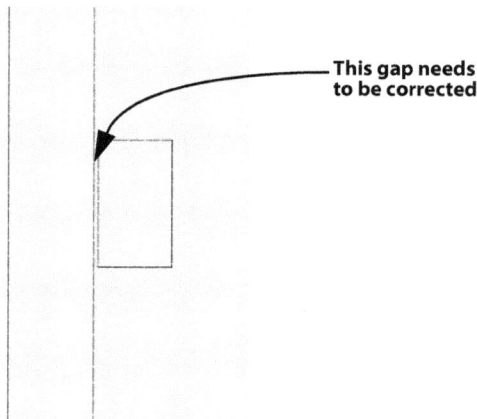

This gap needs
to be corrected

4. Rotate the model similar to that shown in the following image.

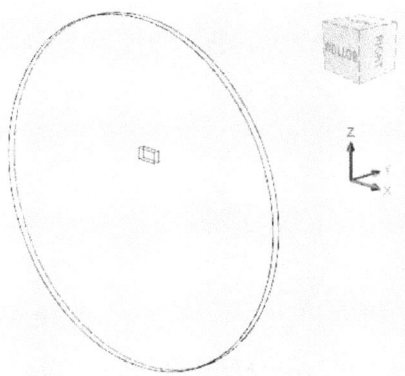

5. Click ▣ (Select Face Priority).

6. Place the cursor over the surface of the LCD and click and hold the left mouse button until the selection menu displays, as shown in the following image.

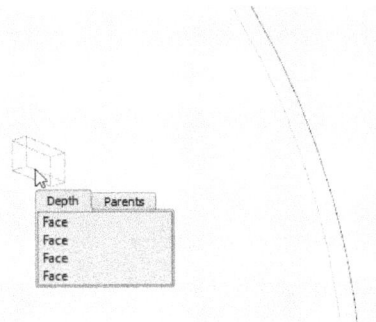

7. Release the left mouse button and then select the face of the LED, the third Face in the list, as shown in the following image.

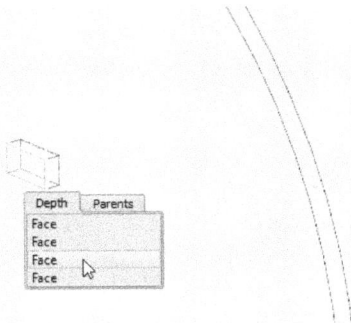

8. Right-click and select Press Pull, as shown in the following image.

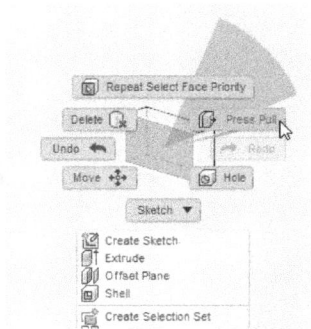

9. In either the dimension entry box or the OFFSET FACES panel, click the arrow next to the distance and select Measure, as shown in the following image.

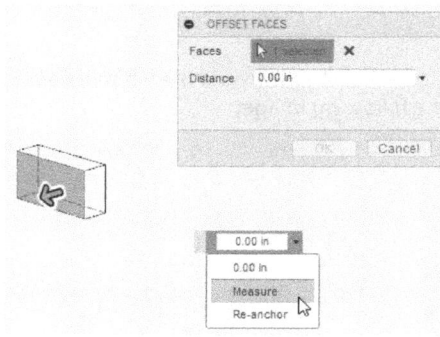

10. Select the surface of the LED again using the preceding selection technique.

11. Click and hold on the PCB surface, then select the second Face in the list, as shown in the following image.

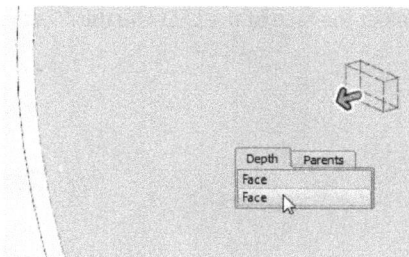

12. A measured value of 0.003in is entered for you. Click OK.

13. On the ViewCube, click RIGHT and zoom in to orient the model, as shown in the following image.

   ▪ Note the gap between the PCB and the LED has been removed. The original LED was smaller than the others, thus the offset. By offsetting its face, it is now aligned with the PCB and is the same size as the other LEDs.

14. Right-click on the screen and select Undo Isolate.

Repair the interference between the third LED and the PCB.

In this task, you will use Press Pull to repair the issue with the LED that intersects the PCB.

1. Orient the model as shown in the following image. In the Select panel, click [icon] (Select Body Priority) and select the LED.

   ▪ Recall that interference was identified between this LED (first LED in the negative Z direction from the center) and the PCB.

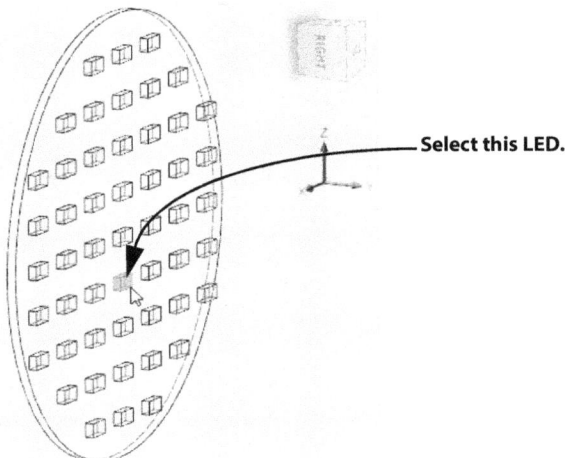

Select this LED.

2. Hold <Ctrl> and select the PCB board. Right-click and select Isolate.

3. Only the single LED and the PCB board should be displayed. On the ViewCube, click RIGHT and zoom in to display the model, as shown in the following image.

- Click in the graphics window to clear the selection of the components.
- Note the interference between the PCB and the LED.
- You can use the ⊞ (Interference) tool to correct this issue.

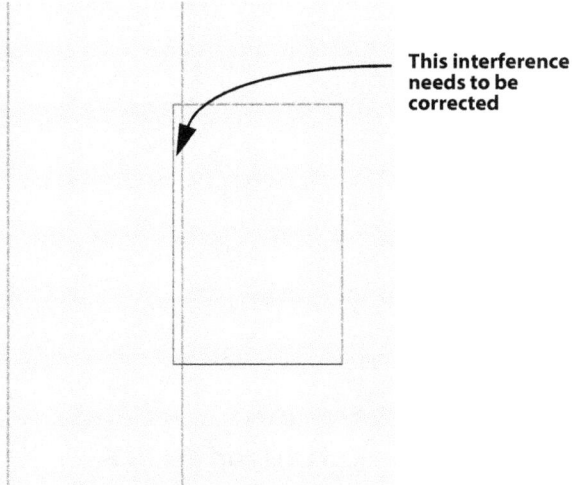

This interference needs to be corrected

4. Expand the INSPECT panel and select ⊞ (Interference).

5. Select the PCB, hold <Ctrl>, and select the LED. Click ⊞ (Compute) in the INTERFERENCE dialog box, as shown in the following image.

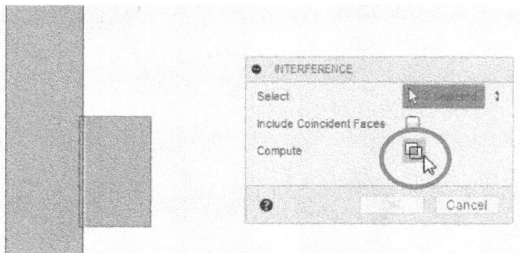

6. The Interference results dialog box opens, showing the volume of interference, as well as the objects to Cut From and Preserve, as shown in the image below.

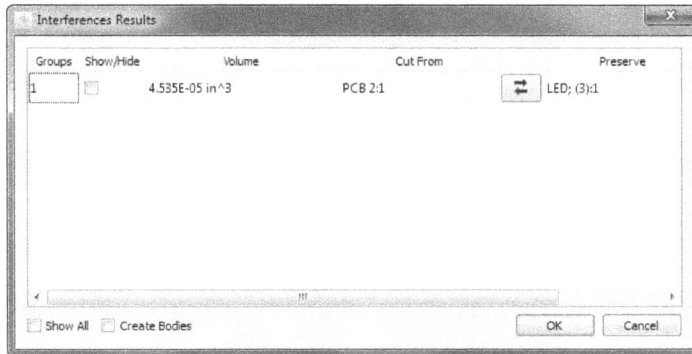

7. If you were to accept the current settings, material would be removed from the PCB to resolve the interference. You want to remove the interfering material from the LED.

- The components assigned to the Cut From and Preserve fields are dependent on the order of selection. Depending on your selection order, you may not have to switch them.

- Click ⇄ to switch the objects, so you Cut From the LED and Preserve the PCB, as shown in the following image.

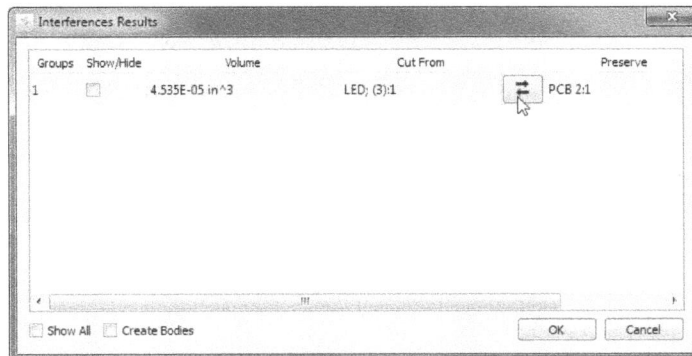

8.   Click OK to complete the interference repair.

   ▪ Note that the interference between the PCB and the LED has been removed. The interference was originally created because the depth of the LED was too large. This interference repair modified the LED's geometry so that it is now the same size as all of the other LEDs.

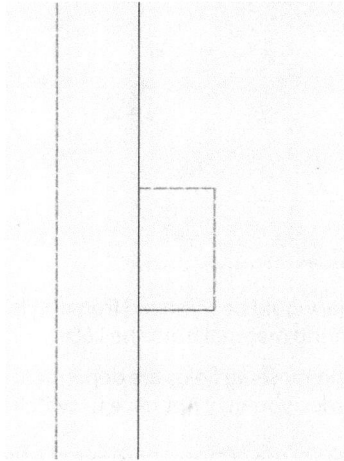

Run the MAT again to verify the fixes.

In this task, you will run the MAT once again and verify that the fixes were made.

1.   Expand the ADD-INS panel in the ribbon and select CFD Model Assessment Tool.

2.   In the Model Assessment browser, select the Potential Issues tab.

3.   In the Model assessment tools drop-down list, select the Edge lengths and note that no LEDs are listed as they were previously, as shown in the following image. The other edge lengths are acceptable.

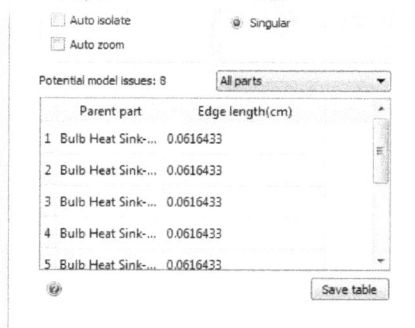

4. In the Model assessment tools drop-down list, select Surface slivers and note that no LEDs are listed as they were previously, as shown in the following image. The other surface slivers are acceptable.

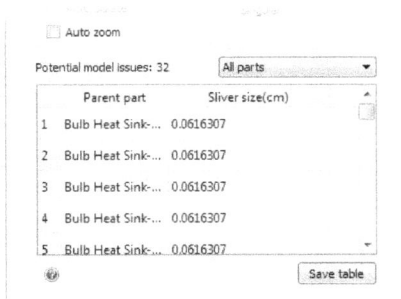

5. In the Model assessment tools drop-down list, select Model gaps and note that the LEDs listed are not those near the center of the model, but rather on the perimeter near the wall. This gap is acceptable, as you do not want the LEDs touching the wall.

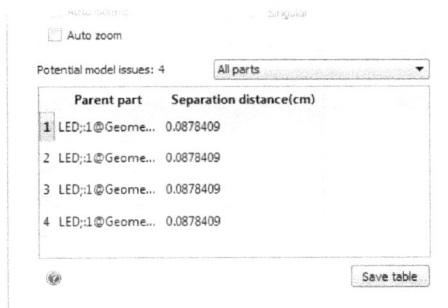

6. Finally, note that the only Interference is the friction fit between the PCB and the heat sink, as shown in the following image. This is also acceptable. With all issues corrected, you could return to the design study and complete your setup.

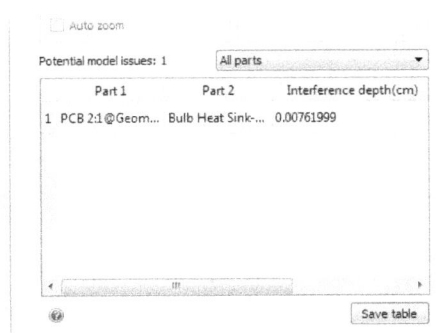

7. Close the MAT window and the Autodesk CFD application.

8. Save and close the open simulation in the SimStudio Tools application.

Materials and Devices

After establishing the model and fluid geometry, you must apply material to those objects, so that the system understands the material properties required to correctly analyze the model. This chapter discusses the material library and how to apply these materials to various components in a model. Materials can be edited or changed to modify the parameters for the analysis. Additionally, you can use special material types, referred to as Devices, that have been setup to mimic the behaviors of common physical devices, such as fans and blowers. Using devices can greatly simplify and speed up an analysis.

Objectives

After completing this chapter, you will be able to:

- Describe the various material databases.
- Identify when to use the Default database and when to create a custom database.
- Create a new database.
- Reuse existing materials to create new materials.
- Describe the process of applying materials.
- Apply materials to individual and multiple components.
- Describe the use of Scenario Environment settings.
- Describe the use of devices.
- Describe some of the devices available in the Autodesk® CFD software.

Lesson: Overview of Materials

Overview

In this lesson, you will review the standard material database.

Objectives

After completing this lesson, you will be able to:

- Describe the various material databases.
- Identify when to use the Default database and when to create a custom database.
- Create a new database.
- Reuse existing materials to create new materials.

Using Materials

Until the solid parts and fluid volumes are assigned materials, the Autodesk CFD software cannot analyze your designs because the flow, heat transfer, thermal conductivity, and other properties of those models are unknown. Materials represent physical substances and are the foundation of the Autodesk CFD analysis. To analyze a model, materials must be assigned to each component.

For example, some of the properties found in the ABS Polycarbonate material are shown in the following image.

Property	Value	Units	Underlying variation
X-Conductivity	0.000181	W/mm-K	Constant
Conductivity			Same as X-dir.
Conductivity			Same as X-dir.
Density	0.00115	g/mm3	Constant
Specific heat	1.81	J/g-K	Constant
Emissivity	0.9	none	Constant
Transmissivity	0	none	Constant
Electrical resistivity	1.46e+17	ohm-mm	Constant
Wall roughness	0	millimeter	Constant

There are two distinct material types available in an analysis: fluids and solids. In general, you will use both types when setting up your analyses. For example, consider the valve shown in the following image. Each component must have an appropriate material applied.

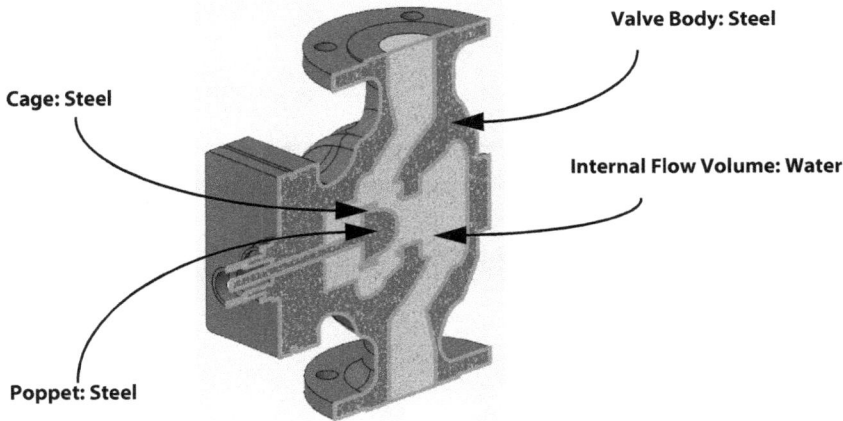

Valve Body: Steel

Cage: Steel

Internal Flow Volume: Water

Poppet: Steel

The material database installed with Autodesk CFD is called Default and contains an extensive library of fluids and solids. It also contains devices such as fans and blowers, which will be discussed later in this chapter.

Materials in this database cannot be changed, but they can be copied to a custom database and modified, as required, to establish custom materials or to organize materials for quick access. A custom database called My Materials is included with the installation of Autodesk CFD, but you can create additional databases, as required. You can also create materials in a Local database. This is a database that exists locally in each design study, so it cannot be shared with others.

> If you share a file with someone that does not have your material database, the custom material will show up as a local material. This can be saved to My Materials custom database.

Material databases are created in the Material Editor dialog box, which is accessed by clicking

(Material Editor) in the Materials panel. The Material Editor dialog box opens as shown in the following image.

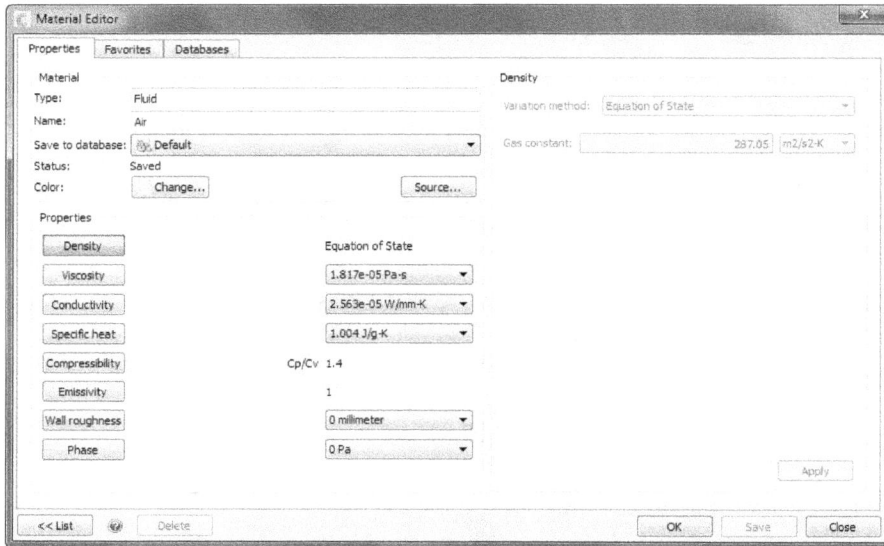

To review the databases that are available, select the Databases tab in the Material Editor, as shown in the following image.

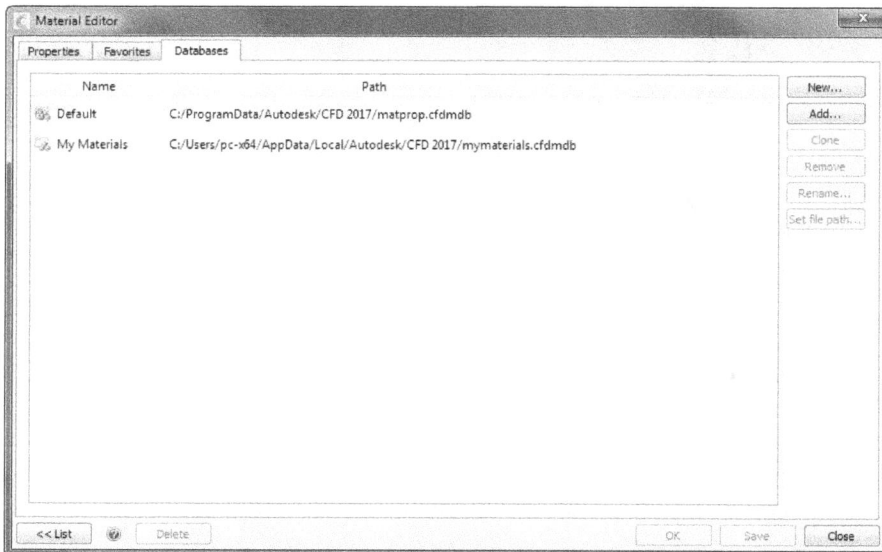

The following options are available when working with databases:

- Click New to create a new database.
- Click Add to import a database from another user.
- Select an existing database and click Clone to copy an existing database to a new name.

Creating Materials

Although the Default material database is extensive, you may still find that the exact material you are looking for in terms of fluid dynamic properties is not available. There are three basic scenarios for manipulating a material. You can create a material from an existing material, create a brand new material, or modify an assigned material.

Create From an Existing Material

Creating a material by using another similar material as a starting point can save you a great deal of time. To create a material from an existing material, use the Material Editor to display the full list of available materials and select one to use, as shown in the following image.

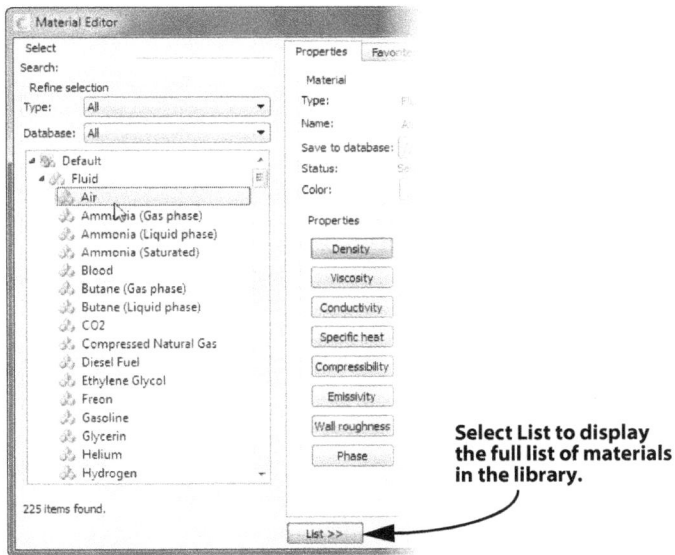

Select List to display the full list of materials in the library.

Once the starting material is selected, complete the following steps to create a new material:

1. In the Properties tab, in the Save to database drop-down list, select the database.

2. Enter a new name for the material.

3. Edit any properties that need to be customized. To edit any of the properties, follow these steps:

   a. Select the applicable property button, such as Density, as shown in the image below.

   b. Select the Variation method such as Constant, Equation of state, etc.

   c. Enter a value in the Value field.

   d. Select the appropriate units.

   e. Click Apply to make the change.

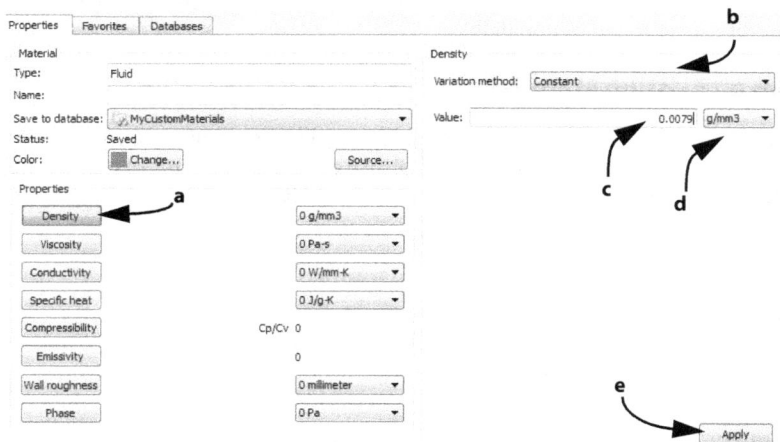

4. After you have set all of the required parameters, click Save. The new material will be available for selection from the database you specified.

Create New Material

It is sometimes easier to simply create a completely new material. This can be done in the Material Editor through the material list. In the expanded list, right-click on a custom material database, select New Material, and select the material type from the list shown in the following image. In the Properties tab, specify a name for the material, customize any properties, and click Save.

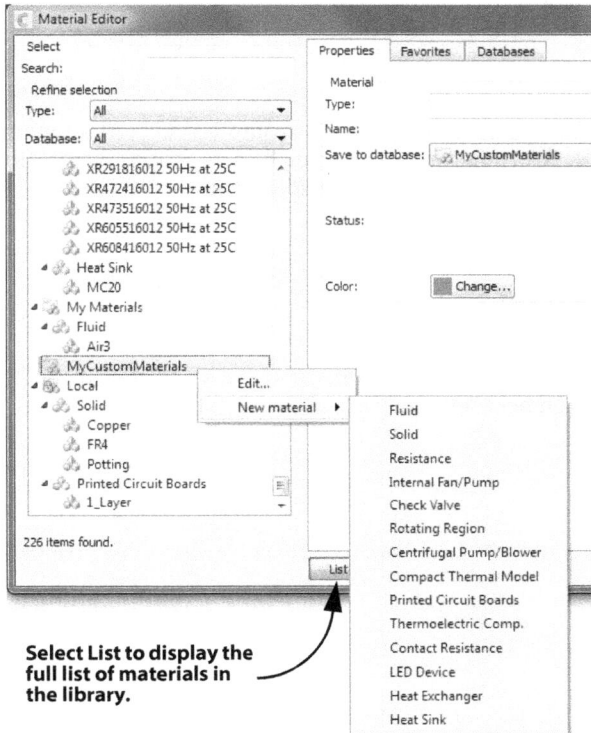

Select List to display the full list of materials in the library.

Modify an Assigned Material

You may have to edit a material that has been assigned to a part. To edit, complete the following steps:

1. In the graphics window, right-click the part that uses the material and select Edit to open the Materials dialog box. Alternatively, you can right-click the Design Study Bar's Material node to access this dialog box.

2. Click Edit adjacent to the Material parameter in the Materials dialog box to open the Material Editor.

3. Modify any properties, as required.
   - If the material is in the Default database, you will have to create a copy to a custom database before making changes.

4. Select Save.

Lesson: Assigning Materials

When a design study is created and the CAD model is brought into Autodesk CFD, all components are listed as an Unassigned material type. To conduct an analysis, you have to assign materials to every component. In this lesson, you will learn how to assign fluid, solid, and device materials.

Objectives

After completing this lesson, you will be able to:

- Describe the process of applying materials.
- Apply materials to individual and multiple components.
- Describe the use of Scenario Environment settings.

Assigning Materials

When a design study is initially created, all components have an Unassigned material, as shown in the following image.

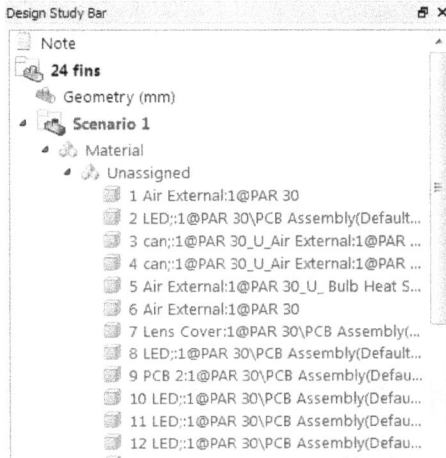

To assign a material, complete the following steps:

1. In the Setup tab, in the Setup Tasks panel, ensure that ⬡ (Materials) is the active Setup Task.

2. Select a component in the Design Study Bar or a volume directly in the graphics window, right-click and select Edit, as shown in the following image. Alternatively, in the Materials Panel, you can select Edit.

    - The Materials dialog box opens enabling you to assign the material database, select the material type and name, and where applicable, assign an environment.

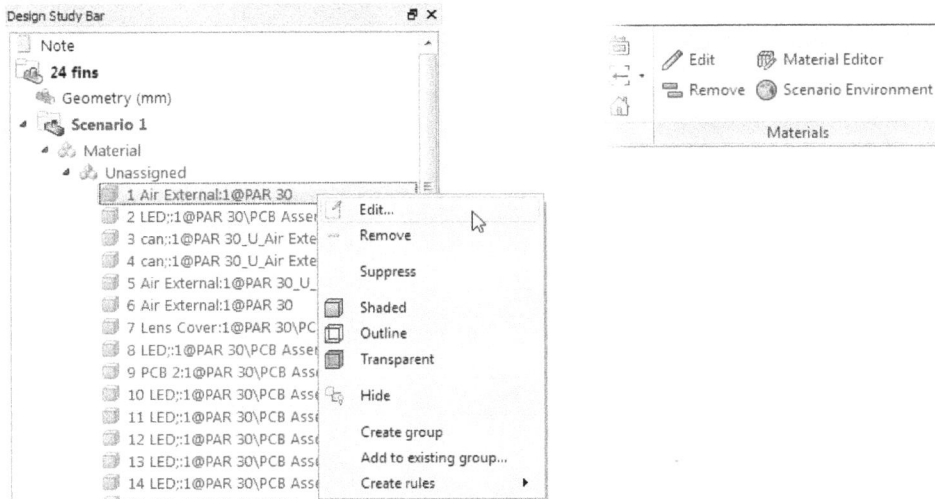

> You can apply materials to multiple components at the same time. Hold <Ctrl> while selecting the components, or use a selection rectangle to click and drag around the objects you want to include.

3. In the Materials dialog box, select the Type drop-down list and set the material Type as either Fluid or Solid, as shown in the following image. The default type is Fluid. The Device materials, such as Resistance, Centrifugal Pump/Blower and so on, are covered later in this chapter.

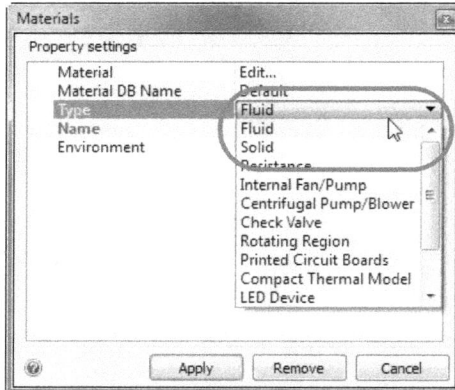

4. In the Materials dialog box, select the Name drop-down list and select the material. The list of materials will vary depending on whether you have set the Type to Fluid or Solid, as shown in the following image.

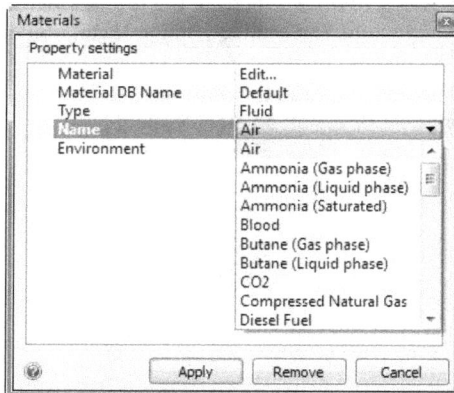 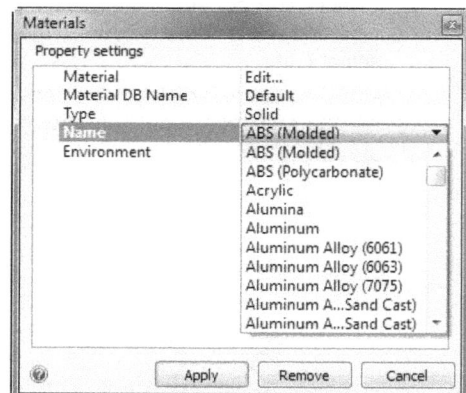

Type: Fluid **Type: Solid**

5. Click Apply to assign the material to the selected component(s).

Each material has a color assignment. The color of the components in the model are set based on the assigned color. A color legend displays in the graphics area to clearly define the objects that the material applies to, as shown in the following image.

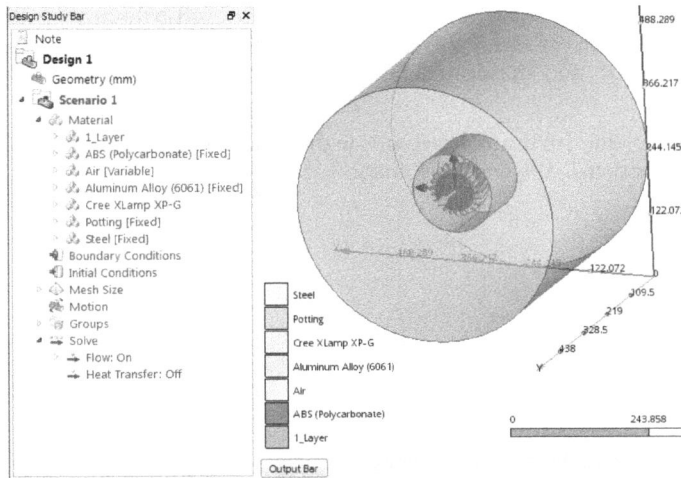

Environment-Driven Properties

In many simulations, material properties are constant. In other simulations, for example where natural convection occurs, the material properties must be allowed to vary. The Environment property can be set to Fixed or Variable to control the operating conditions throughout the scenario. If Variable is selected, the material's initial properties are applied and will vary as the scenario proceeds.

To specify a material with a Constant or Variable property, complete the following steps:

1. In the Materials dialog box, click Set, adjacent to the Environment parameter. If the current material has variable properties, the Material Environment dialog box opens, as shown in the following image.
   - Note that the property values are derived from the material database, so they are presented in this dialog box for reference. You cannot edit these values.

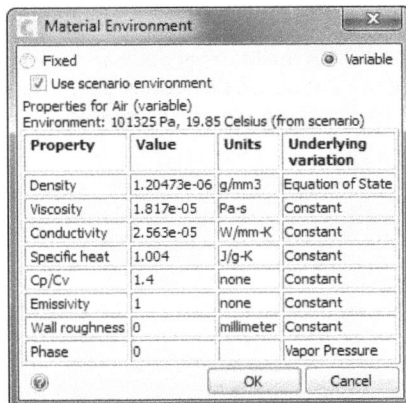

2. In the Material Environment dialog box, select Fixed or Variable.

3. Click OK.

Only those properties that have been defined with a variable method will update during the analysis. The values provided in the table are the initial starting values that will be used in the analysis. All others will remain constant. For example, in the Material Environment dialog box shown in the previous image, you can see that the Density and Phase are defined with a variable method, but all others are constant.

Once a material is assigned, it is added to the Material node in the Design Study Bar, with either [Fixed] or [Variable] adjacent to it, as shown in the following image.

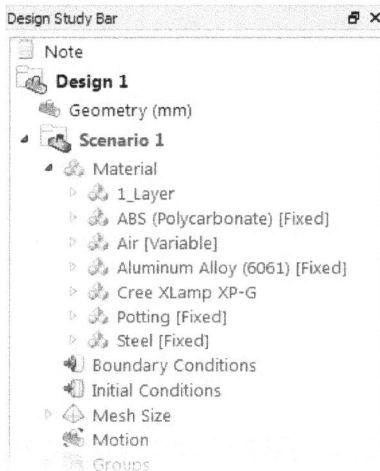

Scenario Environment Settings

Each Scenario has a default environment applied, consisting of temperature and pressure. The scenario environment settings affect all materials that have the Use scenario environment option enabled on the Material Environment dialog box. For example, an environment can be set up to indicate that the scenario is analyzed at a set elevation. The required temperature and pressure would be set for that elevation and all of the materials can be set as subject to this environment.

To change the scenario environment settings, right-click on the Material node and select the Edit scenario environment reference. The Scenario Environment dialog box opens, as shown in the following image. You can change the pressure and temperature values, as required.

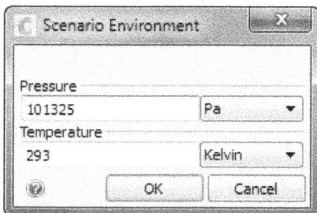

Lesson: Using Devices

CAD systems are capable of creating incredible levels of detail. In many cases in a CFD analysis, when running an analysis on a CAD model with a high level of detail, it can have a heavy requirement on system resources and take a great deal of time to complete. Even attempting to setup attributes to model the flow and heat transfer characteristics of these models can be very difficult. Autodesk CFD addresses this by providing a library of devices that can be applied to these components as materials. These materials have the same characteristics (both flow and thermal) as the models they represent, but allow for much faster and less resource intensive analyses.

Objectives

After completing this lesson, you will be able to:

- Describe the use of devices.
- Describe some of the devices available in the Autodesk CFD software.

Using Devices

There are situations in which a lot of detail may cause the model to require more mesh and longer analysis times. In some of these situations, you can replace some of the detail with material representations to improve both the mesh count and simulation time.

Several of the available devices are discussed in this chapter.

Distributed Resistance

Distributed resistances are used to represent flow obstructions in a model. The left-hand image shown in the following image is a detailed CAD model that details a sheet with perforated holes. This detail can be useful when trying to study the detailed velocities of each orifice and how that velocity profile changes. However, in a larger system where this is one component of many, this will introduce a pressure loss in the system. Using materials, you can replace this detailed CAD model with a Distributed Resistance device, as shown in the right-hand image.

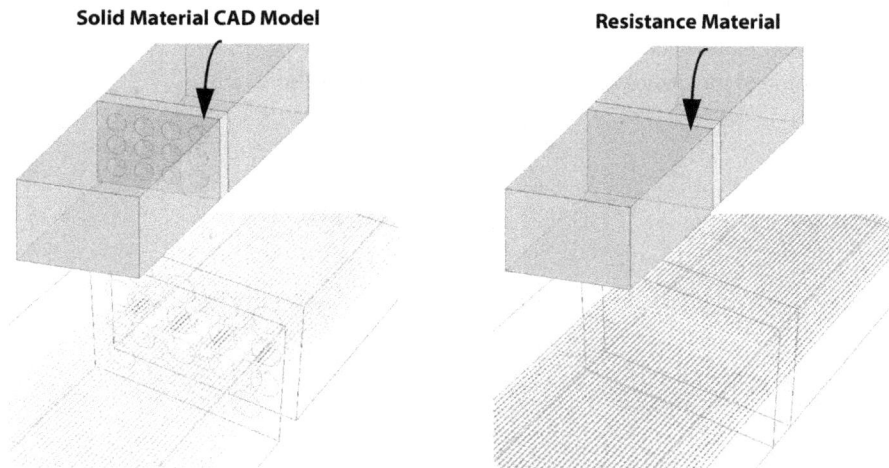

Solid Material CAD Model   **Resistance Material**

The Distributed Resistance device will average out some of the detail on the velocity profiles, predict a similar pressure drop to that of the detailed model, and allow the analysis to run much more efficiently.

- Resistances have a number of different variation methods from simple loss factors, to having a tabular performance curve.
- With distributed resistances, there is no need to assign any flow or pressure boundary condition to them directly. This will unfortunately have a negative impact on the calculations being done in the resistance material. For this reason, if there is a distributed resistance at an inlet or outlet of your model representing a screen, mesh or filter, you would add an additional CAD volume act as a fluid extension that you would assign the boundary conditions to.
- If you have a number of resistances in series, you do not want them directly touching. They should be modeled in CAD such that there is a fluid gap between them, along with an appropriate mesh across that gap.
- With meshing resistances, to achieve best results, strive for two to three elements across the thickness in the primary flow direction, as well as an element at each end.

Centrifugal Pump/Blower

To incorporate a centrifugal blower's detailed geometry in an analysis, you would use a transient model, as you would have to deal with the movement of the spinning blades. This would give a very detailed flow solution, but would also mean notably longer run times because the software tries to take the transient model to a steady state solution. Autodesk CFD provides Centrifugal Blowers with similar simplifications as resistances. The following images show the CAD model and the simplified Centrifugal Blower material device.

Centrifugal Blower CAD Model

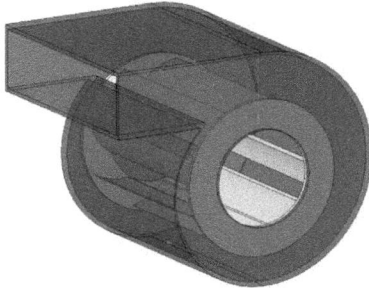

Simplified Blower Material

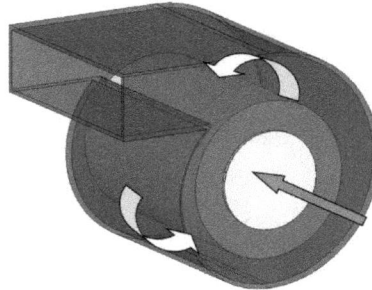

With the Centrifugal Blower device, performance information such as the RPM and the flow rate are included enabling a quicker steady-state running model.

As with resistances, you do not want to assign any boundary conditions directly to the material. Under the material assignment, the inlet surface(s) will have to be designated as well as the outlet surface(s), as shown in the following image.

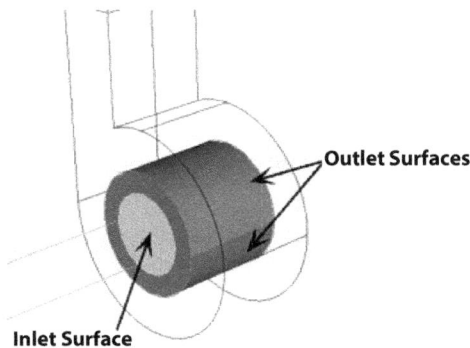

Outlet Surfaces

Inlet Surface

- With the CAD model, isolation is required between the inlet and outlet surfaces of the blower. In particular, the outer edge of the inlet surface and the outlet surface should not be shared (note the annular surface above that separates them).
- You can also model the blower as an annulus where the inlet surfaces would be the interior of the annulus and the outlets would be the exterior.

Internal Fans and Pumps

Internal Fans or pumps can also incorporate the use of a material device for simplification. Similar to a Centrifugal Blower, fans and pumps involve motion requiring larger run times. To incorporate a material device, you model the complex geometry (i.e., fan) as a simple cylinder or as an annulus to account for the center hub, as shown in the following image. Once the Internal Fan/Pump material device is assigned, a given performance curve and rpm is set.

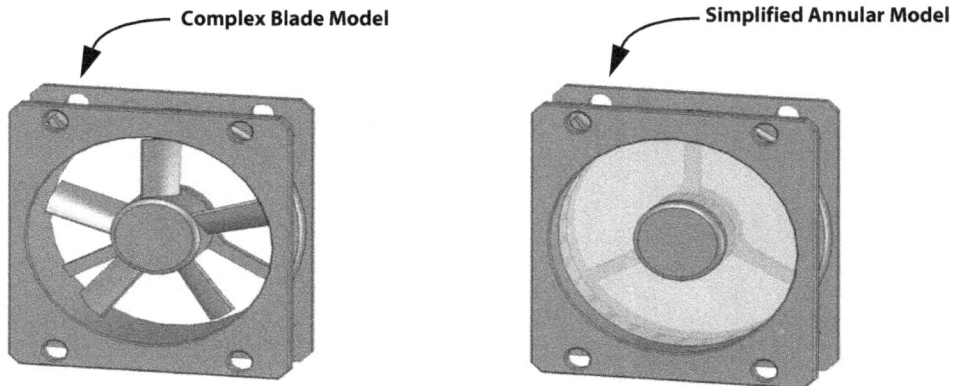

Complex Blade Model   **Simplified Annular Model**

- No flow boundary conditions should be assigned to the fan material. If located near an inlet or outlet, a fluid extension will be required to assign the boundary condition.
- Fans/pumps use local cartesian components for dictating the through-flow direction. These are specified when the material is applied to the volume.
- Fans/pumps should not be stacked in series and should contain a fluid gap between them.
- Fans/pumps should have an appropriate mesh around the circumference such that they display round. Additionally, they should have two to three elements through the thickness.

Heat Exchanger

The Heat Exchanger material device is useful for closed-loop setups to represent air conditioners or heaters.

- Specific requirements for the geometry require that the inlet and outlet of the heat exchanger material to touch the meshed domain. The rest of the model should be external or encompassed by a volume that is suppressed in meshing.
- No other boundary conditions are required for this device as its properties will dictate the flow and thermal parameters of the heat exchanger.

Heat Sink

A Heat Sink material device is a progression from smart resistances. They enable you to represent highly detailed heat sinks and use a simple block to understand how its performance would impact the chip temperature or system as a whole, as shown in the following image.

Complex Heat Sink Model

Simplified Heat Sink Model

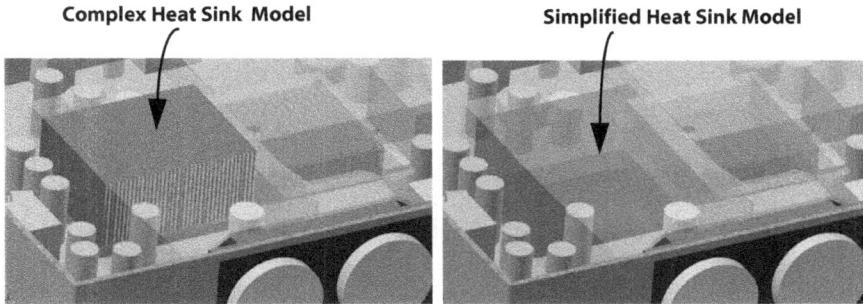

Heat Sinks can represent a number of configurations, including but not limited to the following:

- Micro channels or extruded fins
- Pin fins in either an aligned or staggered arrangement
- Offset strip

During the assignment, you will need to select an Approach Surface and Base Surface to dictate where flow enters and which side represents the base of the sink. You can also enter additional performance data for the material.

Compact Thermal Model (CTM)

The Compact Thermal Model material device is a simplification used for chips. For most chips, there is a large amount of small scaled detail as compared to the system as a whole. If modeled, this would create an excessively large model that may be somewhat impractical to analyze.

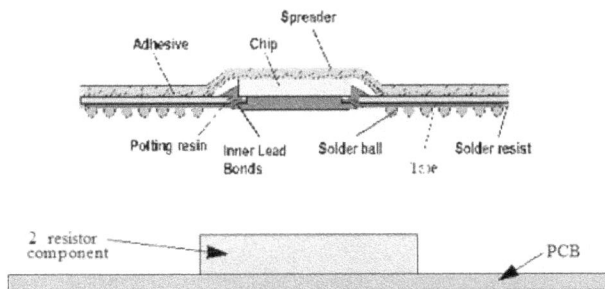

The CTM is a simple cuboid used to efficiently model the characteristics of a detailed chip. There are several restrictions and requirements to use CTMs:

- They must be a six-sided cuboid.
- They must touch either a PCB material type or Solid material type that contains PCB in its name.
- They are assumed to have adiabatic sides and transfer all heat from their junction to either the board or the case of the chip.

The required material properties, theta JC and theta JB, represent the thermal resistance between junction and case, or board respectively, as shown in the following image.

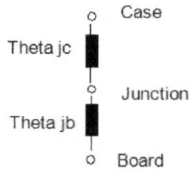

Light Emitting Diode (LED)

An LED material device is similar to a CTM material device. For example, the same time savings benefits are seen when representing the LED as a simple cuboid. A complex LED and the simplified cuboid are shown in the following image.

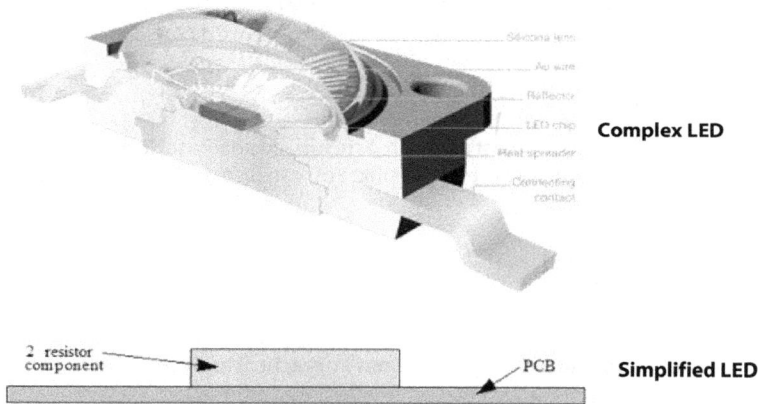

The restrictions and requirements for the use of an LED material device are described as follows:

- They must be a six-sided cuboid.
- They must touch either a PCB material type, or Solid material type that contains PCB in its name.
- They are assumed to have adiabatic sides and transfer all heat from its junction to either the board or the case of the chip.

The required material properties, theta JC and theta JB, represent the thermal resistance between junction and case, or board respectively.

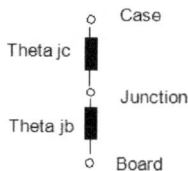

Printed Circuit Board

Printed Circuit Boards can be difficult to model in detail because the scale of the trace layers versus the board or systems scale can be notably different. The Printed Circuit Board material device type enables you to do the following:

- Specify the number of layers
- Specify the Trace and Dielectric material types and thickness

These enable you to have an appropriate in-plane versus orthogonal conductivity, as well as other associated properties.

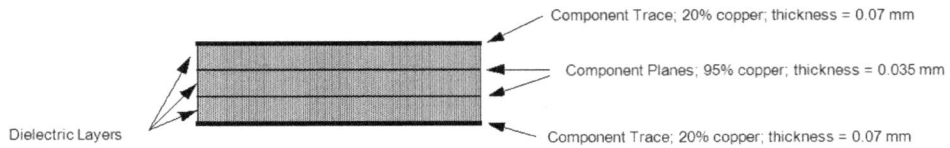

Component Trace; 20% copper; thickness = 0.07 mm

Component Planes; 95% copper; thickness = 0.035 mm

Dielectric Layers

Component Trace; 20% copper; thickness = 0.07 mm

Exercise: Applying Materials

In this exercise, you will open an existing design study in Autodesk CFD. You will then assign appropriate materials to the various objects in the model, including the interior and exterior air volumes, to prepare it for the next step in the setup process. You will also use device materials for PCB and LED components to simplify the analysis. The objectives in this exercise are to:

- Assign materials from the Default database to model components.
- Create custom materials and store them in the Design Study's local database.
- Assign standard Devices to simplify the analysis.

Open a Design Study in the Autodesk CFD Environment and review the components.

1. Launch Autodesk CFD, if not already running.

2. In the Home tab, click 📂 (Open).

3. In the Open dialog box, browse to the *C:\Autodesk CFD 2017 Essentials Exercise Files\Materials\ Assigning Materials LED* folder. Select and open *Assigning Materials LED.cfst*. The model displays as shown in the following image.

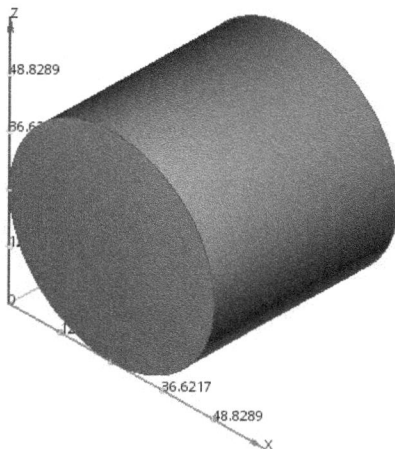

4. In the Design Study Bar, right-click on Geometry (cm) and select Change length units to and select mm.

5. Hover the cursor over the model, hold <Ctrl> and press the middle mouse button to hide the components one by one. This is a good technique to review the components in the model.

    ▪ Remove components from display until only the LED's display, as shown in the following image.

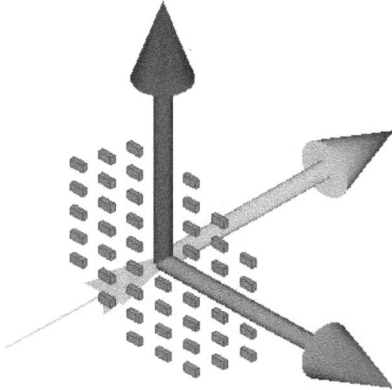

Create a group to help with manipulation of the LEDs.

Manipulating the individual LEDs takes considerable time, so you can create a group that enables you to apply a material to all of them at the same time.

1. Click and drag a rectangle around the LEDs to select all of them.

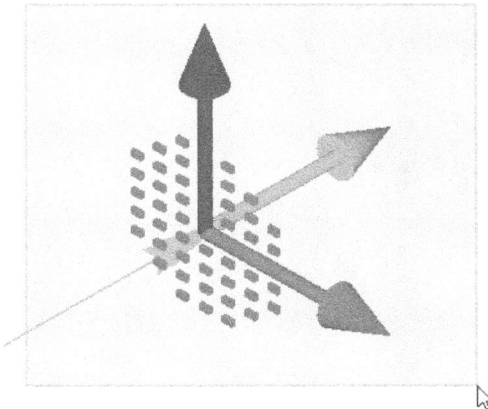

2. Right-click on the screen and select Group>Create group.

   - In the Group name field enter **LEDs**.
   - Click OK.

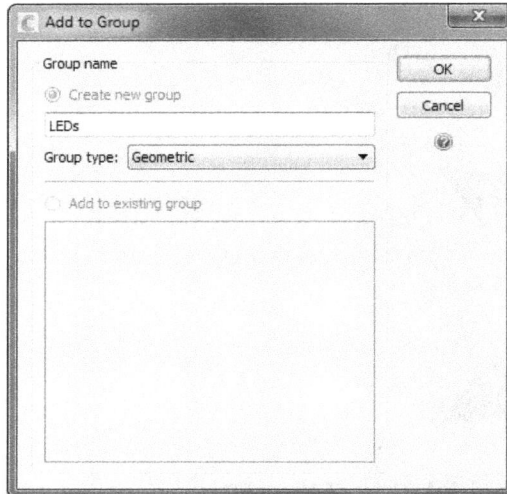

3. Note that the LEDs group is added to the Groups node, as shown in the following image. This group will be used later in this exercise to quickly assign material to the LEDs.

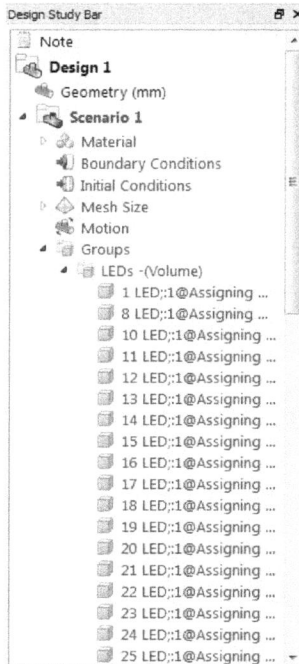

Investigate the Material node.

When a Design Study is initially created, all parts have an Unassigned material. In this task, you will review the current status of the materials.

1. In the Design Study Bar, expand the Material node and the Unassigned node, if not already expanded.

   - All parts in the model are listed in the Unassigned node, as none have a material assigned.
   - Note that the LED components are listed here. Adding them to a Group does not remove them from the Material list.

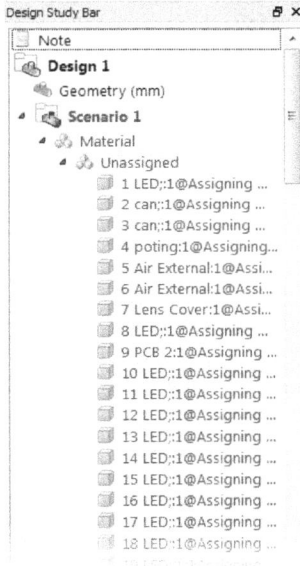

2. Hold <Ctrl> and roll the scroll wheel up until all components display. In the Quick Access Toolbar, click (Visual Style) and select Transparent, as shown in the following image, to see the internal components.

   Note: Although transparency is beneficial to help identify models during training, it may lead to graphical performance issues when dealing with larger models.

3. In the Material>Unassigned node, select 5 Air External 1 and note that it highlights.

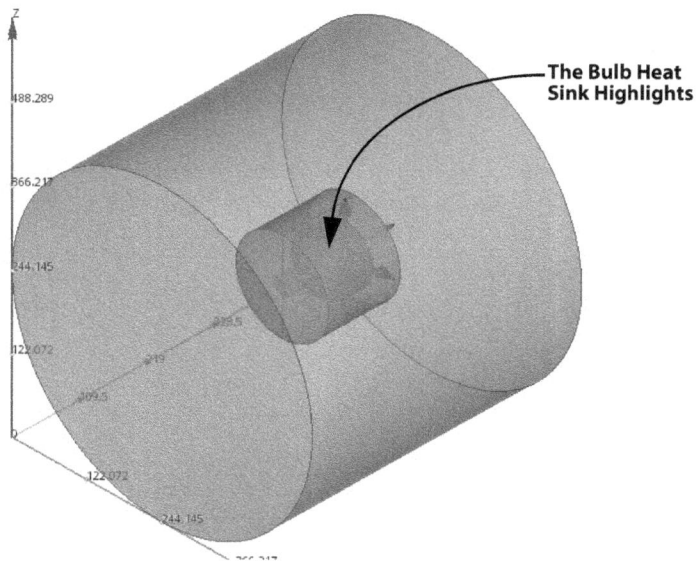

The Bulb Heat Sink Highlights

- Select several objects in the Material>Unassigned node so that you know which components they represent.
- You may have to zoom in on some objects or even hide some objects to see others.
- Once you have investigated the objects, show all of them.

Apply the Air material to two Air volumes.

In this model, an air volume exists that surrounds the model (59 Air External). Another volume exists between the PCB and the lens (6 Air External). These volumes have convective flow, which means the air properties need to be able to fluctuate during the analysis. To fluctuate, the air material must be set as variable.

1. In the Material>Unassigned node, select 6 Air External. Scroll to the last object in the Unassigned node, press <Ctrl>, and select 59 Air External.

    ▪ Right-click and select Edit to open the Materials dialog box.

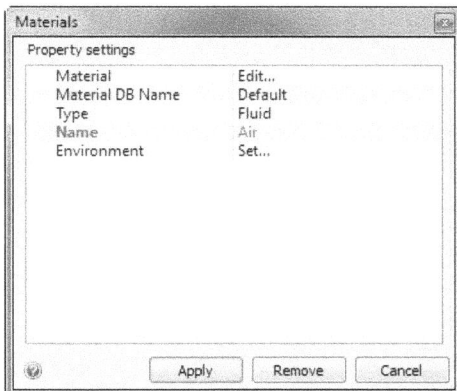

    ▪ Ensure that the Type is set to Fluid.
    ▪ Ensure that the Name is set to Air.
    ▪ Click Set in the Environment row.

2. The Material Environment dialog box opens. Select Variable to enable the properties of the air to vary throughout the analysis. Review the properties listed and click OK. Note that the values shown are the initial values used and they may vary throughout the analysis.

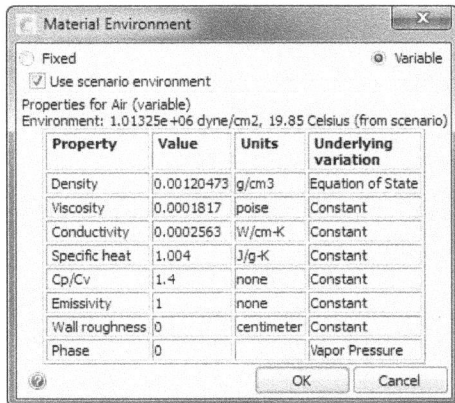

3. Click Apply in the Materials dialog box and note that the two air volumes have been removed from the Unassigned node and placed under a new node called Air [Variable], as shown in the following image.

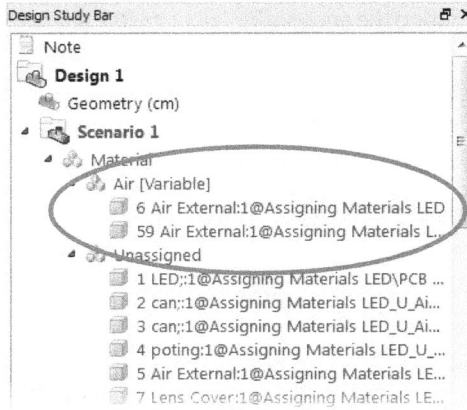

4. Collapse the Air [Variable] node.

Apply several solid materials.

In this task, you will add materials to several solid objects. Remember that an analysis cannot be completed until all objects have been converted into assigned materials.

1. Apply an ABS material for the lens cover.

   - In the Unassigned node, select 7 Lens Cover.
   - Right-click and select Edit to open the Materials dialog box.
   - In the Type drop-down list, select Solid.
   - In the Name drop-down list, select ABS (Polycarbonate).
   - The Materials dialog box should display as shown in the following image.
   - Click Apply when complete. An ABS (Polycarbonate) [Fixed] node is added.

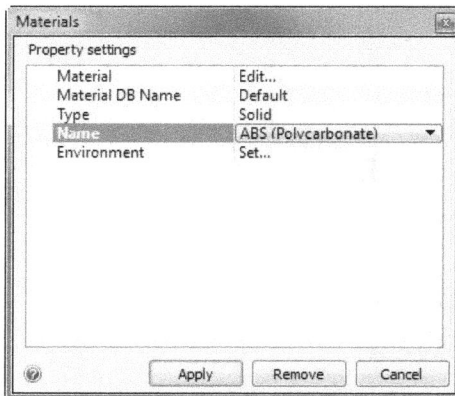

2. Note that the legend in the lower left of the window updates with each new material assignment. To view each component in its respective color, in the Quick Access Toolbar, click

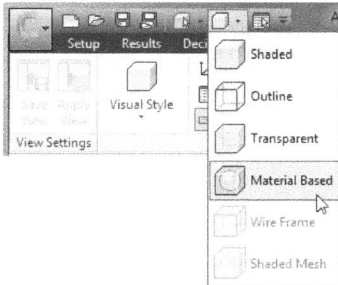 (Visual Style) and select Material Based, as shown in the following image.

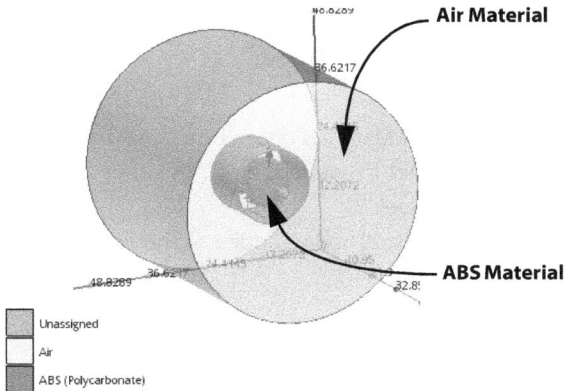

3. Assign Steel material to the housing that surrounds the LED.

- As an alternative to selecting geometry from the Design Study Bar, you can also select directly in the graphics window. In the graphics window, select the two halves of the housing (2 can and 3 can) that surrounds the LED, as shown in the following image.

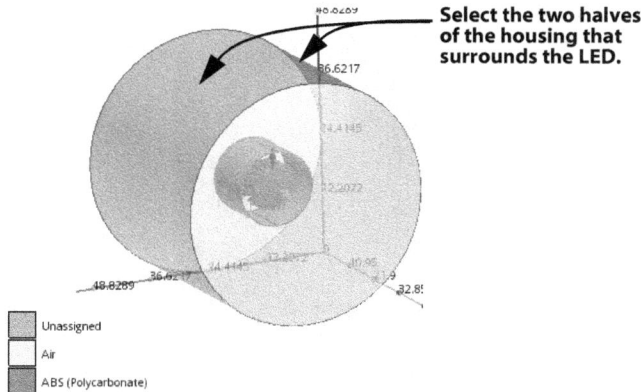

Select the two halves of the housing that surrounds the LED.

- Unassigned
- Air
- ABS (Polycarbonate)

- Right-click and select Edit to open the Materials dialog box.
- In the Type drop-down list, select Solid, if required.
- In the Name drop-down list, select Steel.
- Click Apply when complete. A Steel [Fixed] node is added, as shown in the following image.

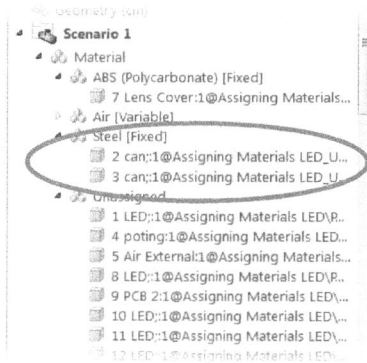

4. Assign an aluminum alloy to the bulb heat sink.

- In the Unassigned node, select 5 Air External.
- Right-click and select Edit to open the Materials dialog box.
- In the Type drop-down list, select Solid, if required.
- In the Name drop-down list, select Aluminum Alloy (6061).
- Click Apply when complete. An Aluminum Alloy (6061) [Fixed] node is added, as shown in the following image.

Create a custom material, and store it in the local database.

The potting between the bulb heat sink and the PCB is made of a material not contained in the default database. In this task, you will create the material and store it in the Local database. Storing it here will ensure that it does not change, as the Local database is only accessible in this design study.

1. In the Unassigned node, select 4 potting, right-click and select Edit.

2. In the Materials dialog box, click Edit in the Material row. The Material Editor opens as shown in the following image.

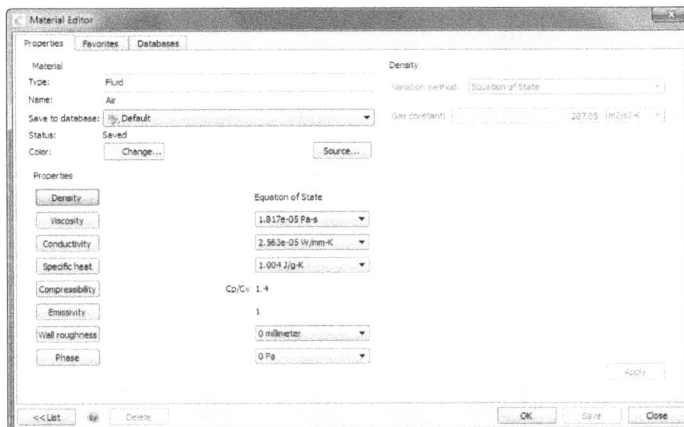

3. The Type and Name cannot currently be edited in the text fields, because the dialog box is showing the values for the default material.

- Create a new material by clicking List in the lower left of the Material Editor dialog box.
- The dialog box expands to list the available materials, as shown in the image below.

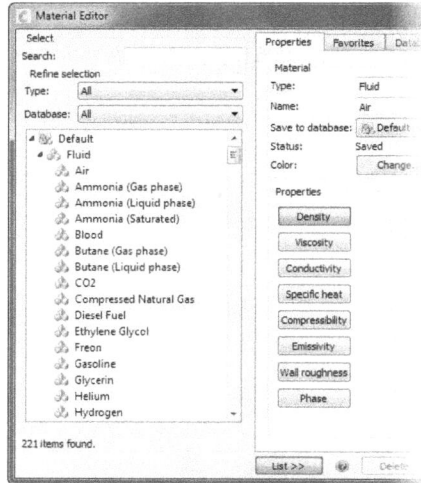

4. Scroll down in the list until you find the Solid node, then scroll further and select Potting Compound (Silicon). This will be used as the basis for your custom material.

- Click List to close the selection panel.
- The Material Editor updates as shown in the following image.

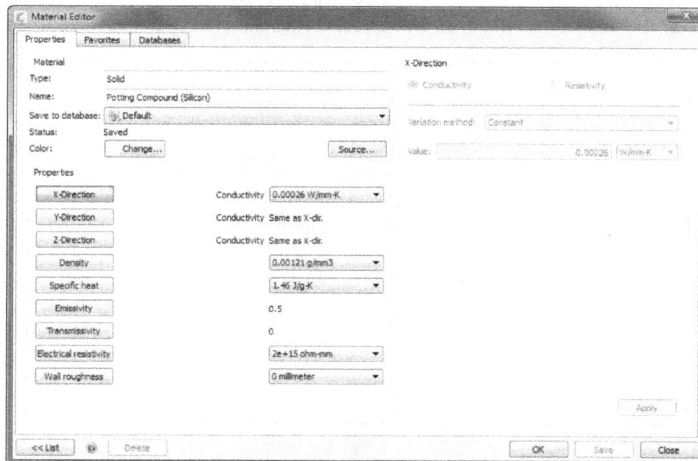

5. The material properties are similar to those required for this design, but do need to be edited.

   - In the Name Field, edit the name to **Potting**.
   - In the Save to database drop-down list, select Local.
   - The dialog box updates as shown in the following image.

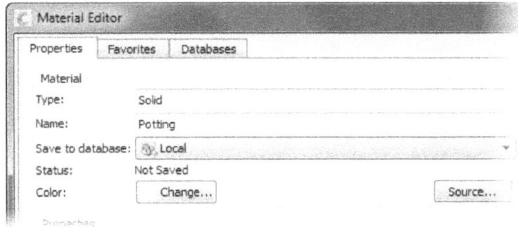

6. Change the color of the potting material.

   - In the Material Editor, click Change next to Color to open the Select Color Editor.
   - Select the Cyan color shown in the following image and click OK.

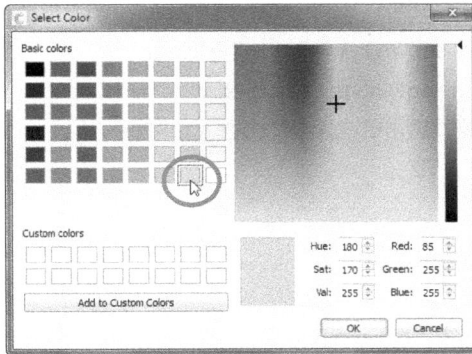

7. Change the value for the X-Direction Conductivity.

   - In the Value field, edit the value to **0.00037** and ensure that the units are set to W/mm-K.
   - Click Apply.
   - The X-Direction value updates as shown in the following image.

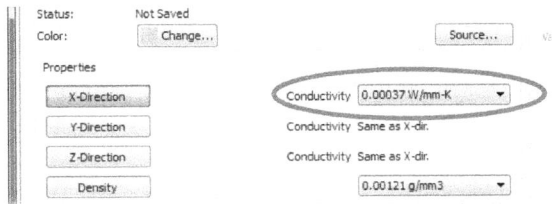

8. Leave both the X-Direction and Y-Direction Conductivity as Same as X-dir.

9. Change the Density value.

- Click Density.
- In the Value field, edit the value to **0.00105** and ensure that the units are set to g/mm3.
- Click Apply.
- The Density value updates as shown in the following image.

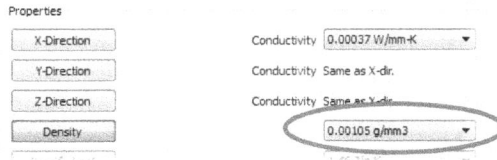

10. Follow the previous step to change the following values. Click Apply after changing each value.

- Specific Heat: **2.05 J/g-K**
- Emissivity: **0.2**
- Electrical resistivity: **3.66e-05 ohm-mm**

11. The Material Editor should display as shown in the following image.

- Click OK when you have finished applying the changes.

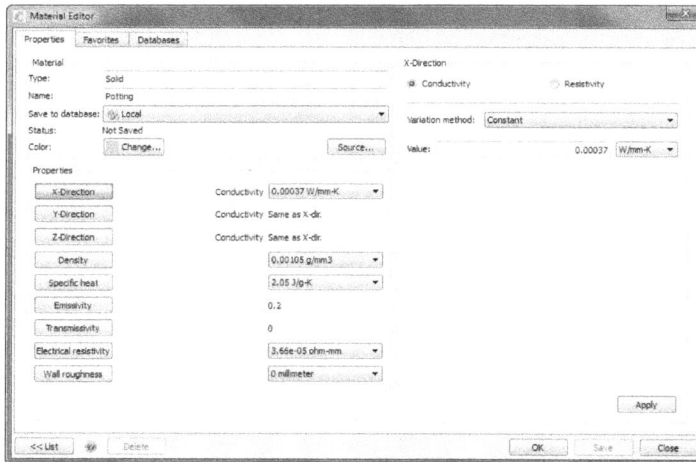

- In the Materials dialog box, click Apply to add the new material.

12.   A Potting node is added, as shown in the following image.

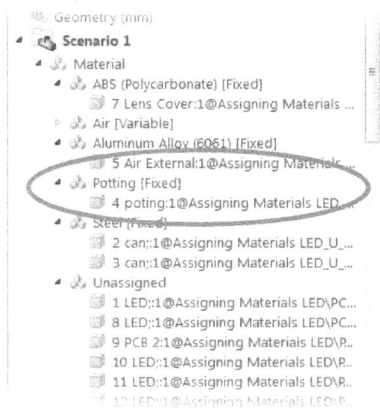

Use a PCB device as the material for the PCB model.

Devices are materials that have the properties of more complex components, but that require much less computation time and resources. In this task, you will apply a PCB device to the PCB component. Generally, you will replace a complex CAD component with a simplified version. In this exercise, the PCB is already modeled as a simple disc shape, so you can simply apply a PCB material to it. The required device needs to be created, since it does not exist in the Default database with the correct parameters.

1.   In the Unassigned node, select 9 PCB 2, right-click, and select Edit.

2.   In the Materials dialog box, in the Type drop-down list, select Printed Circuit Boards. Since there is only one device for this type, it is automatically used.

3.   The material properties are close to those required for this design, but do need to be edited. Select Edit in the Material row.

- In the Name Field, edit the name to **1_Layer**.
- In the Save to database drop-down list, select Local.
- The dialog box updates as shown in the following image.

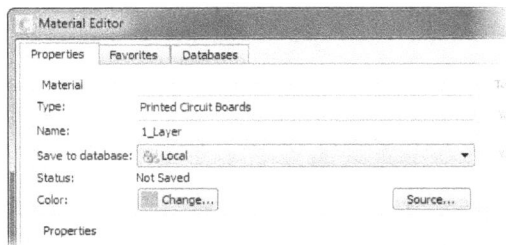

4. Change the value for the total PCB thickness.

- In the Value field, edit the value to **0.06** and ensure that the units are set to inch.
- Click Apply.
- The Total PCB thickness value updates as shown in the following image.

5. Since the PCB is a material that mimics the behavior of a device, it needs to calculate an Effective Planar Conductivity. The Traces and Planes material, thickness, and percentage metal are required to correctly calculate the PCB's properties. Edit the Traces and Planes values as follows.

- Click Traces and Planes.
- Ensure that the Material is set to Copper.
- Select the first thickness listed and click Delete.
- Click Delete until all thicknesses are removed.
- In the Thickness column, enter **0.00137**.
- In the %Metal column, enter **40**.
- Edit the Coverage Exponent E value to **1**, to define the layout.
- Click Apply.
- The Material Editor dialog box displays as shown in the following image.

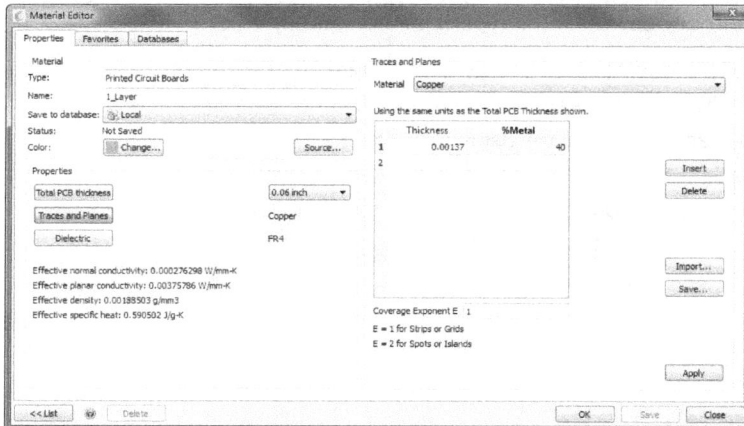

6.   Click OK in the Material Editor and Apply in the Materials dialog box. A node named 1_Layer is added to the Material node, as shown in the following image.

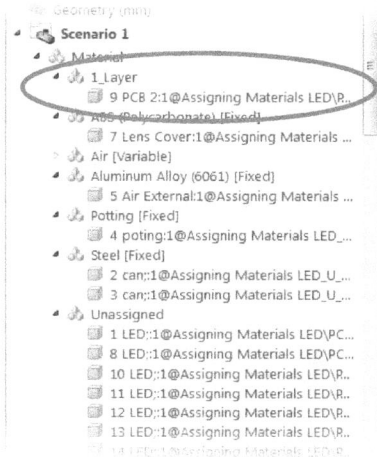

Use an LED device as the material for the array of LEDs.

The material database includes many brand name devices. In this task, you will apply a Cree XLamp XP-G LED device to all of the LED components. The group that you created earlier in this exercise will be used to quickly apply the device to all LED objects in one step.

1.   In the Design Study Bar, scroll down to the Groups node and expand it, if not already expanded.

2.   Select the LEDs -(Volume) group, as shown in the following image.

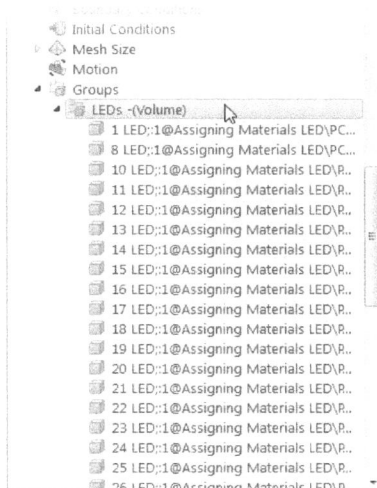

3. In the Setup tab, in the Materials panel, select ✎ (Edit) to open the Materials dialog box.

4. Expand the Type drop-down list and select LED Device, as shown in the following image.

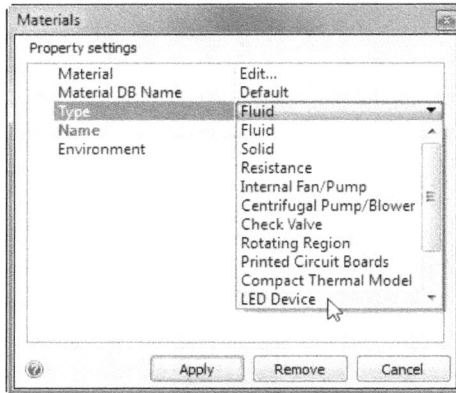

5. Expand the Name drop-down list and select Cree XLamp XP-G, as shown in the following image.

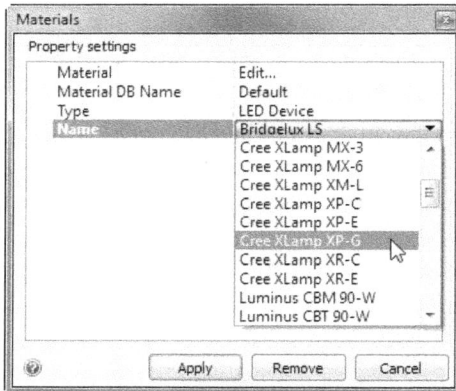

6. Click Apply to complete the application of the device to all of the LEDs. Note that if any LEDs are missed from the Group and are not assigned the LED device, you can simply drag and drop the missed component onto the Cree XLamp XP-G node to assign it.

7. Collapse all of the individual Material nodes and note that there is no Unassigned node. Note that the legend in the main window no longer has any objects displayed with the Unassigned color, as shown in the following image.

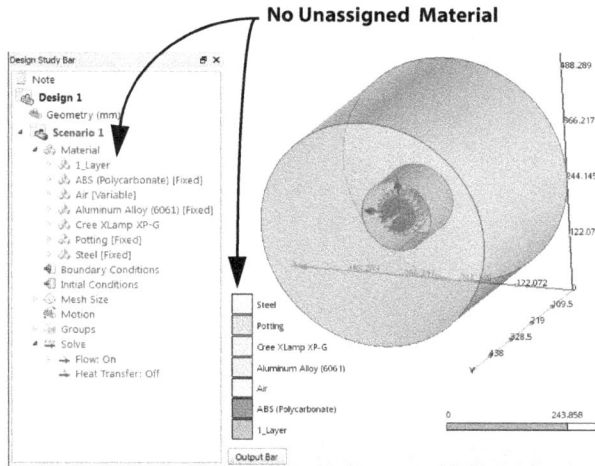

No Unassigned Material

8. In the Quick Access toolbar, click 🖫 (Save) to save the study.

- With all materials defined, you will be able to add boundary conditions, mesh the model, and so on. These topics will be discussed in the upcoming chapters.

9. Close the Autodesk CFD application.

Boundary Conditions

Boundary conditions are used in Autodesk CFD to represent the actual flow and thermal conditions the model will experience. Assigning the correct boundary conditions in a CFD analysis is a critical step in achieving accurate and useful results. In this chapter, you will learn how to assign flow and thermal boundary conditions to geometry in the model.

Objectives

After completing this chapter, you will be able to:

- Describe what boundary conditions are used for.
- Understand the need for Inlet extensions.
- Describe the difference between flow and thermal boundary conditions.
- Describe the various Flow and Thermal Boundary Conditions.
- Describe the different properties required to setup boundary conditions.
- Apply boundary conditions to volumes and surfaces.

Lesson: Boundary Conditions

Overview

Boundary conditions are used to define the inputs of the simulation model. Some boundary conditions, like velocity and volumetric flow rate, define how a fluid enters or leaves the model, while others, like film coefficient and heat flux, define the interchange of energy between the model and its surroundings.

Objectives

After completing this lesson, you will be able to:

- Describe what boundary conditions are used for.
- Understand the need for Inlet extensions.
- Describe the difference between flow and thermal boundary conditions.

Using Boundary Conditions

Boundary conditions connect the simulation model with its surroundings. Without them, the simulation is not defined, and in most cases, cannot proceed. Most boundary conditions can be defined as either steady-state or transient.

- Steady-state boundary conditions persist throughout the simulation.
- Transient boundary conditions vary with time and are often used to simulate an event or a cyclical phenomena.

In most situations, you assign boundary conditions to external faces. External faces have a meshed volume on only one side of the surface, which represents the external face. If there is no boundary condition assigned to an external face, and it is a fluid volume, the face is treated as a wall with a velocity of zero. For thermal analyses, you can assume that the external faces without conditions are adiabatic (without gain or loss of heat) and are treated as perfectly insulated.

For example, consider the faucet shown in the following image. A Flow Rate and Temperature can be assigned at each inlet to represent the hot and cold water coming in, as well as a pressure on the outlet. Consider the following:

- If no other boundary conditions were assigned, any and all heat from the hot water will be mixed and dissipated with the cold water and out the outlet.
- If another condition (such as a Film Coefficient) is added, the heat loss the faucet experiences to the surroundings can be represented, enabling more heat to be dissipated. This boundary condition is one example of how you can achieve a more conservative or realistic result by including additional boundary conditions.

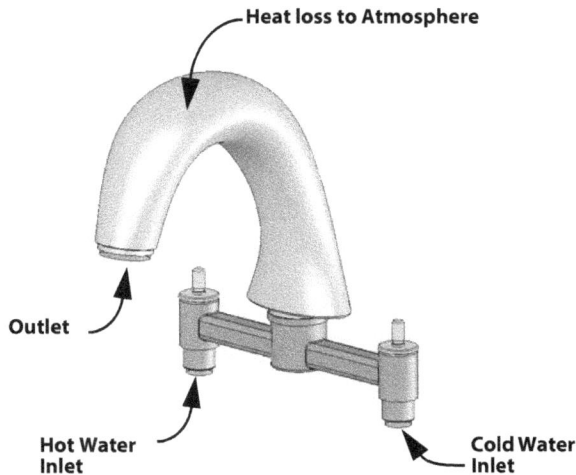

Heat loss to Atmosphere

Outlet

Hot Water Inlet

Cold Water Inlet

Inlet and Outlet Extensions

In some situations, you will want to include a fluid extension to an inlet or outlet. The intent of these extension is to avoid having a large recirculation region crossing an inlet or outlet. For thermal models, an inlet extension allows for better temperature solutions as the inlet temperature is only assigned to a fluid and is not in contact with a neighboring solid. Generally, the extension is five times the size of the diameter, to ensure that the recirculation regions are captured correctly.

- Consider the following images of a valve and its flow volume. A temperature boundary condition applied to an inlet that is too close to the solid portions of the model will affect the temperature of the solids, as shown on the left in the following image. This is an undesirable result. To prevent this, extend the inlet region of the model and apply temperature and flow boundary conditions to surfaces further from the solid, as shown on the right.

Inlet Too Short   Inlet Extended

Flow Boundary Conditions

When applying boundary conditions, you have to determine the factors that drive the flow of the fluid, such as:

- Pressure drop
- Flow rate
- Fan (balance between flow rate & pressure drop)
- Buoyancy (natural convection)

Common combinations for incompressible flow are as follows:

INLET CONDITION	OUTLET CONDITION
Flow Rate	$P_{static} = 0$
$P_{static} = 0$	Flow Rate
$P_{static} > 0$	$P_{static} = 0$
External Fan (Push)	$P_{static} = 0$
$P_{static} = 0$	External Fan (Pull)
Internal Fan	
$P_{static} = 0$	$P_{static} = 0$

Thermal Boundary Conditions

For thermal boundary conditions, all inlets must have a temperature boundary condition assigned to set the inbound fluid temperature. Autodesk CFD will solve the temperature distribution through the model so that thermal conditions on the outlet are not required. When assigning Thermal conditions, use the following guidelines:

- Assign a temperature on the flow inlet face.
- Assign a thermal condition at any point (on the model) where thermal energy enters or leaves the model (except the outlet).
- Define a temperature, as required.

> Thermal surface boundary conditions are meant to be external. For internal heat generation, use a volume heat generation.

For example:

- Heat loss to surrounding environment: Film coefficient.
- Power dissipation from an internal component: Heat generation or Total heat generation.

Lesson: Flow and Thermal Conditions

Autodesk CFD uses both flow and thermal boundary conditions to load the model for analysis. Without the assignment of boundary conditions, there is no fluid flow or heat transfer to analyze.

Objectives

After completing this lesson, you will be able to:

- Describe the various Flow and Thermal Boundary Conditions.
- Describe the different properties required to setup boundary conditions.

Flow Boundary Conditions

Flow boundary conditions typically represent a quantity or state at a model opening. Flow boundary conditions are applied to surfaces in 3D models and edges in 2D models. The Boundary Conditions are defined in the Boundary Conditions dialog box, as shown in the following image.

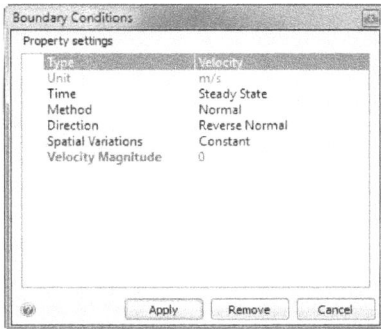

The following are some of the common flow boundary conditions, along with their required properties.

Velocity

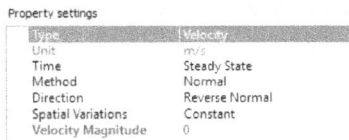

- Velocity is generally used as an inlet boundary condition, specified as normal to the selected surface but can be vectored by entering Cartesian coordinates. You can apply a velocity to an outlet, provided the direction of that velocity vector is defined as out of the model.

- Spatial Variation is an optional property that defaults to Constant, but can be set to either Fully Developed or Linear Variation. The Fully Developed property is useful if the model entrance length is not long enough to allow for the natural development of the flow.

> In general, entry length is over 20 diameters in most pipe flow applications. To calculate the entry length, consider the following equations:
> - For laminar flow, calculate the entry length using Le / d = .06 * Re (d)
> - For turbulent flow, calculate the entry length using Le / d ~ 4.4 Re (d) 1/6

Rotational Velocity

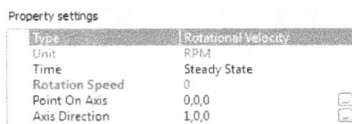

- A Rotational Velocity boundary condition simulates a rotating object surrounded by a fluid, by applying a rotating velocity to a wall.

- This boundary condition requires a Rotation Speed value in either revolutions per minute or radians per second.

Volume Flow Rate

Property settings

Type	Volume Flow Rate
Unit	l/min
Time	Steady State
Volume Flow Rate	380
Direction	Reverse Normal
Fully Developed	☐

- A Volume Flow Rate boundary condition is applied to a planar opening. It is most often used as an inlet condition and is particularly useful if the density is constant throughout the analysis. A volume flow rate can be applied to an outlet, provided the flow direction is out of the model, if not the Direction must be reversed.

- You can apply a Volume Flow Rate to multiple surfaces, but they must be flowing in the same direction.

Mass Flow Rate

Property settings

Type	Mass Flow Rate
Unit	kg/s
Time	Steady State
Mass Flow Rate	0
Direction	Reverse Normal

- A Mass Flow Rate boundary condition is most often applied as an inlet condition, although it can also be applied to an outlet if the flow direction is out of the model. The boundary condition must be applied to a planar surface.

Pressure

Property settings

Type	Pressure
Unit	Pa
Time	Steady State
Pressure	0
Gage / Absolute	Gage
Static / Total	Static

- The Pressure boundary condition is typically applied as an outlet condition. It is recommended to apply the outlet condition as a static gage pressure with a value of 0. When applied, no other conditions are required at an outlet.

- You can apply a non-zero pressure as an inlet condition. Therefore, if you know that the pressure will drop through a device, you can apply a static gage pressure value for the pressure drop at the inlet, and a static gage pressure value of 0 at the outlet.

- The default setting is Gage pressure, which is a relative pressure. You can also use Absolute pressure, which is the sum of the gage and the Material Environment pressures.

For most incompressible flows, Static pressure is the recommended setting.

External Fan

Property settings

Type	External Fan
Unit	RPM
Rotational Speed	0
Direction	Reverse Rotation
Fan Characteristic	Edit...
Slip Factor	1

- You can apply an External Fan boundary condition to move flow in or out of a device. The external fan boundary condition is defined as a head-capacity curve, resulting in an inlet flow rate that varies with the pressure drop of the device.

- The Slip Factor is the ratio of the true rotational speed of the flow to the rotational speed of the fan blades. Slip can result in a slower tangential flow velocity than expected due to inefficiencies in the fan. Autodesk CFD determines the flow tangential velocity component by multiplying the slip factor by the user-supplied fan rotational speed. By default, the slip factor is set to 1.0, which means that the rotational speed of the flow is the same as the rotational speed of the fan.

Thermal Boundary Conditions

The section below describes some of the most common Thermal boundary conditions, along with their required properties. These are divided into Surface and Volumetric boundary conditions.

Surface Boundary Conditions

- Surface-based Thermal boundary conditions represent either a known physical state, such as temperature, or an amount of heat entering or leaving the device, such as a heat flux. Temperature is the only condition that can be applied to both openings and wall surfaces. You should apply the others only to wall surfaces.

Temperature

Property settings

Type	Temperature
Unit	Celsius
Time	Steady State
Spatial Variations	Constant
Temperature	0
Static / Total	Static

- A temperature boundary condition should be specified at all inlets when conducting heat transfer analyses. In most situations, a Static temperature condition is recommended, but you can use Total temperature as an inlet temperature for compressible heat transfer analyses.

> If a surface is both an inlet and an outlet (such as a bucket type natural convection analysis), you must specify the temperature using a film coefficient.

Heat Flux

Type	Heat Flux
Unit	W/m2
Time	Steady State
Heat Flux	0

- Heat Flux imposes a set amount of heat directly to the applied surface. Heat flux is calculated as a heat value divided by the area.
- You should only apply Total heat flux to outer wall surfaces.

Film Coefficient

Property settings

Type	Film Coefficient
Time	Steady State
Coefficient Units	W/m2/k
Film Coefficient	0
Temperature Units	Celsius
Ref Temperature	0

- The Film Coefficient is often used to simulate a cooling effect for heat transfer analyses. You can assign film coefficients to external surfaces. This boundary condition, also known as a convection condition, is used to simulate the effect of the environment that is external to the device. You should only apply the film coefficient boundary condition to external surfaces.
- The Film Coefficient boundary condition is often used to simulate convection from exterior surfaces to regions that are outside of (and not modeled in) the physical model. A film coefficient value between 5 and 25 W/m^2K is typically a good approximation (equivalent of convection to still air). Moving air or using conductive fluids (e.g., water, glycol, etc.) can warrant a higher value.

Radiation

Property settings

Type	Radiation
Time	Steady State
Emissivity	0
Temperature Units	Celsius
Ref Temperature	0

- The Radiation boundary condition simulates the radiative heat transfer between the selected surfaces and a source that is external to the model. It is a "radiation film coefficient" in that it exposes a surface to a given heat load using a source temperature and a surface condition.

Applying the Radiation boundary condition does not require you to enable Radiation in the Solver.

Volumetric Boundary Conditions

Volumetric conditions are used to generate heat. You can use Volume selection for 3D models and Surface selection for 2D models.

Heat Generation

Property settings

Type	Heat Generation
Unit	W/m3
Time	Steady State
Temperature Dependent	Disabled
Heat Generation	0

- The Heat Generation boundary condition must be applied to a volume. The specified value is divided by the volume of the part.
- This boundary condition is typically applied to simulate heat-dissipating components in electronics assemblies.

Total Heat Generation

Property settings

Type	Total Heat Generation
Unit	W
Time	Steady State
Temperature Dependent	Disabled
Total Heat Generation	0

- The Total Heat Generation boundary condition is similar to Heat Generation, but the heat load is not divided by part volume. This condition is recommended for most heat-load applications because the value does not have to be adjusted if the part volume changes.

Lesson: Assigning Boundary Conditions

Overview

Now that you are familiar with the various boundary conditions, you can learn how to apply those boundary conditions to the geometry in your model.

Objectives

After completing this lesson, you will be able to:

- Apply boundary conditions to volumes and surfaces.

Assigning Boundary Conditions

To activate the Boundary Condition assignment task, select ⬇ (Boundary Conditions) in the Setup Tasks panel in the Setup tab, or select the Boundary Conditions node in the Design Study Bar.

Once the Boundary Conditions task is active, Boundary Conditions are assigned using the Boundary Conditions dialog box.

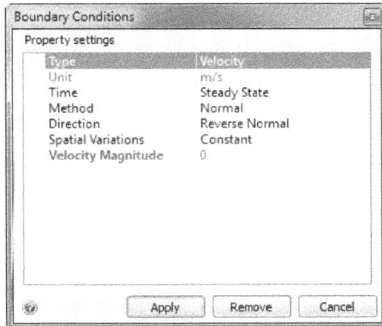

To open the Boundary Conditions dialog box, use one of the following methods:

- Left click on the surface or volume and click the ▱ (Edit) on the context toolbar.
- Right-click on the surface or volume and click Edit for an existing boundary condition, or click New BC to create a new one.
- Click ✎ (Edit) in the Boundary Conditions context panel.

Surface and Volume Selection

Depending on the type of boundary condition you want to assign, in the Setup tab, in the Selection panel, enable either ▱ (Volume) or ▱ (Surface). For example, to apply a Total Heat Generation boundary condition, use ▱ (Volume) to select the entire volume of the applicable component and not just a single surface.

Assigning Properties

You can assign a boundary condition to one or more surfaces or volumes at a time. Once the appropriate objects have been selected, the Boundary Condition dialog box opens and you can edit the values of any properties required to define the condition. You can set the properties by adding values directly in their respective fields or by selecting them in the drop-down lists. In the example shown in the following image, the Type property provides a drop-down list of selectable options, while the Total Heat Generation property requires a value to be directly entered.

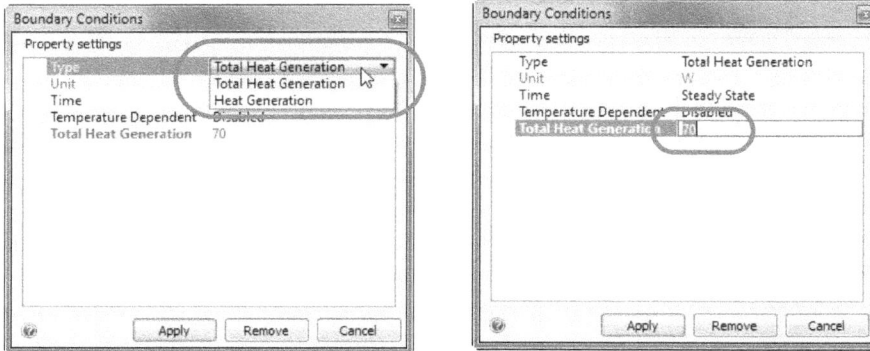

When you have defined the properties appropriately, click Apply. The Boundary Condition is added to Boundary Conditions node in the Design Study Bar, as shown in the following image.

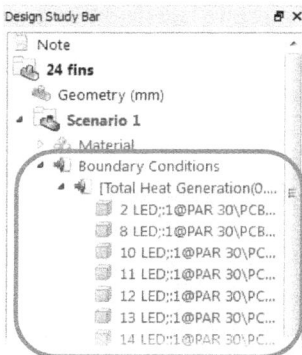

In addition, a stripe is applied to either a single surface (in the case of Surface boundary conditions) or all surfaces (in the case of Volume boundary conditions). In the example shown in the following image, a Total Heat Generation volumetric boundary condition was applied, so a strip is placed on each surface.

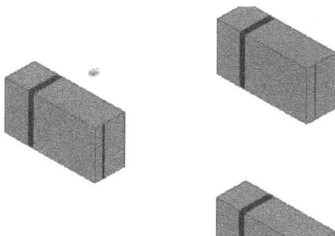

In another example, a pressure boundary condition is applied to the surface shown, so the stripe is only added to that surface.

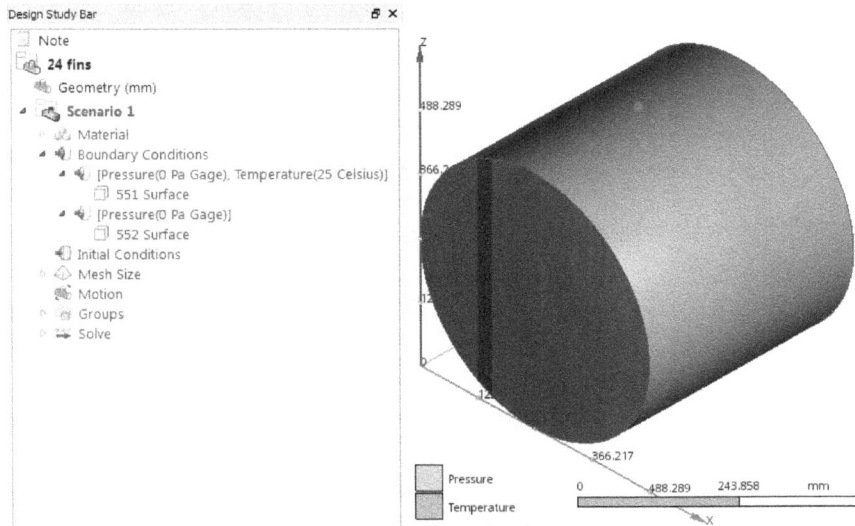

Each boundary condition is identified by a colored strip on its assigned surface. For visual reference, a color legend displays on the screen to help you identify the type of condition.

Note that multiple boundary conditions can be assigned to the same surface or volume as required, to fully define your model. In the preceding image, 551 Surface has a pressure or 0 Pa Gage and Temperature of 25 degrees Celsius applied.

> If a boundary condition has been created and you want to reuse it, simply select it in the Design Study Bar and drag it onto the geometry reference (Surface or Volume) to which it will apply. All properties from the original boundary condition will be assigned to the new geometry. If the geometry already had other boundary conditions assigned, they would also remain.

Removing Boundary Conditions

You can remove a boundary condition by right-clicking it in the Boundary Conditions node in the Design Study Bar and selecting Remove. Alternatively, if you want to remove all assigned boundary conditions, right-click directly on the Boundary Conditions node and select Remove All.

Exercise: Assigning Boundary Conditions I

In this exercise, you will open an existing design study and add boundary conditions to provide the foundation for analyzing the flow. You will also add both an entry flow rate and an exit pressure. The objectives in this exercise are to:

- Add a flow rate boundary condition.
- Add a pressure boundary condition.
- Observe the legend added to the display once a boundary condition is established.

Open the Model in the Autodesk CFD Environment.

1. Launch Autodesk CFD, if not already running.

2. In the Home tab, click ![folder icon] (Open). If prompted to save an open design study, click Yes.

3. In the Open dialog box, browse to the *C:\Autodesk CFD 2017 Essentials Exercise Files\ BoundaryConditions\Control Valve BC* folder. Select and open *Control Valve BC.cfdst*. The model displays as shown in the following image.

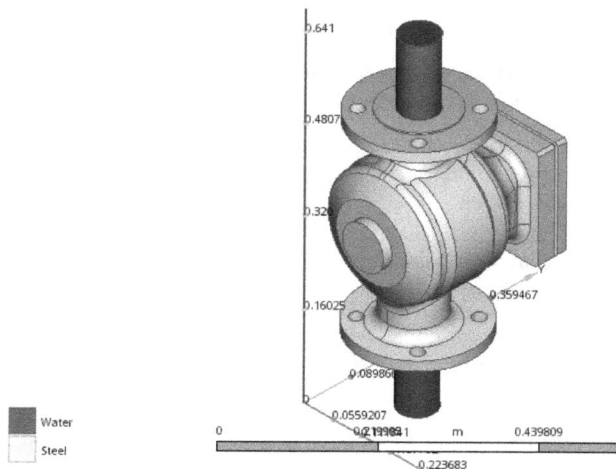

Note that two materials have been applied to the model - Water and Steel.

Add a boundary condition for the inlet of the valve.

Once the materials have been applied, you can add boundary conditions. For a flow analysis such as this, you are not concerned with any thermal characteristics, but rather the flow and pressure characteristics at the inlet and outlet. In this task, you will apply a volume flow rate of 380 liters per minute to the inlet of the valve.

1. In the Setup tab, in the Setup Tasks panel, click (Boundary Conditions) to activate this stage of the design study setup. The Boundary Conditions context panel displays.

2. Select the surface shown in the following image. Hover the cursor over it until the mini-toolbar displays.

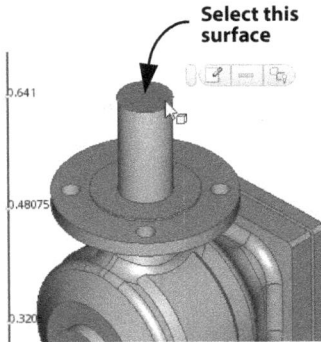

3. Select (Edit) in the mini-toolbar to open the Boundary Conditions dialog box, as shown in the following image. If the mini-toolbar is no longer visible, in the Boundary Conditions panel,

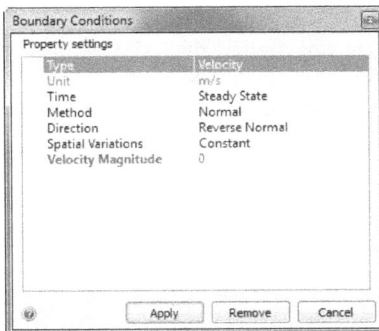

    click (Edit).

4. In the Boundary Conditions dialog box, in the Type drop-down list, select Volume Flow Rate, as shown in the following image.

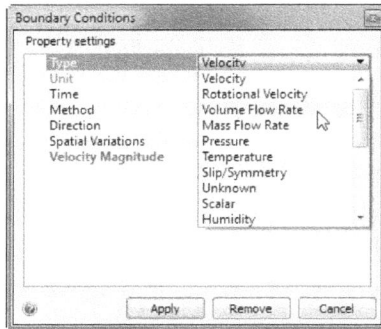

The available properties will change based on the boundary condition Type selected.

5. Use the Boundary Conditions dialog box to set the following properties (leave all others as default):

    - Unit: **l/min**
    - Volume Flow Rate: **380**

    The model and Boundary Condition Dialog box should display as shown in the following image.

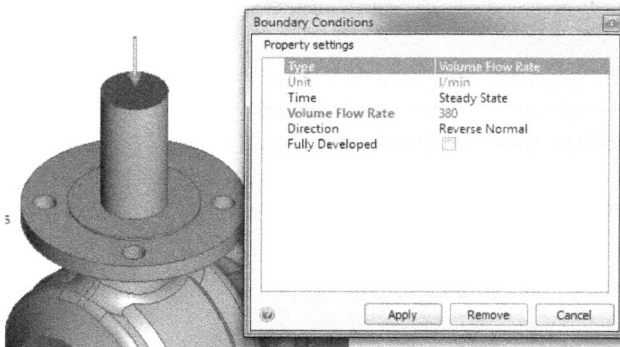

The flow direction is pointing into the value, as indicated by the arrow. If the arrow were pointing outwards, you could select Reverse Normal to change it.

6. Click Apply to complete the Boundary Condition Definition.

- Note the stripe that is added to the surface, indicating that a boundary condition has been applied.
- A legend is added, so you can quickly reference the boundary condition type (Volume Flow Rate) to the surface it is applied to.
- The volume flow rate is added to the Boundary Conditions node.

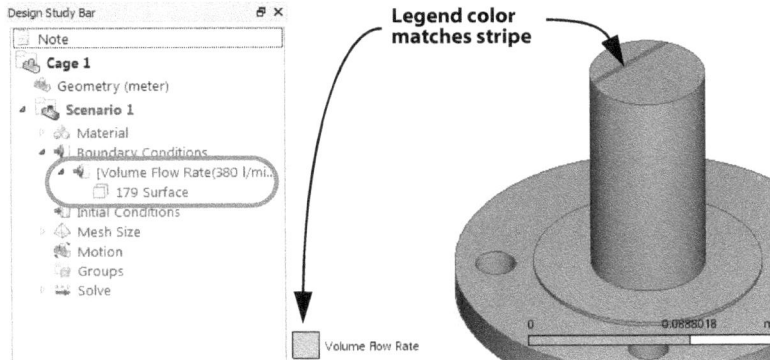

Add a boundary condition to the outlet.

In this task, you will add an outlet pressure boundary condition of 0 Pa Gage, so that when the analysis is run, you can determine the pressure drop across the valve.

1. Rotate the model so you can see the bottom of the flow volume, similar to that shown in the following image.

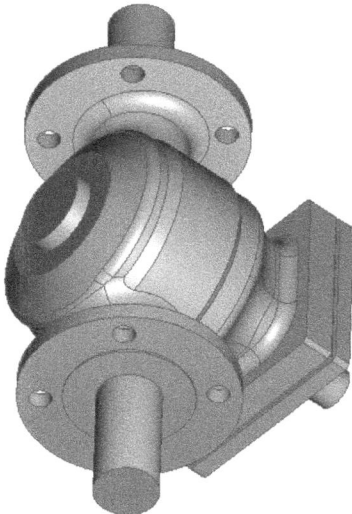

2. Select the surface shown in the following image. Hover the cursor over it until the mini-toolbar displays.

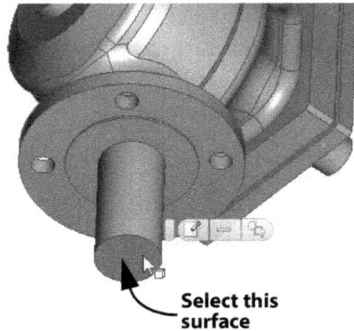

Select this surface

3. Select ☑ (Edit) in the mini-toolbar to open the Boundary Conditions dialog box. If the mini-toolbar is no longer visible, in the Boundary Conditions panel, click ✐ (Edit).

4. In the Boundary Conditions dialog box, in the Type drop-down list, select Pressure, as shown in the following image.

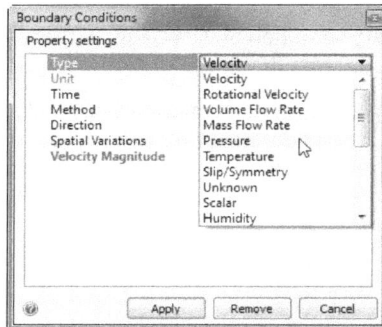

5. Ensure that the properties in the Boundary Condition Dialog box are set as shown in the following image.

    ▪ Setting the pressure to 0 Pa Gage reflects releasing the flow to atmosphere.
    ▪ It also provides a baseline for quickly measuring pressure drop across the valve. Note that the unit isn't important when using a 0 Gage.

6. Click Apply to complete the Boundary Condition Definition. The model updates as shown in the following image.

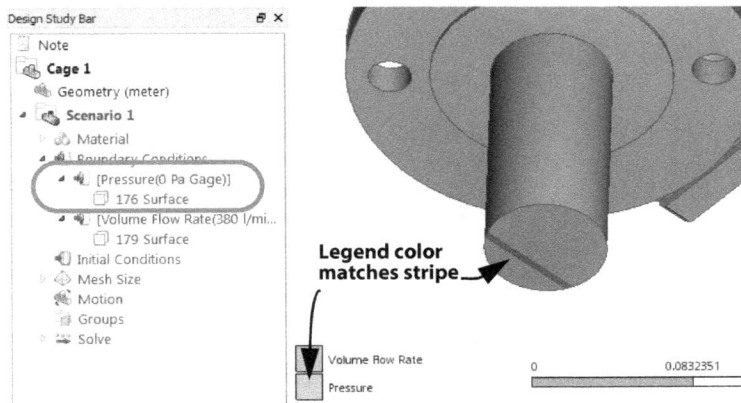

7. In the Quick Access toolbar, click ⊟ (Save) to save the study. With the boundary conditions set, the model mesh can be applied. This topic is covered in more detail in the next chapter.

Exercise: Assigning Boundary Conditions II

In this exercise, you will assign boundary conditions to prepare an LED light for analysis. You will setup the conditions to analyze the temperatures and convective air flow. The objectives in this exercise are to:

- Assign a Temperature boundary condition.
- Assign Pressure boundary conditions.
- Assign a Total Heat Generation boundary condition to several volumes.

Open the Model in the Autodesk CFD Environment.

1. Launch Autodesk CFD, if not already running.

2. In the Home tab, click �} (Open). If prompted to save an open design study, click Yes.

3. In the Open dialog box, browse to the *C:\Autodesk CFD 2017 Essentials Exercise Files\ BoundaryConditions\LED BC* folder. Select and open *LED BC.cfdst*. The model displays as shown in the following image.

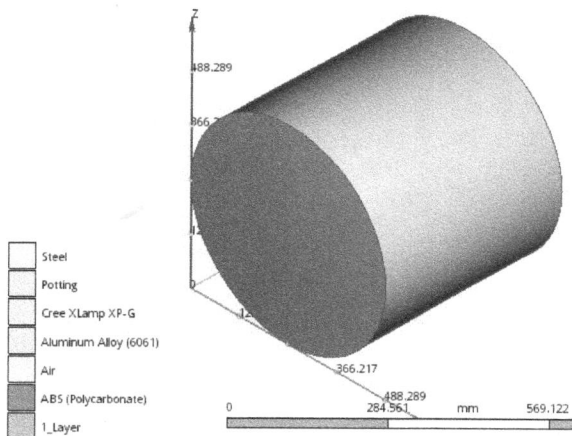

Note that many materials have been applied to the model.

4. Hover the cursor over the model, hold <Ctrl> and press the middle mouse button to hide objects so you can review the various components of the model.

5. Hold <Ctrl> and scroll up with the middle mouse button until all objects display again.

Add a boundary condition for the ambient air volume.

Once the materials have been applied, you can add boundary conditions. The model has an ambient air volume that surrounds the geometry. You will set the surrounding temperature to 25 degrees Celsius.

1. In the Setup tab, in the Setup Tasks panel, click ⬇ (Boundary Conditions).

2. Rotate the model and select the surface shown in the following image. This is the end of the air volume that faces into the room in which this LED will be installed.

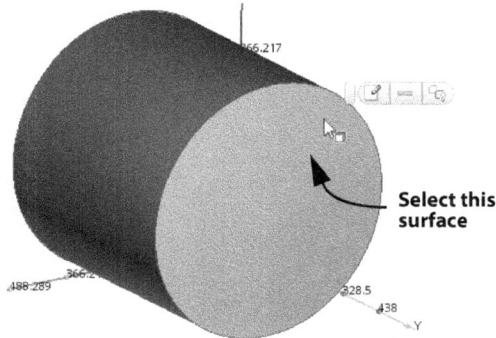

Select this surface

3. Select ⬚ (Edit) in the mini-toolbar to open the Boundary Conditions dialog box.

4. In the Boundary Conditions dialog box, in the Type drop-down list, select Temperature, as shown in the following image.

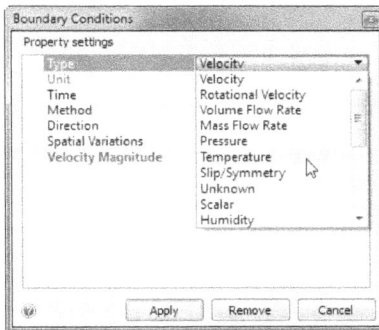

5. Ensure that the Unit is set to Celsius and set the Temperature to **25**. Leave all other properties at their default values. The Boundary Conditions dialog box should display as shown in the following image.

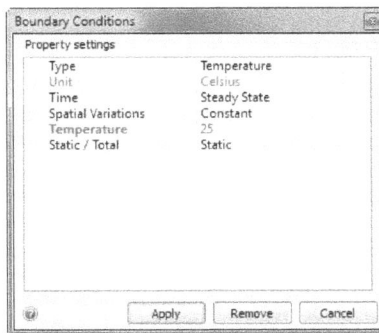

6. Click Apply to complete the Boundary Condition Definition.

- Note the stripe that is added to the surface and legend added to the main window.
- The temperature is added to the Boundary Conditions node.

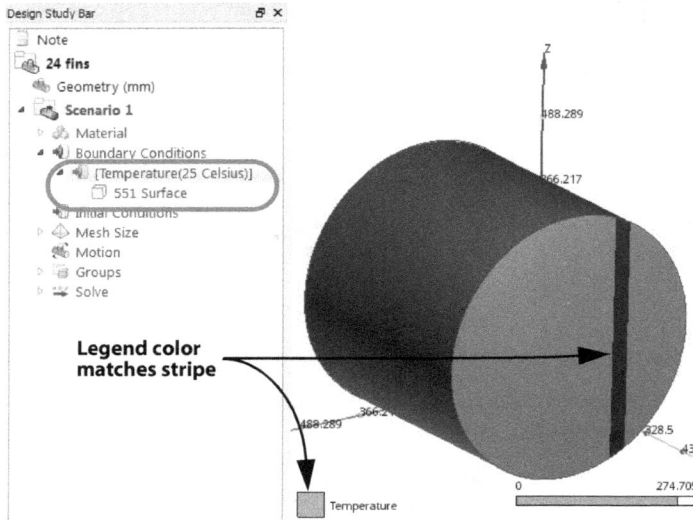

Add a pressure boundary condition to the same end as the ambient air volume.

In this task, you will add a pressure boundary condition of 0 Pa Gage to the same end of the ambient air volume to which you added the temperature boundary condition.

1. Select the surface shown in the following image.

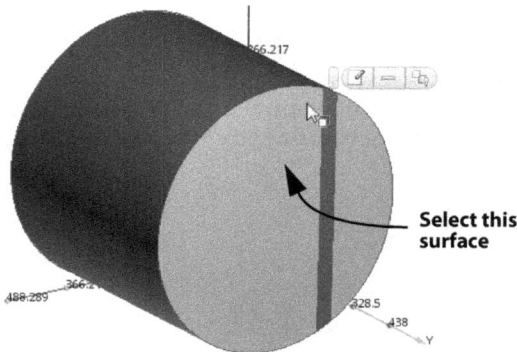

2. Select ☑ (Edit) in the mini-toolbar to open the Boundary Conditions dialog box.

3. In the Boundary Conditions dialog box, in the Type drop-down list, select Pressure and accept the default properties and values shown in the following image.

4. Click Apply to complete the Boundary Condition Definition.

- Note the additional stripe that is added to the surface, indicating a pressure boundary condition has been assigned.
- The pressure is added to the same node as the temperature boundary condition, as shown in the following image.

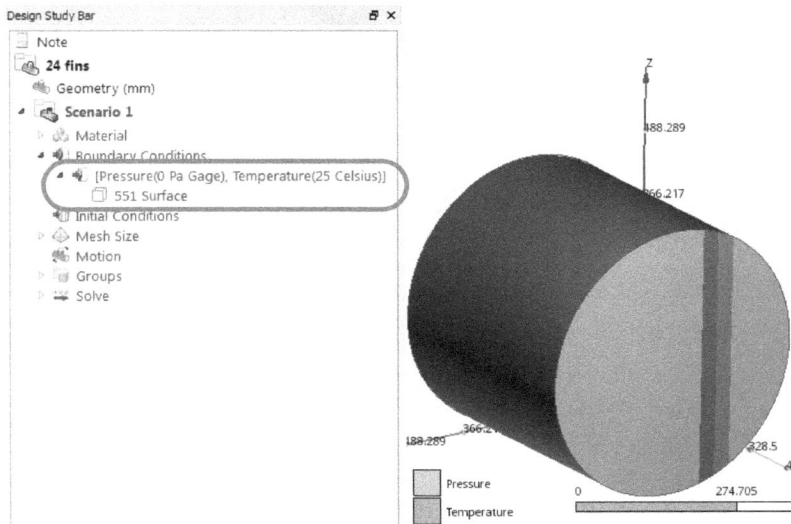

Add another pressure boundary condition to the opposite end of the ambient air volume.

In this task, you will add another pressure boundary condition of 0 Pa Gage to the opposite end of the ambient air volume. The two 0 Pa pressure boundary conditions indicate that the system is open to the surrounding environment.

1. Select on the ViewCube to return to the model's default Home view and select the surface shown in the following image.

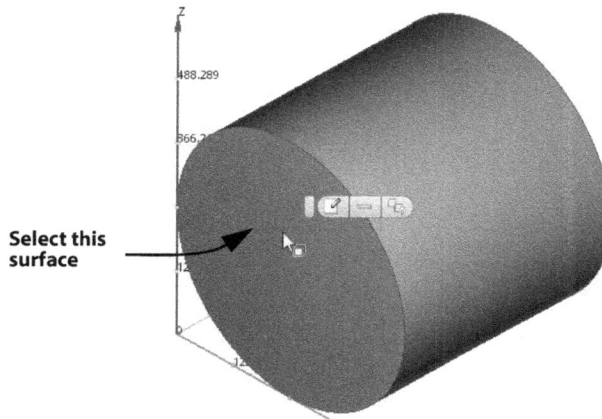

Select this surface

2. Select (Edit) in the mini-toolbar to open the Boundary Conditions dialog box.

3. In the Boundary Conditions dialog box, in the Type drop-down list, select Pressure and accept the default properties and values shown in the following image.

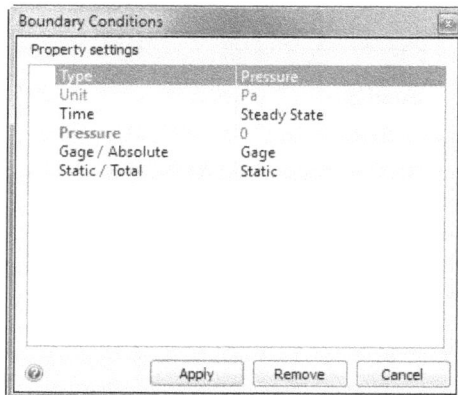

4. Click Apply to complete the Boundary Condition Definition.

Note: Both pressure boundary conditions could have been added at the same time by selecting the two surfaces at one time and then creating the 0 Pa Gage boundary condition.

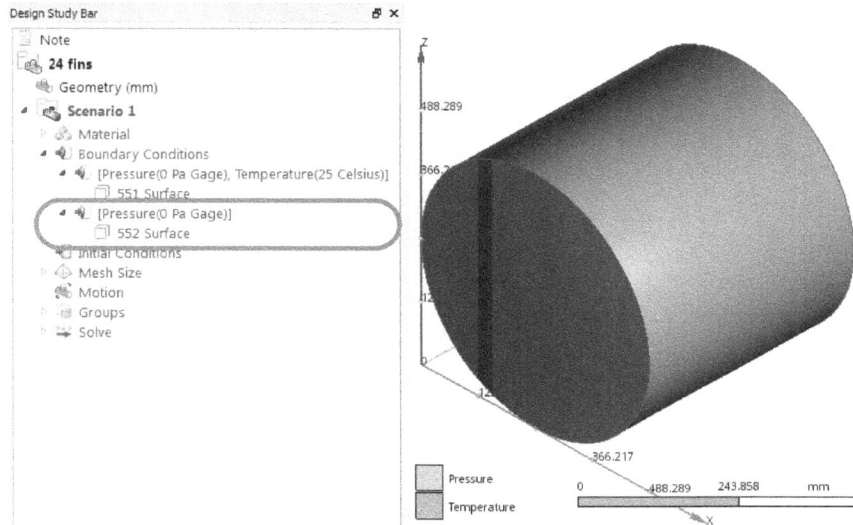

Add a heat generation boundary condition to account for the heat generated by the LED lights.

In this task, you will add a total heat generation boundary condition to each of the LEDs. Each LED accounts for 0.2 Watts. Total Heat Generation is applied to bodies, not surfaces, so you will have to change your selection filter.

1. In the Setup tab, in the Selection panel, click 🔲 (Volume).

2. Hover the cursor over the model, hold <Ctrl> and press the middle mouse button to hide components. Hide all components until only the LEDs display, as shown in the following image.

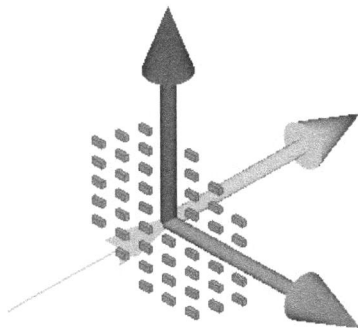

3. Click and drag a selection rectangle around the components. Alternatively, you can select the LED group that exists in the model.

4. Select 🖉 (Edit) in the mini-toolbar to open the Boundary Conditions dialog box. If the mini-toolbar is not available, in the Boundary Conditions Panel, click 🖉 (Edit).

5. In the Boundary Conditions dialog box, ensure that the Type is set to Total Heat Generation and the Unit is set to W. Then, enter a Total Heat Generation of **0.2**. Accept the default properties and values. The Boundary Conditions dialog box displays as shown in the following image.

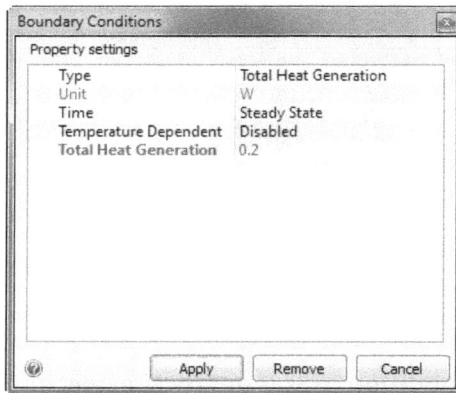

6. Click Apply. Zoom in on the model and note that because this is a volume related boundary condition, the stripe is added to all external surfaces, as shown in the following image.

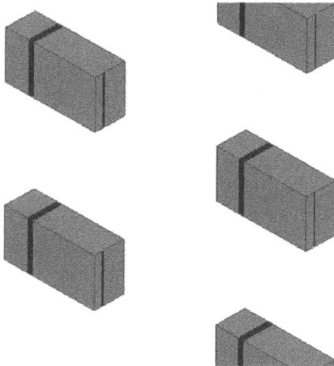

7. Hold <Ctrl> and scroll up with the middle mouse button until all objects display again. Alternatively, you can hold <Ctrl> and press the middle mouse button away from the model geometry to display all geometry.

8. In the Quick Access Toolbar, click [⬜▾] (Visual Style) and select Transparent, as shown in the following image, so that you can see the internal components.

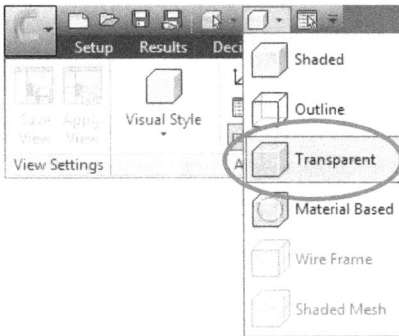

9. Select [⌂] on the ViewCube to return to the model's default Home view, if not already set.

The model with boundary conditions displays as shown in the following image.

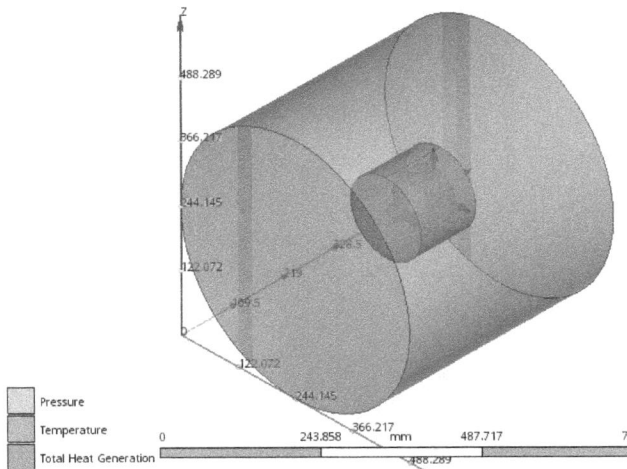

10. In the Quick Access toolbar, click [💾] (Save) to save the study. With the boundary conditions set, the model mesh can be applied. This topic is covered in more detail in the next chapter.

Exercise: Assigning Boundary Conditions III

In this exercise, you will look at a typical office setting and apply appropriate boundary conditions. The materials have already been applied, but you have to account for the heating and cooling sources. In this example, the heat from two occupants must be added to the boundary conditions. Additionally, a curtain style slot diffuser as well as three ducted plaque diffusers are used for cooling, so they also require the application of boundary conditions. The objectives in this exercise are to:

- Assign Total Heat Generation boundary conditions to the occupants of the building.
- Assign Volume Flow Rates and Temperatures for several air conditioning outlets.
- Assign a Pressure boundary condition at the return outlet of the air conditioning system.

Open the Model in the Autodesk CFD Environment.

1. Launch Autodesk CFD, if not already running.

2. In the Home tab, click [] (Open). If prompted to save an open design study, click Yes.

3. In the Open dialog box, browse to the *C:\Autodesk CFD 2017 Essentials Exercise Files\ BoundaryConditions\Office Lobby BC* folder. Select and open *Office Lobby BC.cfdst*. The model displays as shown in the following image.

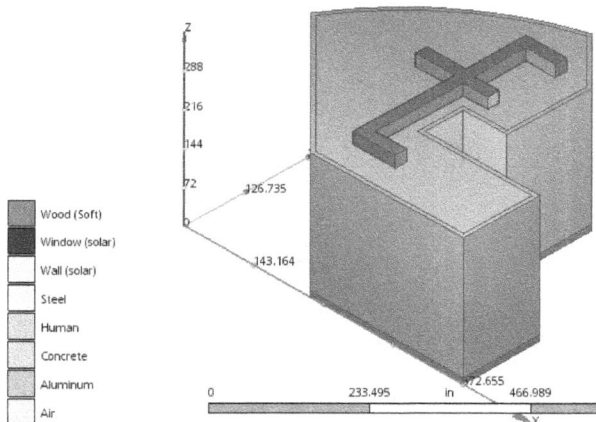

Note that the materials have already been applied to the model.

4. Since this is the first time you have seen this model, investigate its structure. In the Quick Access Toolbar, click ⬛ (Visual Style) and select Outline, as shown in the following image, to see the internal components.

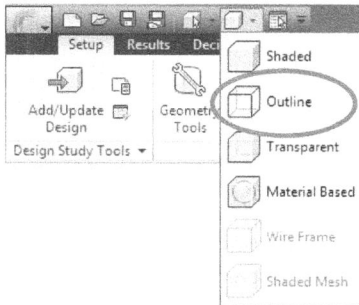

5. Hold <Shift> and the middle mouse button to rotate the model until it displays approximately as shown in the following image.

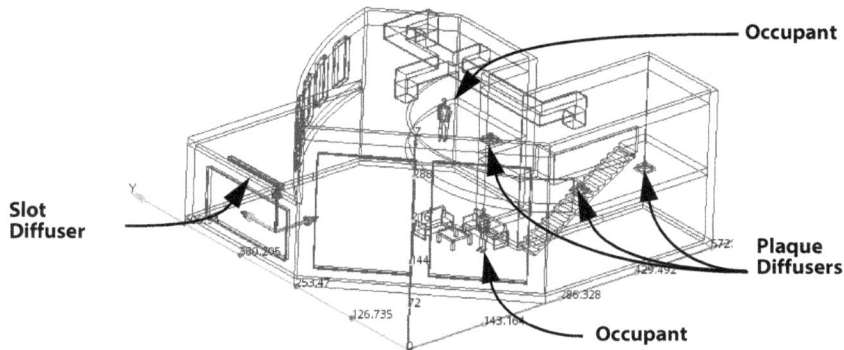

6. Select 🏠 on the ViewCube, then in the Quick Access Toolbar, click ⬛ (Visual Style) and select Transparent. The model displays as shown in the following image.

    Note the surface of the air volume at the ducting outlet. This will have a pressure of 0 Pa applied when you add the boundary conditions.

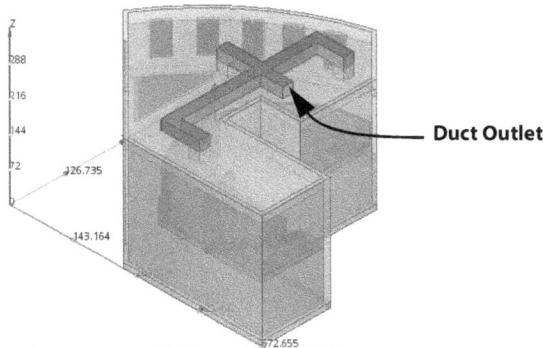

Add a boundary condition to the duct outlet.

In this task, you will add a Pressure boundary condition to the outlet of the duct to enable airflow. You will set the pressure to 0 Pa.

1. In the Setup tab, in the Setup Tasks panel, click ⬇ (Boundary Conditions).

2. Select the surface shown in the following image. Hover the cursor over it until the mini-toolbar displays.

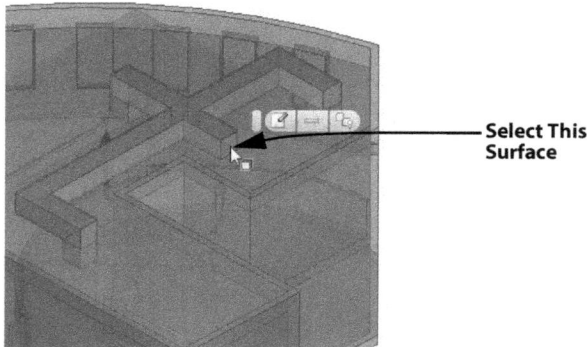

Select This Surface

3. Select ✎ (Edit) in the mini-toolbar to open the Boundary Conditions dialog box. If the mini-toolbar is not available, in the Boundary Conditions Panel, click ✎ (Edit).

4. In the Boundary Conditions dialog box, in the Type drop-down list, select Pressure. Set the Unit to **Pa** and leave the Pressure property value as **0**. The Boundary Conditions dialog box should display as shown in the following image.

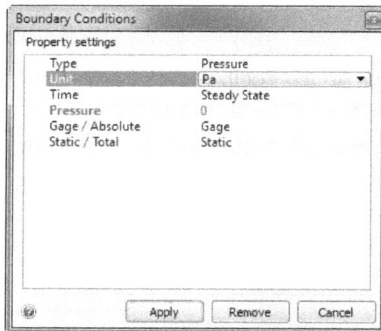

5. Click Apply to complete the Boundary Condition Definition. The Design Study Bar displays as shown in the following image.

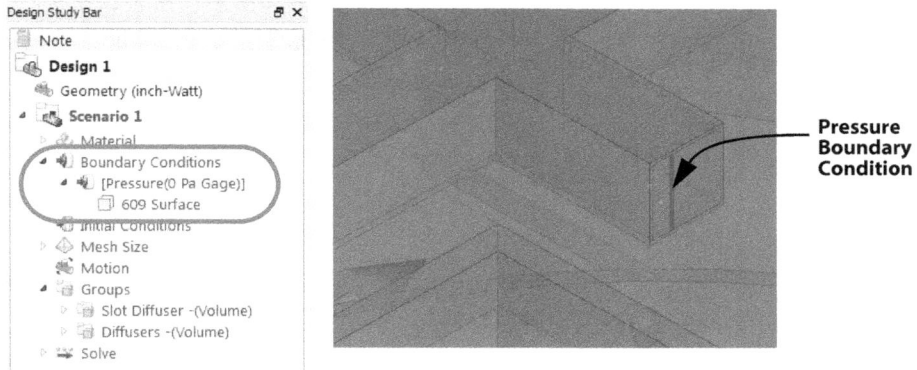

Pressure Boundary Condition

Add a Total Heat Generation boundary condition for each occupant.

An occupant of a room contributes approximately 70 W of total heat generation. In this task, you will add the appropriate boundary condition to each occupant.

1. First, hide objects to clear the display. A quick way to do so is to hide using the materials.

- Expand the Material node in the Design Study Bar.
- Select Air [Variable], right-click, and select Hide.
- Select Wall (solar) [Fixed], right-click, and select Hide.
- Select Window (solar) [Fixed], right-click, and select Hide.
- Select Wood (Soft) [Fixed], right-click, and select Hide.

The model displays as shown in the following image.

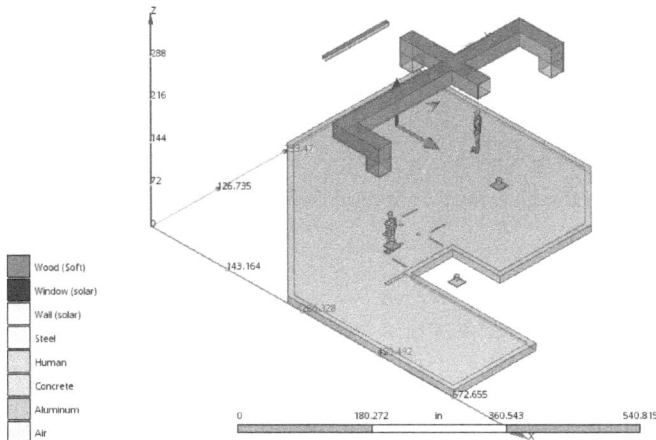

2. In the Setup tab, in the Setup Tasks panel, click ⬇ (Boundary Conditions).

3. In the Setup tab, in the Selection panel, click 🔲 (Volume) and select the two occupants, as shown in the following image.

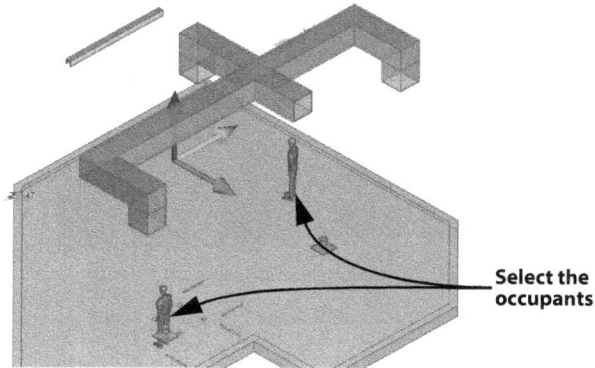

Select the occupants

4. Select ✏ (Edit) in the mini-toolbar to open the Boundary Conditions dialog box.

5. Accept the default options and edit the Total heat Generation to **70**, as shown in the following image.

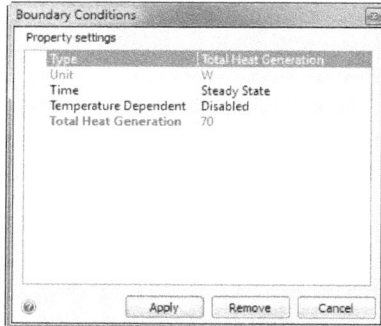

6. Click Apply to complete the Boundary Condition Definition.

7. Verify that the Design Study Bar displays as shown in the following image to ensure that the boundary conditions were all added correctly.

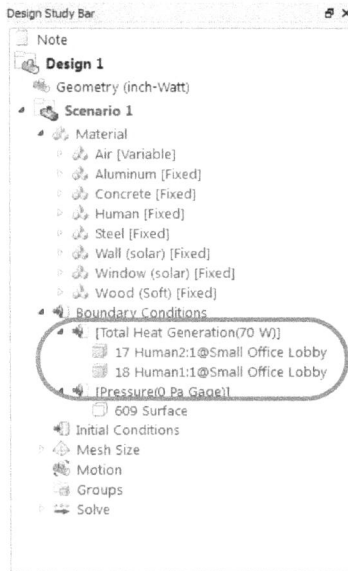

Add boundary conditions to setup the air conditioning.

In this task, you will add a volume flow rate of 500 ft3/min and temperature boundary condition of 52 degrees Fahrenheit to the slot diffuser. The diffuser is separate from the ducting and has its own air volume.

1. In the Design Study Bar, expand the Groups node, if not already expanded. Select Slot Diffuser, right-click, and select Hide to clear the casing for the slot diffuser from the display.

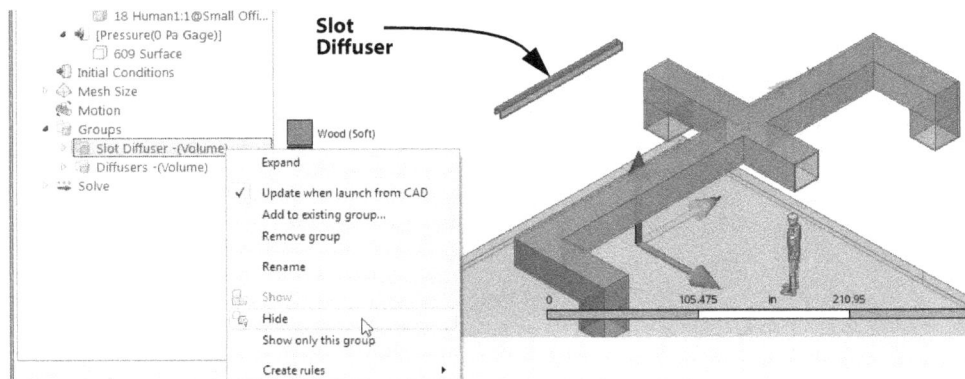

2. In the Design Study Bar, expand the Air [Variable] node and select 2 Main Body:1. Right-click and select Show. Right-click and select Deselect All. The air volume, which was enclosed in the slot diffuser, displays as shown in the following image. You can identify that it is the air volume if it displays in the light blue air color. Now that the air volume displays, the boundary condition can be assigned to it.

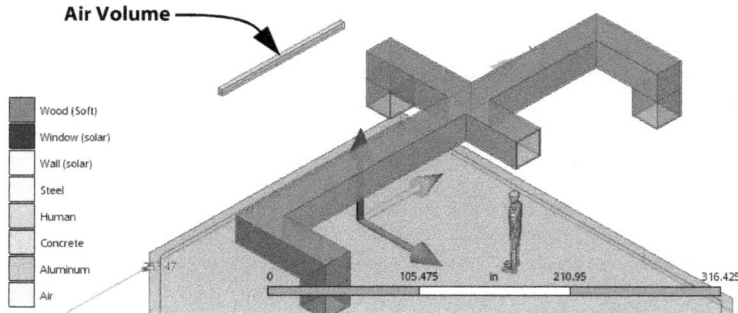

3. In the Setup tab, in the Setup Tasks panel, click (Boundary Conditions).

4. Zoom in on the air volume that you just displayed for the slot diffuser. Select the top surface of the air volume. Select (Edit) in the mini-toolbar to open the Boundary Conditions dialog box. Edit the following properties:

    - Type: **Temperature**
    - Unit: **Fahrenheit**
    - Temperature: **52**
    - The Boundary Conditions dialog box displays as shown in the image below.
    - Click Apply to complete the boundary condition.

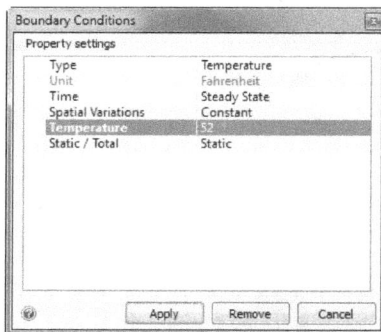

5. Select the top surface of the air volume again. Select ☑ (Edit) in the mini-toolbar to open the Boundary Conditions dialog box. Edit the following Properties:

- Type: **Volume Flow Rate**
- Unit: **ft3/min**
- Volume Flow Rate: **500**
- Direction: Click Reverse Normal
- The Boundary Conditions dialog box and model display as shown in the image below.
- Click Apply to complete the boundary condition.

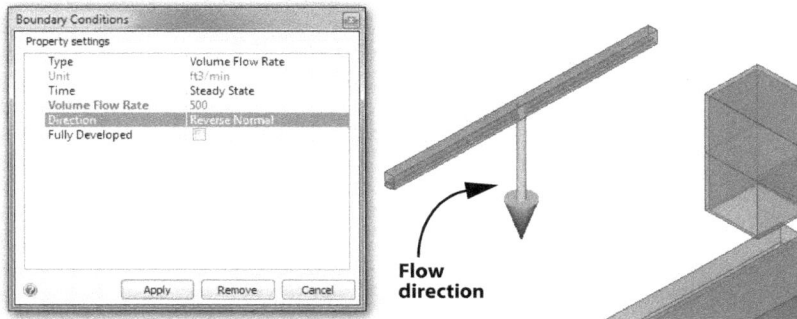

Flow direction

The Direction defaults to the outside of a selected surface, but in this case, the flow has to be reversed to ensure that it exits the diffuser and that it enters the room.

Add boundary conditions to setup the plaque diffusers.

In this task, you will add a volume flow rate of 350 ft3/min and temperature boundary condition of 52 degrees Fahrenheit to the three plaque diffusers.

1. Select 🏠 on the ViewCube to reposition the model in the center of the graphics window.

2. In the Groups node, right-click on the Diffusers group and select Show only this Group. Zoom in until the model displays similar to that shown in the following image. Only the three steel diffuser components display. The air volumes for these components do not display.

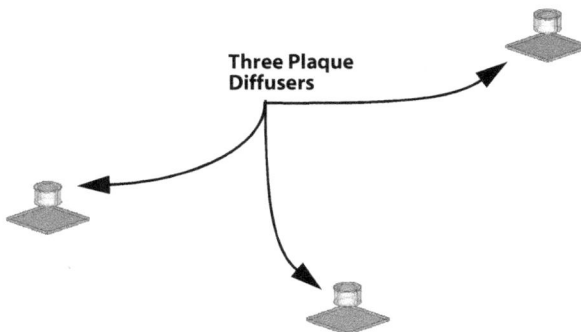

Three Plaque
Diffusers

3. In the Design Study Bar, in the Material node, select the Steel [Fixed] node, right-click and select Hide. The circular steel diffusers have now been cleared from the display.

4. The air volumes must now be displayed so that a boundary condition can be assigned to them.
   - In the Design Study Bar, in the Air [Variable] node, select 5 main body:1, hold <Shift> and select 12 main body:1.
   - Right-click and select Show.
   - Right-click and select Deselect all.
   - The air volumes display in a light blue color, as shown in the following image.

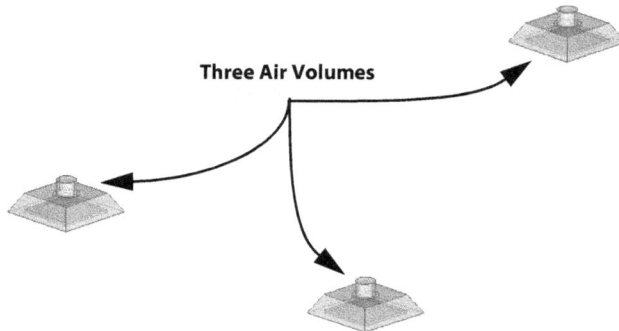

Three Air Volumes

5. In the Setup tab, in the Setup Tasks panel, click (Boundary Conditions).

6. Select the top circular surface on each of the three air volumes, as shown in the following image.

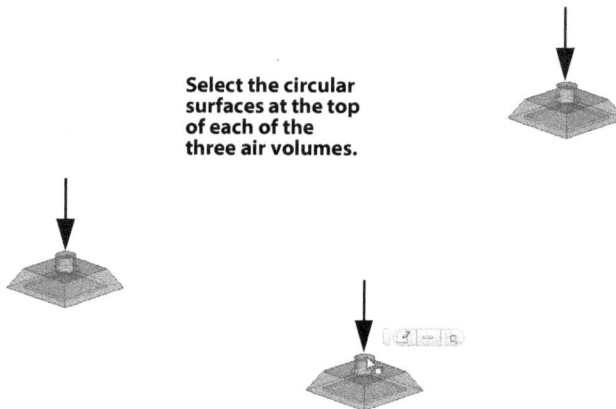

Select the circular surfaces at the top of each of the three air volumes.

7. Select ✎ (Edit) in the mini-toolbar to open the Boundary Conditions dialog box, as shown in the following image. Edit the following properties:

   ▪ Type: **Temperature**
   ▪ Unit: **Fahrenheit**
   ▪ Temperature: **52**
   ▪ The Boundary Conditions dialog box displays as shown in the image below.
   ▪ Click Apply to complete the boundary condition.

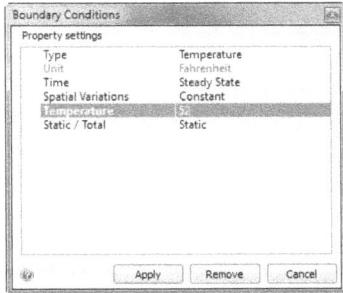

8. Once again, select the same three circular surfaces on each of the air volumes. Alternatively, right-click and select Previous to reselect the previously selected surfaces. Use the Edit command in either the mini-toolbar or the Boundary Conditions panel to open the Boundary Conditions dialog box. Edit the following Properties:

   ▪ Type: **Volume Flow Rate**
   ▪ Unit: **ft3/min**
   ▪ Volume Flow Rate: **350**
   ▪ Direction: Click Reverse Normal
   ▪ The Boundary Conditions dialog box and model display as shown in the image below.
   ▪ Click Apply to complete the boundary condition.

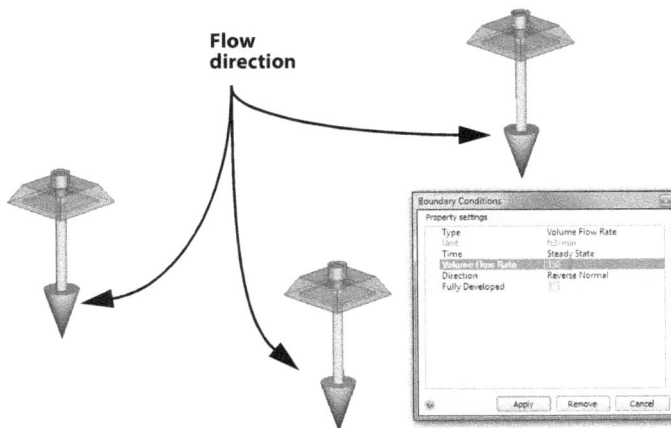

The Direction defaults to the outside of the selected surface, so it had to be reversed in order to send the flow out of the diffuser and into the room.

Clean up the display.

In this task, you will return all components to the display and save the design study.

1. Right-click in the graphics window and select Show all.

2. Select ⌂ on the ViewCube.

3. In the Quick Access toolbar, click 🖫 (Save) to save the study. With the boundary conditions set, the model mesh can be applied. This topic is covered in more detail in the next chapter.

> The diffuser flow conditions are technically applied to internal surfaces. In most situations, this can lead to instability in the solution, or even solution failure. Flow conditions should only be applied to external surfaces in a simulation model (see page 3 of this chapter). To comply with this, the metal parts covering the inlets to all diffusers will be suppressed in the meshing process in the next chapter. By suppressing these components, there will be mesh on only one side of the flow boundary condition, so it complies with the "outer surface" rule.

Meshing

To analyze your models, the Autodesk® CFD software breaks the model down into small elements and analyzes flow and heat transfer at each of those elements. Establishing a quality, well defined mesh, is an important step in achieving meaningful analysis results.

Objectives

After completing this chapter, you will be able to:

- Recognize how meshes are used to break models into elements for analysis.
- Describe how to apply automatic mesh sizing.
- Describe the advantages of using automatic mesh sizing.
- Describe why mesh refinement may be required in a design.
- Describe the tools available for manipulating the mesh.
- Use the diagnostic tools to locate problem areas in CAD geometry.
- Refine meshes using regions.
- Remove components from being included in the mesh.
- Describe the manual mesh options.
- Assign mesh size manually.
- Describe the default mesh display.
- Display a preview of the mesh elements and distribution.
- Display the model with a shaded mesh.

Lesson: Meshing Overview

Overview

A well defined mesh is required to achieve quality analysis results. In this lesson, you will learn how meshes in Autodesk CFD are comprised of elements and nodes.

Objectives

After completing this lesson, you will be able to:

- Recognize how meshes are used to break models into elements for analysis.

Meshing

Meshing is a required step in analyzing a model when using Autodesk CFD. The process of meshing breaks the model down into small elements across the entire geometry of the model (internally and externally). Flow and heat transfer can be are analyzed at each of the element nodes that are generated by the mesh. The following image shows the original CAD model and the meshed model.

CAD Model　　　　　　**Meshed Model**

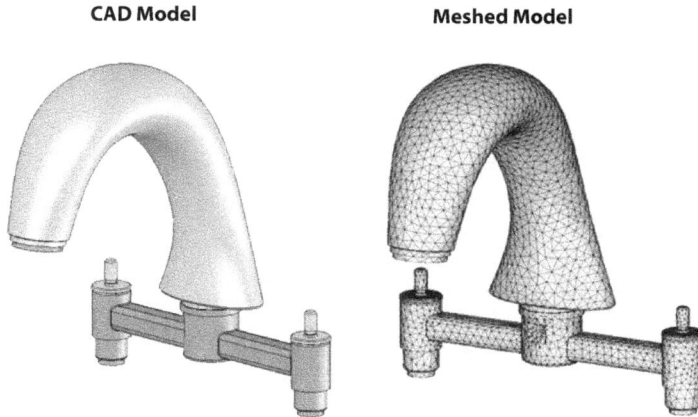

In three dimensional models, most elements are tetrahedrals: a four sided, triangular-faced element. In two dimensional models, most elements are triangles, as shown in the following image.

3D Element　　　　　**2D Element**

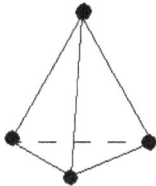

The corner of each element is a node, which is where the calculations are performed. The mesh is comprised of elements, where adjacent elements share nodes. Autodesk CFD automates much of the mesh creation process to help you create a quality mesh for your simulation.

Lesson: Automatic Mesh Sizing

Overview

The automatic mesh that Autodesk CFD creates uses the geometry of the model to determine an appropriate mesh size and distribution, and applies it to the model. This mesh generally represents a good starting point but it will typically require refinement.

Objectives

After completing this lesson, you will be able to:

- Describe how to apply automatic mesh sizing.
- Describe the advantages of using automatic mesh sizing.

Automatic Mesh Sizing

The mesh can be defined by automatically or manually determining the mesh density. It is common to begin an analysis using the automatically defined mesh size and distribution.

To begin the application of the mesh, in the Setup tab, in the Setup Tasks panel, click (Mesh Sizing) to activate this setup task and open the Type and Automatic Sizing panels in the ribbon, as shown in the following image.

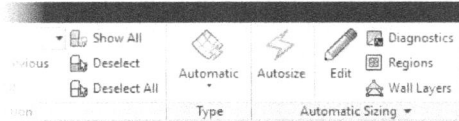

To apply Automatic Sizing, use one of the following methods:

- In the Setup tab, in the Type panel, ensure that (Automatic) displays in the Type panel, indicating that automatic meshing is set, and click (Autosize).

- Left click on or near the model and click (Autosize) in the mini-toolbar.

- Right-click in the Graphics window or on the Mesh Size branch of the Design Study bar, and click (Edit). In the Mesh Sizes quick edit dialog box, click Automatic size, as shown in the following image.

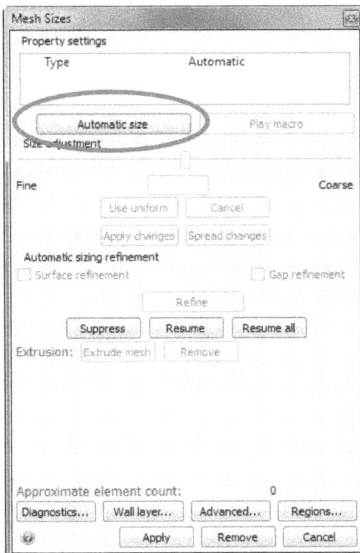

When the auto-sizing of the mesh is complete, a series of dots are added to the model display, as shown in the following image. These dots provide a preview of the mesh sizing and distribution, indicating where the elements will be located on the model edges.

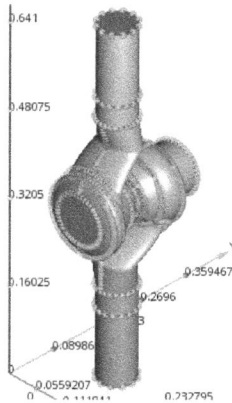

Advantages of Automatic Mesh Sizing

Autodesk CFD performs a comprehensive topological interrogation of the model geometry and determines the mesh size and distribution on every edge, surface, and volume in the model. When assigning element sizes and mesh distributions, Autodesk CFD accounts for geometric curvature, gradients, and proximity to neighboring geometry. The advantages of using automatic sizing are as follows:

- Greatly simplified set-up of analysis models, resulting in less time spent assigning mesh sizes.
- More efficient mesh distributions. The mesh is fine where required and coarse where it can be.
- Improved solution accuracy due to better mesh quality and mesh transitions.
- Improved solution robustness. Good mesh transitions lead to a well-posed mathematical model.

The automatic meshing process is fast, but can take a few minutes for models that contain more than 3000 edges.

Mesh History

Unlike materials and boundary conditions, an automatic mesh definition is a set of commands issued in a specific order. As such, the history of the mesh settings is maintained, enabling full visibility to every step that defines the mesh.

The Mesh History is stored in the Mesh Size node of the Design Study Bar. Each step is listed as a separate item (e.g., automatic sizing, mesh size adjustment) and each can be modified, disabled, or deleted. All steps in the recorded history constitute the mesh definition.

Consider the following:

- New steps that are added to the definition may change the distribution and may even "undo" the effects of earlier steps.
- You can "roll back" a mesh definition by disabling or eliminating one or more steps to review the effect of a change or to fix errors.
- Reviewing the history makes it easy to recreate the same mesh on a different model or at a later time.

Lesson: Mesh Refinement

After you have automatically defined the mesh, refinement is often required to create a finer or coarser mesh than what the system assigned values have generated. Refinement can be done to selected volumes, edges or surfaces.

Objectives

After completing this lesson, you will be able to:

- Describe why mesh refinement may be required in a design.
- Describe the tools available for manipulating the mesh.
- Use the diagnostic tools to locate problem areas in CAD geometry.
- Refine meshes using regions.
- Remove components from being included in the mesh.

Refining the Mesh

Adjusting the mesh distribution will depend on the goal for the analysis and what is being simulated.

- For a first pass run, consider using a coarser mesh to save some computation time. This will provide an initial result set to review.
- For more complexity and more accurate material property variation, a finer mesh might be needed. More simulation time might be required to solve these types of analyses.

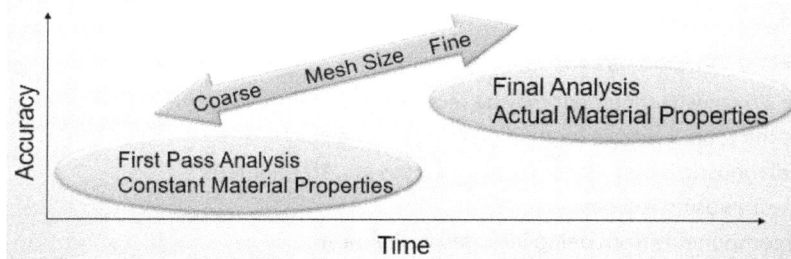

In general, the mesh size is adjusted to capture high gradients of velocity, pressure, and temperature as well as basic geometric shapes. Consider the following images.

Mesh is too coarse
- **Does not capture curvature**
- **Does not capture gradient**
- **Less than 6 nodes across the gap**

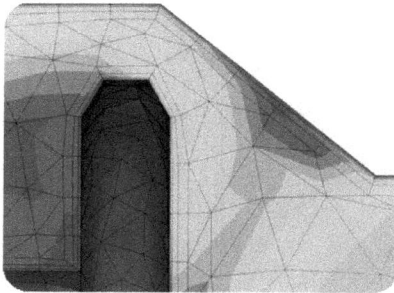

Mesh is adequate
- **Captures curvature of poppet**
- **Roughly one element through gradient**
- **More than 6 nodes across the gap**

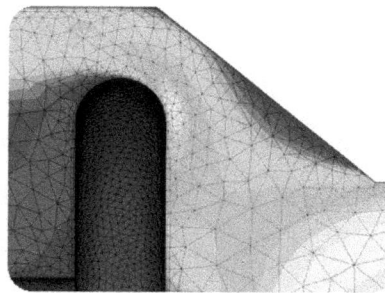

- The image on the left is a generic poppet valve. For a first pass, running this mesh might be adequate to determine where the critical gradients reside and where to focus the mesh. However, it is not an appropriate mesh for doing any form of results comparisons with geometry.
- The image on the right captures the curvature of the poppet as well as the gap between the poppet and valve seat. By refining the mesh, it captures critical gradients, whether that is a critical pressure, velocity, or thermal gradient.

In most situations, you should have a minimum of 6 nodes across a gap and 6 nodes around the circumference of circular geometry. More nodes might be required based on the curvature or the gradient across the gap.

You can refine the automatic mesh using the meshing tools found in the Mesh Sizes dialog box. Many of the mesh commands are also available on the mini-toolbar and on the Automatic Sizing panel in the ribbon.

- **Mini-Toolbar** - The mini-toolbar, shown in the following image, displays by left-clicking on the model. You can edit the mesh for the selected object, or suppress, resume or hide it.

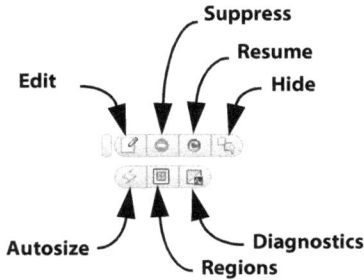

> It is important to note that suppression in the context of meshing is not the same as suppression in a CAD system. In the context of Autodesk CFD, suppression simply removes the selected objects from the list of objects to which the mesh is applied.

- **Automatic Sizing Panel** - Many of the same options available in the mini-toolbar can also be found in the Automatic Sizing panel in the ribbon, as shown in the following image.

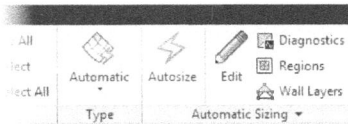

To refine the mesh in specific areas, while maintaining the automatic mesh elsewhere, select a volume, surface, or edge, right-click, and select (Edit) in the mini-toolbar. Use the options available in the Mesh Sizes dialog box, in the Size adjustment and Automatic sizing refinement areas, as shown in the following image.

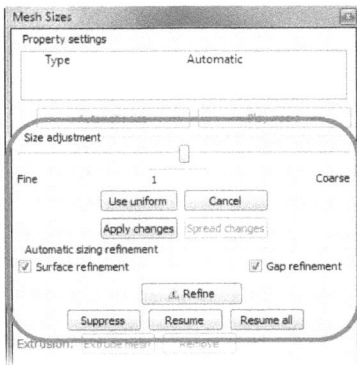

In the Size adjustment area, you can adjust the local mesh density by dragging the slider from Fine to Coarse, or by entering a value. This is a scaling factor that runs from 0.2 to 5. You can also use the following buttons:

- **Use uniform:** This command creates a mesh where all of the elements are the size of the smallest element in a volume.
- **Apply changes:** As the Size adjustment slider is moved, the modified distribution updates dynamically. Apply changes locks in the required slider position.
- **Spread changes:** With this command, all modified settings are resolved with neighboring settings to ensure correct element transitions. The slider position for each adjusted entity resets to 1, so the newly assigned size becomes the default size for subsequent adjustments.
- **Cancel:** This option returns the slider position to 1, effectively undoing any adjustments made to an entity after either the automatic size specification or since the last Spread Changes command.

In the Automatic sizing refinement area, you can enable Surface refinement to produce a better mesh on surfaces with small curvature or few edges, and Gap refinement to control the mesh within gaps between closely oriented surfaces, as shown in the following image.

Mesh in Gap is coarse
before Gap refinement

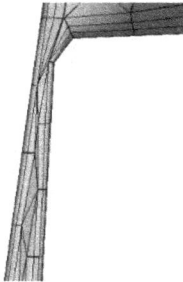

Mesh in Gap is finer
after Gap refinement

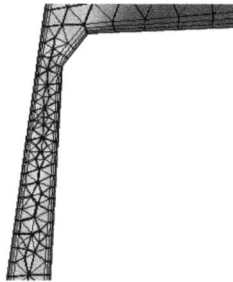

- Click Refine to apply Surface and Gap refinements.

Note that the Mesh Size node in the Design Study Bar updates to reflect the application of these settings, as shown in the following image. When set, Surface refinement or Gap refinement are marked true, otherwise they are marked false.

Tools for Improving the Mesh

It is important to have enough mesh to capture flow and heat transfer gradients. It is also important to conserve computer resources so that analyses run quickly. Autodesk CFD provides tools to help you modify the default mesh to match your design and optimize performance and reliability. These tools enable you to do the following:

- Locally adjust mesh sizes to accommodate flow details that need additional mesh density, as previously discussed.
- Run a diagnostic on the CAD geometry to locate problem areas.
- Modify the Minimum Refinement Length to adjust the threshold edge size that will be permitted to influence the mesh in neighboring features. This is one of the most powerful tools for improving the mesh.
- Create refinement regions for concentrating the mesh locally.
- Use suppression to remove objects from meshing.

> Consider adding a cut plane using the Plane functionality to visualize the internal mesh. Creating planes is discussed in detail in the next chapter.

Diagnostics

To locate problem areas in CAD geometry, click the (Diagnostics) icon in the Automatic Sizing panel or by clicking Diagnostics in the Mesh Sizes dialog box. In either case, the Mesh Sizes dialog box opens as shown in the following image.

This set of tools interrogates the geometry to determine the location of potential problem areas. These areas may cause difficulty in the determination of mesh sizes, the mesh generation, and in the solution stability of the analysis.

You can also set the Minimum Refinement length here to adjust the edge size that is permitted to influence surrounding elements.

Refinement Regions

Refinement regions enable you to create a volume to encapsulate one or more volumes in the model, and to apply a modified mesh to objects within the volume. To define a region, click ▦ (Regions) in the Automatic Sizing panel to open the Mesh Refinement Regions dialog box. Alternatively, left-click in the graphics window to open the mini-toolbar and click ▦ . Click Add to create the region. The system displays a default refinement volume.

- There are three preset volume shapes available: Box Region, Cylinder Region and Sphere Region.
- Change the size and orientation of the region using the text fields or by dragging the arrows.
- Set the mesh density within the region, as required.

In the example shown in the following image, refinement is required on the fins of the heat sink. The Cylinder Region was selected as the shape. Once the default cylindrical volume is added it is resized as required.

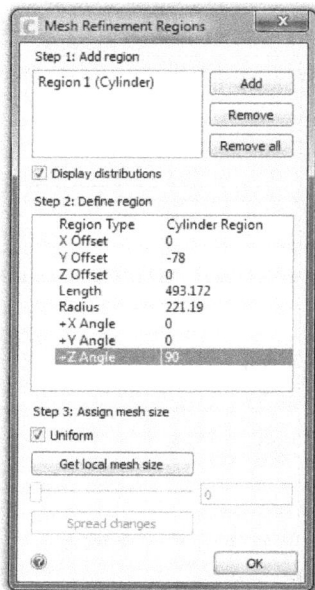

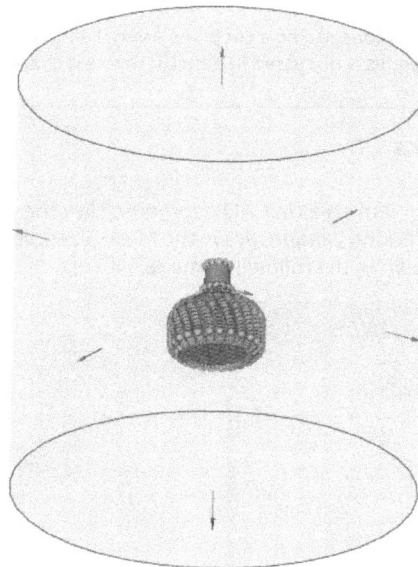

The refinement region's size was set to only enclose the fins.

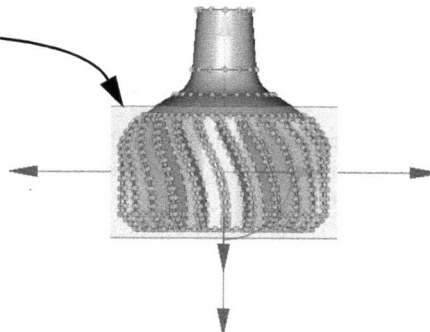

It is recommended use mesh regions to increase the results resolution in areas that have localized flow behavior or areas that do not have geometric features. For example, adding a cylindrical mesh region above the LED light canister provides a more accurate representation of the plume of heat rising above the fixture.

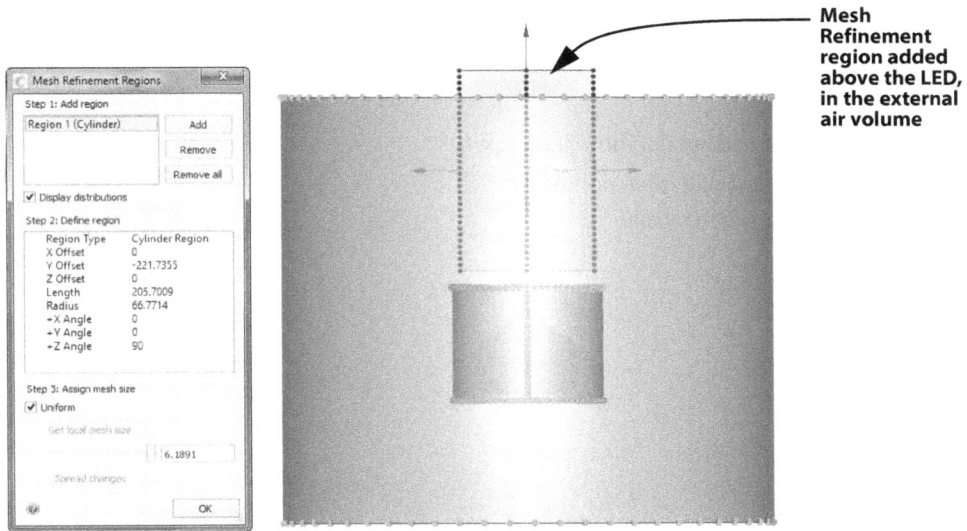

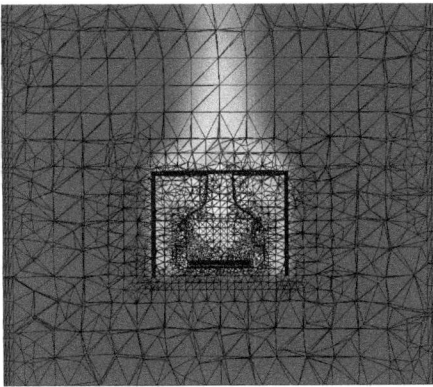

Mesh Refinement region added above the LED, in the external air volume

Default mesh density

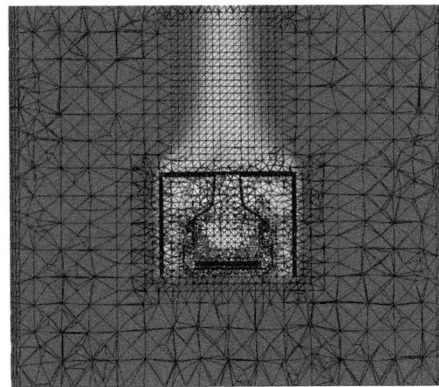

Refined, coarser mesh density in refinement region

Note that any changes made to the mesh in the refinement region will apply to all objects in that region.

Suppression

You can use ⊖ (Suppress) to prevent one or more parts from being meshed. In this case, suppression eliminates parts from the analysis by not meshing them. If suppressed, components display in blue in the meshing view.

Lesson: Manual Mesh Sizing

You can manually size the mesh in an Autodesk CFD analysis to provide control over where the mesh is concentrated, and how it is distributed.

Objectives

After completing this lesson, you will be able to:

- Describe the manual mesh options.
- Assign mesh size manually.

Manually Defining the Mesh

There are two main considerations when deciding to manually mesh the model.

- First, you must ensure that the geometric shapes are adequately defined. You have to be certain that none of the geometric features are mis-represented. For example, if you mesh a round tube and used too few elements, the tube will be approximated as a square duct, as shown in the following image.

- Secondly, you must ensure that elements are concentrated where flow gradients occur. You must concentrate elements where there is a lot of fluid movement and use a coarser mesh where there is little fluid movement.

To manually define the mesh, select Manual in the Type panel, or in the Mesh Sizes dialog box, in Type drop-down list, select Manual, as shown in the following image.

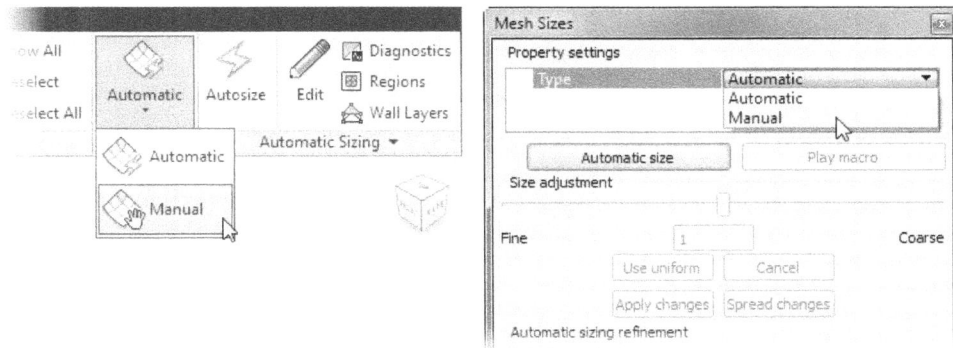

When you automatically apply a mesh, Autodesk CFD assigns element sizes to the surfaces and volumes in the model. These values vary for the different entities, and Autodesk CFD keeps track of them for you.

If you change the Type from Automatic to Manual, you will be promoted to convert the mesh distribution on all model surfaces, as shown in the following image.

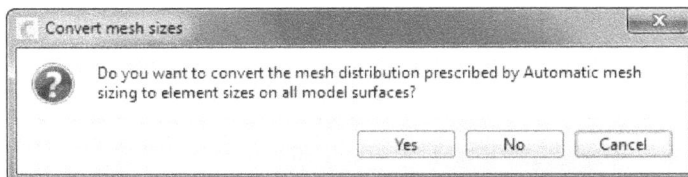

If you click No, the automatic mesh settings are maintained by the system. If you click Yes, the Mesh Sizes dialog box updates to remove the Automatic options, as shown in the following image.

In addition, the element sizes that were automatically assigned to the various surfaces and bodies in the model are extracted and listed out individually in the Design Study Bar, as shown in the following image.

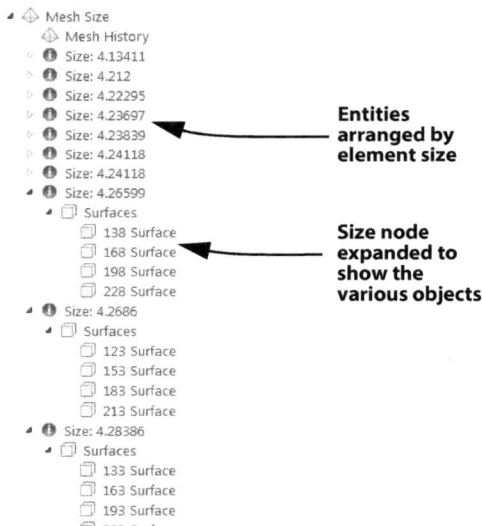

When using a manually define mesh, consider the following:

- You can edit the element size for any object listed. Note that using the manual mesh option increases the strain on system resources.
- You can return to Automatic sizing by selecting Automatic in the Mesh Sizes dialog box, but you will lose any manually applied element sizes.

Lesson: Shaded Mesh

The mesh is initially displayed in a lightweight view. To display the mesh elements, you have to set the display to Shaded Mesh.

Objectives

After completing this lesson, you will be able to:

- Describe the default mesh display.
- Display a preview of the mesh elements and distribution.
- Display the model with a shaded mesh.

Visualizing the Mesh

During the Mesh setup task, preview dots display on the edges of all volumes to be meshed, as shown in the following image. These dots indicate the location of nodes on edges once the mesh is generated.

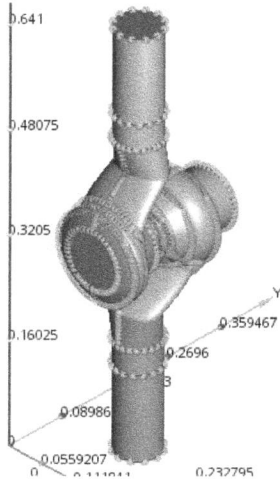

To view the mesh prior to generating the entire three-dimensional mesh, select the surfaces or volumes you want to preview. Right-click and select Preview, as shown in the following image on the left. The mesh will preview only on the visible surfaces of the selected volumes, as shown in the following image on the right. Mesh will not display on non-selected objects.

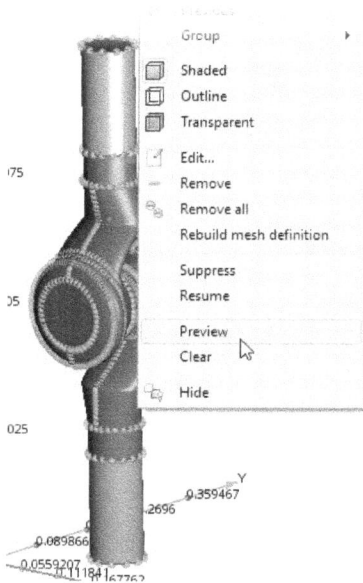

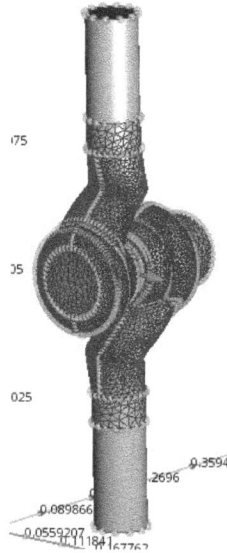

To remove the previewed element faces, simply right-click on the surface or volume and select Clear.

Generating the Mesh

To generate the full mesh prior to running an analysis, right-click on the Scenario branch or the Mesh Size branch in the Design Study bar and select Generate mesh. The mesh is generated according to the established element distribution, whether automatically or manually generated, as shown in the following image.

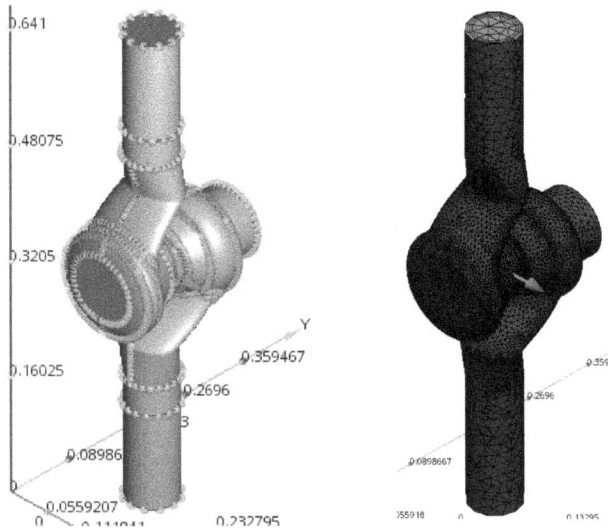

Once generated, check the mesh to ensure that it resolves the geometry correctly, prior to initiating an analysis.

> **Note:** As you will see in the next chapter, you can also generate the mesh as part of initiating the analysis by clicking Solve in the Solve dialog box. In this circumstance, if a mesh already exists and you are simply continuing the analysis, a new mesh is not created.

Viewing Internal Mesh Elements

Note that the options covered so far display the mesh on the surface of the model. However, in fluid analyses, the internal mesh can be far more important. One way to view the internal mesh is using the Planes option in the Results tab.

This option will be discussed in more detail in *Chapter 7: Results Visualization*. Essentially, you can create a cutting plane through the model that shows the internal elements, as shown in the following image.

Since the elements in a solid are 3D, you may notice some splintering or slivers in the elements, as shown in the following image. This is due to the plane cutting through the elements. As previously mentioned, in areas across narrow passages, where there is generally an increase in velocity, it is recommended that a minimum of 6 nodes be used.

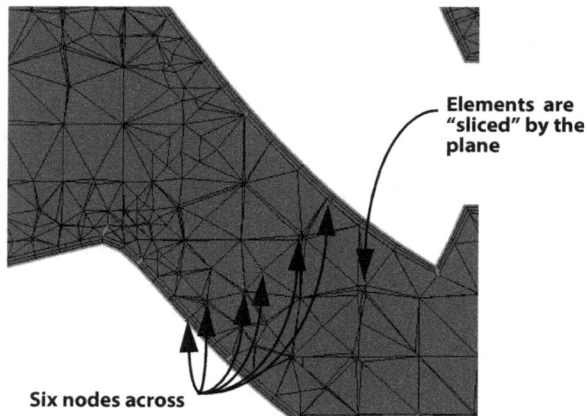

Exercise: Meshing a Model

In this exercise, you will open an existing design study and apply a mesh using the Autosize option. You will also learn how to use the suppress option to remove the mesh from components that are not required and impact the analysis. The objectives in this exercise are to:

- Automatically assign a mesh in a design study.
- Investigate the mesh.
- Use suppress to remove the mesh from components that will not impact the analysis.

Open a design study in the Autodesk CFD Environment.

1.   Launch Autodesk CFD, if not already running.

2.   In the Home tab, click ⌗ (Open). If prompted to save an open design study, click Yes.

3.   In the Open dialog box, browse to the *C:\Autodesk CFD 2017 Essentials Exercise Files\Mesh\ ControlValveMesh* folder. Select and open *ControlValveMesh.cfdst*. The model displays as shown in the following image.

   - Note that the materials and boundary conditions have been applied to the model.

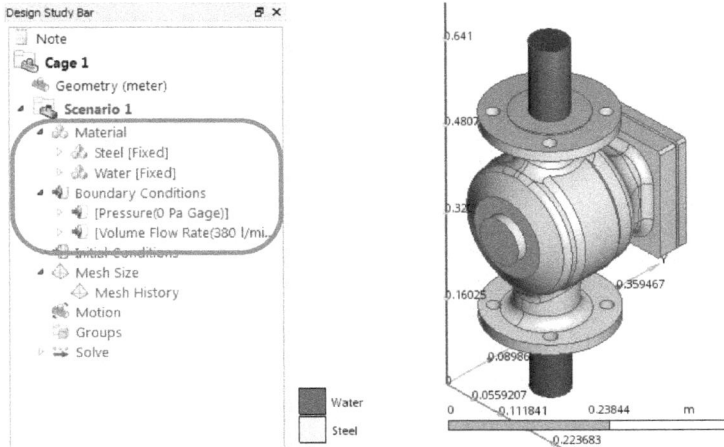

Assign a mesh to the flow volume.

Once the materials and boundary conditions have been applied, you can add the mesh. In this task, you will use the automated tools to apply the mesh.

1. In the Setup tab, in the Setup Tasks panel, click (Mesh Sizing) to activate this stage of the model setup. The Mesh Sizing context panels displays.

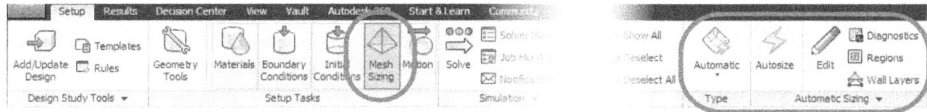

2. In the Type panel, ensure that (Automatic) displays in the Type panel, indicating that

    automatic meshing is set. In the Automatic Sizing panel, click (Autosize).

    -   Note that all geometry, including the casing has the mesh preview applied.
    -   The cyan dots indicate where mesh points will be on the edges of the model.

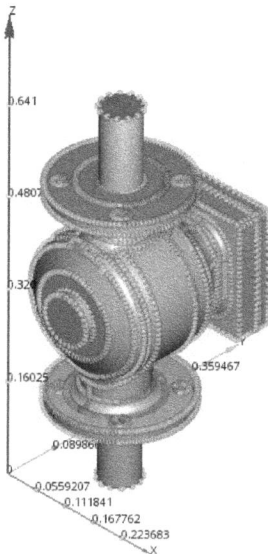

3. This is a flow-only simulation, so heat transfer through the solids will not be calculated. Therefore, it is not necessary to mesh the solids. To suppress the steel casing, click the casing and select (Suppress) in the mini-toolbar, as shown in the following image.

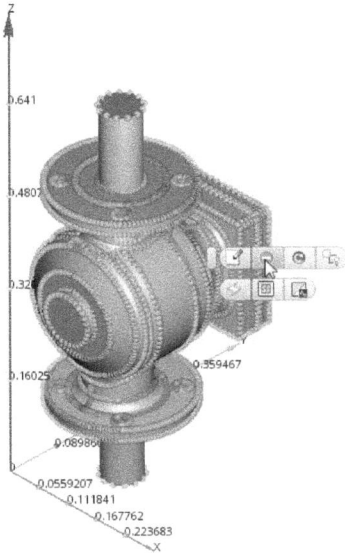

4. A window displays a warning that the mesh will be removed when the part is suppressed and that you will have to reapply the mesh.

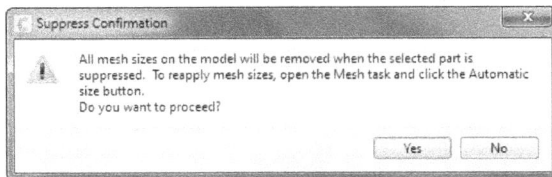

- Click Yes.

5. In the Automatic Sizing panel, click ⚡ (Autosize).

    ▪ The mesh is removed from the valve casing, as shown in the following image.
    ▪ Blue bodies will not be meshed.

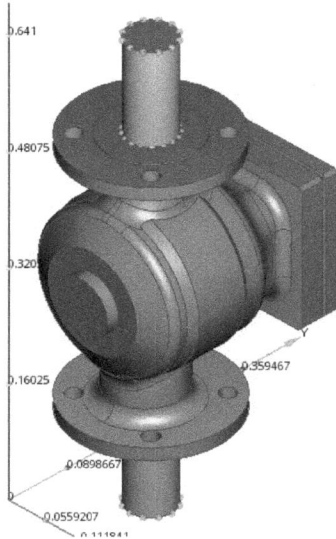

6. Hold <Ctrl> and press the middle mouse button on the casing to remove it from display. The model displays as shown in the following image.

    ▪ Note the greater concentration of dots near the center of the valve.
    ▪ Small edges and tight curvatures are often areas where flow and thermal gradients are high. Automatic Meshing refines the mesh in these areas.

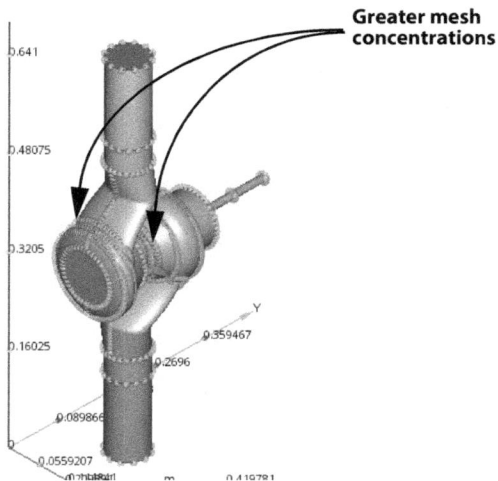

Greater mesh concentrations

7.   Hold <Ctrl> and press the middle mouse button on the middle of the flow volume to remove it from display. The model displays as shown in the following image.

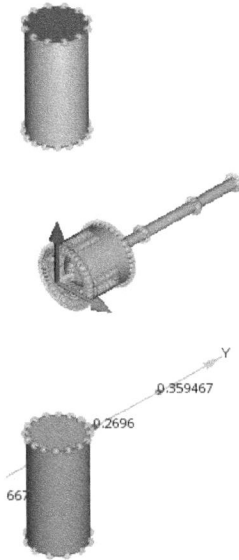

8.   Since this is a flow-only simulation and you will not be calculating heat transfer through the solids, they can be suppressed. Select the cage and valve stem and select ⊖ (Suppress) in the mini-toolbar, as shown in the following image.

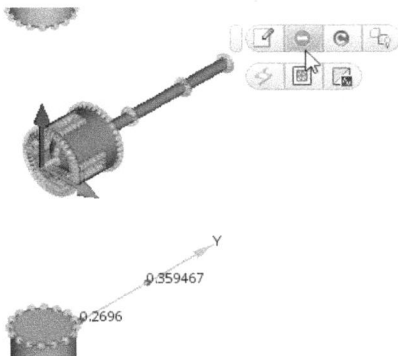

9.   Click Yes in the Suppress Confirmation dialog box.

10. In the Automatic Sizing panel, click ⚡ (Autosize) and the mesh updates as shown in the following image.

   ▪ Note that the cyan mesh preview dots appear on the suppressed (blue) solid parts. CFD shows where nodes from the neighboring fluid mesh will be.

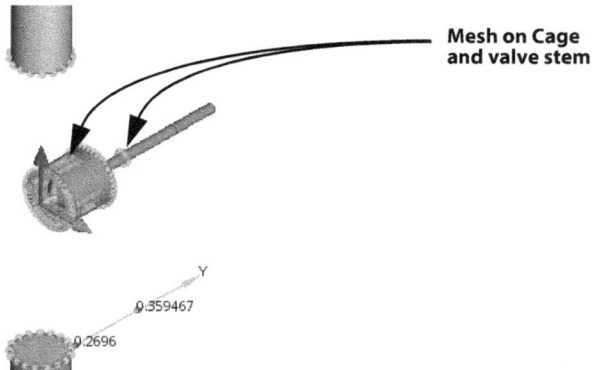

Mesh on Cage and valve stem

11. Hold <Ctrl> and scroll up on the mouse wheel to show the flow volume.

   Note: As a general best practice, you can save time if you suppress by assigned material. For example, in this exercise, you could have selected the Steel material in the Design Study Bar, right-clicked and selected Suppress, as shown in the following image. This would have suppressed all steel components with one action.

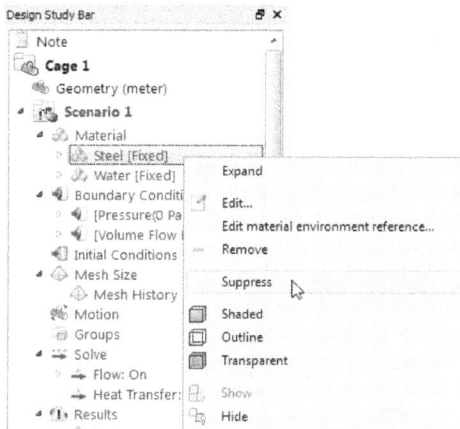

Preview the mesh.

In this task, you will preview the mesh.

1. Select the middle section of the flow volume, right-click and select Preview, as shown in the following image.

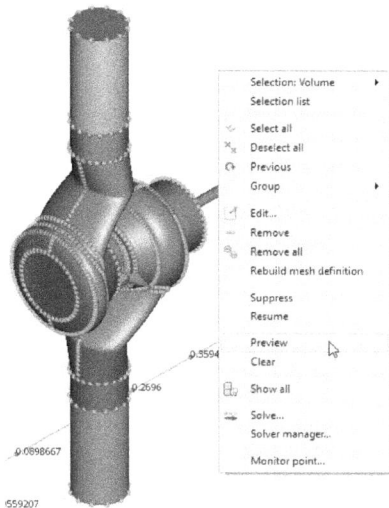

2. The mesh previews as shown in the following image.

    ■ Note how quickly the mesh is generated.
    ■ This is not the final mesh, but rather a representation of the mesh on the surfaces of this body. There is no mesh inside the part yet.

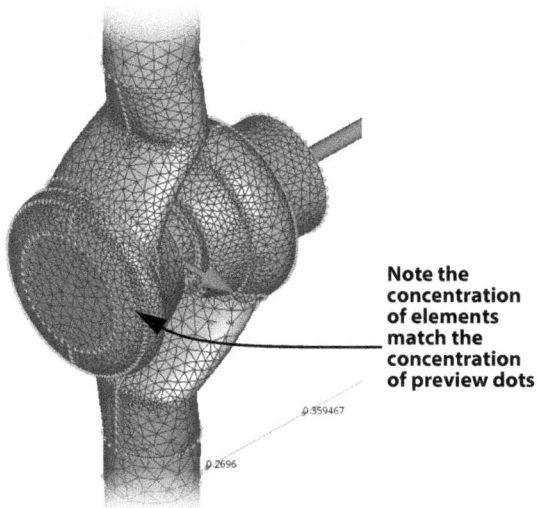

Note the concentration of elements match the concentration of preview dots

3. Right-click on the mesh and select Clear to remove the preview.

Generate the full mesh.

In this task, you will generate the full mesh.

1.   In the Design Study Bar, right-click on Mesh Size (auto) and select Generate mesh.

   - In the Mesh Generation Confirmation dialog box, click Yes.

2.   It will take longer to create the full mesh than it did to create the preview. The Output Bar provides feedback during the meshing process. Once the mesh calculations are complete, the model displays as shown in the following image.

   - Note that the Velocity magnitude appears constant throughout the flow volume, except where boundary conditions are applied. This is because the analysis has not yet been run and you are looking at the model with its initial setup only.

   - The display settings need to be changed before you can see any elements or nodes.

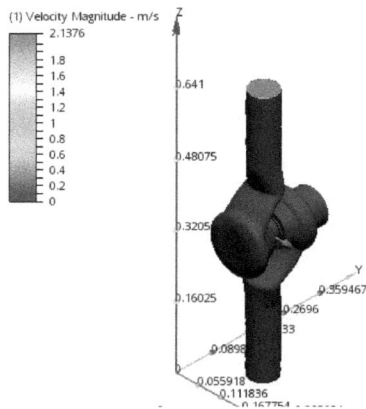

3.   In the Quick Access Toolbar, expand ⬜ (Visual Style) and select Shaded Mesh.

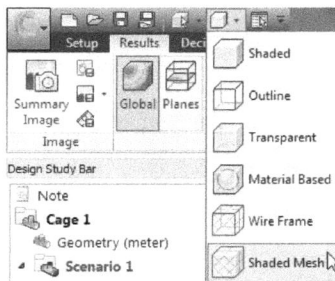

4. The mesh displays as shown in the following image.

- As with the previewed mesh display, note the areas of concentration of elements.

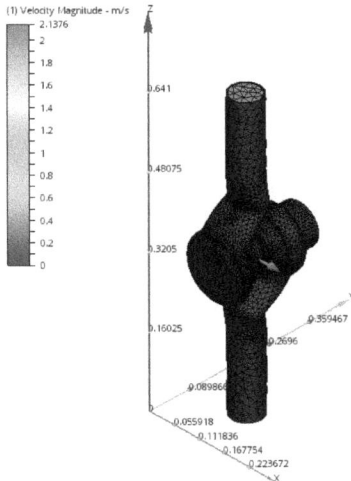

View the internal mesh using a plane through the model.

1. Select the Results tab in the ribbon, if not already selected.

2. In the Results Tasks panel, click 🔲 (Planes).

3. In the Planes panel, click ➕ (Add). A plane through the center of the model is established, as shown in the following image.

- If the model is not displayed as shown, in the Quick Access Toolbar, expand 🔲▾ (Visual Style) and select Outline.

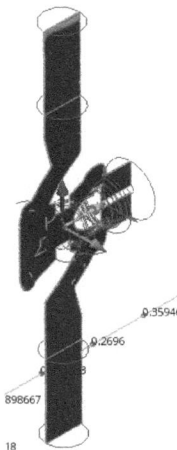

4. In the graphics window, right-click on the plane and select Shaded mesh.

5. On the ViewCube, click RIGHT. Hover over the ViewCube and click the counter-clockwise arrow, as shown in the following image, to rotate the model.

   - The model should display as shown in the following image.

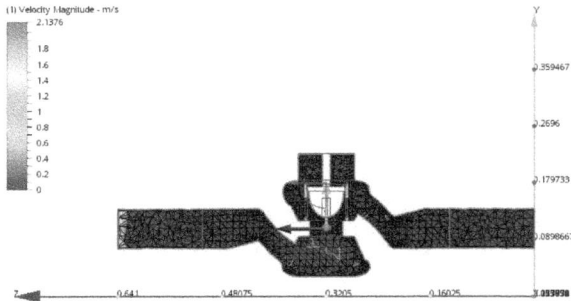

6. Zoom in on the model, as shown in the following image. Note the following:
   - You are looking at the elements and nodes inside the flow volume.
   - Elements that appear fractured or splintered are being visually cut by the plane.
   - The automatic mesh appears satisfactory, with the recommended 6 nodes across narrow areas.

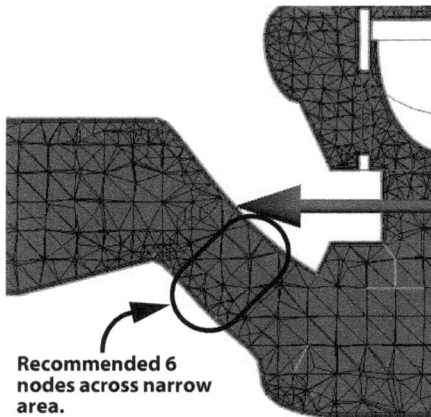

Recommended 6 nodes across narrow area.

7. In the Quick Access toolbar, click 💾 (Save) to save the study. With the mesh established, the analysis is set to run. This topic is covered in more detail in the next chapter.

Exercise: Customizing a Mesh

In this exercise, you will open an existing design study that has been meshed. You will investigate the mesh and customize it to adjust its spacing around the fins of the heat sink. The objectives in this exercise are to:

- Investigate a mesh.
- Use a refinement area to customize the mesh.
- Use a selected volume to adjust the mesh.

Open a design study in the Autodesk CFD Environment.

1. Launch Autodesk CFD, if not already running.

2. In the Home tab, click ⬜ (Open). If prompted to save an open design study, click Yes.

3. In the Open dialog box, browse to the *C:\Autodesk CFD 2017 Essentials Exercise Files\Mesh\ LEDMesh* folder. Select and open *LEDMesh.cfdst*. The model displays as shown in the following image.

    - Note that the materials, boundary conditions and mesh settings have been applied to the model for you.

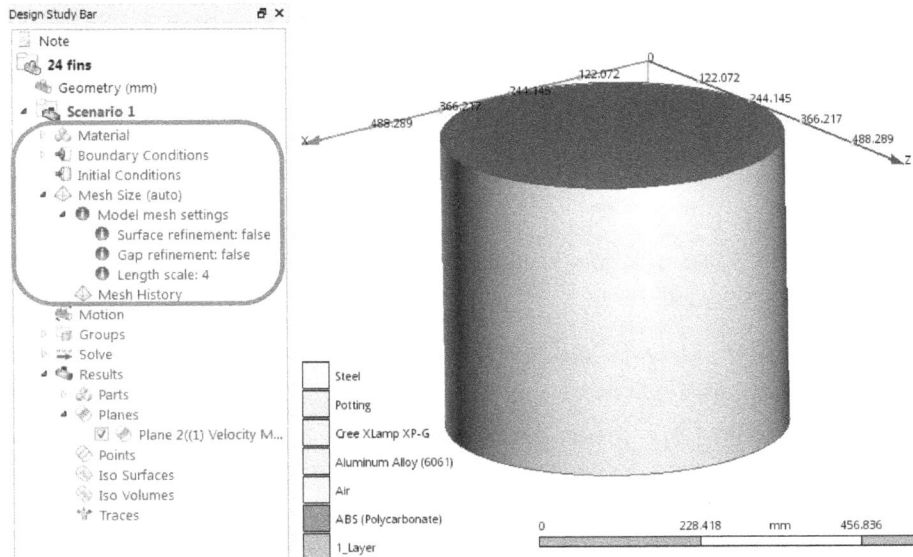

Generate the Autosize mesh.

Once the materials, boundary conditions, and mesh have been defined, you can generate the Autosize mesh.

1. In the Quick Access Toolbar, expand ⬛ (Visual Style) and select Transparent.

2. In the Design Study Bar, select the Mesh Size (auto) node and note that the mesh preview displays as shown in the following image.

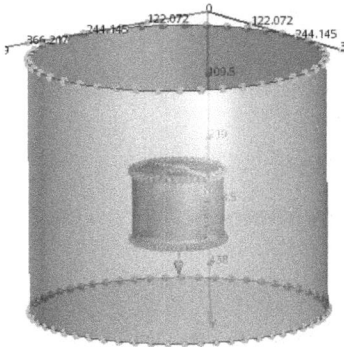

3. Hold <Ctrl> and press the middle mouse button to remove the external air volume and cannister from display.

   - Ensure that you click both halves of the cannister to remove it.
   - Zoom in until the model displays similar to that shown in the following image.
   - The mesh around the fins of the heat sink are of interest.

4. Remove the axes from display.

   - Select the View tab.
   - Expand Axes and remove the check next to each type, as shown in the following image.

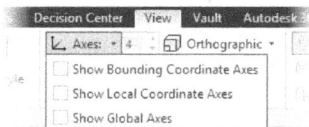

5. Select the Setup tab to return to the mesh setup.

6. In the Design Study Bar, right-click on the Mesh Size (auto) node and select Generate mesh. Click Yes when prompted to confirm. Make note of how long the analysis takes.

7. In the Quick Access Toolbar, expand ▢▾ (Visual Style) and select Transparent, if the view display has changed. The model should display as shown in the following image.

(1) Velocity Magnitude - mm/s

8. Autodesk CFD assigns a minimum and maximum value for the legend scale. In later tasks in this lesson, these values can vary depending on your exact settings. To ensure that the mesh elements are easily visible at this point, manually set the scale as shown in the following image:

- Right-click on the legend and select Options.
- In the Legend Options dialog box, enable User specified range.
- Edit the Min value to **-1**.
- Edit the Max value to **1** and click Close. The model should display as green.

9. Review the Output Bar and the number of elements and nodes that were generated, as shown in the following image.

```
** FINITE ELEMENT SUMMARY FOLLOWS...
55172 Total Nodes,   52280 Fluid Nodes ,   2892 Solid Nodes
220029 Total Elements,   182802 Fluid Elements ,   37227 Solid Elements
0 Inlets   2 Outlets   0 Unknowns
```

10. In the Quick Access Toolbar, expand ▭▣ (Visual Style) and select Outline.

- On the ViewCube, click BACK.

11. Hold <Ctrl> and press the middle mouse button away from the geometry to return all components to the display.

12. In the Design Study Bar, expand the Results node, if required. In the Planes node, right-click on Plane 1(1) Velocity Magnitude, and select Shaded mesh. This plane was setup to slice the model through the fins of the heat sink. The model displays as shown in the following image.

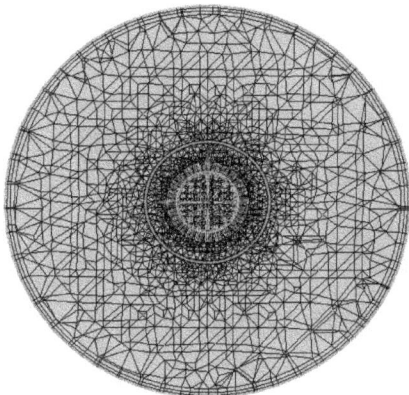

13. Zoom in to see the mesh concentration around the fins, as shown in the following image.

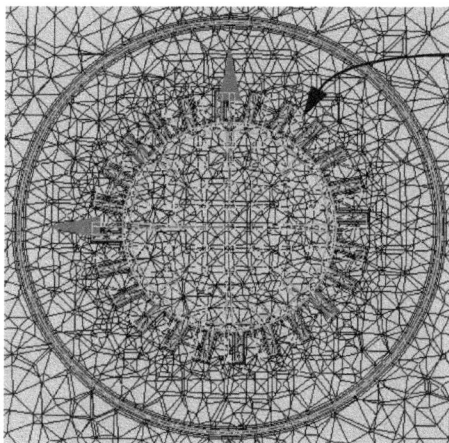

The Automatic mesh spacing is shown

Clone the scenario and use a Region to refine the mesh on the heat sink.

In this task, you will adjust the mesh to refine the spacing by using a region. You will clone the scenario so that you don't lose the current settings that were setup in the current scenario.

1. In the Design Study Bar, right-click Scenario 1 and select Clone.

   - Edit the name to **Scenario 2 - Region**.
   - Click Include mesh and results, as shown in the following image.
   - Click OK.

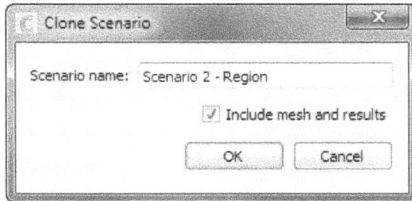

2. In the Design Study Bar, select the Mesh Size (auto) node to activate the Mesh Sizing setup task.

3. Hide the outer air volume and the cannister, and rotate the model so it displays similar to that shown in the following image.

4. Select the surface of the heat sink and click ⊞ (Regions) in the mini-toolbar, as shown in the following image.

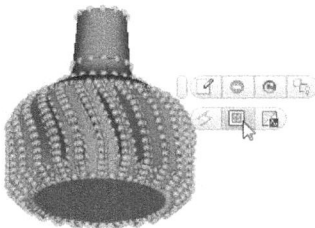

5. In the Mesh Refinement Regions dialog box, click Add. Then, edit the following:

- In the Region Type drop-down list, select Cylinder Region.
- In the +Z Angle field, type **90** and press <Enter>.
- The dialog box and model should display as shown in the following image.

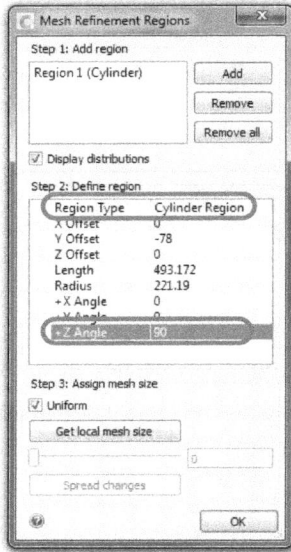

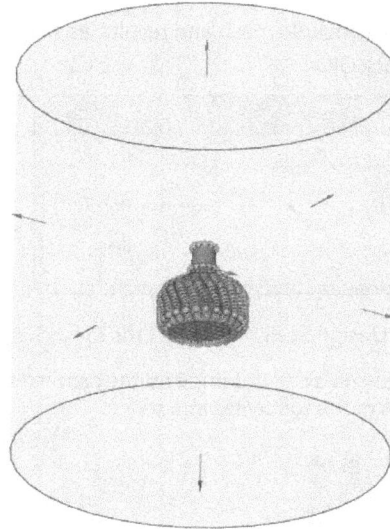

6. On the ViewCube, click BACK. Drag one of the arrows so that the cylinder is approximately the same size as the outer diameter of the heat sink, as shown in the following image.

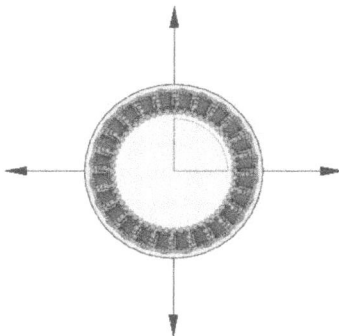

7. Select the arrow on the top of the ViewCube to rotate the model to the TOP orientation.

    ▪ Use the arrows on the cylinder to resize it so that it only encompasses the heat sink fins, as shown in the image below.

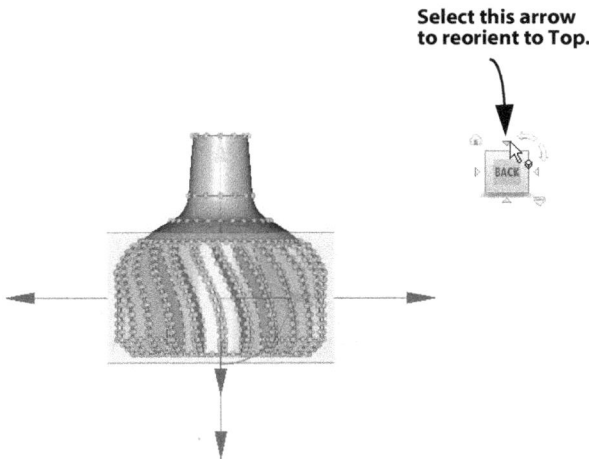

**Select this arrow
to reorient to Top.**

8. In the Mesh Refinement Regions dialog box, click Get local mesh size and drag the slider approximately to the middle. This will roughly double the mesh density by reducing the spacing between elements.

    ▪ Click Spread changes to apply the mesh.
    ▪ Click OK.

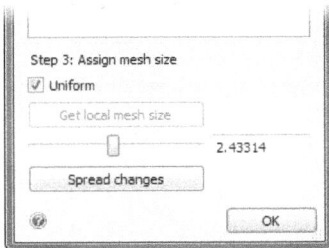

9. In the Design Study Bar, right-click on Mesh Size (auto) and select Generate mesh. Click Yes when prompted to confirm.

    ▪ Click Yes in the Delete Results? dialog box shown in the following image.
    ▪ Since the mesh settings have changed, any existing results have to be deleted. This is the reason the scenario had been cloned, to avoid losing the original results.

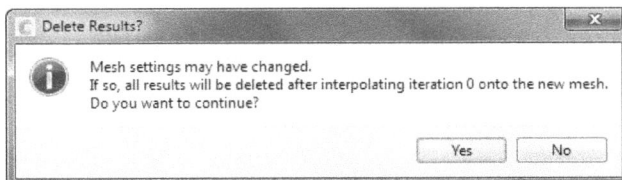

10. The increase in mesh density significantly increases the time required to mesh the geometry. Depending on the size set with the slider, the number of elements and nodes displayed may vary as compared to those shown in the following image.

```
** FINITE ELEMENT SUMMARY FOLLOWS...
272167 Total Nodes,   209837 Fluid Nodes ,   62330 Solid Nodes
1198873 Total Elements,  788554 Fluid Elements ,   410319 Solid Elements
0 Inlets   2 Outlets   0 Unknowns
```

11. Zoom out to review the model and hide the outer air volume and the cannister from the display.

12. In the Results tab, in the Results Tasks panel, click (Planes).

13. In the Planes panel, click (Add).

14. Rotate the model similar to that shown in the following image. Select the surface of the plane and click (Align Y) in the mini-toolbar, as shown in the following image, to cut the model through the Y-Axis.

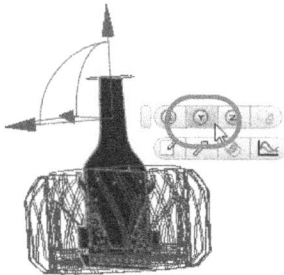

15. Drag the indicated arrow to move the plane so it intersects the heat sink fins, similar to that shown in the following image.

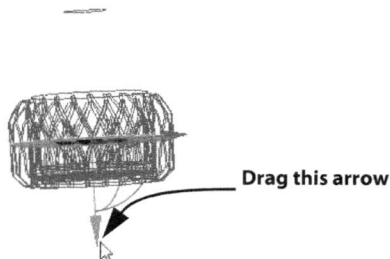

Drag this arrow

16. In the ViewCube, click BACK.

- Right-click Plane 1(1) Velocity Magnitude and select Shaded mesh.
- Set the legend scale range from -1 to 1. Refer to the previous task for detailed steps, if required.
- Hold <Ctrl> and press the middle mouse button on the screen to show all hidden components.
- The model displays as shown in the following image.

17. Zoom in to view the mesh concentration. Note the increased density near the fins.

18. Note however that when you use a refinement region, you increased the mesh on any objects contained within the volume of the region. Therefore, you also increase the mesh on the PCB, LEDs and so on. Although this may be acceptable in some cases, it can cause unnecessary strain on system resources.

Clone Scenario 1 and refine the mesh on the heat sink volume.

In this task, you will once again adjust the mesh to refine the spacing, but you will apply the changes only to the heat sink volume. You will clone the first scenario so that you do not lose the current settings.

1. In the Design Study Bar, complete the following:

    ▪ Right-click Scenario 1 and select Activate.
    ▪ Right-click Scenario 1 and select Clone.
    ▪ In the Clone Scenario dialog box, edit the name to **Scenario 3 - Volume**.
    ▪ Click Include mesh and results, as shown in the following image.
    ▪ Click OK.

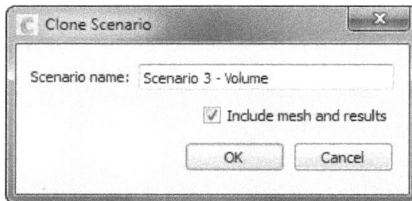

2. In the Design Study Bar, select the Mesh Size (auto) node. This activates the Mesh Sizing setup task.

3. ▪ Hide the outer air volume and the cannister, then rotate the model so that it displays similar to that shown in the following image.

4. Select the heat sink and click (Edit) in the mini-toolbar, as shown in the following image.

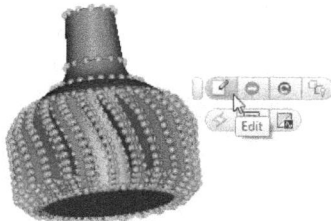

5. In the Mesh Sizes dialog box, use the Size adjustment slider or enter a value of **0.3** to create a finer mesh, as shown in the following image. Click Apply changes and then click Apply.

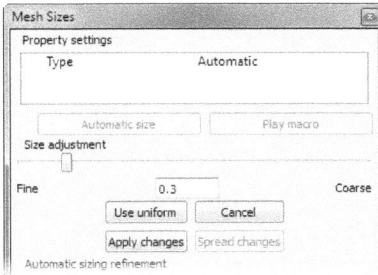

6. In the Design Study Bar, right-click on the Mesh Size (auto) node and select Generate mesh. Click Yes when prompted in both dialog boxes. Note the relative time it takes to complete. The number of nodes and elements should be as shown in the following image.

```
** FINITE ELEMENT SUMMARY FOLLOWS...
320899 Total Nodes,   222126 Fluid Nodes ,   98773 Solid Nodes
1466031 Total Elements,  774425 Fluid Elements ,   691606 Solid Elements
0 Inlets   2 Outlets   0 Unknowns
```

7. Zoom out to review the model and hide the outer air volume and the cannister from the display.

8. In the Results tab, in the Results Tasks panel, click (Planes).

9. In the Planes panel, click (Add).

10. Rotate the model similar to that shown in the following image. Select the surface of the plane and click (Align Y) in the mini-toolbar, as shown in the following image, to cut the model through the Y-Axis.

11. Drag the indicated arrow to move the plane so it intersects the heat sink fins, similar to that shown in the following image.

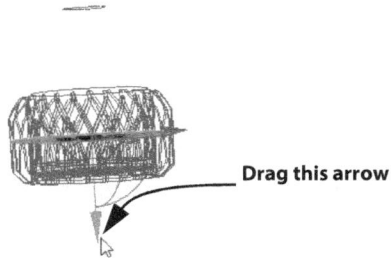

Drag this arrow

12. In the ViewCube, click BACK.
    - Right-click Plane 1(1) Velocity Magnitude and select Shaded mesh.
    - Set the legend scale range from -1 to 1.
    - Hold <Ctrl> and press the middle mouse button on the screen to show all hidden components.
    - The model displays as shown in the following image.

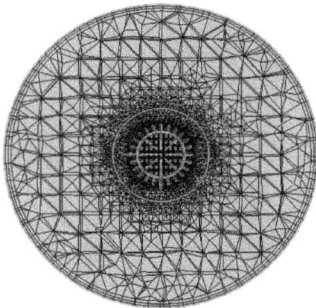

13. Zoom in to view the mesh concentration. Note the increased density near the fins. Only the density of the heat sink component was changed and not all of the internal components.

14. The following image shows the three meshes side by side for comparison.

Default Mesh   **Refinement Region**   **Size Adjustment**

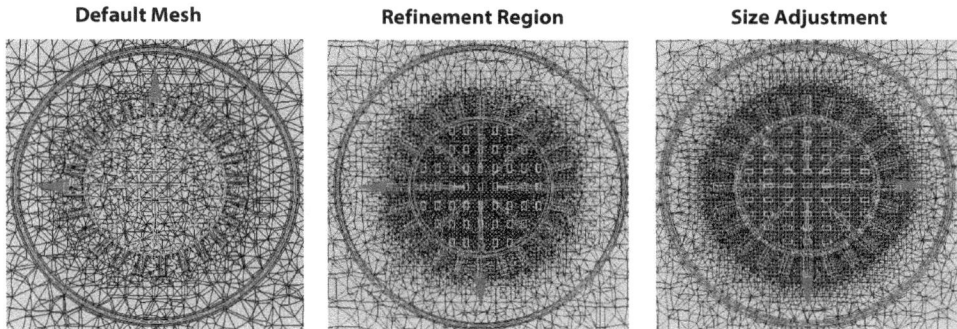

To summarize, this exercise showed that the default mesh did not create the required node spacing between the heat sink fins. The addition of a mesh refinement region or increasing the mesh density on a volume were both good methods for increasing the mesh density. Note that more elements require longer run times. Consider using the method that provides an adequate mesh in the areas of concern while minimizing the element count. This provides a robust solution while using less computer resources and time.

Tip: If the areas of concern are not easily enhanced with these methods, it is recommended to create your own mesh refinement region in the CAD model before starting the CFD simulation. Define the CAD volume as a fluid material and increase the mesh resolution on that volume alone.

15. In the Quick Access toolbar, click 🖫 (Save) to save the study.

- In upcoming chapters, you will run analyses and see the impact of changes to your meshes.

Chapter

6

Solver Settings

Once the materials, boundary conditions, and mesh have been setup in the model, the study can be solved using the Solve dialog box. In this chapter, you will learn how to simulate a design study scenario to report the required results and how to use the parameters available in the Solve dialog box to customize a solution. Additionally, you will learn how to manage and monitor a simulation's progress using Autodesk® CFD tools.

Objectives

After completing this chapter, you will be able to:

- Set the parameters in the Solve dialog box.
- Solve a design study scenario.
- Interpret the messages and plots that appear in the Output Bar while an analysis is being run.
- Use the Solver Manager to setup multiple scenarios for efficient simulation.
- Use the Job Monitor to review the progress of executed simulations.
- Use email notifications to indicate when specific milestones are reached during a simulation.

Autodesk

Autodesk

Lesson: Solving a Simulation

Overview

This lesson provides an overview of how you can setup the parameters in the Solve dialog box to ensure that the required results are generated for a simulation. Additionally, you will learn how the Autodesk CFD software reacts during an analysis.

Objectives

After completing this lesson, you will be able to:

- Set the parameters in the Solve dialog box.
- Solve a design study scenario.
- Interpret the messages and plots that appear in the Output Bar while an analysis is being run.

Solver Dialog Box

Once the model material setup tasks, boundary conditions, and mesh are complete, you are able to solve the simulation. There are multiple parameters available during solver setup that can be customized to ensure that the required results are reported. The customization and execution of a simulation is done using the Solve dialog box.

To open the Solve dialog box, use one of the following methods:

- Right click in the graphics window and select Solve.

- In the Setup tab, in the Simulation panel, click ⟹ (Solve).

- In the Design Study Bar, right-click on the Solve node, and click Edit.

- In the Results tab, in the Iteration/Step panel, click ⟹ (Solve).

The Solve dialog box opens similar to that shown in the fowling image.

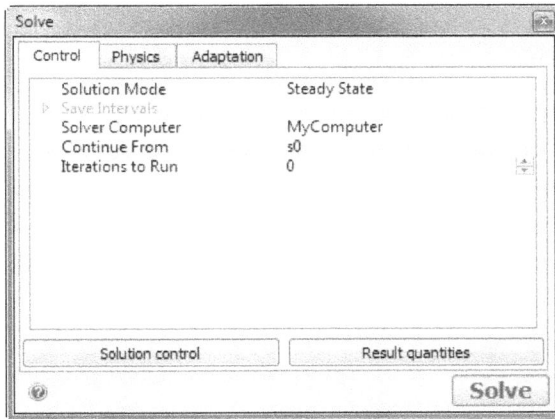

To define how the simulation runs, you can customize the parameters on each of the three tabs: Control, Physics, and Adaptation.

- **Control Tab -** Use the options on this tab to define how the analysis runs.
    - Set the Solution Mode to Steady State (independent of time) or Transient (time dependent). When set as Transient, additional Transient Parameters (time step size, etc.) must be specified.
    - Set the Save Intervals options to save intermediate iterations. This sets how often the results and summary information are stored to the disk.
    - Select the Solver Computer (the local computer is the default) that will be used for the analysis.
        - The Scalable Solver is intended to capitalize on high performance computing (HPC).
        - Solving on the Cloud enables you to solve multiple analyses on the cloud at the same time.
    - To continue an analysis from a previous iteration, enter a value in the Continue From field. By default, the entry continues from last saved iteration or time step.

> **Changes to a Design Study Setup**
>
> Changes made to mesh definitions, boundary conditions, or materials are automatically incorporated into the analysis. If you change the mesh size, but do not reset the Continue From menu to 0, the following occurs:
>
> - a new mesh will be generated
> - the current results are interpolated onto this new mesh
> - the analysis iteration count is reset to 0
>
> All intermediate saved results files (and time steps) will be deleted. The analysis will proceed with the saved results mapped to the new mesh.

- Enter the number of Iterations to Run (or Time Steps to Run) in the Iterations to Run field. By default, the iteration value is set to 100. It is recommended to run an analysis to convergence. Depending on the physics required and other settings, the iteration value may vary.
- Solution control enable you to modify convergence settings and set numerical schemes called advection schemes. For more information on analysis intelligence, search for "Solution Control" in the online Help documentation.
- Result quantities enable you to add additional results for viewing after the analysis is solved. **Hint:** Rerunning for 0 iterations from the end of an analysis will make these variables available without having to rerun the analysis.

- **Physics Tab** - Use the options on this tab to enable physical models such as flow and heat transfer. The Physics tab shown in the following image displays the default settings.

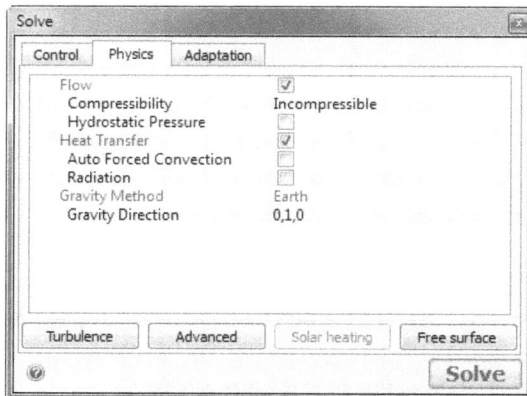

The following options are available in the Physics tab:

- **Flow:** Use this option whenever fluid movement needs to be calculated. This option is on by default and only needs to be disabled for simulations that deal solely with conductive heat transfer.
    - **Compressibility:** The default setting is set to Incompressible and it is appropriate for most design simulations. Changing this option to Subsonic or Compressible increases solution complexity and lengthens simulation time. For more information on this advanced topic, search for "Compressibility" in the online Help documentation.
    - **Hydrostatic Pressure:** Use this option when the weight of the fluid needs to be included in the simulation. Since most simulations do not require this, the option is off by default. For more information, search for "Hydrostatic Pressure" in the online Help documentation.

- **Heat Transfer:** Use this option to include thermal effects in the simulation. This option is off by default, which causes the simulation to be adiabatic.
  - **Auto Forced Convection:** This option stages the flow and heat transfer solvers. This ensures that the flow is solved and that the heat transfer is run afterwards with a locked flow solution. This saves time when buoyant flow fields are not present. For more information, search for "Heat Transfer" in the online Help documentation.
  - **Radiation:** This option includes surface-to-surface radiation effects. It is useful for cases where radiation is a significant factor in heat transfer. Radiation calculations significantly increase computations time. For more information, search for "Radiation" in the online Help documentation.
- **Gravity Method:** For natural convection and hydrostatic problems, it is imperative that the downward direction of the model be specified. Entering a Gravity Direction vector enables temperature-driven density changes in fluids to drive fluid movement. Fluid materials assigned must have densities that vary with temperature. This option increases calculation time and is therefore disabled (set to 0,0,0) by default.

- **Adaptation Tab** - Use the options on this tab to enable adaptation that will progressively improve the mesh by running the simulation multiple times. At the end of each run, the mesh is automatically modified based on the results, and the new mesh is used for the next cycle. The result is a mesh that is optimized for the particular simulation. The mesh is finer for high gradient regions and coarser elsewhere. The Adaptation tab is shown in the following image.

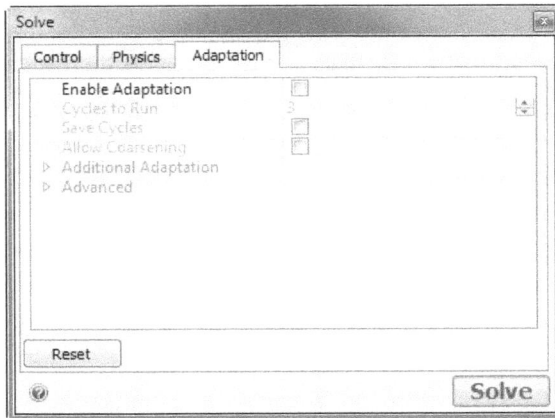

Select Enable Adaptation to enable this adaptive analysis strategy and define values for the cycles to run. This is helpful for refining the mesh around areas where flow phenomenon are difficult to predict without heavily meshing the entire model. It requires multiple simulations to be performed sequentially and therefore takes longer to produce a solution. Adaptation is not required for most simulations. For more information on this advanced strategy, search for "Adaptive Meshing" in the online Help documentation.

Solving a Scenario

Once the parameters are all defined in the Solve dialog box, click Solve to begin running the analysis. While running, the following occurs:

- The Scenario icon in the Design Study Bar displays as ![icon].
- The Message Window tab in the Output Bar displays the progress of the analysis, similar to that shown in the following image.

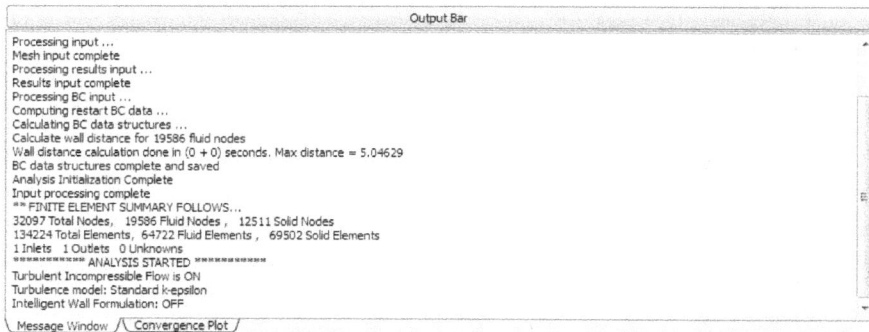

- The graph in the Convergence Plot tab in the Output Bar displays the progress of the analysis, similar to that shown in the following image. Note that early in the analysis, the results can change a lot from one iteration to the next. The convergence lines might oscillate up and down. Horizontal convergence lines indicate when the results stop changing and the solution is "converged."

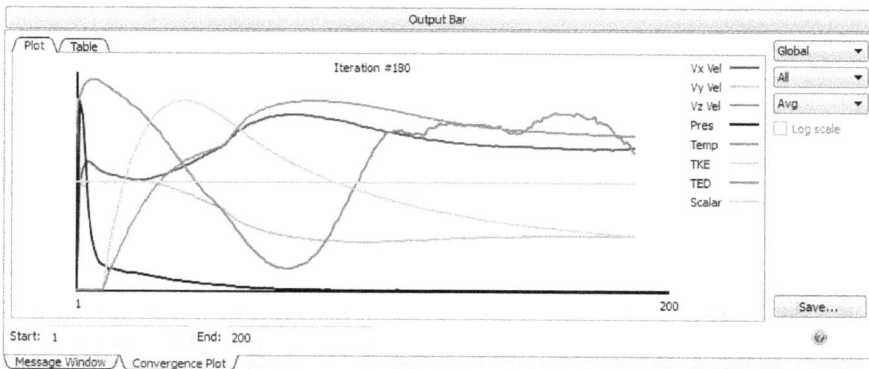

> As an analysis is running, limited interaction in the software is permitted. For example, you can manipulate the model orientation and use most results visualization tools; however, you cannot make changes to the setup parameters.

Once the analysis is complete, consider the following:

- The Scenario icon in the Design Study Bar displays as ![icon].
- The Message Window tab in the Output Bar displays a message that the "Analysis completed successfully". If the analysis failed to complete a failure message will display.
- To rerun the study, consider using the Continue From options to restart from a specified iteration.

Convergence

Every Autodesk CFD analysis requires multiple iterations. An iteration is a numerical sweep through the entire model. The convergence of each degree of freedom (quantity) is plotted on the Convergence Plot tab, in the Output Bar. Note that early in the analysis, the results can change a lot from one iteration to the next. The convergence lines might oscillate up and down. A horizontal convergence line indicates when the result has stop changing and the solution is converged. Numerous iterations are required to attain full convergence. The number varies based on the application and the physics of the model.

In the following convergence plot, visual inspection of key variables such as pressure, temperature, and the primary velocity component show that the solution has converged.

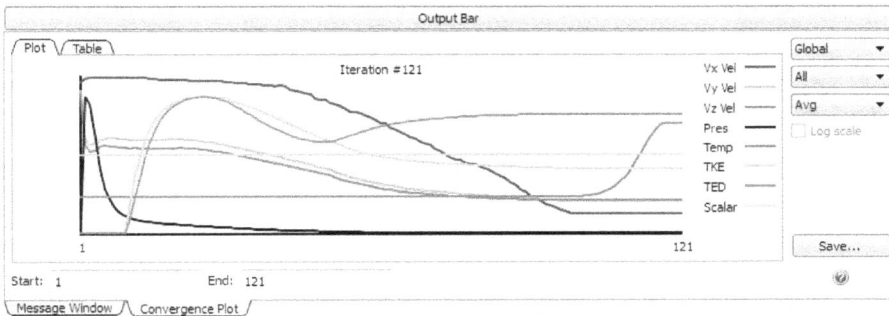

In addition to the manual parameters (e.g., Continue From and Iterations to Run) that are defined in the Solve dialog box to control solution convergence, Autodesk CFD contains a great deal of analysis intelligence. This automatically controls the rate of convergence and determines when the analysis is no longer changing (converged). Although convergence must be reached before you can quantitatively assess the results, trends can be assessed much earlier in the analysis.

Convergence can be determined automatically or manually:

- Automatic convergence detection uses analysis intelligence in Autodesk CFD to assess the progress of the solution and stops the analysis when it satisfies certain numerical criteria. Autodesk CFD constantly examines small and large frequency changes throughout the solution field and evaluates the local and global fluctuations of each degree of freedom. This is indicated by the conclusion of the analysis prior to reaching the number of iterations defined by the user. It is also accompanied with a message in the Output Bar confirming that flat lines have been detected.

- Manual convergence assessment is required in situations where flow phenomena such as recirculation naturally causes some quantities to fluctuate. The curves might not flatten and automatic convergence might not be attained. To manually determine convergence, review the variable values in the Table tab and determine if the fluctuations are acceptable.

> If manual convergence assessment determines that convergence of the key variables has not been reached, you can start the solver again using the Solve dialog box. Because a previous solution already exists, the Continue From value will default to the last saved iteration.

Lesson: Solving Multiple Designs

Overview

This lesson provides an overview of how you can use the Solver Manager and Job Monitor tools to efficiently run and monitor the progress of multiple design study scenario simulations at the same time. Using theses tools as opposed to individually solving each scenario, enables you to assign a computer resource and execution time to solve the study. You will also learn how to set up notifications so that a defined list of recipients can receive notifications during a simulation.

Objectives

After completing this lesson, you will be able to:

- Use the Solver Manager to setup multiple scenarios for efficient simulation.
- Use the Job Monitor to review the progress of executed simulations.
- Use email notifications to indicate when specific milestones are reached during a simulation.

Solver Manager

The Solve tool enables you to run the currently active scenario in the Design Study. The Solver Manager tool enables you to schedule and run multiple scenarios at the same time, eliminating the need to activate and run each scenario individually.

To open the Solver Manager use one of the following methods:

- Right-click in the graphics window and select Solver manager.

- In the Setup tab, in the Simulation panel, click ⊞ (Solver Manager).

- In the Design Study Bar, right click on the Solve node, and click Solver Manager.

All scenarios in the Design Study are listed in the Solver Manager, similar to that shown in the following image.

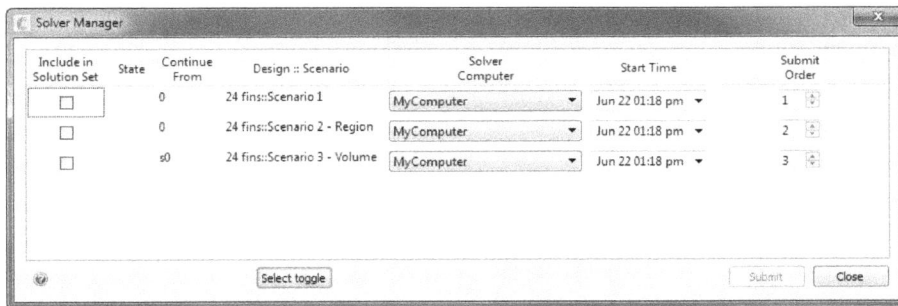

Use the Solver Manager to set the following for each scenario:

- Enable or disable the checkbox in the Include in Solution Set column to specify whether the scenario is to be included in the simulation or not.

- Select in the Continue From or Design: Scenario fields to open each scenario's specific Solve dialog box. Using this dialog box, you can modify the same solver parameters that are set when running an individual simulation.

- Select the computer name that will be used to solve each scenario.

- In each Start Time cell, set the required date and time for the simulation to be run.

- Change the Submit Order numbers as required, to customize the execution order for situations where the start times are all the same.

> Remote Computing enables you to run analyses on remote computers on a network. This facilitates the solving process without sacrificing your own machine's resources. Cloud solving enables you to run solves in parallel. For more information on setting up remote computing, search for "Remote Solving" in the online Help documentation.

To run the simulation for the selected design study scenarios, click Submit. Once submitted, the State column identifies the included scenarios as submitted. Additionally, the Scenario node in the Design Study Bar updates to show that the simulation is being run (🗂). Once the scenario is completed, the Scenario node in the Design Study Bar updates to show that the simulation is finished (🗂). While running, the Solver Manager can be closed.

Job Monitor

The Job Monitor is an external utility that tracks analysis activity. If multiple computers are available, it identifies the following information for each computer:

- Simulations running on each solver computer and their respective owners.
- The current iteration of each simulation.
- The amount of CPU resources used on each solver computer.

To open the Job Monitor use one of the following options:

- In the Setup tab, in the Simulation panel, click ▦ (Job Monitor).
- In the Design Study Bar, right-click on the Solve node, and click Job Monitor.
- From the Windows® Start menu, click All Programs>Autodesk>CFD 2017>CFD 2017 Job Monitor.

All scenarios that are currently begin solved display similar to that shown in the following image. If multiple computers are being used, they are each listed.

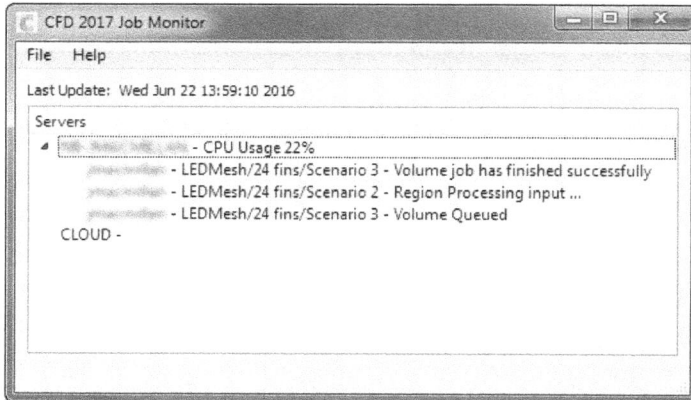

The Job Monitor is not used when running in the cloud. Instead, you can use the Simulation Job Manager to monitor solution progress.

To stop a job, use either of the following two methods:

- In the Job Monitor dialog box, right-click on the job, and click Stop Job.
- In the Solve dialog box, click Stop.

In both situations, the simulation will stop after the current iteration is complete and results will be saved up to that point. If required, a simulation can be restarted from any saved iteration by choosing that iteration from the drop-down list in the Continue From cell. By default, the Continue From cell will contain the value of the last saved iteration.

Solver Notifications

Autodesk CFD enables you to receive notification emails on specific milestones during the simulation.

To open the Solver Notifications dialog box, use one of the following methods:

- In the Setup tab, in the Simulation panel, click ⊠ (Notifications).
- In the Design Study Bar, right-click on the Solve node, and click Notifications.

The Solver Notifications dialog box opens as shown in the following image.

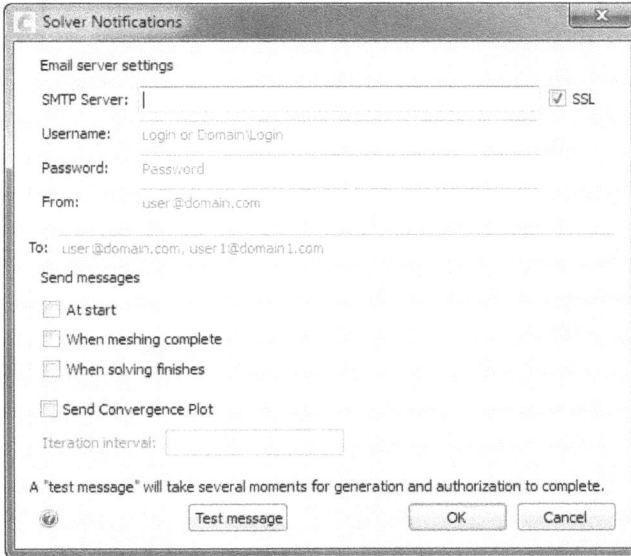

To enable notifications, define the email server settings from which the email is sent and the target e-mail address that will receive the notifications. To enter multiple target addresses, separate each with a comma. In the Send messages area, select the events that will trigger a notification. If you select Send Convergence Plot, indicate how many iterations should elapse between plot images in the Iteration Interval box.

Click Test message to confirm the settings and send a test message to all recipients. Notifications will be sent for all subsequent analyses that are launched from your computer, using your Windows login. The analysis conclusion notification contains the status file. If an error occurs, this file includes the error message.

> To receive notifications as text messages, enter the SMS address according to your mobile vendor's specifications in the To: field. For more information on the appropriate SMS address for your specific carrier, search for "Notifications" in the online Help documentation.

Exercise: Solving Multiple Scenarios

In this exercise, you will open an existing design study, that has been setup with materials, boundary conditions, and mesh. The design study involves the valve model you have seen previously. You will work with three designs that have been setup for you, in which a different CAD model of the cage design is used around the valve poppet. You will clone one of the existing design studies to create a fourth alternative cage design, apply solver settings, and solve this single design study. To complete the exercise, you will simultaneously solve the remaining three design studies.

The objectives in this exercise are to:

- Clone a design study and use Autodesk® SimStudio Tools to change the model used in the design study.
- Apply solver settings to ensure that only the flow (not the heat transfer) is evaluated.
- Solve a single design study.
- Solve the three design scenarios simultaneously.

Open a design study in the Autodesk CFD Environment.

In this task, you will open a design study and review the difference between the three designs.

1. Launch Autodesk CFD, if not already running.

2. In the Home, tab click ⬚ (Open). If prompted to save an open design study, click Yes.

3. In the Open dialog box, browse to the *C:\Autodesk CFD 2017 Essentials Exercise Files\Solver\ControlValve_Solver* folder. Select and open *ControlValve_Solver.cfdst*. The model displays as shown in the following image.

- Note that the materials, boundary conditions, and mesh have been applied to the designs.
- Note that three designs have been created: Cage 1, Cage 2 and Cage 3. Each have a slightly different CAD model for the cage design and contain a single scenario.

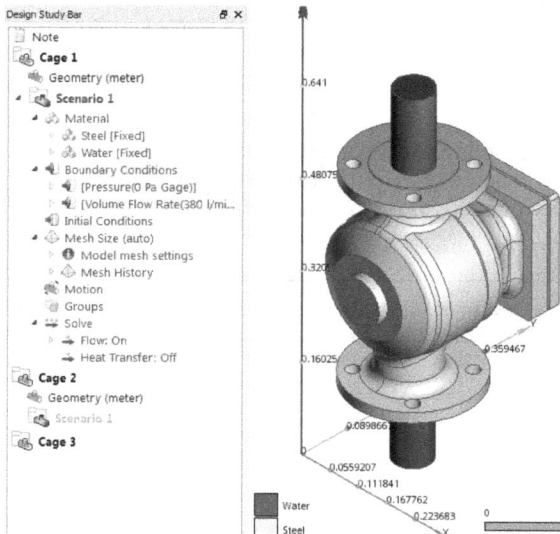

4. Note that in the Design Study Bar, Cage 1>Scenario 1 is active. Hold <Ctrl> and press the middle mouse button on the valve casing and the internal flow volume to expose the cage and valve stem, as shown in the following image.

   - Note that the cage has only four openings.
   - Review the Solve node in the Design Study Bar and note that the default Solve setting for Flow is On and for Heat Transfer is Off. These default settings are appropriate for this analysis, as heat transfer is not of concern.

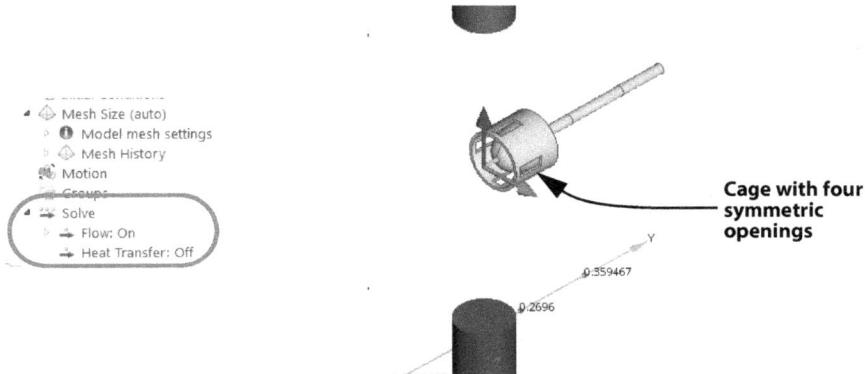

Cage with four symmetric openings

5. Hold <Ctrl> and press the middle mouse button anywhere on the screen to display the hidden objects.

6. In the Design Study Bar, expand Cage 2 if required, and double-click on Scenario 1 to activate it.

7. Hold <Ctrl> and press the middle mouse button on the valve casing and the internal flow volume to expose the cage and valve stem, as shown in the following image.

   - Note that this cage has 24 openings.
   - Ensure that the Solve setting for Flow is On and for Heat Transfer is Off.

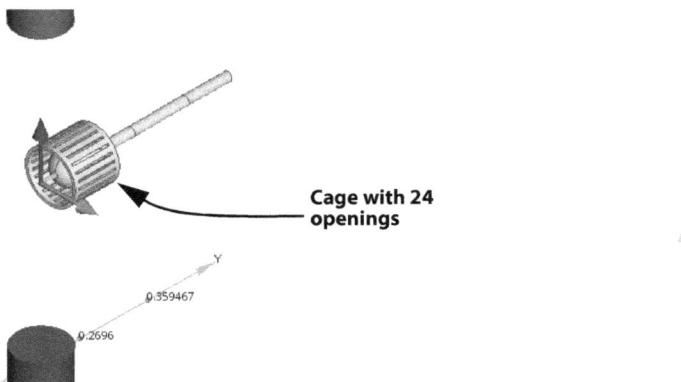

Cage with 24 openings

8. Hold <Ctrl> and press the middle mouse button anywhere on the screen to display the hidden objects.

9. In the Design Study Bar, expand Cage 3 if required, and double-click on Scenario 1 to activate it.

10. Hold <Ctrl> and press the middle mouse button on the valve casing and the internal flow volume to expose the cage and valve stem, as shown in the following image.

   ▪ Note that this cage also has 24 openings.
   ▪ Ensure that the Solve setting for Flow is On and for Heat Transfer is Off.

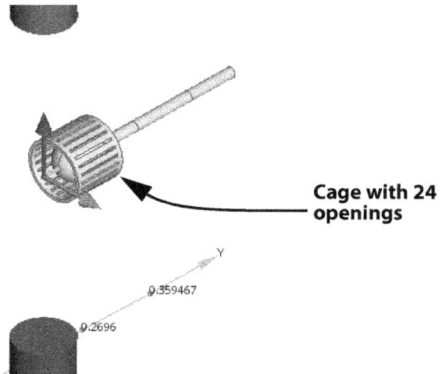

Cage with 24 openings

11. Zoom in and rotate the model. Note that the cage has different sized openings, as shown in the following image.

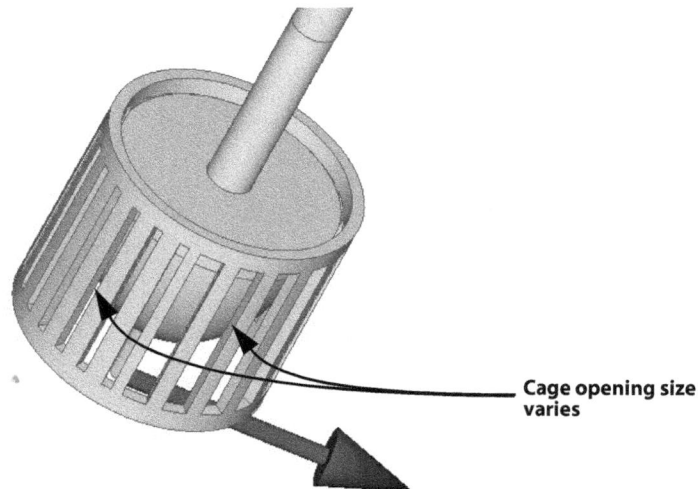

Cage opening size varies

12. Return to the Home orientation, hold <Ctrl>, and press the middle mouse button anywhere on the screen to display the hidden objects.

13. In the Design Study Bar, in the Cage 1 node, double-click on Scenario 1 to activate it.

Clone a Design Study and change a Model in the Design.

In this task, you will clone one of the design studies and replace the cage model with a fourth design to investigate its effect on the analysis. Note that this was the process for creating the three design studies provided when you initially opened the study.

1. In the Design Study Bar, right-click on the Cage 1 design study and select Clone.

    -   In the Clone Design dialog box, in the Design name field, enter **Cage 4**, as shown in the following image.
    -   Leave Include mesh and results unselected.
    -   Click OK.

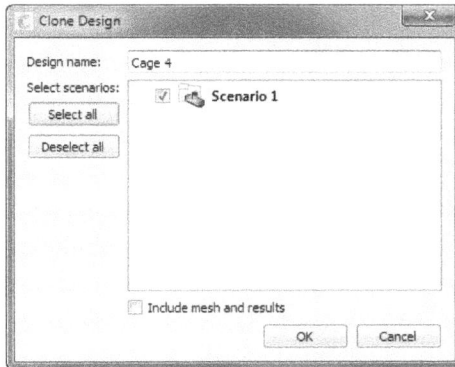

2. Note that the materials and boundary conditions are copied into the Cage 4 design, as shown in the following image.

    -   Hold <Ctrl> and press the middle mouse button on the valve casing and the internal flow volume to expose the cage and valve stem. As a clone of Cage 1, the design model in this new design is same and contains four symmetric openings.

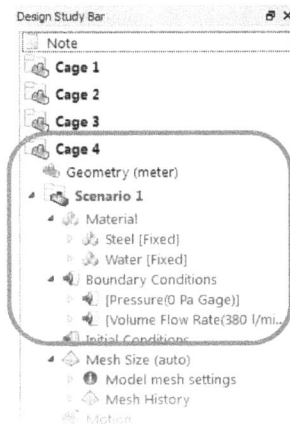

3. Launch Autodesk SimStudio Tools, if not already running.

4. In the Home tab, click (Open).

5. In the Open dialog box, browse to the *C:\Autodesk CFD 2017 Essentials Exercise Files\Solver\ ControlValve_Solver* folder. Select and open *ControlValve.SimStudio*. The model displays as shown in the following image.

  - Cage 1 is being used in the model while Cage 2, Cage 3 and Cage 4 are all suppressed.

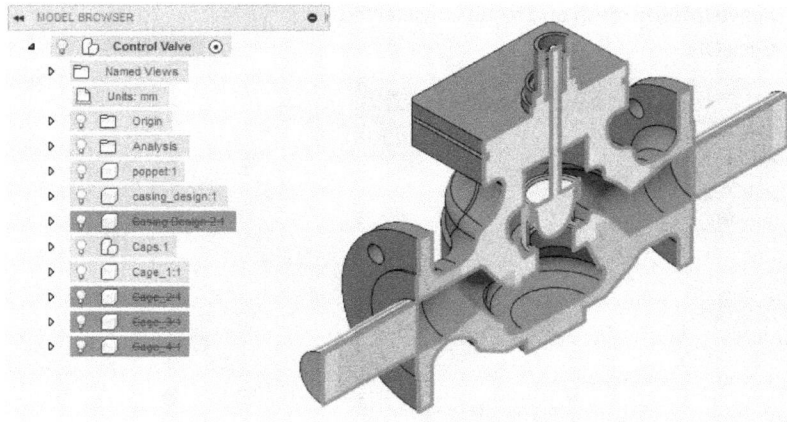

6. Switch the cage design.

  - In the MODEL BROWSER, right-click on Cage_1:1 and select Suppress.
  - Right-click on Cage_4:1 and select UnSuppress.
  - The model should update as shown in the following image.

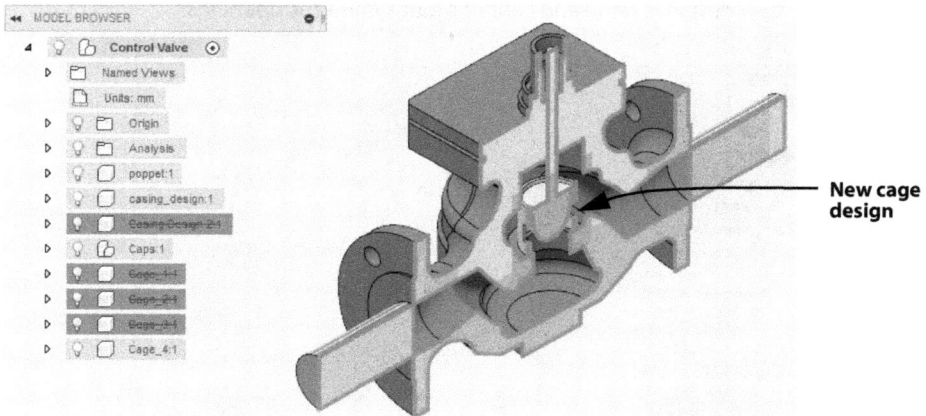

New cage design

7. Review the new cage design.

   - In the MODEL BROWSER, click adjacent to Analysis to hide it.
   - Right-click on Cage 4:1 and select Isolate.
   - Zoom in and reorient the model to review the offset openings in the cage, as shown in the following image.
   - After reviewing the cage, right-click on Cage 4:1 and select Undo Isolate.

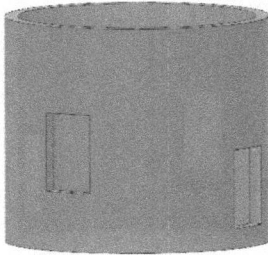

8. Expand the ADD-INS panel and select Simulate in CFD.

9. In the Design Study Manager, select the Update design study tab, as shown in the following image.

   - In the Design study list, expand ControlValve_Solver.
   - Select Cage 4.
   - Click Update design to replace the model in the Cage 4 design study with this revised model.

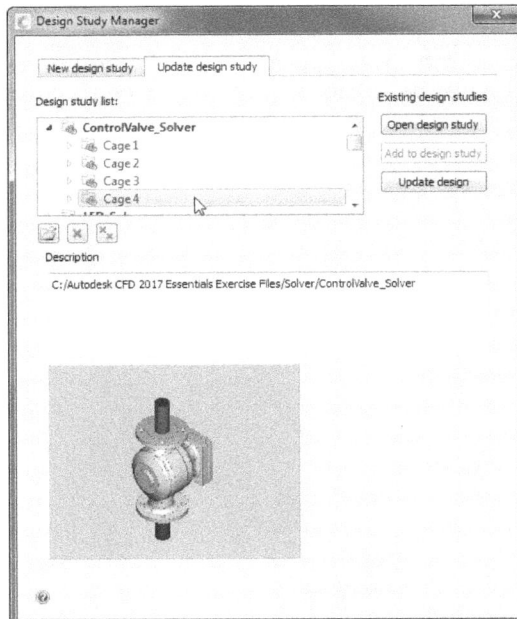

10. Return to the Autodesk CFD window. It will take several seconds to update the design.

11. In the Design Study Bar, in the Scenario 1>Material node, expand Steel (Fixed).

- Note that Cage 4 has been substituted, as shown in the following image.
- Hold <Ctrl> and press the middle mouse button on the valve casing and the internal flow volume to expose the cage and valve stem. Review the offset openings in the cage.
- The steel materials were suppressed in the original design study so that they would not be meshed. That setting is carried forward to the cloned design study.
- Return all components to the display before continuing.

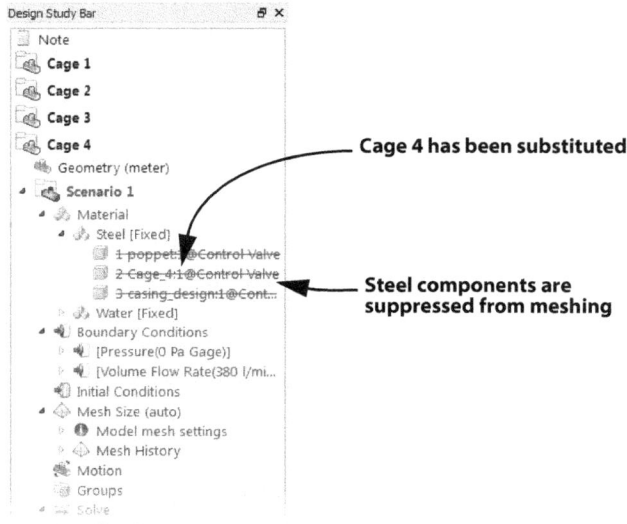

Cage 4 has been substituted

Steel components are suppressed from meshing

Note: After cloning, ensure that your settings are applied correctly for the new design. In cases where geometry is changed, there may be settings applied to the wrong surfaces or volumes.

Apply the solver settings for this design, and run the Solver.

In this task, you will apply the solver settings to ensure the analysis results are as required.

1. Right click in the graphics window and select Solve. The Solve dialog box displays as shown in the following image.

   - Alternatively, in the Setup tab, in the Simulation panel, click ⇨ (Solve).
   - Note that the Solution Mode is set to Steady State and the Iterations to Run are set to 300. These options are acceptable for this analysis.

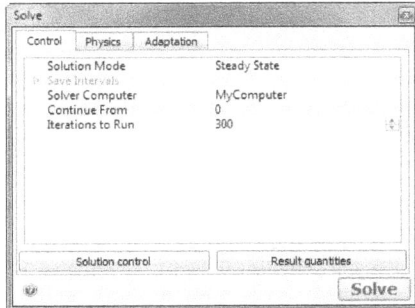

2. Select the Physics tab and ensure that only Flow is selected, as shown in the following image.

   - Ensure that the Compressibility is set to Incompressible.

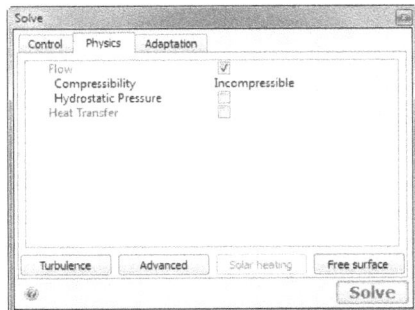

3. Click Solve to run the analysis. Note that this is only solving the Cage 4 design study.

4. The solver begins solving the Cage 4 design. Expand the Output Bar, if not already expanded. Note the convergence plot on the Convergence Plot tab. It will display similar to that shown for Iteration #150 in the following image.

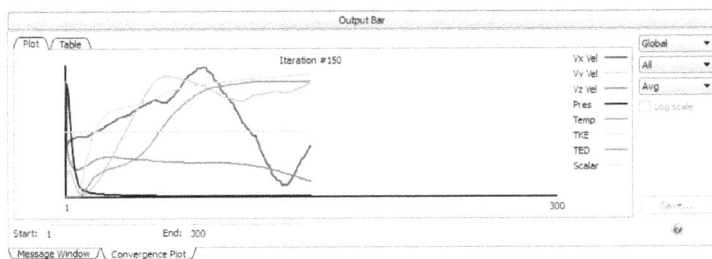

5. The completed convergence plot displays, as shown in the following image.

   ▪ Note that the analysis did not satisfy the criteria for automatic convergence. This is because it considers all variables. In this case, the system stops when the number of iterations is reached.

   ▪ You can generally consider an analysis converged when the change in values approaches zero with each iteration. For example, in the following image, the pressure could be considered converged, as it is no longer changing with each iteration.

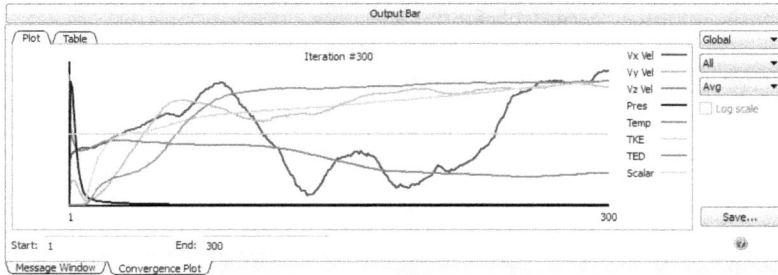

   ▪ Identify the Vx (blue) and Vy (green) variables in the plot. Based on the plot, it appears that this values are changing significantly. These are not dominant flow directions for this analysis so the variation in values is acceptable. The dominant flow in Vz (magenta).

   ▪ Select the Table tab in the Output Bar to display the actual values for the variables, as shown in the following image. The plot view provides a normalized view of the values; however, table view provides actual values which can be useful when reviewing for convergence.

   ▪ Scroll to the top of the table and identify the Vz variable column. This is the dominate flow direction. In the last ten iterations, Vz has been varying by approximately .5%. Depending on the design requirements, this may/may not be enough to conclude convergence.

Analyze three designs using the Solver Manager.

Each design could be analyzed individually by simply selecting Solve in the Solve dialog box. In this task, you will use the Solver Manager to analyze all scenarios in each of the designs at the same time.

1. Right-click in the graphics window and select Solver manager to open the Solver Manager dialog box, as shown in the following image.

    - Alternatively, in the Setup tab, in the Simulation panel, click ⊞ (Solver Manager).
    - Note how the Cage 4 scenario is listed. It shows that 300 iterations have already been run on it.

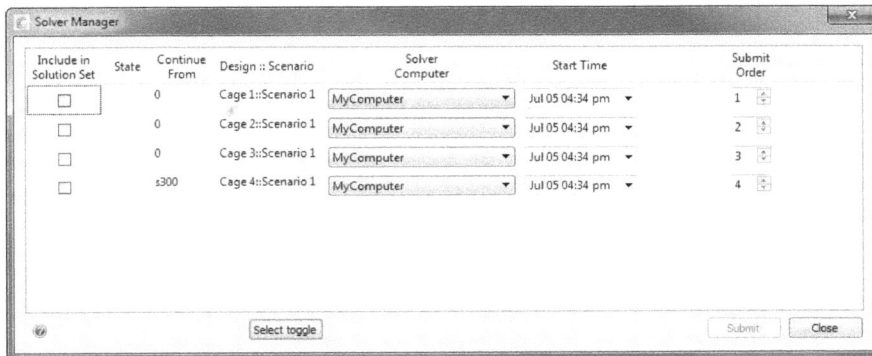

2. In the Solver Manager, select the first three design scenarios for inclusion in the solution set, as shown in the following image.

    - Click Submit.
    - Note that you could change the solver computer to Cloud to reduce runtime by solving in parallel.

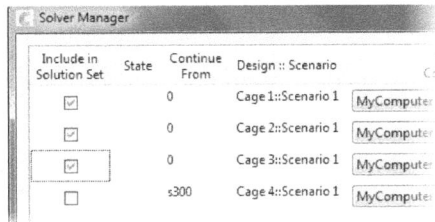

3. The solver begins solving the first design. Because it is not the active Scenario, you must activate it to view its progress. Expand the Cage 1 design, if required, and double-click on Scenario 1 to activate it.

4. Expand the Output Bar, if not already expanded, and display the Plot tab. It will display similar to that shown for Iteration #67 in the following image.

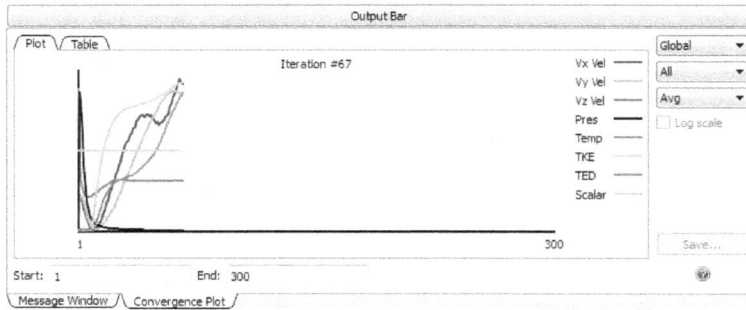

5. In the Design Study Bar, activate Scenario 1 for the Cage 2 design and note that the analysis for it has not started its iterations.

    ▪ You can switch between designs while the analysis is running.

6. In the Design Study Bar, activate Scenario 1 for the Cage 1 design.

    ▪ The convergence plot should be closer to convergence, as shown in the following image.

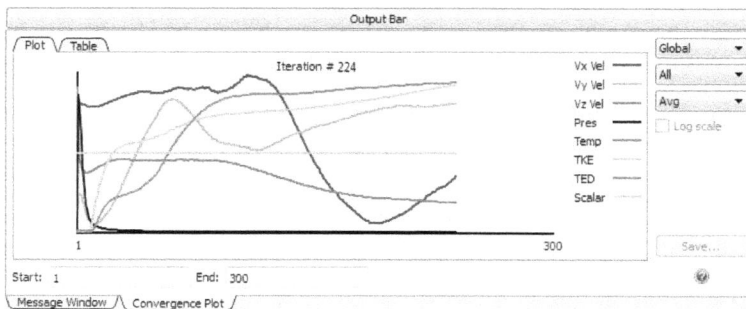

Tip: If Autodesk CFD crashes, the software will stop running; however, the solver is a separate process so it will continue to run. Launch Autodesk CFD and reopen the file to see that the solver has continued running.

7. Select the Setup tab in the ribbon, and in the Simulation panel, click ▦ (Job Monitor).

    - The Job Monitor dialog lists the status of each analysis, similar to that shown in the following image.
    - The current analysis will show the current iteration.
    - Analyses that have not yet started will be listed as "Queued"

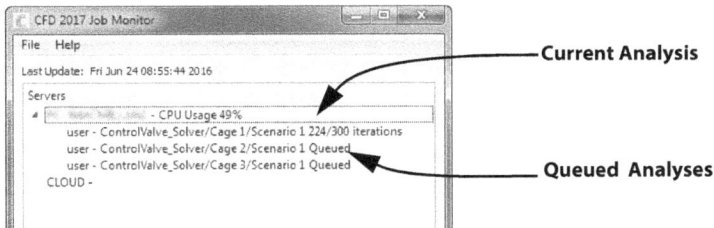

8. Continue to review the remaining scenarios as they are solved.

    - Note that it will take some time before all 3 scenarios are solved (300 iterations each).
    - As each scenario is solved, note that the icons adjacent to the Scenario node display as

      🗀 while running and 🗀 when solved.

    - Allow the analyses to complete or consider the following tip.
    - The completed convergence plot for Scenario 1 for the Cage 3 design is shown in the following image.

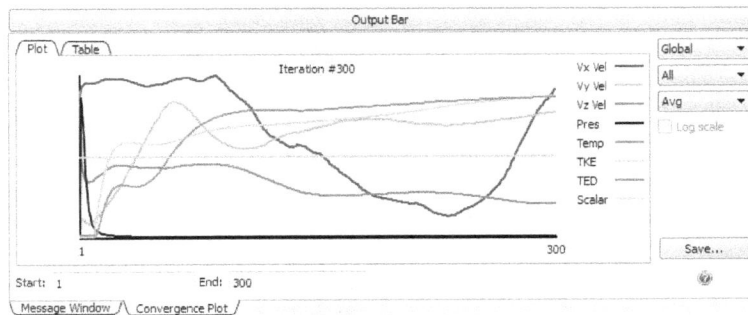

Tip: Once an analysis has started running, it may take some time to complete. To terminate an analysis while it is running, use either of the following methods:

    - In the Setup tab, in the Simulation panel, click Job Manager (if not already open). Once the Job Manager displays, right-click on the current job and select Stop Job.
    - Right-click in the graphics window and select Solve. In the Solve dialog box click Stop.

    All iterations are saved up to the point of stopping an analysis. Completed result files are provided for you in the next chapter so it is not necessary to let all analyses fully run.

9. Once the analysis for all three scenarios is complete or you have stopped them from finishing,

    click 🖫 (Save) in the Quick Access toolbar to save the study. In the next chapter, you will visualize and investigate the results of the analyses.

Exercise: Run an Analysis for Natural Convection

In this exercise, you will open an existing design study that has two designs for an LED light. Each design has a different number of fins on the heat sink. The objectives in this exercise are to:

- Apply Solver settings to account for heat transfer.
- Solve for convective flow and heat transfer.

Open a design study in the Autodesk CFD Environment.

In this task, you will open a design study and review the difference between the three designs.

1. Launch Autodesk CFD, if not already running.

2. In the Home tab, click [icon] (Open). If prompted to save an open design study, click Yes.

3. In the Open dialog box, browse to the *C:\Autodesk CFD 2017 Essentials Exercise Files\Solver\ LED_Solver* folder. Select and open *LED_Solver.cfdst*. The model displays as shown in the following image.

   - Note that the materials, boundary conditions, and mesh have been applied to the designs.
   - Note that two designs have been created: 24 fins and 36 fins. Each use a slightly different CAD model for the number of fins on the heat sink and contain a single scenario.

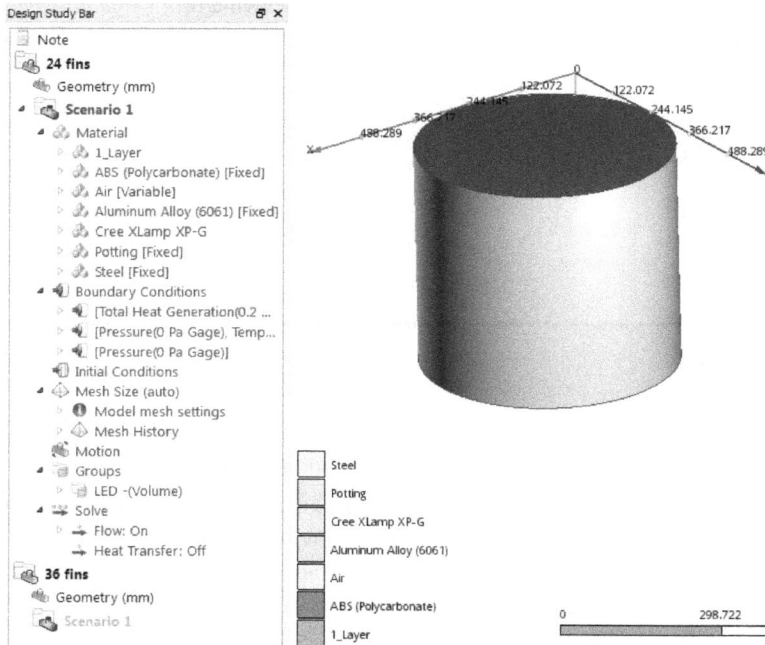

4. Note that in the Design Study Bar, 24 fins>Scenario 1 is active. Hold <Ctrl> and press the middle mouse button on the external air volume and both sides of the cannister to expose the heat sink, as shown in the following image.

    ▪ Note that the heat sink has 24 fins.

    ▪ Review the Solve node in the Design Study Bar and note that the default Solve setting for Flow is On and Heat Transfer is Off. You will have to change these settings in a later task to account for convective heat transfer.

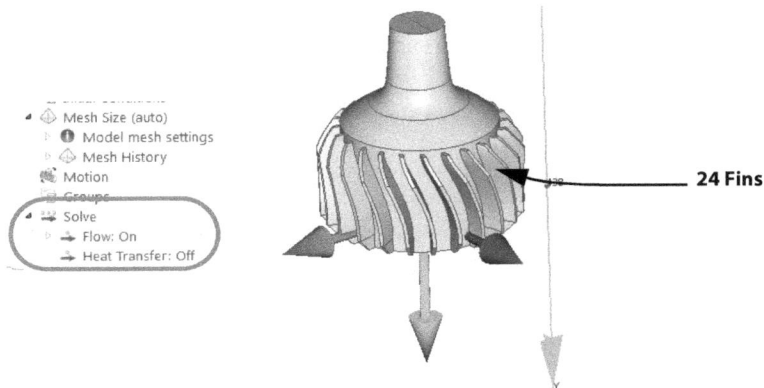

24 Fins

5. Hold <Ctrl> and press the middle mouse button anywhere on the screen to display the hidden objects. Zoom out to see the entire model.

6. In the Design Study Bar, expand 36 fins if required, and double-click on Scenario 1 to activate it.

7. Hold <Ctrl> and press the middle mouse button on the external air volume and both sides of the cannister to expose the heat sink, as shown in the following image.

    ▪ Note that this heat sink has 36 fins.

    ▪ Ensure that Flow is On and Heat Transfer is Off.

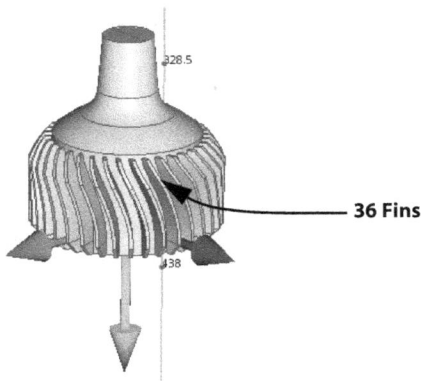

36 Fins

8. Hold <Ctrl> and press the middle mouse button anywhere on the screen to display the hidden objects. Zoom out to see the entire model.

9. In the Design Study Bar, in the 24 fins node, double-click on Scenario 1 to activate it.

Apply the Solver Settings.

The materials, boundary conditions and mesh have already been defined in this model. In this task, you will apply the solver settings. The analysis must account for convective heat transfer.

1. In the Quick Access Toolbar, expand ☐ (Visual Style) and select Transparent. The model displays as shown in the following image.

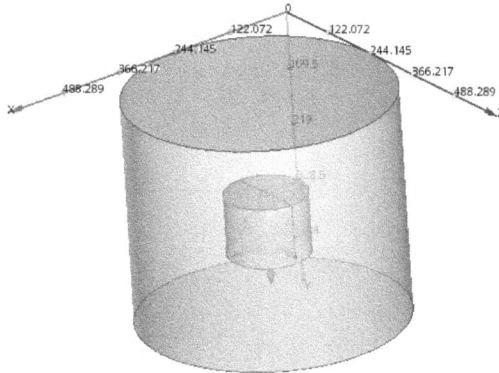

2. Right-click in the graphics window and select Solve. The Solve dialog box displays as shown in the following image.

- Alternatively, in the Setup tab, in the Simulation panel, click ⇨ (Solve).
- Note that the Solution Mode is set to Steady State.
- Change the Iterations to Run from 200 to **300** to help ensure it reaches convergence.

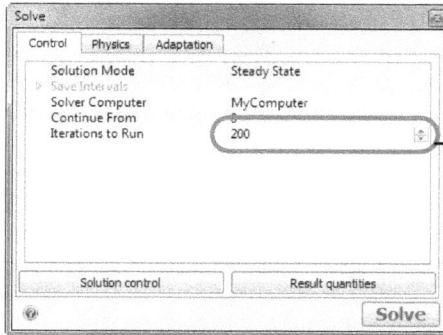

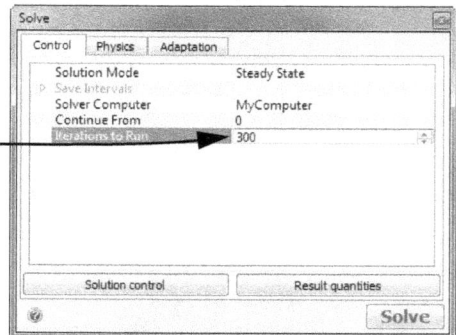

3. Select the Physics tab.

   - Note that Flow is selected and the Compressibility is set to Incompressible.
   - Select Heat Transfer. The settings expand as shown in the following image.

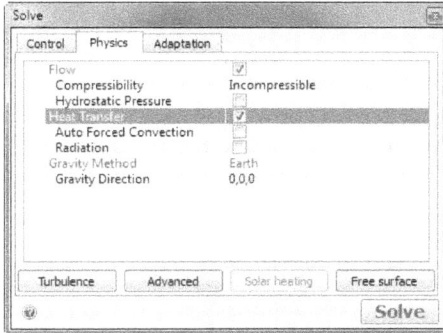

4. You want to account for the natural convection that will occur as the LEDs heat up. This will require flow and heat transfer to be run at the same time and gravity to be applied.

   - The Gravity Method defaults to Earth, which is correct for this analysis.
   - Note that the direction of gravity would be in the positive Y direction, since the current orientation is how the LED would be installed in a ceiling. Edit the Gravity Direction field to be **0, 1, 0** (these are the directions gravity pulls in the X,Y, and Z axes).

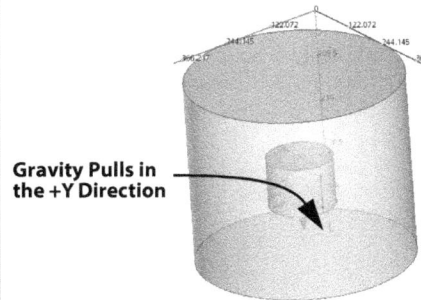

Gravity Pulls in the +Y Direction

5. Do not click Solve, as that would solve only this design. In the next task, you will solve both designs at the same time.

   - Close the Solve dialog box by selecting [icon] in the top right-hand corner.

6. In the Design Study Bar, in the Solve node, expand the Heat Transfer: On node, if not already expanded.

   - Note that Gravity is set to 0,1,0 and Radiation is set to Off, as shown in the following image.

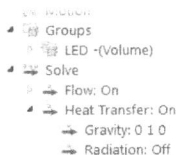

7. In the Design Study Bar, in the 36 fin node, double-click ON Scenario 1 to activate it.

    ■   Right-click in the graphics window, and select Solve.
    ■   Repeat Steps 2 through 5 from the previous task to apply the heat transfer settings. Once complete, close the Solve dialog box.

Analyze both designs.

In this task, you will use the Solver Manager to analyze the scenarios in each of the designs at once.

1. Right-click in the graphics window and select Solver manager to open the Solver Manager dialog box, as shown in the following image.

    ■   Alternatively, in the Setup tab, in the Simulation panel, click ▦ (Solver Manager).

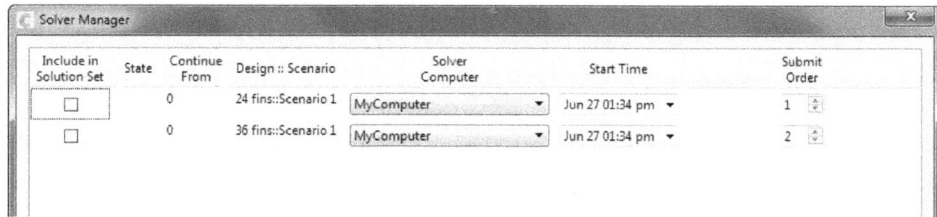

2. In the Solver Manager, click Select toggle at the bottom of the Solver Manager dialog box and click Submit.

3. In the Design Study Bar, in the 24 fins node, double-click on Scenario 1 to activate it.

4. The solver begins solving the first design. Expand the Output Bar, if not already expanded. Note the convergence plot in the Convergence Plot tab. It will appear similar to that shown for Iteration #87 in the following image.

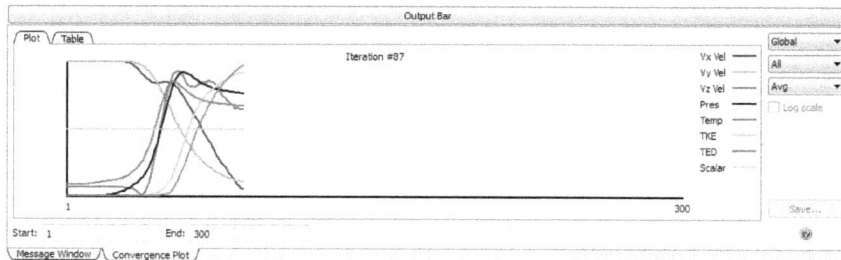

5. Note that as the analysis continues, the model display dynamically updates to provide a visual representation of the values, as shown in the following image. The Visualization tools topic will be discussed in more detail in the next chapter.

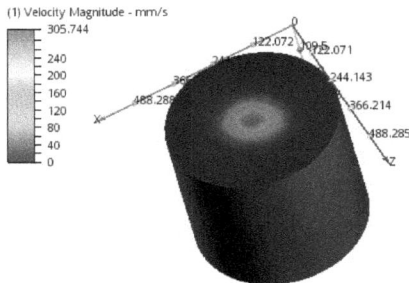

6. This may take some time to complete. Allow both analyses to complete or consider the following tip. The resulting Convergence Plots display as shown in the fowling image.

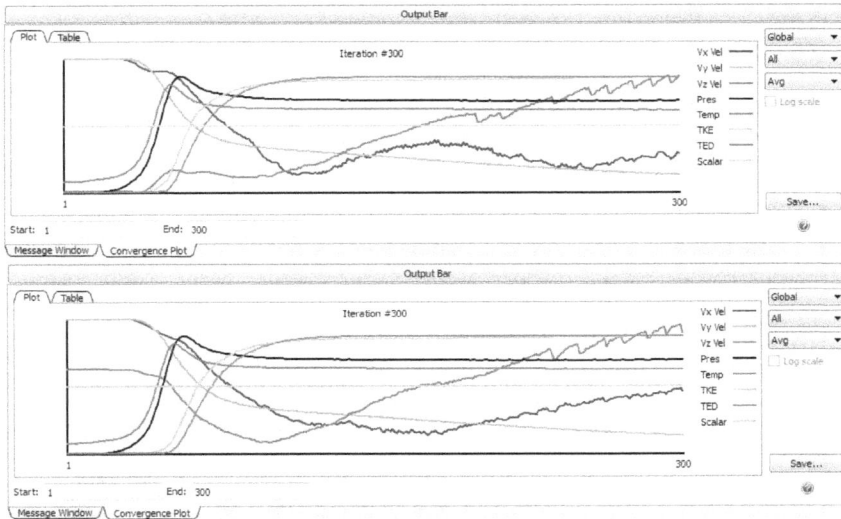

Tip: Once an analysis has started running, it may take some time to complete. To terminate an analysis while it is running, use either of the following methods:

- In the Setup tab, in the Simulation panel, click Job Manager. Once the Job Manager displays, right-click on the current job and select Stop Job.
- Right-click in the graphics window and select Solve. In the Solve dialog box, click Stop.

All iterations are saved up to the point where the analysis is stopped. Completed result files are provided for you in the next chapter so it is not necessary to let all analyses fully run.

7. Once the analysis for both scenarios is complete or you have stopped them from finishing, click 🖫 (Save) in the Quick Access toolbar to save the study. In the next chapter, you will visualize and investigate the results of these analyses.

Exercise: Run an Analysis for Forced Convection and Radiation

In this exercise, you will open an existing design study for a small office lobby. The office has windows and walls that are subject to external conditions, while the interior has air conditioning. The objectives in this exercise are to:

- Apply Solver settings to account for heat transfer and radiation.
- Apply solver settings to account for solar heating.
- Solve the analysis.

Open a design study in the Autodesk CFD Environment.

In this task, you will open a design study and review the current setup.

1. Launch Autodesk CFD, if not already running.

2. In the Home tab, click ⌷ (Open). If prompted to save an open design study, click Yes.

3. In the Open dialog box, browse to the *C:\Autodesk CFD 2017 Essentials Exercise Files\Solver\ OfficeLobby_Solver* folder. Select and open *OfficeLobby_Solver.cfdst*.

4. In the Quick Access Toolbar, expand ⌷ (Visual Style) and select Transparent. The model displays as shown in the following image.

    - Note that the materials, boundary conditions, and mesh have been applied to the designs.
    - Note the internal objects such as the mezzanine, occupants, furniture, etc.
    - Note that a single design with a single scenario has been setup.

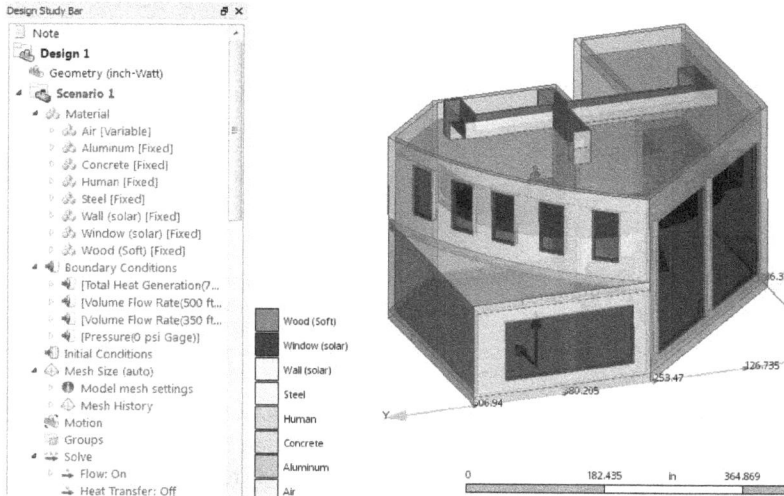

Apply the Solver Settings.

Once the materials, boundary conditions, and mesh have been defined, you can apply the solver settings. The analysis must account for heat transfer and solar energy.

1. Right-click in the graphics window and select Solve. The Solve dialog box displays as shown in the following image.

    - Note that the Solution Mode is set to Steady State.
    - Edit the Iterations to Run from 200 to 500 to help ensure it reaches convergence.

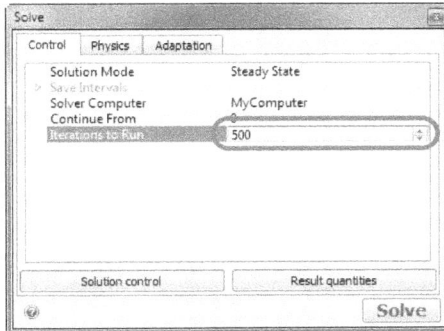

2. Select the Physics tab and note that Flow is selected and the Compressibility is set to Incompressible. Make the following edits in the dialog box:

    - Select Heat Transfer.
    - Select Radiation to account for radiant heat loss and gain.
        - **Note:** If you do not have the advanced solver license, do not add radiation. Skip directly to the next task, *Analyze the design.*
    - Set the Gravity Direction to be in the negative Z direction by entering 0,0, -1 as the Gravity Direction value.
    - The Solve dialog box should display as shown in the following image.

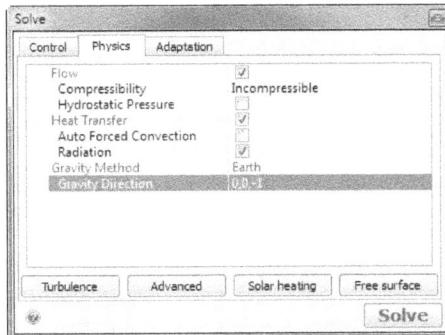

3.   You need to account for the effects of solar energy. In the Solve dialog box, click Solar heating.

■   The Solar Heating dialog box opens as shown in the following image.

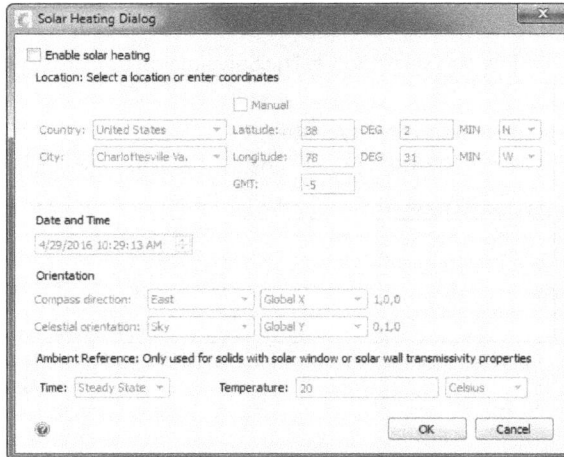

4.   Click the Enable solar heating option.

■   Accept the default location as United States and Default City as Charlottesville, Va.
■   Set the Compass direction as East, Global -X.
■   Set the Celestial orientation as Sky, Global Z.
■   Set the Temperature to 70 Fahrenheit.
■   The Solar Heating dialog box should display as shown in the following image.
■   Click OK to set the values.

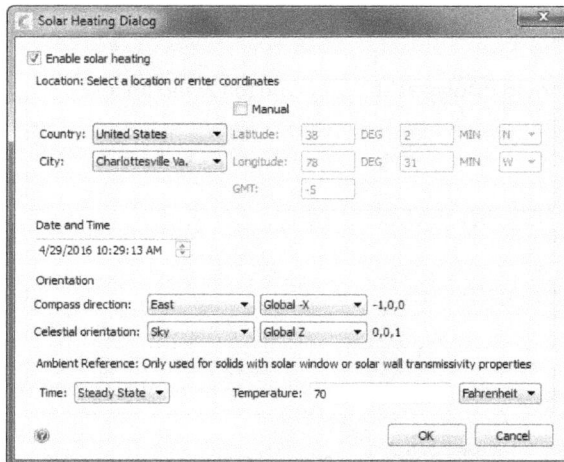

Analyze the design.

In this task, you will analyze the scenario.

1. In the Solve dialog box, click Solve.

   - **Note:** If an error message, as shown in the following image, opens indicating that you do not have the proper level of licensing for running radiation models, you must correct this to continue the analysis. Open the Solar Heating dialog box and disable solar heating. Additionally, un-check the radiation checkbox in the Solver dialog box. The results going forward will vary from the rest of this guide.

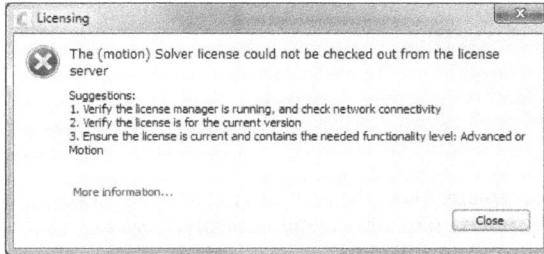

2. The solver begins solving the design. Expand the Output Bar, if not already expanded. Note the convergence plot in the Convergence Plot tab. It will display similar to that shown for Iteration #111 in the following image.

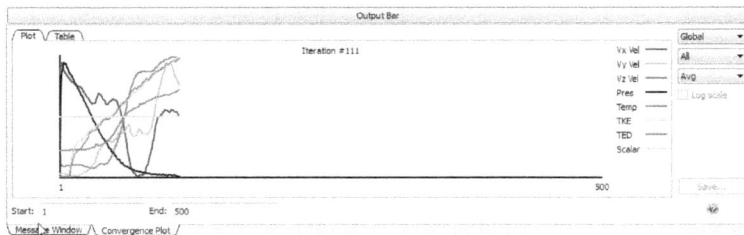

3. In the Quick Access Toolbar, expand (Visual Style) and select Transparent.

4. In the Results tab, in the Global panel, in the Global Result drop-down list, select Temperature. The global result options are discussed in more detail in the next chapter.

    ▪ The temperature gradient throughout the model continuously updates as the analysis runs, as shown in the following image.

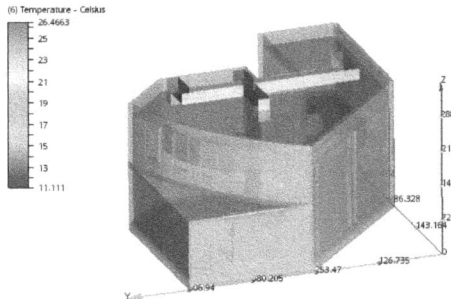

5. This may take some time to complete. Allow the analyses to complete or consider the following tip. The plot, which shows up to 500 iterations, displays as shown in the following image. Because we have buoyant flow and radiation, this model has still not reached convergence after 500 iterations.

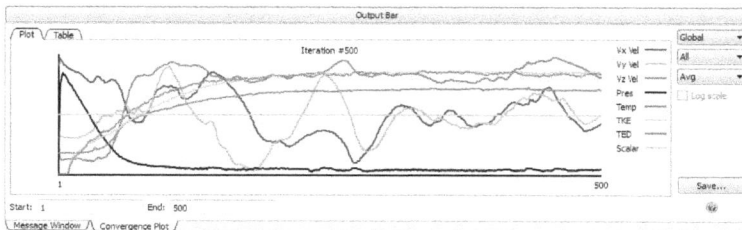

Tip: Once an analysis has started running, it may take some time to complete. To terminate an analysis while it is running, use either of the following methods:

    ▪ In the Setup tab, in the Simulation panel, click Job Manager. Once the Job Manager displays, right-click on the current job and select Stop Job.

    ▪ Right-click in the graphics window and select Solve. In the Solve dialog box, click Stop.

    All iterations are saved up to the point of stopping an analysis. Completed result files are provided for you in the next chapter so it is not necessary to let the analysis fully run.

6. Once the analysis is complete or you have stopped it from finishing, click 🖫 (Save) in the Quick Access toolbar to save the study. The design has been analyzed. In the next chapter, you will visualize and investigate the results of the analysis.

Results Visualization & Interpretation

Once a design study is setup and solved, you are ready to visualize and extract any required results data to ensure that the model meets the design requirements. Autodesk® CFD has various different tools that are available to review your results, create reports, and share the data with other stakeholders. In this chapter, you will learn how to create visually appealing and useful result views and extract result values. You will also learn how you can use the Decision Center tool to easily compare identical result views and values in multiple designs and scenarios.

Objectives

After completing this chapter, you will be able to:

- Identify the Result Tasks that can be used to visually represent results.
- Identify the Result Tasks that can be used to extract result values.
- Describe the tools that enable you to share results, images, and animations with stakeholders not using the Autodesk CFD software.
- Set the global result and global vector settings.
- Create a results plane and position it interactively in the model.
- Modify the result and vector setting on the results plane.
- Manipulate the display of the plane in the model.
- Use Bulk Calculator to quickly calculate and show bulk-weighted results on a results plane.
- Create an XY Plot on a results plane.
- Define the 2D seed distribution settings that will form the foundation from which the traces will extend.
- Create a trace set on a reference surface.

- Modify a trace set.
- Animate a trace set to visually represent the flow path of the trace particles.
- Create an iso surface and iso volume.
- Review a created iso surface and iso volume and interpret its results.
- Change the appearance and displayed result quantity for a created iso surface or iso volume.
- Select surfaces that are to be used as references during wall calculations.
- Use the Wall Calculator result tool to generate a report on selected flow-induced forces on solid and wall surfaces.
- Review and save the results of the Wall Calculator tool.
- Use the Parts result task functionality to report on the temperature of selected components.
- Use the Points result task functionality to create points in the model.
- Create a plot that shows the result type as a function of time/iteration history.
- Create summary objects for later design comparison using Decision Center.
- Access the Decision Center environment.
- Update all summary objects to propagate the data across all scenarios.
- Review all summary objects using the tools in the Decision Center environment.

Lesson: Visualizing Your Results

The visualization tools in Autodesk CFD enable you easily view, extract, and present analysis results once a simulation is setup and run. In this lesson, you will be introduced to the tools that can be used to visually display the results and to extract result values for explicit comparison. These tools will be taught in depth throughout the remainder of this chapter.

Objectives

After completing this lesson, you will be able to:

- Identify the Result Tasks that can be used to visually represent results.
- Identify the Result Tasks that can be used to extract result values.
- Describe the tools that enable you to share results, images, and animations with stakeholders not using the Autodesk CFD software.

Visualization Tools

Overview

Autodesk CFD has a powerful set of results visualization tools to help view, extract, and present analysis results quickly, easily, and efficiently. This includes a graphical, CAD-like set of tools and several ways to output graphical images and data, which make communicating analysis results with other members of the design supply chain very easy.

The full suite of visualization tools is available while the scenario is running and after completion, to provide constant graphical feedback on the analysis. This powerful run-time environment is extremely helpful for understanding the progression of the solution.

The followings images show some of the results views that can be created to help you visualize the design.

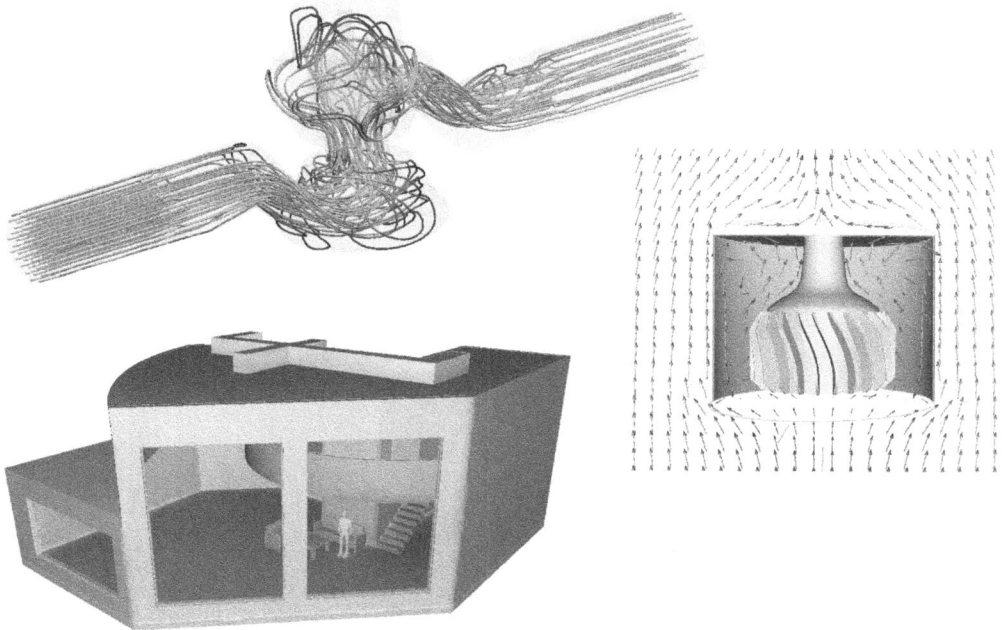

Workflow

The following are the two primary goals in analyzing the results of a simulation.

- Visualize Results
- Extract Results Values

The Autodesk CFD results tasks provide access to the tools that enable you to accomplish both of these goals. Unlike many tools, how you visualize and extract the results is not a sequential procedure. The requirement for result views and/or result value reports is dependent on the design and what is being studied. The visualization tools are available on the Results tab, as shown in the following image.

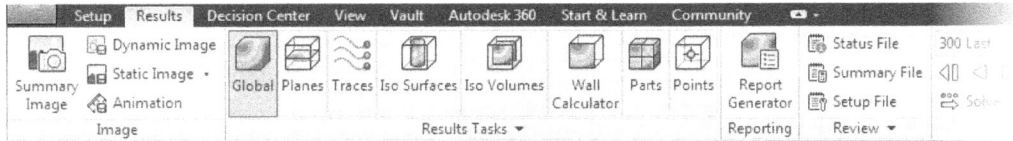

The Planes, Traces, Iso Surfaces, and Iso Volumes result tasks can be used to create visual results. To extract specific values, consider using the Wall Calculator, Parts and Points tools.

Image panel

The Image panel is a key panel available as you create all of the result views that hep you visualize your simulation. The main command in this panel enables you to create Summary Images of your result views. This, in conjunction with the use of the Decision Center, enables you to quickly create a similar result in each design study scenario to easily compare the results of multiple designs and scenarios. The Decision Center is discussed in more depth later in this chapter.

The remaining options on the Image Panel provide tools for visualizing the results using other software tools. These tools enable you to do the following:

- Use the Dynamic Image option to create an image file that can be view using the Autodesk CFD Viewer. The dynamic image file (.VTFX), contains the model geometry, results, display attributes, and animation settings. They are fully navigable, so unlike static images, they allow direct interaction for a deeper understanding of the results.
- Use the Static Image and Set Resolution options to save an image of the current view. The available file types include GIF, TIF, BMP, and JPG.
- Use the Animate option to create an animation of the saved analysis intervals.

Results Tasks panel

The items listed in the Results Tasks panels are used to visualize the simulation results. Unlike the Setup Tasks that were previously discussed, there is no recommended work flow sequence. The tools are arranged from left to right in the order that most users access them. As each tool is selected for use in creating visualization results, an associated context menu is added to the ribbon that provides the required tools. The options in the Results Tasks panel and their associated context panels are discussed in more depth in the upcoming lessons.

Reporting panel

The Report Generator tools can be used once the simulation is complete and all required result views are created. It enables you to compile required information into a Microsoft® Word document to easily share the results. For more information on how to create a report, search for "Report Generator" in the online Help documentation.

Review panel

All data generated during the execution of the analysis can be reviewed using the options in the Review panel. The following are the three most commonly used options for reviewing the data:

- **Status File:** Enables you to review the startup and progress messages, iteration residuals, and error messages that are recorded during the analysis.
- **Summary File:** Enables you to review and save the completed results data. This file also contains details of the mesh count.
- **Setup File:** Enables you to review and save a complete list of the model parameters that were used in setup of the design.

Component Display

During the visualization step, the component display settings can be customized, as required, to best show a result. In some cases, the component display is automatically set for you when a result view is created.

The visibility, transparency, and color of components (including suppressed components) can always be changed, as required.

Lesson: Global Results

The Global option in the Results tab enables you to quickly assign the default result settings that will display as you use the various visualization tools to create result views. In this lesson, you will learn to set the global options.

Objectives

After completing this lesson, you will be able to:

- Set the global result and global vector settings.

Global Results and Vector Settings

Although the Global option in the Results Tasks panel does not explicitly create a result, it enables you to control the display of results on all model surfaces. The Global result task is the active task when the Results tab is selected. The Global context panel is also always available on the View tab. To control the global results, select (Global) in the Results Task panel. This activates its controls and displays the Global context menu, as shown in the following image.

The Global context panel contains useful controls for clear visualization on model surfaces that enable you to control how the results display. These are described as follows:

- **Global Result:** Select the scalar results quantity to display on all model surfaces. The available list of results is shown in the following images. To change the result quantity that displays on model surfaces, without having to use the Global context menu, right-click in the graphics window, expand Global result, and select the required result.

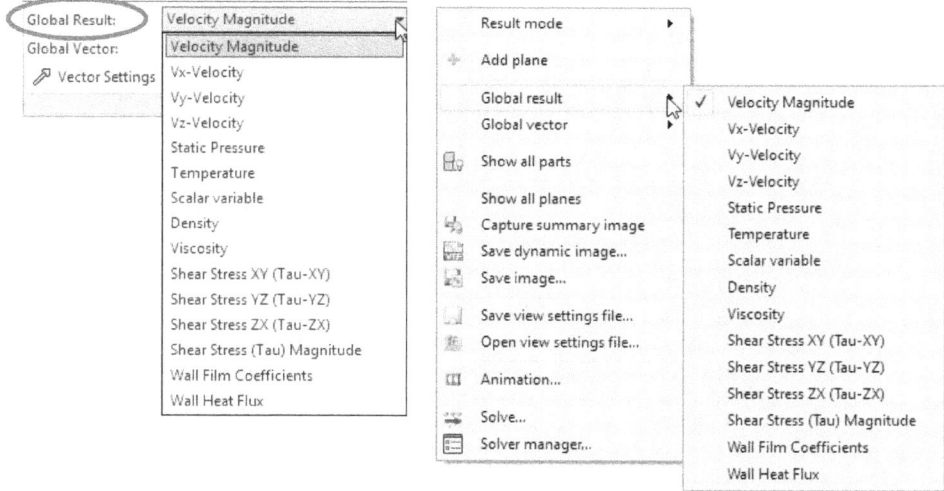

> The currently assigned global result is reflected in the Legend that displays in the top left-hand corner of the graphics window. This also sets the result quantity displayed in the Status Bar when probing with the mouse. (To probe, hover the cursor over the location of interest.) When different result variables are shown on different result tasks or objects, multiple legends will display.

■ **Global Vector:** Select the vector results quantity to display on all model surfaces. The available list of results is shown in the following image. The global vector can also be set using context menu, as shown on the right image. Global vectors display independently of the global result setting. A vector is not required and is generally used to verify flow direction.

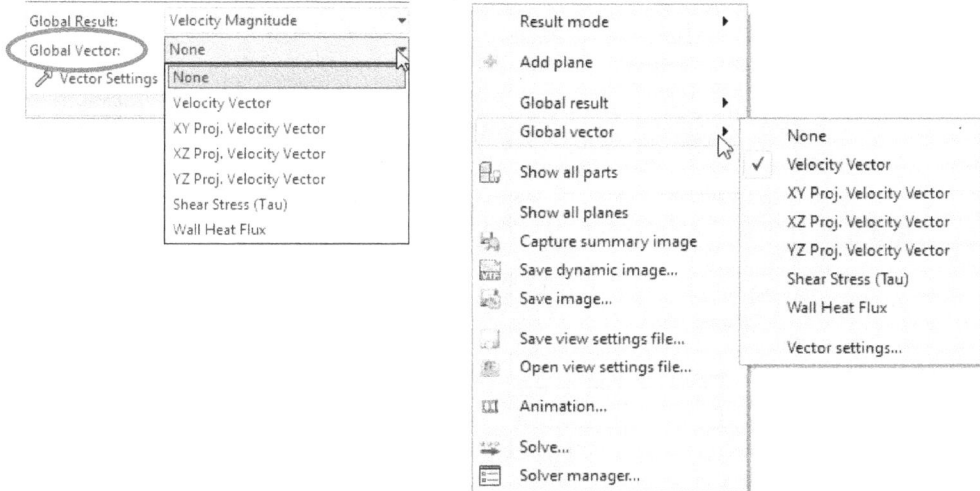

■ **Vector Settings:** Controls the appearance of global vectors throughout the model. If a global vector result has not been selected in the Global Vector drop-down list, select a vector results quantity directly in the Vector Settings dialog box. Vectors are generated with their tail at every mesh node on every surface. Although the quantity cannot be modified, the length slider can be used to modify the size of the arrows. Click More to display all vector options.

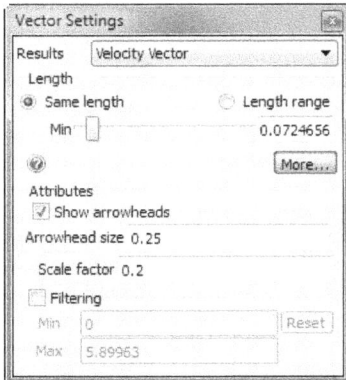

Once a result is selected, you can the change vector appearance for that result using any of the following options:

- To vary the vector length, use the Length area. By default, all vectors display with the Same length. To change the vector length, drag the Length slider, as required. To display vectors with lengths relative to the legend, click the Length range. Drag the Min and Max sliders to vary the range.
- To disable arrowheads, uncheck Show arrowheads.
- To change the size of vector arrows, specify a value for the Arrowhead size. The arrowhead size is scaled based on the vector length.
- To scale all vectors by the same amount, modify the value of the Scale factor.
- To show regions where the active vector is within a specified range, enable Filtering and enter a range in the Min and Max fields. Click Reset or clear the Filtering option to display the entire model.
- The current vector settings for the current CFD session will persist until changed. You can use the Planes, Iso Surfaces, and Iso Volumes result task context menu to specify the Vector settings.

> The Custom Result Quantities option is an advanced tool that enables you to create custom, derived result quantities to analyze and visualize quantities critical to your application. Equations are setup in the Custom Result Quantities dialog box. This advanced tool is not discussed in this student guide.

Lesson: Planes Result Task

In this lesson, you will learn how to use the Planes results task. This results task is the primary tool for visualizing data on three dimensional models. Planes provide a section view for easier visualization. They are also a starting point for the creation of XY Plots and the Bulk Calculator tool for graphical and tabular data. To compare the results between multiple designs and scenarios, you create summary planes and images that are reviewed in the Decision Center.

Objectives

After completing this lesson, you will be able to:

- Create a results plane and position it interactively in the model.
- Modify the result and vector setting on the results plane.
- Manipulate the display of the plane in the model.
- Use Bulk Calculator to quickly calculate and show bulk-weighted results on a results plane.
- Create an XY Plot on a results plane.
- Create summary objects for later design comparison using Decision Center.

Planes Result Task

Planes are the primary tool for visualizing data on three dimensional models. Planes provide a wide array of visualization functionality, including the following:

- Planes graphically present results on cross-sections.
- Planes enable the extraction of bulk data through planar cross sections.
- Planes serve as a basis for XY-plots.

To create a plane to visualize a result, select the (Planes) task in the Results Task panel. This activates the task and enables you to create a plane in the model. The Planes context menu displays as shown in the following image.

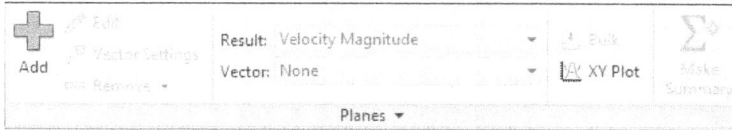

To create a plane, use any of the following three methods:

- In the Planes panel, click (Add).
- Right-click in the graphics window and select Add Plane.
- In the Design Study Bar, right-click on the Planes node and select Add Plane.

By default, a plane appears through the middle of the model in the ZY plane. To manipulate the plane, left-click on the plane to access the mini-toolbar (shown in the following image) or drag the triad that displays on the plane. In the following image, the Static Pressure result in the Global panel has been set and no vectors are being displayed.

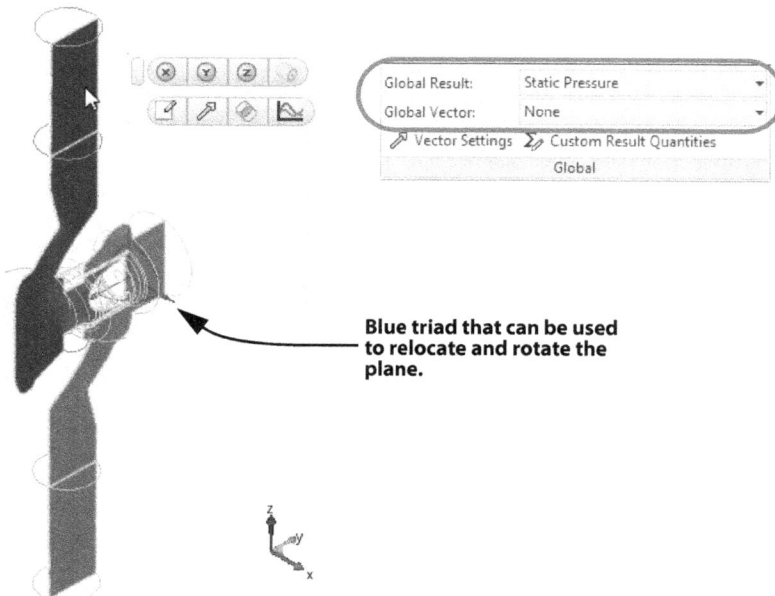

Blue triad that can be used to relocate and rotate the plane.

Mini-toolbar Commands

The following list describes the commands in the mini-toolbar.

- The tools in the top row of the mini-toolbar (⊗ Ⓨ Ⓩ) enable you to change from the default alignment of the plane. By default, the plane is aligned to the X axis (⊗). To change the alignment to the y or z planes, select Ⓨ or Ⓩ, respectively.

- To align to a specific (non, x, y, or z) planar surface, select and select a surface on the model to relocate the plane.

- Drag the handles on the plane's triad to relocate the plane or rotate it.

- Select in the mini-toolbar to open the Plane Control dialog box. This can be used to control the result displayed, the plane's location, and the model's appearance display setting (shaded, outline, etc). The vector settings can also be defined using the Vector settings tab.

- Select in the mini-toolbar to open the Vector settings tab in the Plane Control dialog box. The standard vector settings that were previously discussed can also be modified using this dialog box.

- Select in the mini-toolbar to conduct a bulk calculation. This option is also available in the Planes context panel. This is discussed in more detailed later in this lesson.

- Select in the mini-toolbar to create an XY plot. This option is also available in the Planes context panel. This is discussed in more detailed later in this lesson.

The new plane is added to the Planes node, as shown in the following image. When a plane is created, the visual style for the model automatically changes to Outline. This enables you to easily visualize the plane and results. Note that the current Global Result setting that is assigned to the plane is also listed.

         ▷ ⤳ Flow: On
         ⤳ Heat Transfer: Off
     ◢ 🐾 Results
       ▷ 🐾 Parts
       ◢ 🔷 Planes
          ☑ 🔷 Plane 1((1) Static Pressure)
       🔷 Points
       🔷 Iso Surfaces
       🔷 Iso Volumes
       Traces

To view and work with the plane to visualize your result, consider the following notes:

- The result that initially displays on the plane is based on the Global Result setting that was assigned. To assign a specific visualization result to a plane, right-click on the plane and select a new result in the plane's result list. The result specified for the review in this way will be maintained with the plane, regardless of the global result setting.

- The result that displays on the plane, is automatically set as the last iteration that exists in the model. To control which iteration displays, you must have previously set the Save Intervals parameter in the Solve dialog box so that intervals are saved. You can then use the Iterations/Steps panel options to navigate between iterations.

- To rename a plane, right-click on the plane name in the Design Study Bar and select Rename. Once renamed, the Result setting is maintained regardless of the name entered.

- To toggle off the display of the Plane, clear the checkbox adjacent to the plane name in the Design Study Bar or right-click on the plane in the graphics window and select Hide Plane.

- Add additional planes as required, to visualize all required results.

- Planes that exist in a scenario will update to reflect changes to the results, when rerun.

- To View a Plane on a shaded model, you can use clipping. This is a powerful way to display vectors when the model is shaded and it improves the visibility of specific model regions. To enable clipping, right-click on the results plane and select Clip. Click Reverse Clip if the wrong side of the model displays. To disable clipping, right-click on the results plane and uncheck Clip.

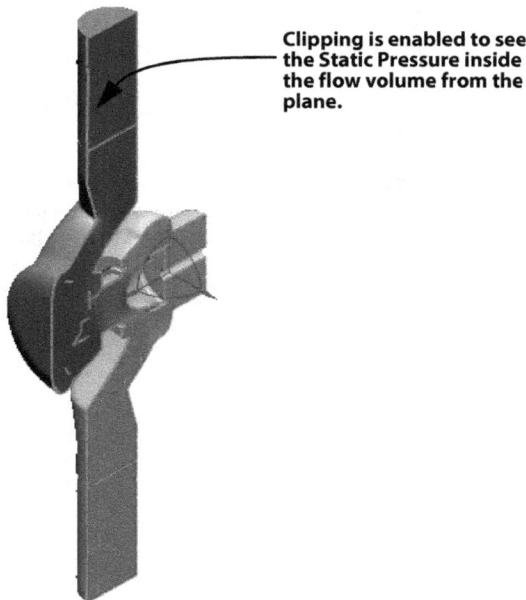

Clipping is enabled to see the Static Pressure inside the flow volume from the plane.

- To remove a plane, right-click on the plane name in the Design Study Bar and select Remove. You can also select Remove All to quickly remove all planes in the scenario.

Bulk Calculator Results

The Bulk Calculator quickly calculates and shows bulk-weighted results on a results plane. Bulk (mass-weighted) results are automatically updated as the active Plane is moved. Once the tool is active, select the desired quantities for bulk calculation, change the units of the output quantity, as required, and click Calculate. The bulk results are written to the Output tab.

In the following image, the Bulk Results dialog box is shown on the left with a number of bulk-weighted settings enabled, while the Output tab is shown on the right displaying the results. This data can be exported to a spreadsheet (.CSV file) using the Save button.

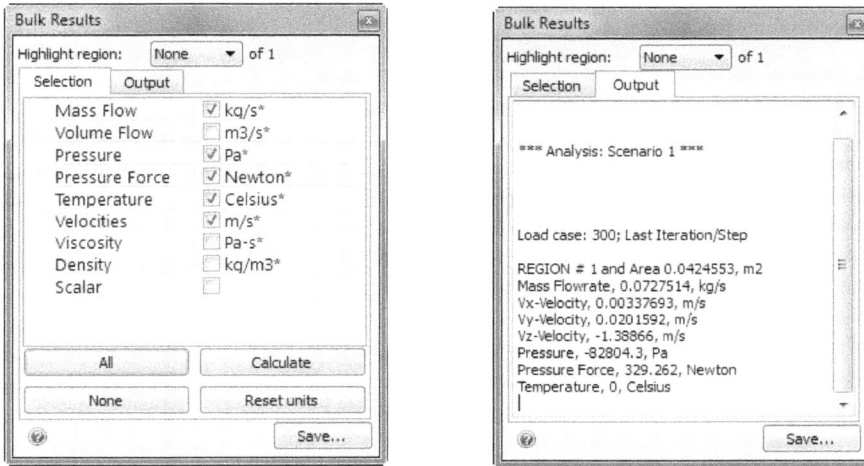

If there is recirculation across a plane, the resulting bulk calculation value will be reduced due to the recirculation that is experienced.

XY Plot Results

With a plane created, you can create an XY plot of the analysis results that exist on that plane. This provides a convenient way to extract and present analysis results data by selecting points on a cutting surface, by entering point coordinates, or by using points saved from a previously created plot.

To create an XY plot, complete the following steps:

1. Create a Results Plane.

2. In the Plane panel, click (XY Plot) to open the XY Plot dialog box.

3. Select the points to define the XY plot using any one of the followings methods. The maximum number of points in an XY plot is 500.

    *   To add by picking points, click Add points and select locations on the cutting plane through which the plot will pass. The Point List Region displays the points. A minimum of two points is required.

    *   To add by entry, specify X, Y, and Z coordinates separated by a comma in the field. (Do not use brackets or parentheses.) Click Add.

- To read from an existing file, the point locations from a previous XY plot must have been saved using the Save Points option. Select Read from File and select the file to read the points. The file is saved as an XYP file. **Note:** Saved point locations can be used to create a plot in a different design study.

4. Enter a Title for the XY Plot. The default name for unnamed plots is Untitled.

5. Change the Number of Divisions to change the plot resolution. The default number of divisions between every point is 20 and the entered value must be between 2 and 500.

6. Click Plot to create the Plot. The resulting plot displays in a separate window, similar to that shown in the following image.

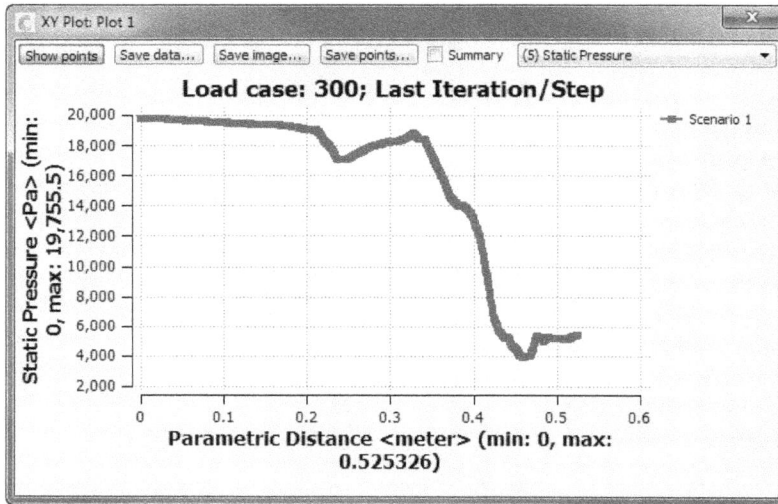

7. Modify the plot's appearance, as required. The following options can be changed in the plot by right-clicking on the graph:
    - The plotted result quantity for the Y axis.
    - The Y axis units of measure.
    - The axis labels.
    - The min/max axis values.
    - The background color.

Comparing Results using Summary Objects

The preceding topics describe how to create a results plane and plot results data from a single design scenario. This helps to understand the performance and characteristics of that one scenario. To make educated design decisions, it is essential that the same data is compared between multiple scenarios in a design study. In the Planes result task, you can create three types of summary objects for comparison in the Decision Center. The Decision Center uses these summary objects to quickly compute the same result object in every scenario in the design study. Once all data is generated, you have access to the complete design results for accurate comparison. For more information on how to compare the summary objects, refer to the *Decision Center* lesson later in this chapter.

- The Summary Plane functionality enables you to generate tabular data to compare results in multiple scenarios or against critical values. To save a result plane as a Summary Plane, click

  $\Sigma^{\ast}$ (Make Summary) in the Planes panel or right-click and select Make Summary.

- The Summary Image functionality captures a dynamic image of the graphics window. It enables you to visually compare the results for an active results plane between each scenario in the design study. Summary images automatically apply the same view configuration (orientation, result quantity, visualization features, etc.) to all selected scenarios in the Design Study. To save a result

  plane as a Summary Image, click (Summary Image) in the Image panel.

- The Summary Plot functionality enables you to set a created plot so that it is available for comparison in the Decision Center. To enable a plot for comparison, select the Summary option in the XY Plot dialog box. This designates the plot as a Summary plot and adds it to the XY Plot Data branch of the Decision Center.

Lesson: Traces Result Task

The Traces result task enables you to create a visual representation of the path of the fluid as it passes around solid obstructions. In this lesson, you will learn how traces can be used as a valuable tool when visualizing CFD results. They can help understand and verify the flow movement in a design.

Objectives

After completing this lesson, you will be able to:

- Define the 2D seed distribution settings that will form the foundation from which the traces will extend.
- Create a trace set on a reference surface.
- Modify a trace set.
- Animate a trace set to visually represent the flow path of the trace particles.
- Create summary images for later design comparison using Decision Center.

Traces Result Task

Particle traces show the path of the fluid as it passes around solid obstructions. They are a very powerful way to visualize flow movement, circulation, and regions of swirl. To create a particle traces result set, select the ⟆ (Traces) task in the Results Tasks panel. The context menus that display when the Traces Results Task is selected are shown in the following image.

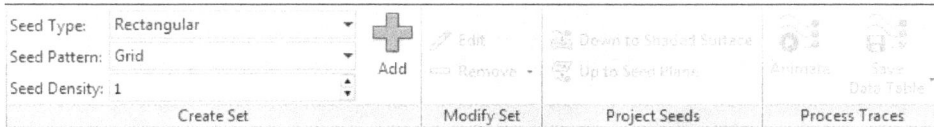

Seed Type:	Rectangular	▼		✎ Edit	Down to Shaded Surface		
Seed Pattern:	Grid	▼	Add	Remove ▼	Up to Seed Plane	Animate	Save Data Table ▼
Seed Density:	1						
	Create Set			Modify Set	Project Seeds	Process Traces	

In the following example, traces show the fluid path through a control valve. The traces are colored by velocity so regions of fast and slow fluid flow can be identified. Flow circulation shows as circular portions of the paths. Areas without traces may be areas of stagnant flow and might be examined more closely with traces and/or planes.

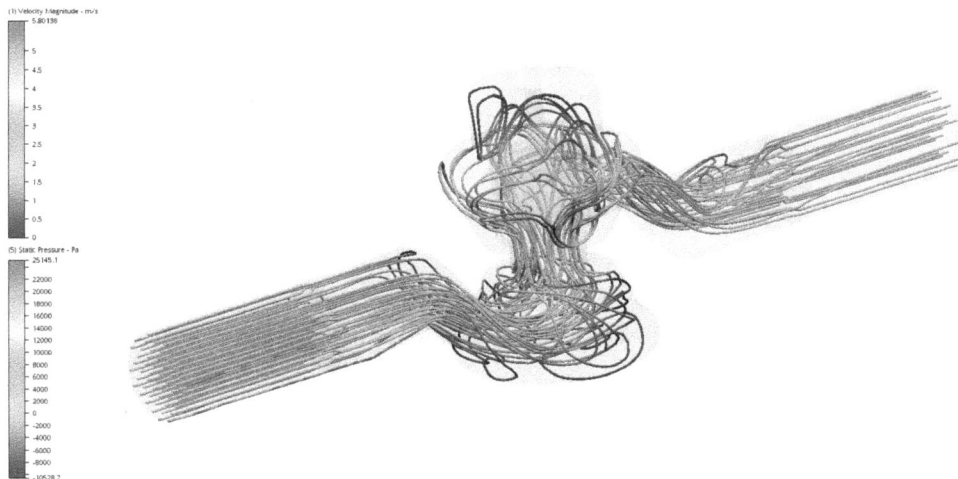

Understanding the Seed Distribution

The trace path layout is defined using the seed settings. These settings define the 2D distribution that will form the foundation from which the traces will extend (grow). The Seed settings include the following options:

- Seed Type
- Seed Pattern
- Density

The option that is assigned for each setting is selected in their respective drop-down list. The options are described as follows:

Seed Type

The Seed Type menu options control how seeds will be arranged. Some of these options are useful for creating large numbers of seeds, while others are ideal for creating a few seeds in specific locations. Seeds positioned on solid geometry will not generate a trace path because flow does not move through a solid. The various Seed Type options available are described as follows:

- **Point:** Enables you to create individual trace seeds on model surfaces. In the following image, note that the seeds positioned at the outlet have traces.

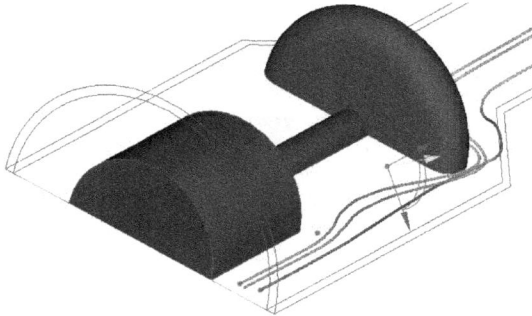

- **Line:** Enables to create a single row of trace seeds.

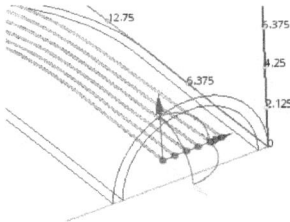

- **Ring:** Enables you to create an unfilled circular shape of trace seeds.

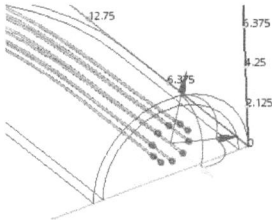

- **Circular:** Enables you to create a filled circular shape of trace seeds.

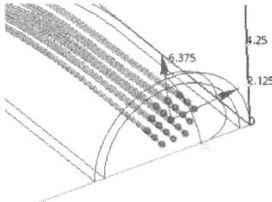

- **Rectangular:** Enables you to create an ordered grid.

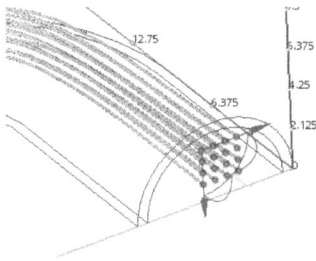

- **Region:** Enables you to apply the trace seed distribution directly to the geometry plane or to the results plane. It also enables you to create a uniform distribution of traces throughout the entire results plane. This method is useful when computing Erosion.

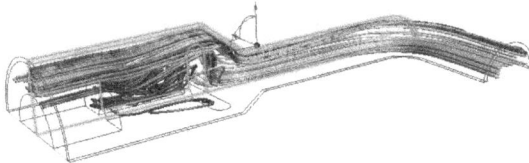

- **Key-in:** Enables to enter exact X, Y, and Z coordinates. Separate each coordinate with a comma. Do not use brackets or parentheses for the coordinates.

Seed Pattern

The Seed Pattern options enable you to control how seed points are spaced on the definition grid. The Seed Pattern cannot be defined for Point, Line and Ring Seed types. The available Seed Pattern options are described as follows:

- Diamond - This pattern option staggers the seed points through the plane.
- Grid - This pattern creates an ordered distribution.
- Hexagon - This pattern option staggers the seed points into a hexagonal distribution.

Diamond Seed Pattern   **Grid Seed Pattern**   **Hexagon Seed Pattern**

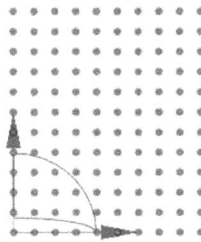

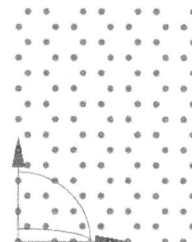

Creating a Trace Set

To create a traces set, complete the following steps:

1. In the Create Set panel, select the Seed Type.

2. In the Create Set panel, select the Seed Pattern layout.

3. In the Create Set panel, enter the Seed Density value.

    *   Modifying the density value enables you to increase or decrease the spacing between the traces. By default, the value is set to 1. Decrease the value to decrease spacing or increase it to enlarge the spacing between the resulting traces.

4. In the Create Set panel, click ➕ (Add).

5. Select a surface of the model to locate the seed reference or in the case of the Key in Seed Type, enter the coordinates. Depending on the Seed Type assigned, the placement requirements will vary. You may have to click and drag, click multiple times, or simply click on specific locations to define the seed distribution.

    *   Point - Click once on a surface to locate the single trace set.
    *   Line- Click once at one end of the line, drag to the required length, and click again to complete the line.
    *   Ring - Click once at the center of the circle, drag to the desired radius, and click to complete the ring.
    *   Circular - Click once at the center of the circle, drag to the desired radius, and click to complete the circle.
    *   Rectangular - Click once to define the first corner, drag to the required width, and click again. Drag to the required height and click a third time to complete the rectangle.
    *   Region - Select an existing plane in the model to locate the trace set that covers the entire region.

> **Seed Surface Selection**
>
> When you click on a surface, the seed point is created on the first shaded geometric surface or results plane in line with the cursor. If there are no shaded surfaces in line with the cursor, the seed point is created on the first visible surface (which can display as outline).
>
> *   If the surface represents a flow opening (or an internal surface between two flow regions), traces grow from the seeds.
> *   If the surface is an external solid surface, trace are not drawn from the seeds.

As soon as the seed reference is defined, the Trace set automatically displays on the model using the pattern and density settings that were previously specified. The set is also added to the Traces node in the Design Study Bar, as shown in the following image. The set's node indicates the number of traces and the result displayed by the trace.

```
      Iso Volumes
   ▲  Traces
        ☑  Set 1 (2 traces)((1) Static Pressure)
        ☑  Set 2 (49 traces)((1) Velocity Magnitude)
```

To view and work with a Trace Set to visualize your result, consider the following notes:

- The result initially displayed by the Trace set is based on the Global Result setting that was assigned. To assign a specific visualization result, right-click on the Traces set in the Design Study Bar and select a new result in the Color by result list. Alternatively, you can right-click on the set in the graphics window and use the same option. The result specified for the Trace set will be maintained, regardless of any changes to the Global Result setting.

- To move a seed set, ensure that it is displayed, left-click on an axis in the triad and drag it to the required location anywhere in the model. Rotate the trace set by dragging the arc on the triad.

- The result displayed by the Trace Set is automatically set as the last iteration that exists in the model. To control which iteration displays, you must have set the Save Intervals parameter in the Solve dialog box so that intervals are saved. You can then use the Iterations/Steps panel options to navigate between iterations and select specific ones.

- To rename a Trace Set, right-click on its name in the Design Study Bar and select Rename. Once renamed, the bracketed Result setting is maintained regardless of the name entered.

- To toggle off the Traces Set display, clear the checkbox adjacent to its name in the Design Study Bar or right-click on it in the graphics window and select Hide trace set.

- To modify a Trace Set, select its name in the Traces node in the Design Study bar and click

  ✏ (Edit) to open the Modify Set dialog box. The Edit Trace dialog box options enable you to remove individual traces from the set, change the displayed result, or modify its properties (such as the shape of the trace).

- Add additional traces as required, to visualize all required results.

- Traces that exist in a scenario will update to reflect changes to the results, when rerun.

- To save the results from the traces set, right-click in the graphics window and select Save Data

  Table or select ⊟ (Save Data Table) in the Process Traces panel to save a CSV file of the results.

- To save a trace set for use later, right-click off the model and select Save view settings file. Enter "traces" (or similar) as the view settings file name to clearly identify it.

- The commands in the Project Seeds panel enable you to set the advanced positioning of traces onto specific surfaces or on a seed plane. These commands are useful for positioning traces at specific locations on or just off of the model for visualizing flow very close to solid objects. For more information on the use of projection options, search for "Projecting Trace Seeds" in the online Help documentation.

- Use ⌇ (Animate) to display and save an animation of the flow path of a traces set. A trace set must be visible to access this option.

- To remove a set of traces, right-click on its name in the Design Study Bar and select Remove or click ▭ (Remove) in the Modify Set panel. Remove All can also be selected to quickly remove all traces in the scenario.

> By default, particle traces are the path a particle without mass would take when released into the flow. A more physically real visualization technique is to include the effects of mass on the particle. For example, to represent a physical contaminant or other material mass can be added to the particle trace. The resulting trace behaves more like a physical substance in a flow system. You can enable Mass in the Edit Trace Set dialog box. For more information on the use of Mass in a Trace set, search for "Massed Particle Traces" in the online Help documentation.

Comparing Results using Summary Images

The use of the Summary Image functionality enables you to visually compare the results for all scenarios using the traces set in a source scenario. Summary Images automatically apply the same view configuration (orientation, result quantity, visualization features, etc.) to all selected scenarios in the Design Study. The Decision Center enables you to quickly view the same traces image in every scenario in the design study. For more information on how to compare the summary images, refer to the *Decision Center* lesson later in this chapter.

- To save a Summary Image, click (Summary Image) in the Image panel on the Results tab.

Lesson: Iso Surface & Iso Volume Results Tasks

The Iso Surfaces and Iso Volumes result tasks are useful for visualizing and presenting complicated flow results, as well as temperature distributions, for a simulation. In this lesson, you will learn how these results display visually in three dimensions showing the physical shape of the flow characteristics. The color graphical representation on the shape indicates the result values in the model. The difference between an iso surface result and an iso volume result is simply that the volume enables you to specify a range (min and max) for the result quantity value.

Objectives

After completing this lesson, you will be able to:

- Create an iso surface and iso volume.
- Review a created iso surface and iso volume and interpret its results.
- Change the appearance and displayed result quantity for a created iso surface or iso volume.
- Create summary images for later design comparison using Decision Center.

Iso Surfaces Result Task

An Iso Surface is a three dimensional tool that shows the physical shape of the flow characteristics as well as a graphics representation (color) of result values in the model. It creates 3D surfaces in the model that correspond to a specific result quantity. They are useful for visualizing velocity distributions in complicated flow paths and temperature distributions in thermal simulations. You can also use iso surfaces to determine the locations of the maximum and minimum values of a quantity.

In the following example, a velocity magnitude iso surface was created and it is colored using the static pressure results. The iso-surface shape indicates all the areas in the model that have a specific velocity magnitude. The colors indicate the static pressure at these locations.

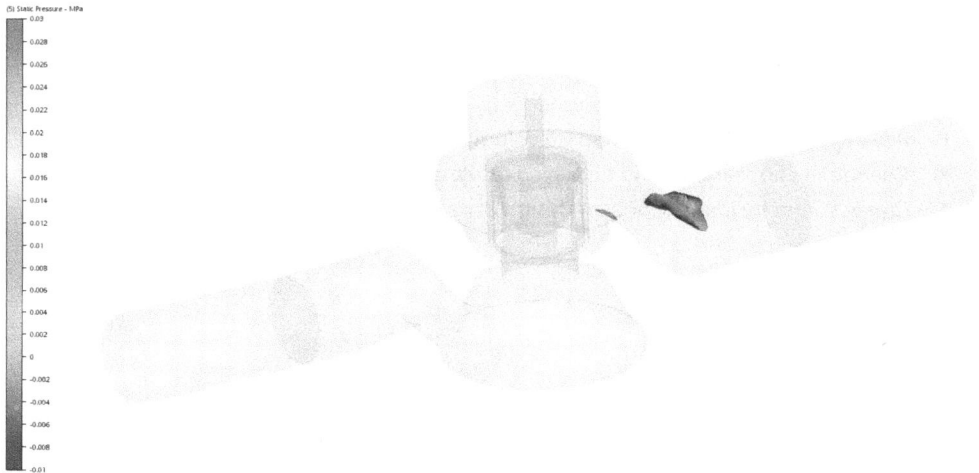

To create an Iso Surface, select the (Iso Surfaces) task in the Results Task panel. The context menu that displays when the Iso Surfaces Results Task is selected, is shown in the following image.

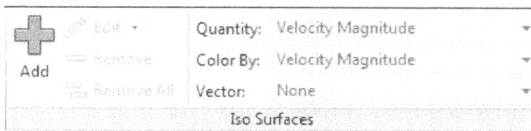

To create an Iso Surface, use any of the following three methods:

- In the Iso Surfaces panel, click (Add).
- Right-click in the graphics window and select Add iso surface.
- In the Design Study Bar, right-click on the Iso Surfaces node and select Add iso surface.

As soon as the Iso Surface's Add/Add iso surface option is selected, it is created and it automatically displays in the model. By default, the iso surface displays, representing the flow volume. The Iso Surface is also added to the Iso Surfaces node in the Design Study Bar, as shown in the following image. The node indicates the name of the Iso Surface and the result quantity that is being displayed.

To modify the iso surface, select its name in the Iso Surfaces node in the Design Study bar and click

✎ (Edit) in the Iso Surfaces panel. Alternatively, right-click the iso surface name and select Edit. The Iso Surface Control dialog box shown in the following image enables you to do the following:

- Change the displayed quantity result and the color by result.
- Modify the value of the iso quantity or the value being mapped to the iso surface.
- Change the appearance of the iso surface.
- The Vector settings tab can also be used to incorporate vectors to the iso surface display and customize them.

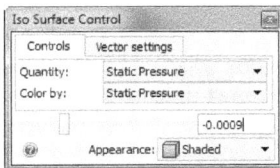

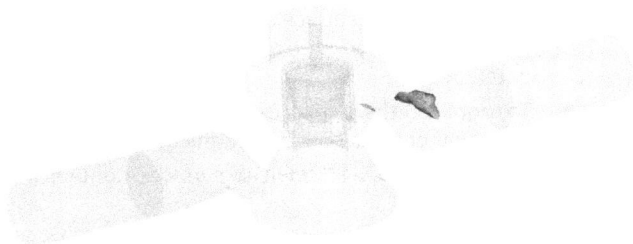

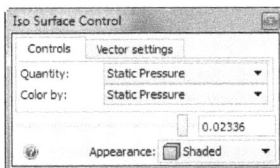

To view and work with a Iso Surfaces to visualize your result, consider the following:

- The quantity result that is initially displayed by the Iso Surface is based on the Global Result setting that was assigned. To assign a specific quantity result, use one of the following methods:
  - Select a new result quantity in the Quantity drop-down list in the Iso Surfaces panel.
  - Right-click on the Iso Surface name in the Design Study Bar and select a new result in the Iso quantity drop-down list.
  - Right-click the Iso Surface in the graphics window and select a new result in the Iso quantity drop-down list.
- The color result that initially displayed by the Iso Surface is the same as the quantity result. To assign a specific color result, use one of the following methods:
  - Select a new result color in the Color By drop-down list in the Iso Surfaces panel.
  - Right-click on the Iso Surface name in the Design Study Bar and select a new color result in the Color by result drop-down list.
  - Right-click the Iso Surface in the graphics window and select a new result in the Color by result drop-down list.
- Use the Vector drop-down list in the Iso Surfaces panel to include vectors on the iso surfaces display. By default, no vector is assigned.
- The results displayed by the Iso Surface, are automatically set as the last iteration that exists in the model. To control which iteration displays, you must have set the Save Intervals parameter in the Solve dialog box so that intervals are saved. You can then use the Iterations/Steps panel options to navigate between iterations and select specific ones.
- To rename an iso surface, right-click on its name in the Design Study Bar and select Rename. Once renamed, the bracketed result quantity setting is maintained regardless of the name that is entered.
- To toggle off the display of an iso surface, clear the checkbox adjacent to its name in the Design Study Bar or right-click on it in the graphics window and select Hide iso surface.
- To quickly show all hidden iso surfaces, right-click in the graphics window and select Show all iso surfaces.
- Add additional iso surfaces as required, to visualize all required results.
- Iso surfaces that exist in a scenario will update to reflect changes to the results, when rerun.
- To remove an iso surface, right-click on its name in the Design Study Bar and select Remove or click ⊜ (Remove) in the Iso Surfaces panel. You can also select Remove All to quickly remove all traces in the scenario.

Iso Volumes Result Task

Similar to iso surfaces, iso volumes are useful for visualizing and presenting complicated flow results, as well as temperature distributions, from a simulation. The difference between an iso surface result and an iso volume result is simply that the volume enables you to specify a range (min and max) for the result quantity value.

To create an iso volume, select the (Iso Volumes) task in the Results Task panel. The context menu that displays when the Iso Volumes Results Task is selected, is shown in the following image.

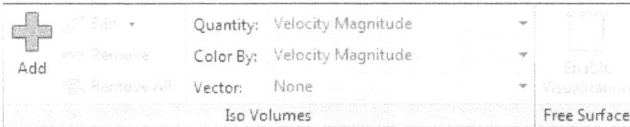

The workflow needed to create an iso volume is the same as that for creating an iso surface. To define the min/max values, edit the iso volume and set the values in the Iso Volume Control dialog box.

The following image shows a velocity magnitude Iso Volume. The shape of the Iso Volume indicates everywhere in the model that falls within a specified range of velocity magnitude. You can set the range in the Min and Max fields.

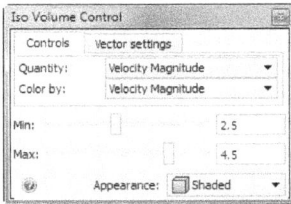

Comparing Results using Summary Images

The use of the Summary Image functionality captures a dynamic image of the graphics window for the active iso surface or iso volume. Once created in a single scenario of the design study, you can use the Decision Center to quickly compute the same image in every scenario of the design study. Once all data is generated, you have access to the complete design results for accurate comparison of the images. For more information on how to compare the summary objects, refer to the *Decision Center* lesson later in this chapter.

- To save a Summary Image, click (Summary Image) in the Image panel on the Results tab.

Lesson: Wall Calculator Result Task

In this lesson, you will learn about the Wall Calculator, a valuable tool for extracting result values, that enables you to calculate and report on selected flow-induced forces on solid and wall surfaces in the design model. Once calculated, the report data can be easily reviewed and compared to critical design data.

Objectives

After completing this lesson, you will be able to:

- Select surfaces that are to be used as references during wall calculations.
- Use the Wall Calculator result tool to generate a report on selected flow-induced forces on solid and wall surfaces.
- Review and save the results of the Wall Calculator tool.

Wall Calculator Result Task

The Wall Calculator tool, found in the Results Task panel, enables you to calculate and report on flow-induced forces on solid and wall surfaces. Once calculated, all the report data can be easily reviewed and saved to a text file. Unlike the other result task tools that are available, there is only a single command in its context panel. This one option, which is also available in the tool itself, simply enables you to calculate results.

The Wall Calculator can be used to report on the following results for a selected volume, or on a surface or edge.

- **Force:** Enables you to report he total (summed) force and the individual forces for all selected surfaces. Note that forces are reported in the global coordinate system.
- **Cutoff pressure:** Enables you to remove very low wall pressures (which may indicate the on-set of cavitation) from the force calculation. Once enabled, specify a minimum pressure value. This value will be assigned to all locations with pressures that fall below the Cutoff. This cutoff does not affect the displayed results fringes or any other output quantity.
- **Pressure:** Enables you to calculate the average pressure exerted by the fluid on the wall surface.
- **Temperature:** Enables you to calculate the average temperature on the wall surface.
- **Heat flux:** Enables you to calculate the heat flux based on the thermal residual from the heat transfer solution.
- **Film coefficient:** Enables you to calculate the film coefficient. The following two methods can be used to calculate this value:
    - By default, this value is calculated using the temperature at every wall node as the local reference temperature (Use near-wall temperatures). In this case, the film coefficient is based on the difference between the wall temperature and temperature at the closest non-wall (flow) node for every node on the wall.
    - Alternatively, you can enable the Temperature option and enter a value for the reference temperate. In this case, the film coefficient is calculated based on the heat flux and the temperature difference between the specified reference temperature and the wall temperature. **Note:** This method is typically required to get expected film coefficient ranges to match hand calculations.
- **Torque:** Enables you to calculate the torque about an axis and the center of force.
    - Enter the coordinates of one point on the axis of revolution using the Point on axis button and enter a unit vector that defines the direction of the axis using the Direction button.

To conduct a wall calculation, complete the following steps:

1. In the Results Tasks panel, click (Wall Calculator). The Wall Results dialog box opens as shown in the following image.

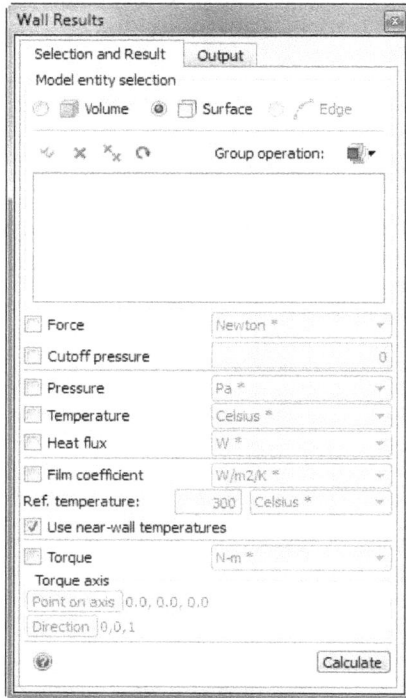

2. Ensure that the Selection and Result tab is active. In the Model entity selection area, select whether the calculation will be done on a volume, surface, or edge by selecting its respective option. Surface is the default option.

3. Select references on the model to be evaluated. Valid surfaces are any wall surface or openings (inlets and outlets).

   - References on the model highlight as the cursor hovers over them. In the case of a volume, the surfaces belonging to a selected volume are actually selected, not the volume itself.

   - To identify that the correct reference is being selected, it may be helpful to display the model in the Shaded or Transparent display style.

   - The IDs of selected references are shown in the list. Use the icons at the top of the list to include all surfaces in the list, delete a selected surface or all surfaces from the list, or restore a previously removed surface.

   - If a group exists in the design prior to running results, it can be easily selected in the Group operation drop-down list.

4. Select the quantities and the required units to report on.

5. Click Calculate from either the Wall Results dialog or from the Wall context panel.

6. Select the Output tab to view calculated wall results for the requested values.
   - A Summary section (bottom of the list) summarizes the total quantities for all of the selected surfaces. Individual values are also provided for each selected reference.
   - To save this data to an Excel CSV file, click Write to file. Click View file to open the saved wall results file.

In the following example, the Wall Calculator is used to summarize the forces on the surfaces of the cage and valve stem. The surfaces were selected, Force was enabled, and the calculation was executed. The Output tab, shown on the right, displays individual data for each surface and a Summary section for the average of all forces.

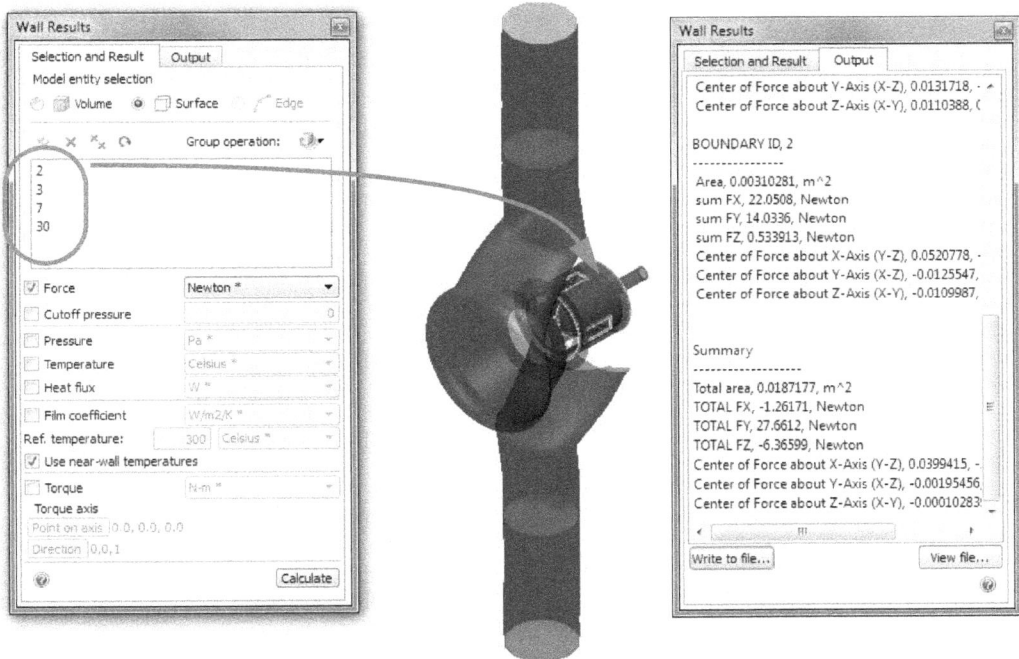

TIPS

- When selecting surfaces, consider using the Surface Blanking command on the View tab to clear surfaces for easier selecting. Once enabled, hold <Ctrl> and press the middle mouse button to select the surfaces that you want to clear.
- For moving solids, the computed force and torque are the hydraulic values and do not include the effect of specified driving and resistance forces or torque as part of the Motion definition. Additionally, heat flux values from moving objects are not available.
- Prior to executing a calculation, you can select an iteration/step to be used if results were saved for intermediate steps. Note that temperature and heat flux values from intermediate saved iterations will not be reported.
- The Wall Calculator outputs tabular data that you can write to a file and review. If required, you can also use the Summary Image command to create a summary image.

Lesson: Parts Result Task

Result Parts are ideal for quickly extracting the result values for the temperature of components (fluids and solids) in a design. For device materials, Result Parts can be used to obtain operational data. In this lesson, you will learn how to use this tool to create report on the temperature of individually selected components. With this data, you can easily compare results to acceptable temperature values.

Objectives

After completing this lesson, you will be able to:

- Use the Parts result task functionality to report on the temperature of selected components.
- Create summary images for later design comparison using Decision Center.

Parts Result Task

The Parts result task enables you to assess the temperature of selected parts in the design study. An example where using the Parts result task is useful is in an electronic power inverter design. In such designs, component temperature must generally remain under a maximum value (i.e., the temperature on components in the design cannot exceed a value of 60°C). After the scenario is run, the Parts result task can be used to obtain the temperature on each component to verify that it remains under the allowable maximum temperature. Device materials can also be selected to report on operational data (e.g., operating point of a fan, or junction temperature of a CTM).

To review part results, complete the following steps:

1. In the Results Task panel, click ⬚ (Parts). The Parts panel and Parts dialog box display as shown in the following image.

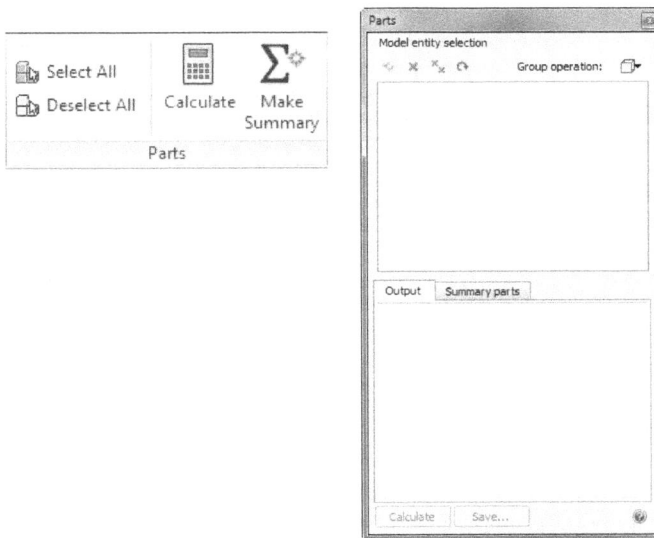

2. Select parts of interest from the design to be assessed. As parts are selected, they are listed in the Parts dialog box.
   - In the Parts panel and Parts dialog box, select ▦ or ✓ (Select All), respectively to select all parts in the design.
   - To select individual parts, select them directly in the graphics window or select them in the Results>Parts nodes in the Design Study Bar.
   - In the Parts panel and Parts dialog box, select ▦ or ✗ₓ (Deselect All), respectively to deselect all parts that were previously selected. Use ✗ in the Parts dialog box to deselect a single selection in the Parts dialog box.
   - If a group exists in the design prior to running results, its parts can easily be assigned for assessment in the Group operation drop-down list.
3. Click Calculate in the Parts dialog box or in the Parts panel in the ribbon. The results display at the bottom of the Parts dialog box in the Output tab.

4. (Optional) To save the results to a text file, click Save at the bottom of the Parts dialog box.

In the following example of an LED light, the two halves of the casing (3 can and 4 can) were selected for assessment and their results were calculated and displayed in the Output tab.

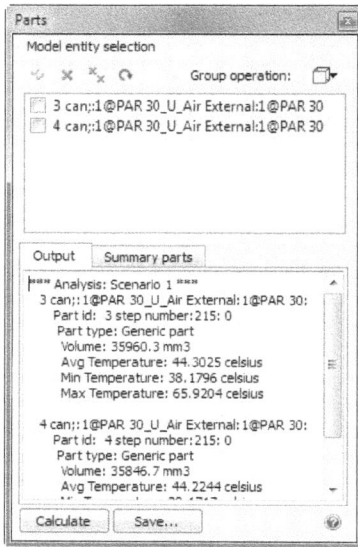

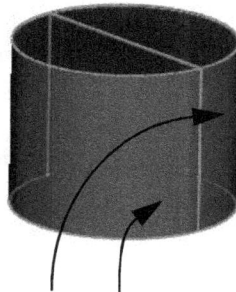

The two halves of the casing were selected for assessment.

Comparing Results using Summary Objects

In the parts result task, you can create summary parts and summary images for comparison in the Decision Center. The Decision Center uses these summary objects to quickly compute the same result object in every scenario in the design study. Once all data is generated, you have access to the complete design results for accurate comparison. For more information on how to compare the summary objects, refer to the *Decision Center* lesson later in this chapter.

■   The Summary Parts functionality enables you to compare the results for the selected parts for each scenario in the design study. For example, you can create summary parts to compare the resultant temperature on the casings in the 24 fin or 36 fin scenarios. To designate a part as a Summary Part, click $\Sigma^{\diamond}$ (Make Summary) in the Parts panel or select the boxes adjacent to the part name on the Parts dialog box. To view the list of summary parts, select the Summary parts tab at the bottom of the Parts dialog box, as shown in the following image. Once the summary parts are created, they are listed in the Decision Center in the Summary Values node.

- The Summary Image functionality captures a dynamic image of the graphics window. It enables you to visually compare the results for image between each scenario in the design study. Summary images automatically apply the same view configuration (orientation, result quantity, visualization features, etc.) to all selected scenarios in the Design Study. To save a result plane as a Summary Image, click (Summary Image) in the Image panel.

Lesson: Points Result Task

In this lesson, you will learn how the Points result task are ideal for creating a plot of the time step/iteration history vs. a selected result type for locations on the model. Additionally, the use of Summary Points enables you to easily created multiple plots and compare them between the scenarios that exist in a design study.

Objectives

After completing this lesson, you will be able to:

- Use the Points result task functionality to create points in the model.
- Create a plot that shows the result type as a function of time/iteration history.
- Create summary images for later design comparison using Decision Center.

Points Result Task

The Points result task can be used to plot the time step/iteration history vs. a selected result at locations in the model. This is done by designating points on the parts. For example, result points can be used to assess time step/iteration history in a pressure relief valve. The time-dependent pressure build-up and subsequent venting of a valve was simulated with a transient design study. To know if the design objective was attained, you can plot the time step/iteration history vs. pressure at critical locations. You can also use it to define the probe points in a test model for temperature measurement.

> **TIP**
> To create an plot result for points on the model, two or more time steps/iterations must exist.

To create the plot for points in the model, complete the following steps:

1. In the Results Task panel, click (Points). The Points panel and Points dialog box displays as shown in the following image.

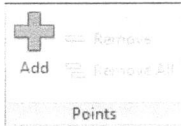

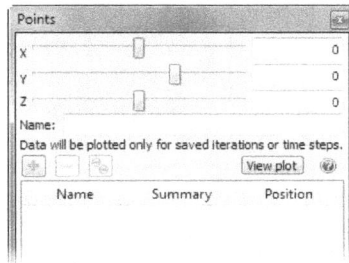

2. Use one of the following methods to define the location for the points:
   - Drag the triad that displays on the model to the required location.
   - Use the X, Y, and Z sliders or the entry fields at the top of the Points dialog box to position the point on the model. The point triad will move to display the location.

3. (Optional) To assign a point name, enter a descriptive name in the Name field prior to creating it.

4. To add the point once it is correctly located, use one of the following methods:

   - In the Points panel, click .

   - In the Points dialog box, click .

   - Left-click on the triad and select in the mini-toolbar.

> **Point Aligned to a Surface**
> To quickly create a point that is aligned to a surface, hover the cursor over the required point on a geometric surface, iso surface, or result plane using the left mouse button and left-click to open the mini-toolbar. Select to create the point aligned to the surface. The selection tool gives higher priority to shaded surfaces. When positioning a point on an outlined surface, ensure that you do not to click too close to a shaded surface.

5. Select the point in the list that is to be plotted. If multiple points are selected, the last point in the list will be plotted.

6. Select the View Plot button to plot the results.

    •   Two or more time steps/iterations must exist before data can be plotted at a Point. Set the Results Save Interval on the Settings dialog to save results at intermediate time-steps/iterations.

    •   By default, the Global Result setting is initially displayed. To change the result that displays, select the Result type drop-down list and select the required result.

In the following example of an LED light, points were setup along the top of the casing to plot the temperature at the outer edges and the center of the casing. The plot that displays at the bottom of the image shows the temperature variation during analysis for a point on the outer edge.

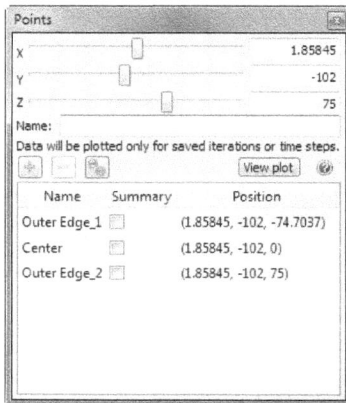

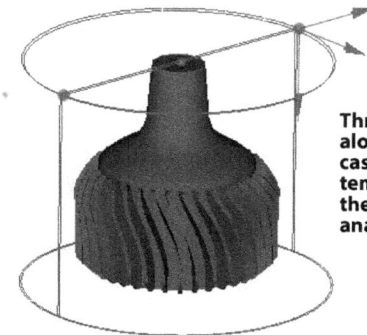

Three points were created along the top of the casing to plot the temperature results for the iteration history of the analysis.

The XY plot is created for the Outer Edge_1 point to report its temperature through the 300 iterations. The save interval was set to 10 so 30 points were plotted.

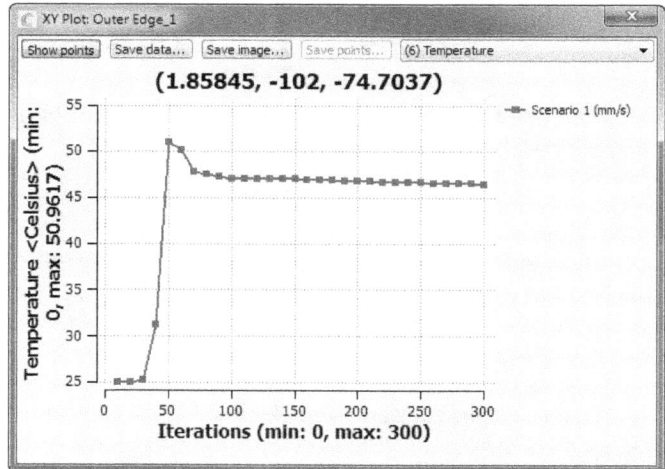

Comparing Results using Summary Objects

Creating result points and plotting the results data for a single design scenario helps to better understand this one scenario; however, a comparison between multiple scenarios in the design study is often required. In the Points result task, you can create both summary points and summary images for comparison in the Decision Center. For more information on how to compare the summary objects, refer to the *Decision Center* lesson later in this chapter.

- The Summary Points functionality enables you to compare the results for the selected points for each scenario in the design study. To designate a point as a Summary Point, select the box adjacent to the point name in the Points dialog box. Once the summary points are created, the comparison is done using the Decision Center.

- The Summary Image functionality captures a dynamic image of the graphics window. It enables you to visually compare the results for an active results plane between each scenario in the design study. Summary images automatically apply the same view configuration (orientation, result quantity, visualization features, etc.) to all selected scenarios in the Design Study. To save a result plane as a Summary Image, click (Summary Image) in the Image panel.

Lesson: Decision Center

Decision Center is an environment in Autodesk CFD used to compare the summary objects created in the result tasks. Using the summary images, summary values, and summary plots that are made available in the Decision Center, you can visually and explicitly compare images and values for all scenarios created in the design study. In this lesson, you will learn how to access and navigate the Decision Center to review and compare results.

Objectives

After completing this lesson, you will be able to:

- Access the Decision Center environment.
- Update all summary objects to propagate the data across all scenarios.
- Review all summary objects using the tools in the Decision Center environment.

Decision Center

The Decision Center is the Autodesk CFD environment used to compare the results of the various design alternatives created in the design study. Visualization objects such as summary images, summary values (parts, planes, and points), and summary plots (XY plots) form the basis of the Decision Center. These items can be used to identify the design scenario that satisfies the design objectives by visually reviewing images and plots or explicitly comparing data values.

In the previous lessons, you learned that as you create results views and extract data in a scenario, you can designate many results as a "summary" objects. The Decision Center uses these summary objects to quickly compute the same result object in every scenario in the study. Once all data is generated, you have access to the complete design results for accurate comparison.

To open the Decision Center and manage all summary objects, click the Decision Center tab. This tab is only available once a design study has been solved. The Decision Center tab displays as shown in the following image.

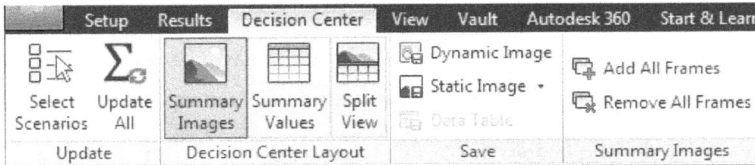

The Decision Center has three main components, as follows:

- Summary Images (Visual)
- Summary Values (Tabular)
- Summary Plots (Graphical)

Summary Images (Visual)

Summary images are used to visually compare the results in multiple scenarios. They can be created during any of the result tasks as they simply capture a dynamic view of the current screen. Summary images are reviewed using the graphics window and the Design Review Center. The Design Review Center is an area in the Decision Center environment that is active when the Summary Images layout is set.

To create and review summary images, complete the following steps:

1. Create the required summary images. In the Results tab, generate the required image for

    comparison using any of the result tasks and click (Summary Image) in the Image panel.

2. Select the Decision Center tab. The Summary Images node displays similar to that shown in the following image. The image shows the three summary images that were created.
   - Each summary image is listed sequentially in the order in which they were created.
   - To rename an image, right-click on its default name, select Rename, and enter a new name.
   - The summary images initially display as out of date (⚠).

3. Update the summary images in the Decision Center. Right-click on an image and select Update image. Additionally, you can right-click directly on the Summary Images header and select Update all images to propagate the data across all scenarios.

4. In the Decision Center Layout panel, ensure that the ▨ (Summary Images) layout is active.

5. Select an image in the list of Summary Images or use the Add All Frames option in the Summary Images panel. The graphics window and the Design Review Center update in the right-hand frame, as shown in the following image. The Design Review Center is used to easily navigate between the images.

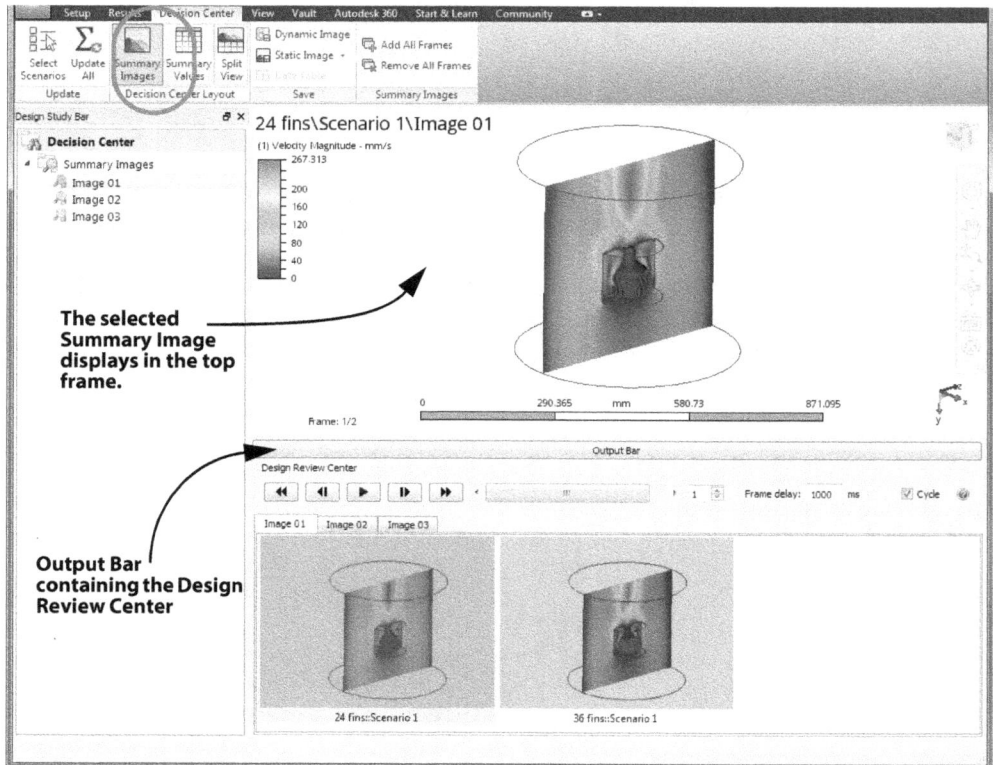

6. The Output Bar contains the Design Review Center, which can be expanded or compressed as required to review the images in a larger frame.

7. Use the Design Review Center to visually compare the summary images.

   - A set of images is provided for each scenario. To review the set of images, select the summary image name in the Decision Center list or select the required tab in the Design Review Center. All images in the set display in the Design Review Center. You can visually compare the images here or you can view them in the graphics window for an enlarged view.

   - Use the Next and Previous control buttons, the slider bar, or the entry field (shown in the following image) to navigate through the set of images in the enlarged graphics window.

Design Review Center

   - Use the Play button to play through the set of images in the graphics window. Use the Frame delay setting to control the playback speed and the Cycle option to cycle through the images.

   - Right-click on a frame in the graphics window area to remove it from the display, or use the Remove All Frames option in the Summary Images panel to remove all frames at once.

Side-by-Side Summary Image Comparison

By default, a single view-port is active in the graphics window, and results are compared by flipping between views using the Design Review Center controls. To view multiple images at once, you can use the Viewports drop-down list in the View tab to select an alternate layout (Vertical Split, Horizontal Split, etc.) for the graphics window.

Controlling Part Appearance

- A Summary Image records the appearance of all parts displayed in the graphics window at the time the option is selected. When a Summary Image is updated, the appearance of every part is applied to the other scenarios in the design study. If a scenario contains parts that are not in the captured scenario, those parts display with a default appearance.

- To change the appearance of a model or a specific part, use the standard appearance controls in either the main menu or the shortcut menu. The changes are stored with the summary image.

- When a summary image is updated, all appearance modifications are removed and the image is reset to its as-captured appearance. To preserve appearance modifications when updating a summary image, right-click on the thumbnail and select Lock. To reset the summary image to its initial appearance, right-click on the thumbnail and select Reset.

Summary Values (Tabular)

Summary Values are used to compare the actual result values in multiple scenarios. Summary Values are evaluated using summary objects from the design study. The following three types of summary objects can be used in the Decision Center to compare result values:

- Summary Parts
- Summary Planes
- Summary Points

In the Decision Center, the results are presented in a summary value table, which is simply a data table in a tabular format. Alternatively, the values can also be displayed as bar graphs. These formats enable you to easily compare scenarios against any known target (reference) values.

To create and review the summary value table in the Decision Center, complete the following steps:

1. Create the required summary objects using the Planes, Parts, and Points Results Tasks tools. The creation of these summary objects was explained in the previous lessons.

2. Select the Decision Center tab. The Summary Values node display similar to that shown in the following image. In this image, two summary parts, a single summary plane, and summary points object were created.

   - Each summary entity is listed in the appropriate branch of the Decision Center (Summary Parts, Summary Planes, or Summary Points, respectively).
   - To rename a summary object, right-click on its default name, select Rename, and enter a new name.
   - The summary objects initially display as out of date (⚠).

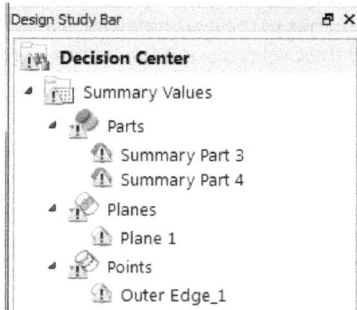

3. Create a summary value table in the Decision Center. Right-click on an summary object branch or the Summary Values header, and select Update summary values to propagate the data across all scenarios.

4. Ensure that the ⊞ (Summary Values) layout is active in the Decision Center Layout panel. This displays the summary values table in the right-hand frame of the graphics window, as shown in the following image.

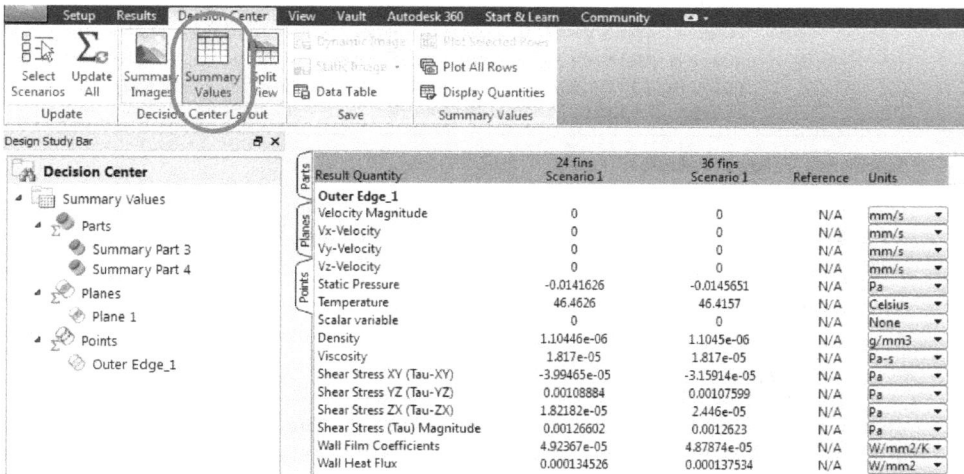

Result Quantity	24 fins Scenario 1	36 fins Scenario 1	Reference	Units
Outer Edge_1				
Velocity Magnitude	0	0	N/A	mm/s
Vx-Velocity	0	0	N/A	mm/s
Vy-Velocity	0	0	N/A	mm/s
Vz-Velocity	0	0	N/A	mm/s
Static Pressure	-0.0141626	-0.0145651	N/A	Pa
Temperature	46.4626	46.4157	N/A	Celsius
Scalar variable	0	0	N/A	None
Density	1.10446e-06	1.1045e-06	N/A	g/mm3
Viscosity	1.817e-05	1.817e-05	N/A	Pa-s
Shear Stress XY (Tau-XY)	-3.99465e-05	-3.15914e-05	N/A	Pa
Shear Stress YZ (Tau-YZ)	0.00108884	0.00107599	N/A	Pa
Shear Stress ZX (Tau-ZX)	1.82182e-05	2.446e-05	N/A	Pa
Shear Stress (Tau) Magnitude	0.00126602	0.0012623	N/A	Pa
Wall Film Coefficients	4.92367e-05	4.87874e-05	N/A	W/mm2/K
Wall Heat Flux	0.000134526	0.000137534	N/A	W/mm2

5. Select the required Parts, Planes, or Points tab in the summary values table to compare the values in the design scenarios.

6. Customize the data presentation in the summary values table using the following options:

    •   To add or remove a result value, ensure that the required tab is active and click Display Quantities (from the right side of the table). Select or deselect the quantities, as required. Click OK.

    •   Change the units of a result by selecting an entry from the Units column.

    •   Set a critical value (or a value important to your design) in the Reference column. Examples include the maximum allowable temperature or the minimum flow rate. This is very useful when plotting the data, to assess which scenarios fall within the allowed design constraints.

7. Plot and visually compare the results in a bar graph. To plot results data, use any one of the following methods. The options are located on the right-hand side of the frame or in the Summary Values panel.

    •   To plot a selected row, select it in the summary values table and click Plot Selected Rows.

    •   To plot multiple rows, hold <Ctrl> and select the rows. Then, click Plot Selected Rows.

    •   To plot all rows, click Plot All Rows.

    Once plotted, the results display as bar graphs in the Results Plots dialog box, as shown in the following image. Use the Scale option to change the Y-axis range and use the Save option to save the plot as a .BMP file.

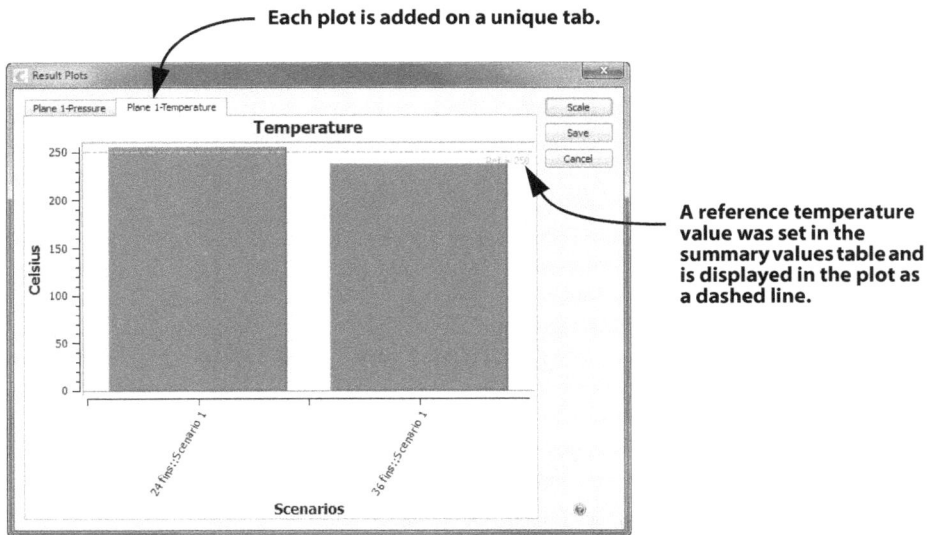

Each plot is added on a unique tab.

A reference temperature value was set in the summary values table and is displayed in the plot as a dashed line.

Summary Plots (Graphical)

Summary Plots are used to graphically compare the XY plot results in multiple scenarios by overlaying them in a single XY plot. They are ideal for determining relative performance of design alternatives. A summary plot can only be created using the Planes result task.

To create and review summary plots, complete the following steps:

1. Create the required summary plot. The creation of a summary plot was previously explained in the *Planes Result Tasks* lesson.

2. Select the Decision Center tab. The Summary Plots node displays similar to that shown in the following image. In this image, a single summary plot was created.
   - Each summary plot is listed sequentially, in the order in which they were created.
   - To rename a plot, right-click on its default name, select Rename, and enter a new name.
   - The summary plots initially display as out of date (⚠).

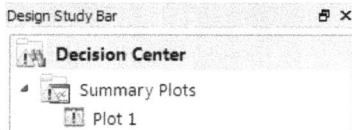

3. Update the summary plots in the Decision Center. Right-click on a plot name or on the Summary Plots header and select Update summary values to propagate the data across all scenarios.

4. Double-click on a plot to display it in the Summary XY Plot dialog box, as shown in the following image. If multiple plots exist, they can all be opened in their own dialog boxes.

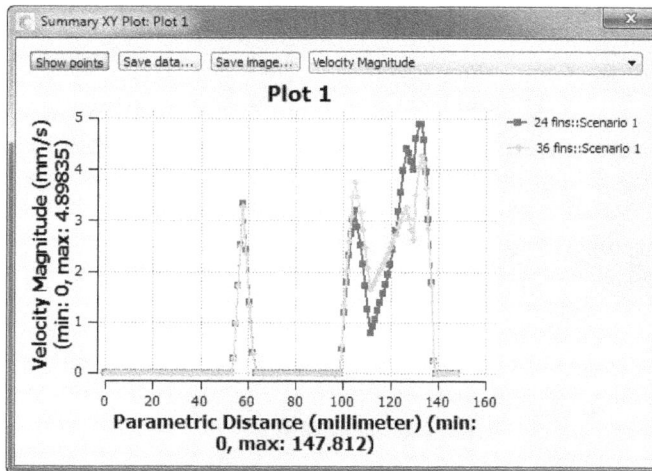

---

5. Use the Summary XY Plot dialog box to visually compare the graphical data.

    •   The results for each scenario are overlay and display in unique colors according to a legend provided on the right-hand side of the dialog box.

    •   By default, the results view that displays is the same as the one set when the XY plot was created. To change the results view that displays, select a new option from the drop-down list.

    •   Enable or disable the Show Points option as required, to show or clear the saved iteration points on the plot.

    •   The Save data and Save image buttons can be selected to save the data or an image file for viewing outside of Autodesk CFD.

6. Close the dialog box to remove the plot from the display.

Managing the Summary Objects

When working in the Decision Center, consider the following tips:

▪   By default, results for each summary object are computed for all scenarios. To change the scenarios, right-click on a particular object and pick Select Scenarios or click ⊟ (Select Scenarios in the Update panel. Select only the scenarios you wish to compare from the list.

▪   Use the ▦ (Split View) layout option in the Decision Center Layout panel to change the display on the right-hand side of the Decision Center. This will show both active summary images in the graphics window and the summary values in the Output Bar.

▪   If a summary entity is moved or a new one is added, the data in the table does not match the summary entity and the warning symbol will display on the branch. Right-click on the entity and select Update summary values.

▪   You can update each summary object individually or update all summary objects for a type (e.g., Summary Images) using the Summary Object node. To update all types at once, click Σ_c (Update All) in the Update panel.

▪   Summary objects can be expanded or compressed in the Decision Center's Design Study Bar to help manage the data that you are reviewing.

▪   To delete any summary object, right-click on its name and select Remove. This only removes the summary object; it does not affect the actual results. **Note:** In the case of Summary Planes, they must be removed as a summary object before the plane can be deleted.

▪   Use the options on the Save panel to save images and/or CSV data tables of the data for review outside of Autodesk CFD.

Exercise: Analyze the Valve Results Set

In this exercise, you will open an existing design study that has been setup and run through the solver. The design study involves the valve model that you have seen previously. The design has been returned to the original three cages. You will compare the results for three cage designs. The objective in this exercise is to:

- Analyze Plane, Traces and Wall results for three designs.

Open a design study in the Autodesk CFD Environment.

In this task, you will open a design study and review the difference between the three designs.

1. Launch Autodesk CFD, if not already running.

2. In the Home tab, click ⬜ (Open). If prompted to save an open design study, click Yes.

3. In the Open dialog box, browse to the *C:\Autodesk CFD 2017 Essentials Exercise Files\Results\ ControlValve_Results* folder. Select and open *ControlValve_Results.cfdst*. The model displays as shown in the following image.

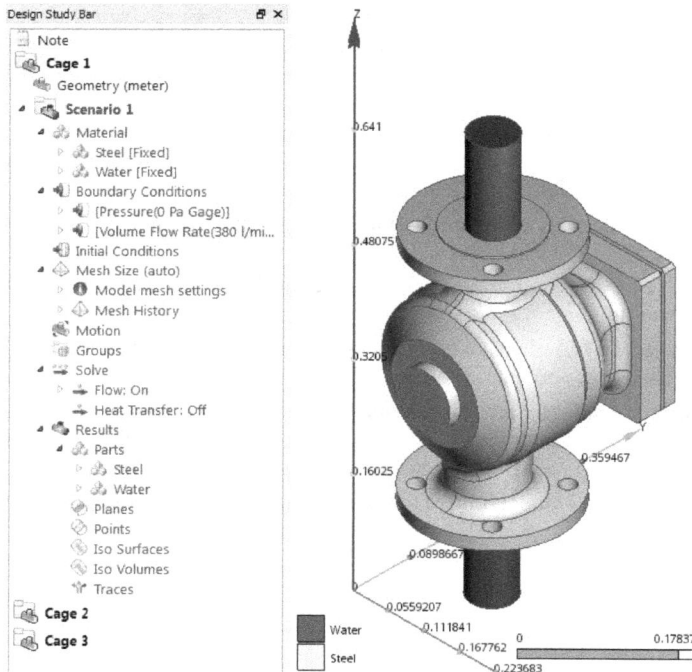

Review the Global results.

In this task, you will review the global pressure.

1. Select the Results tab and note that the model changes color to reflect the last iteration of the analysis, as shown in the following image.

   ▪ The displayed iteration is listed in the Iteration/Step panel.

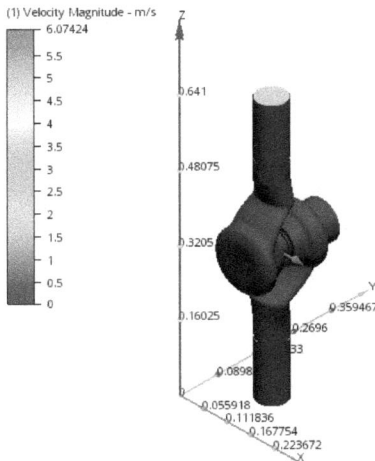

2. In the Results tab in the Global panel, in the Global Result drop-down list, select Static Pressure. The legend and model update as shown in the following image.

   ▪ Changing the Global Result setting sets the Static Pressure as the default result to display for all result tasks that are created.

   ▪ The pressure drops as you follow along the negative Z axis, indicating that the flow is traveling in the -Z direction.

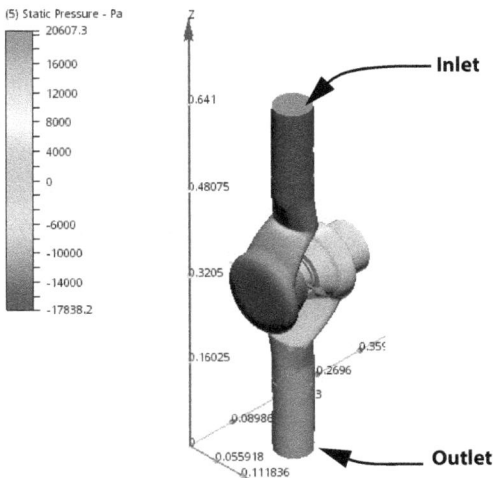

3. In the main graphics window, click Output Bar to minimize it.

4. Place the cursor over the inlet and note that the pressure Value is listed at the bottom of the window, as shown in the following image.

   ▪ Note that your value will be different depending on where exactly the cursor sits.

   ▪ Continue to probe the model for pressure values.

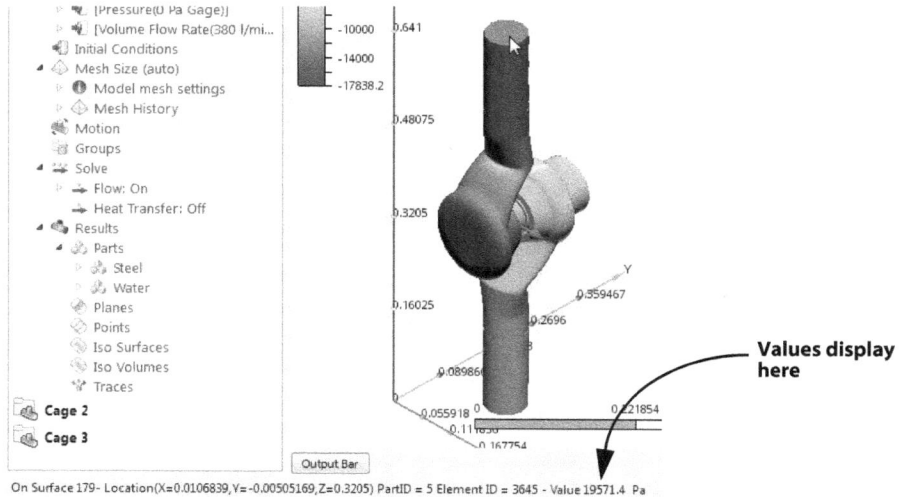

On Surface 179- Location(X=0.0106839,Y=-0.00505169,Z=0.3205) PartID = 5 Element ID = 3645 - Value 19571.4 Pa

5. Select the View tab and click 🔽 ▾ (Axes).

   ▪ Toggle off the display of all axis types, as shown in the following image. This simplifies the display to help visualize the results.

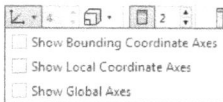

6. In the Quick Access Toolbar, expand 🔲 (Visual Style) and select Transparent to see through the model.

7. When Global is active, the Global panel is available on both the Results and View tabs. In the Global panel, make the following selections:

   ▪ In the Global Vector drop-down list, select Velocity Vector.

   ▪ Click 🖉 (Vector Settings) and in the Vector Settings dialog box, edit the Length to **0.3**, as shown in the following image.

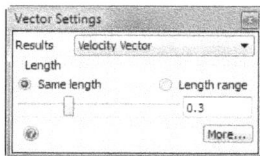

8. Select ⊠ to close the Vector Settings dialog box. The velocity vectors display at the planar surfaces, as shown in the following image.

9. Select the Results tab, if not already active. In the Image Panel, click 📷 (Summary Image) to capture a image.

10. Select the Decision Center tab and click Σ (Update All). The images for all three scenarios update, as shown in the following image.

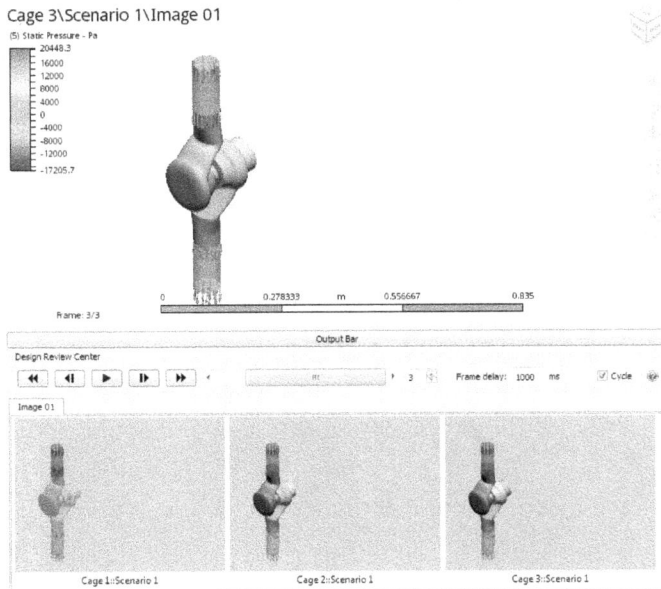

11. In the Design Review Center, click [▶] (Next) to step through the three scenario summary images. Alternatively, you can drag the slider to review the static pressure and vectors for each design scenario in the larger display area.

12. Select the Results tab. In the Global panel, in the Global vector drop-down list, select None.

   ▪ This will clear the vectors from the display. Generally, vectors are best used to confirm the direction of the flow.

Create a Plane result to investigate the internal pressure.

In this task, you will create a plane result to view the internal pressure.

1. In the Results tab, click [⬒] (Planes) to activate the Planes panel.

   ▪ In the Planes panel, click [✚] (Add). Note that Static Pressure is the default result, since it was set as the Global option.
   ▪ In the Quick Access Toolbar, expand [▢] (Visual Style) and select Outline.
   ▪ In the ViewCube, select RIGHT. The model displays as shown in the following image.

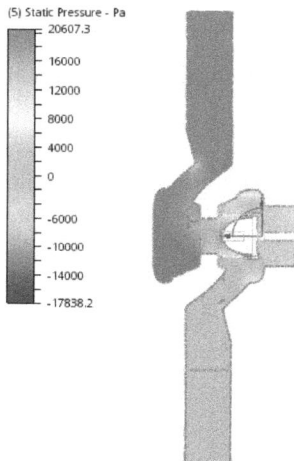

2. In the Planes panel, in the Vector drop-down list, select Velocity Vector.

- Compress the Output Bar to enlarge the graphics window.
- Zoom in on the area near the center of the valve and note that the direction of the flow is from the higher pressure area to the lower pressure area.

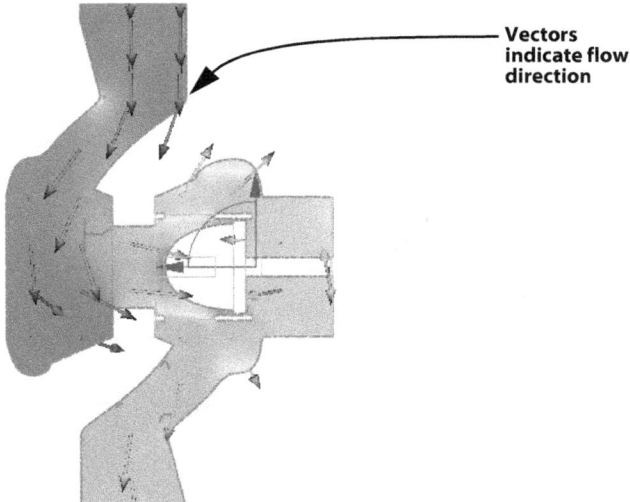

Vectors indicate flow direction

3. In the Planes panel, click ✐ (Vector Settings) to open the Plane Control dialog box, as shown in the following image.

- By default, the Vector Settings tab is active.

4. To refine the vectors, make the following edits:

   - Edit the Length to **0.07**.
   - Edit the Y Grid spacing to **0.003** to increase the vector density.
   - Set the Appearance to Transparent.
   - The dialog box and model displays similar to that shown in the following image. Note the indicated area of low pressure.

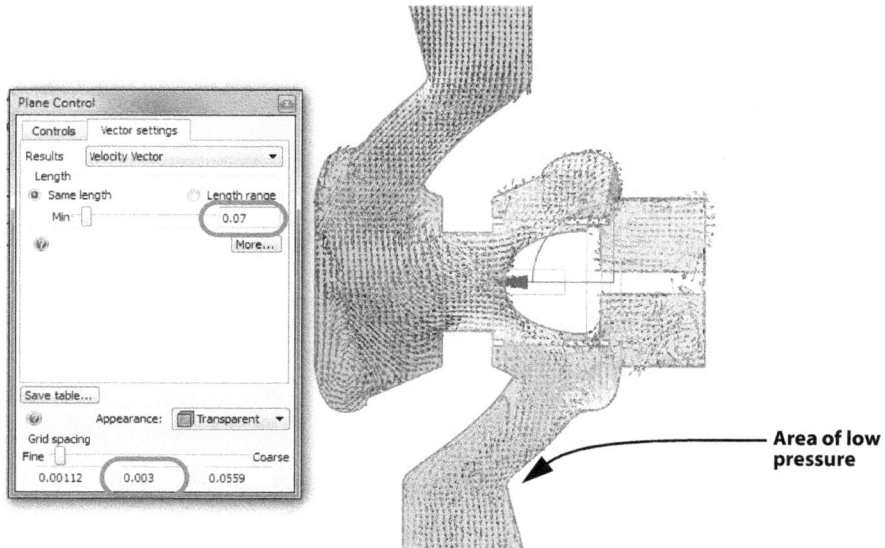

5. Select [×] to close the Vector Settings dialog box.

6. Zoom in on the low pressure area and note the vectors running "against the grain", indicating recirculation.

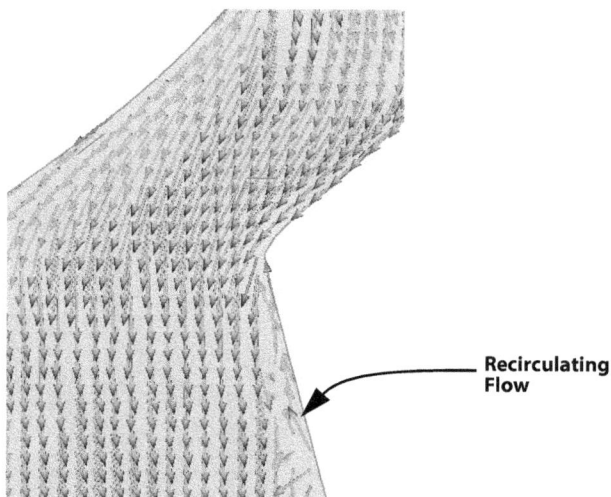

7. In the Image Panel, click (Summary Image) to create an image for comparison.

8. Select the Decision Center tab and click $\sum_\circ$ (Update All).

9. In the Design Study Bar, in the Summary Images node, select Image 02.

10. The images for all three scenarios update as shown in the following image.

    ■ Note that the view orientation and zoom level are stored with the image.

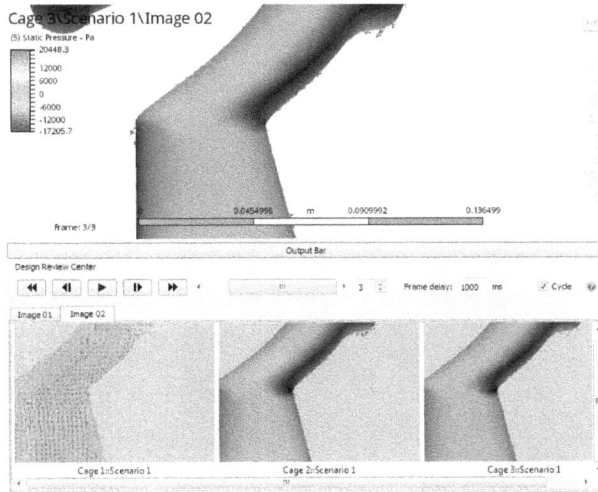

11. Note that the view display for the Cage 2 and Cage 3 design images is still set as Shaded. This is because the view display for these scenarios was not explicitly changed in the design setup.

   - Click ▶ (Next) to step through each summary image.
   - For each image, right-click on the geometry and select Outline.
   - The view displays as shown in the following image.
   - Note that the exclamation marks in the Cage 2 and Cage 3 images simply indicate that they have been changed from the default images.

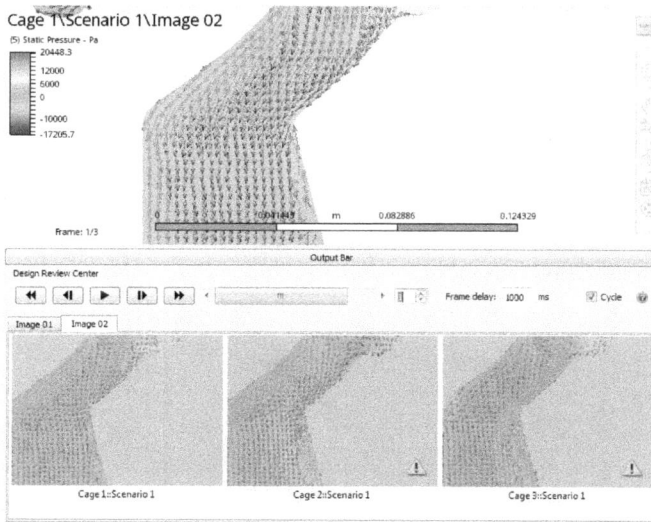

12. In the Design Review Center, click ▶ (Play). This plays through the images in the graphics window.

13. Compress the Output Bar to enlarge the viewing area.

   - Note that the recirculation increases in the Cage 2 and Cage 3 designs.

Create two additional Plane results to investigate the pressure near the cage.

In this task, you will create a plane result through the X and Z axes to view the pressure near the cage.

1. Select the Results tab and click (Planes) to activate the Planes panel.

   - In the Design Study Bar, remove the check mark next to Plane 1.
   - Using the navigation tools, refit the model to full screen. Note that it is still in the Outline display style.
   - In the Planes panel, click (Add).
   - Left-click on the plane and select (Align to Y Axis) in the mini-toolbar to change the plane's default orientation, as shown in the following image.

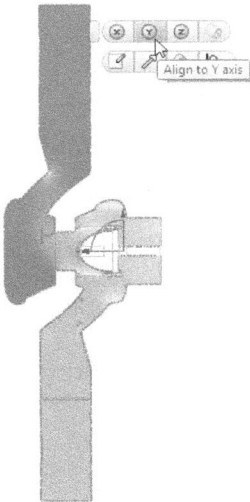

2. Orient the model similar to that shown in the following image.

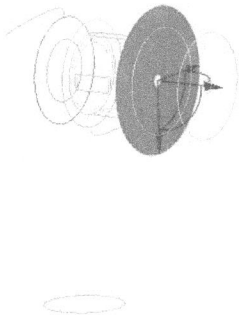

3. Drag the arrow to move the plane so it intersects with the cage, similar to the one shown in the following image.

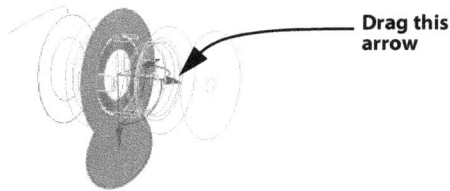

Drag this arrow

4. In the View Cube, select BACK.

5. Right-click on the plane and select Transparent.

6. In the Planes panel, in the Vector drop-down list, select Velocity Vector.

7. In the Planes panel, click 🖋 (Vector Settings) to open the Plane Control dialog box.

   - Edit the Y grid spacing to **0.005**, as shown in the following image.
     - Note that you can also drag the slider.

   - Select 🔲 to close the Vector Settings dialog box.
   - Note that the pressure is high inside the cage, then lowers after it exits through the cage openings.
   - The flow appears to be the same through all outlets of the cage, which is expected given the symmetry.

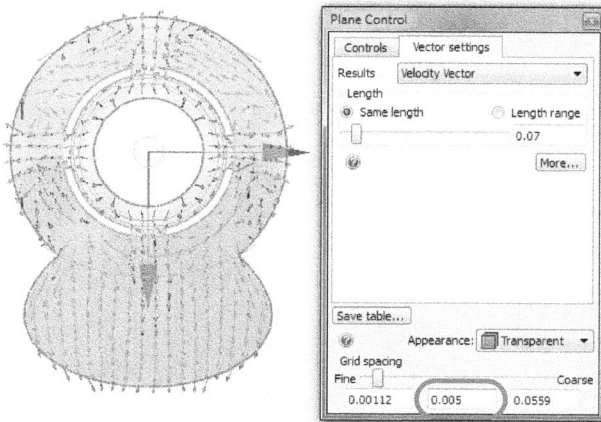

8. In the Image Panel, click 📷 (Summary Image) to create an image for comparison.

9. Add a plane through the Z axis.
In the Design Study Bar, remove the checkmark next to Plane 2.

- In the View Cube, click 🏠 (Home)

- In the Planes panel, click ➕ (Add).

- Left-click on the plane and select (Ⓩ) (Align to Z Axis) in the mini-toolbar.
- The plane is created as shown in the following image.

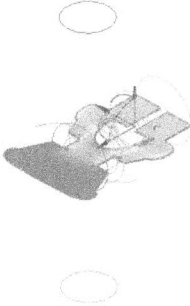

10. In the View Cube, select TOP.

11. Right-click on the plane and select Transparent.

12. In the Planes panel, in the Vector drop-down list, select Velocity Vector.

13. In the Planes panel, click ✏ (Vector Settings) to open the Plane Control dialog box.

- Edit the Y grid spacing to **0.005**, as shown in the following image.

- Select ▣ to close the Vector Settings dialog box.
- The pressure is high entering the cage, then lowers after it exits through the cage openings.

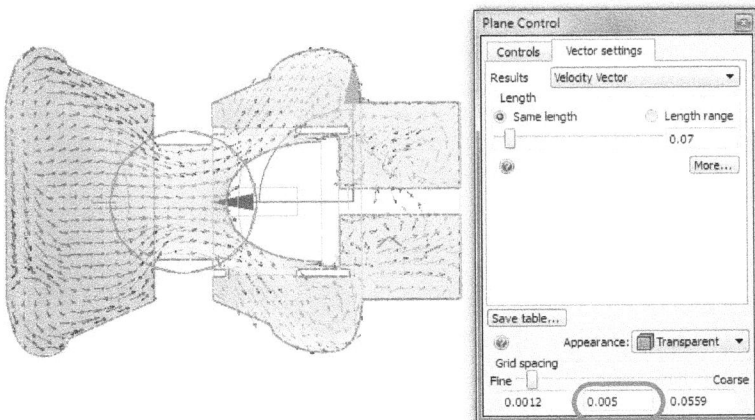

14. In the Image Panel, click 📷 (Summary Image) to create an image for comparison.

15. In the Planes panel, click Σ (Make Summary) to create a summary plane for use in the Decision Center.

16. Select the Decision Center tab and note that the last two summary images and the summary plane are all listed as out of date and require updating. Click Σ (Update All).

17. In the Decision Center, in the Summary values node, select Plane 3. The Summary Values for this plane display in the right-hand frame, as shown in the following image. Your results might vary slightly.

Result Quantity	Cage 1 Scenario 1	Cage 2 Scenario 1	Cage 3 Scenario 1	Reference	Units
Plane 3					
Area	0.016602	0.0167072	0.0167095	N/A	m2
Mass flow rate	-6.27069	-6.3561	-6.43727	N/A	kg/s
Volume flow rate	-0.006282	-0.00638	-0.00644888	N/A	m3/s
Vx-Velocity	-0.00109028	-0.0257775	0.00198087	N/A	m/s
Vy-Velocity	0.942624	0.74483	0.790268	N/A	m/s
Vz-Velocity	-0.378389	-0.381871	-0.38594	N/A	m/s
Density	998.2	995.6	998.202	N/A	kg/m3
Pressure	12374.1	11112.9	9830.7	N/A	Pa
Pressure force	196.319	167.063	150.098	N/A	Newton
Temperature	0	0	0	N/A	Celsius
Viscosity	0.001003	0.00100039	0.001003	N/A	Pa-s
Scalar	0	0	0	N/A	None

18. Select the Results tab.

Create a final Plane result to use the Bulk option.

In this task, you will create a plane result through the inlet to use the Bulk option.

1. Add a plane through the top surface of the flow volume.

   - In the Design Study Bar, remove the checkmark next to Plane 3.

   - In the View Cube, click 🏠 (Home).

   - In the Planes panel, click ➕ (Add).

   - Left-click on the plane and select 🔘 (Align to surface) in the mini-toolbar.
   - Although the model displays in Outline mode, select the surface shown in the following image.

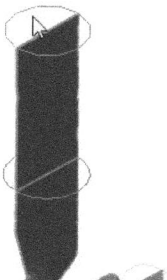

2.   In the View Cube, select TOP. The model updates as shown in the following image.

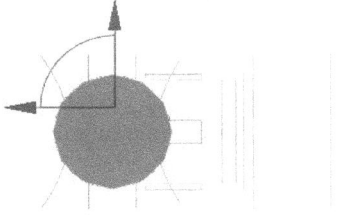

3.   Right-click on the plane and select Transparent.

4.   Left-click on the plane and click (Bulk) in the mini-toolbar to open the Bulk Results dialog box, as shown in the following image.

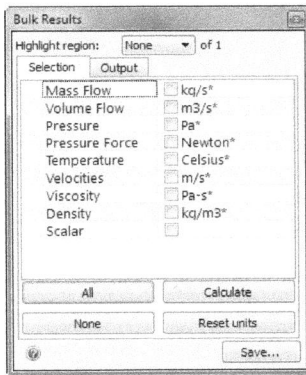

5.   In the Bulk Results dialog box, select the checkboxes adjacent to the Mass Flow and Pressure results.

- Click Calculate and the values for Mass Flowrate and Pressure display in the Output tab, as shown in the following image.
- Note that the massflow rate is -6.32 kg/s and the pressure is 19586.6 Pa for this section.

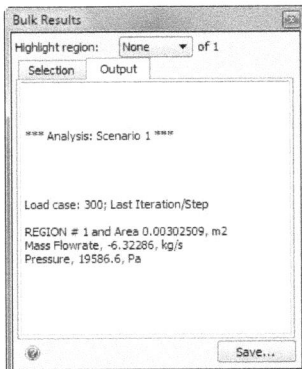

6. Return the model to its default Home view. Do not close the Bulk Results dialog box.

7. Drag the vertical arrow to locate the plane in a position similar to that shown in the following image.

    ■ Ensure that you have positioned the plane such that the flow displays through an opening in the cage.

    ■ Note that the values calculated in the Bulk Results tool automatically update with the plane's change in position.

    ■ This can be used to dynamically inspect various areas in your model.

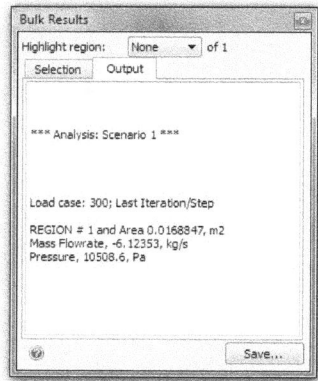

8. Close the Bulk Results dialog box.

9. In the ViewCube, click TOP.

10. Left-click on the plane and click [icon] (XY Plot) in the mini-toolbar to open the XY Plot dialog box, as shown in the following image.

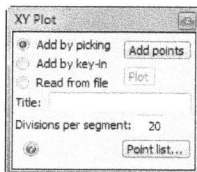

11. In the XY Plot dialog box, enter **Throat Velocity** as the Title.

   ▪ Click Add points and select multiple points similar to that shown in the following image.

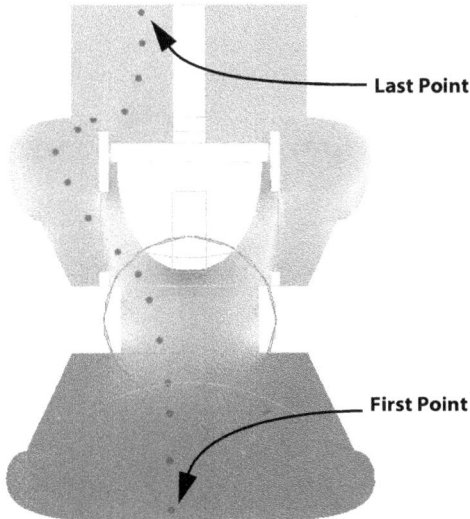

12. In the XY Plot dialog box, click Plot.

13. In the Result drop-down list, select Velocity Magnitude to create a graph of the velocity at each point, similar to that shown in the following image. Your graph may vary depending on the placement of the plane and the points.

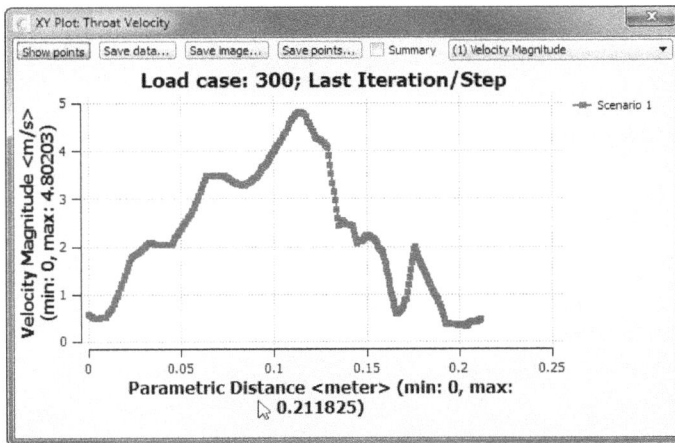

14. In the XY Plot dialog box, select the Summary checkbox to save the plot for use in the Decision Center.

15. Select the Decision Center tab. Note that the Summary Plots node has been added and it displays as out of date.

16. Right-click on the Summary Plots node and select Update summary values.

17. Double-click on the Throat Velocity XY Plot. The Summary XY Plot displays with all three design scenario results plotted in the same plot for easy comparison, as shown in the following image.

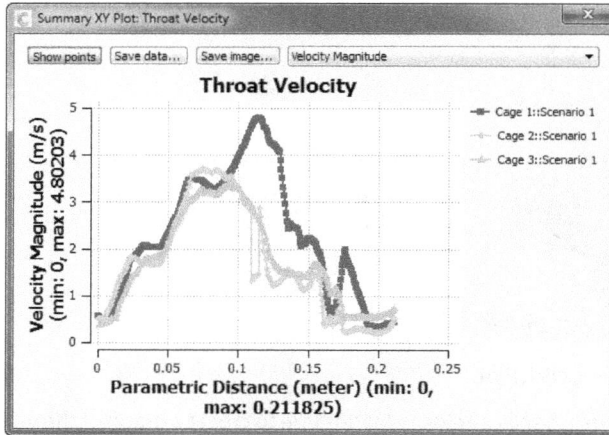

18. Close the two XY Plot dialog boxes.

Analyze the Traces Results.

In this task, you will analyze trace curves to observe the flow pattern.

1. In the Design Study Bar, remove the check mark next to all of the planes. Using the ViewCube, return to the default Home view.

2. In the Results Tasks panel, click (Traces).

3. In the Create Set panel, make the following selections, as shown in the following image:
   - In the Seed Type drop-down list, select Circular.
   - In the Seed Pattern drop-down list, select Diamond.
   - Leave Seed Density as 1 for now.

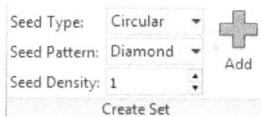

4. In the Create Set panel, click ✚ (Add) and left-click in the approximate center of the inlet surface, then left-click again near the edge of the surface, as shown in the following image.

    ▪ Once placed, you can use the blue drag handles to reposition the seed representation in the surface.

    ▪ Note that although the model displays in the Outline mode, you can still select the surface.

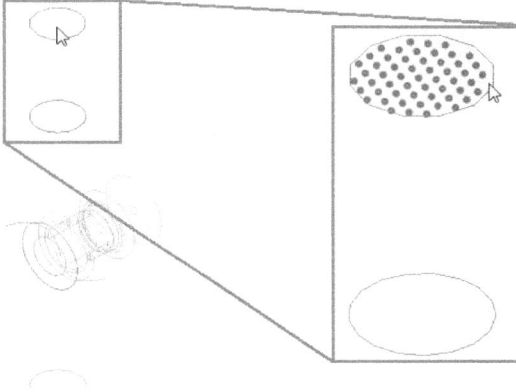

5. The traces display in the model, showing how the flow travels through the valve. Orient and zoom in on the model, similar to that shown in the following image.

    ▪ Your display may vary from that shown depending on the placement of the seed surface and your current orientation.

    ▪ Note that traces that loop back on themselves indicate recirculation.

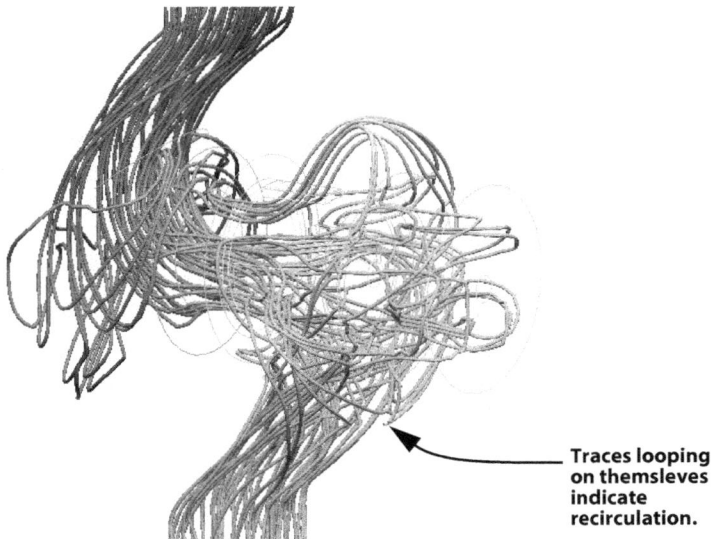

Traces looping on themsleves indicate recirculation.

6.   In the View Cube, click ■ (Home).

7.   To animate the flow, click ◎⁓ (Animate) to open the Animate Traces dialog box.

    ▪ In the Animation Time (sec) field, enter **20**.

    ▪ Click ▶ (Play) to begin the animation. Traces begin at the inlet and flow through the model, as shown in the following image.

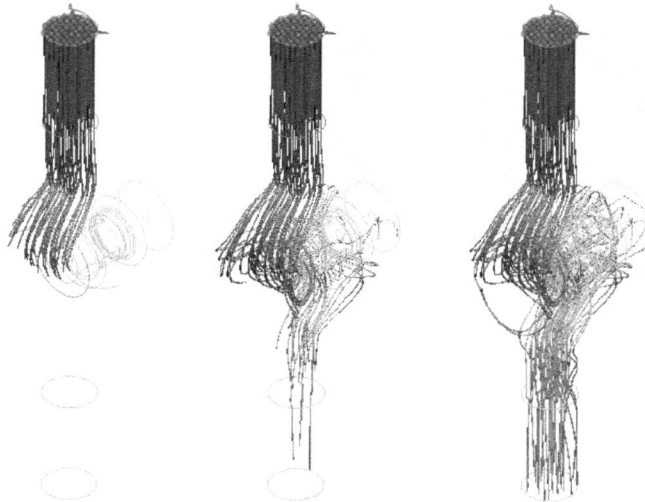

As the animation progreses, the trace curves follow the path of the fluid flow

8.   After reviewing the flow, click ⏸ (Pause) and then ⏭ (Jump to End) to set the display to the last frame of the animation.

9.   In the Design Study Bar, in the Traces node, remove the check mark next to Set 1.

    ▪ Note that Summary Images can be created for a trace set similar to how they were previously created.

Calculate forces on the cage and valve stem.

In this task, you will use the Wall Calculator to summarize the forces on the surfaces of the cage and valve stem.

1. In the Results Tasks panel, click (Wall Calculator). The Wall Results dialog box opens as shown in the following image.

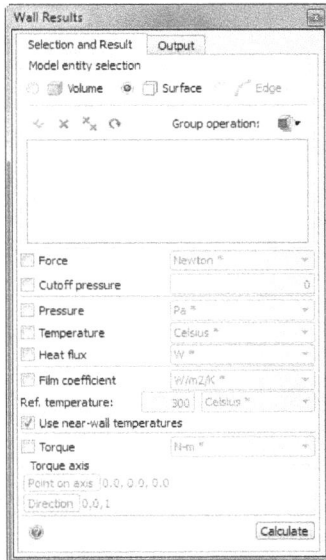

2. In the Quick Access Toolbar, change the view display to Transparent.

3.   In the Wall Result dialog box, expand the Group operation and select Wall_Surfaces, as shown in the following image.

   ▪ This adds the surface of the cage (30), the valve stem (7), and both sides of the poppet (2, 3), which were previously added to the group to make selection easier.

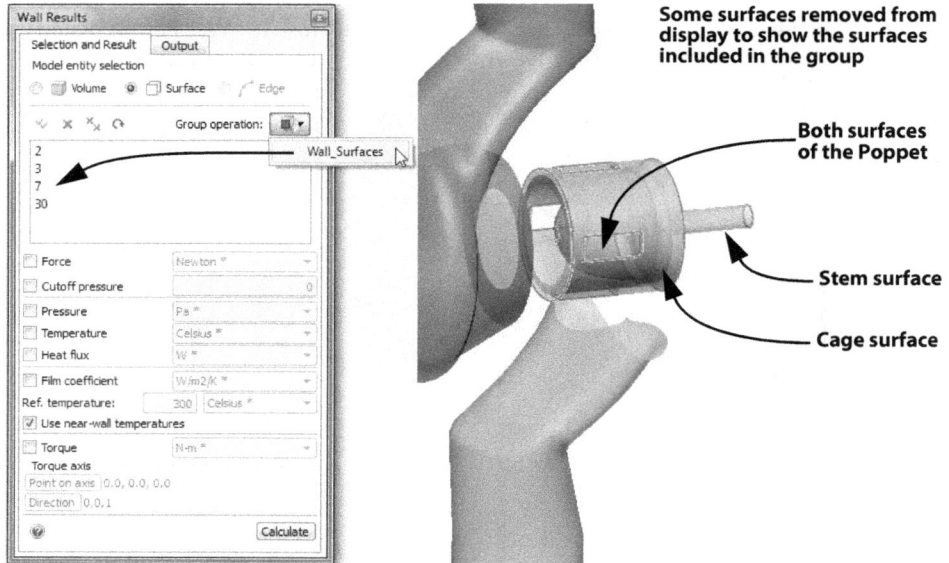

Some surfaces removed from display to show the surfaces included in the group

Both surfaces of the Poppet

Stem surface

Cage surface

4.   In the Wall Results dialog box, click Force to enable it and maintain the default units. Click Calculate.

   ▪ Autodesk CFD calculates the forces on each of the boundaries, as well as an overall summary. The results display in the Output tab, as shown in the following image.

   ▪ Note that the results can be saved to a file for viewing outside of Autodesk CFD.

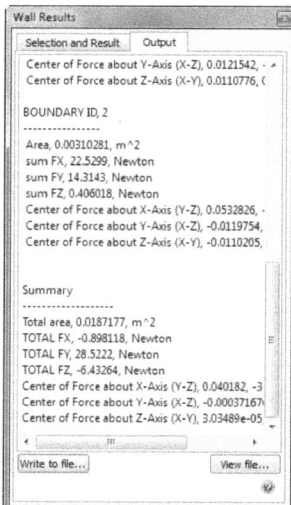

5.   Close the Wall Results dialog box.

Review the Summary File.

In this task, you will use the Summary file to review the values at the inlet and outlet.

1.   In the Review panel, click 🗐 (Summary File) to open the Summary dialog box.

- Scroll to the Inlet section and review the results shown on the left in the following image.
- Scroll to the Outlet section and review the results shown on the right in the following image.

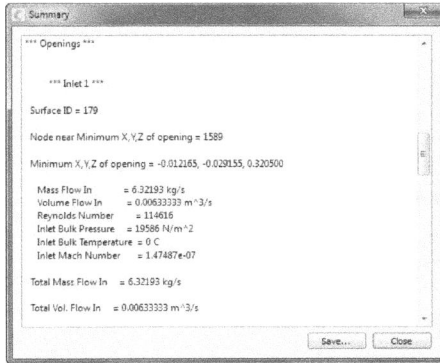

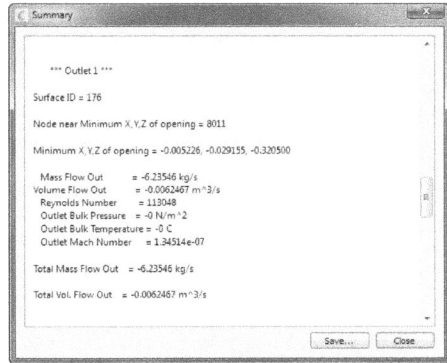

2.   Close the Summary dialog box to complete the exercise.

3.   In the Quick Access toolbar, click 💾 (Save) to save the study, model orientations, etc.

Exercise: Analyze the LED Results Set

In this exercise, you will open an existing design study that has two designs for an LED light. Each design has a different number of fins on the heat sink. The objective in this exercise is to:

- Analyze the result set using a results plane and parts result.

Open a design study in the Autodesk CFD Environment.

In this task, you will open a design study and review the difference between the three designs.

1. Launch Autodesk CFD, if not already running.

2. In the Home tab, click [ ] (Open). If prompted to save an open design study, click Yes.

3. In the Open dialog box, browse to the *C:\Autodesk CFD 2017 Essentials Exercise Files\Results\ LED_Results* folder. Select and open *LED_Results.cfdst*.

4. Select the View tab and click [ ] ▾ (Axes).

    - Ensure all axis types are toggled off, as shown in the following image.

Review the Global results.

In this task, you will review the global Temperature and Heat Flux.

1. Select the Results tab.

2. In the Quick Access Toolbar, expand [ ] (Visual Style) and select Transparent. Note that the model color reflects the last iteration of the analysis, as shown in the following image.

    - You can identify the displayed version from that listed in the Iteration/Step panel.

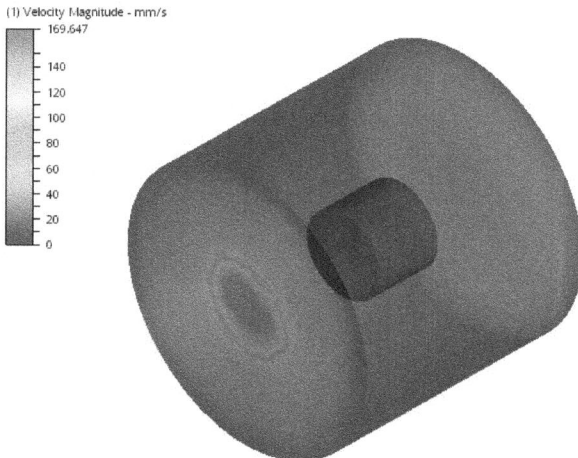

3. Select the View tab and in the View Settings panel, click Apply View. In the *LED Results* folder, select and open the *Installed Orientation.xvs* file. This loads a saved view orientation.

4. In the Results tab, in the Global panel, in the Global Result drop-down list, select Temperature. The model displays as shown in the following image.

   ▪ Note the slight change in temperature near the top center of the external air volume. The air heated by the LED assembly rises due to buoyant forces.

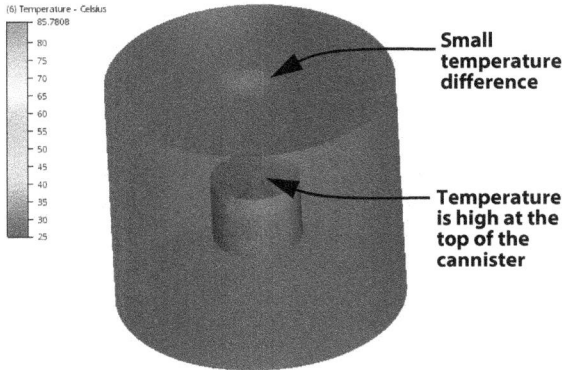

5. In the Global panel, make the following selections:

   ▪ In the Global Vector drop-down list, select Wall Heat Flux.

   ▪ Click ✐ (Vector Settings) and in the Vector Settings dialog box, edit the Length to **0.1**, as shown in the following image.

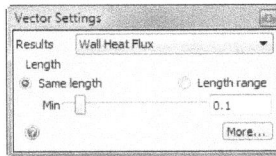

6. Close the Vector Settings dialog box. Hold <Ctrl> and press the middle mouse button on the air volume to hide it. The model displays as shown in the following image.

   ▪ The vectors indicate the rate of heat transfer on the walls of the model.

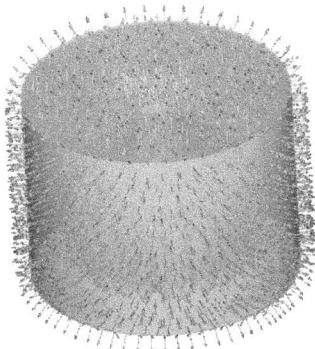

7. In the Global panel, in the Global Vector drop-down list, select None to remove the vectors from display.

8. In the Image Panel, click 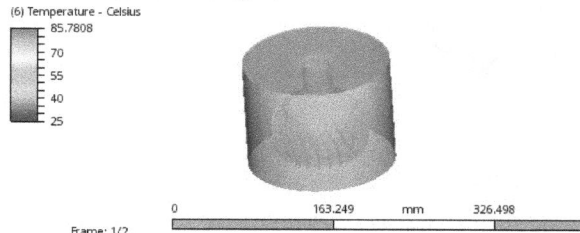 (Summary Image) to create an image for comparison.

9. Select the Decision Center tab and click Σ_{σ} (Update All). The images for two scenarios update.

    ▪ Click  (Next) to step through the scenario summary images.
    ▪ Note that the temperature at the top of the cannister appears to be higher with 36 fins as compared to 24 fins, as shown in the following image.
    ▪ This indicates that it is not dissipating the energy as well.

24 fins\Scenario 1\Image 01

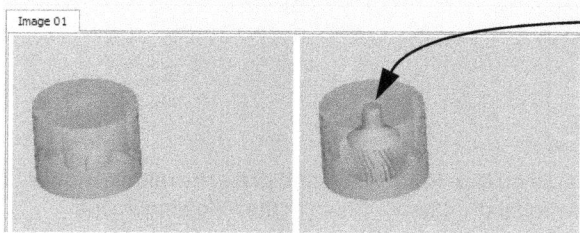

10. Hold <Ctrl> and press the middle mouse button anywhere on the screen to display the hidden objects. Zoom out to see the entire model.

Create a Planes Result.

In this task, you will create a Planes result to observe the temperature distribution near the LEDs.

1. In the Results tab, click (Planes) to activate the Planes panel.

- In the Planes panel, click (Add).
- In the Planes panel, in the Vector drop-down list, select Velocity Magnitude and keep Temperature as the Result setting.
- In the Quick Access Toolbar, expand (Visual Style) and select Outline.
- In the ViewCube, select LEFT. The model displays as shown in the following image.

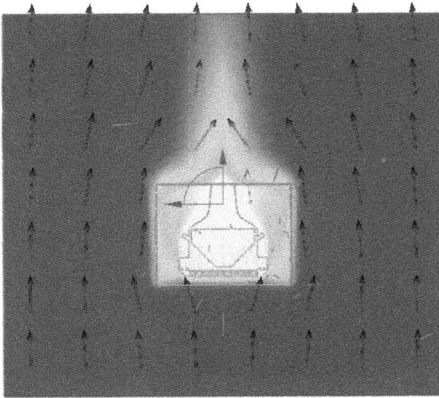

2. In the Planes panel, click ✐ (Vector Settings) to open the Plane Control dialog box. To refine the vectors, make the following edits:

    ▪   Select Length range to display the vectors with lengths that are relative to the velocity magnitude.

    ▪   Edit the Min Length to **0.3**.

    ▪   Edit the Max Length to **0.6**.

    ▪   Edit the Y Grid Spacing to **25**.

    ▪   The dialog box and model display similar to that shown in the following image. Note the higher velocity (larger vectors) above the cannister and heat sink.

    ▪   Close the Plane Control dialog box.

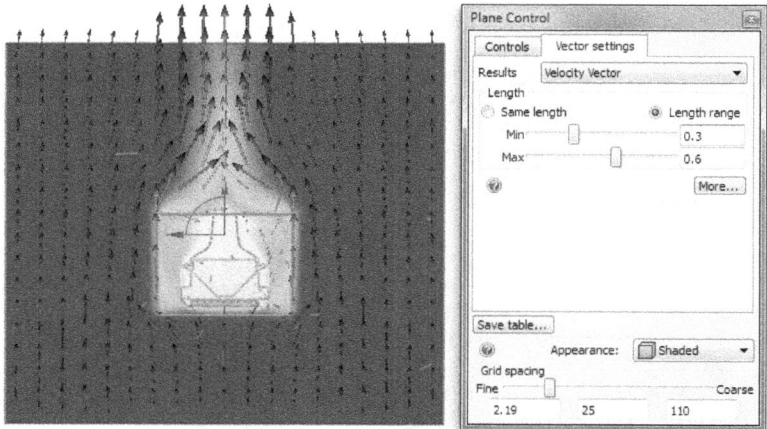

3. Plot the temperature values near the LEDs. Left-click on the plane and click 📈 (XY Plot) in the mini-toolbar to open the XY Plot dialog box, as shown in the following image.

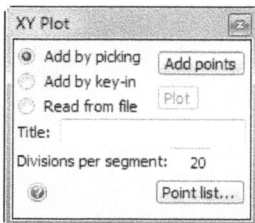

4. Zoom in on the LEDs, and in the XY Plot dialog box, enter **Temperature** as the Title.

   ▪ Click Add Points and select the two points similar to that shown in the following image.

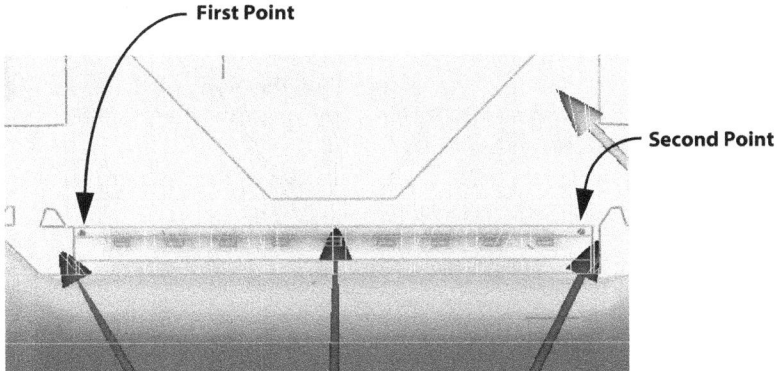

First Point

Second Point

5. In the XY Plot dialog box, click Plot to create a graph of the velocity at each point, as shown in the following image.

   ▪ Click Summary to create a summary plot.

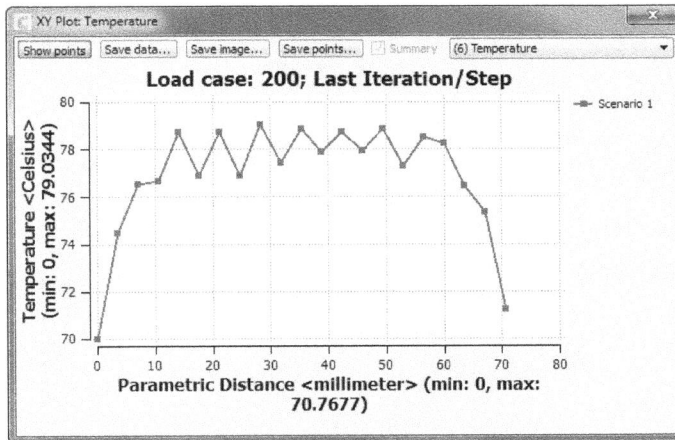

6. Close the two XY Plot dialog boxes.

7. Select the Decision Center tab.

8. In the Design Study Bar, right-click on the Summary Plots node and select Update summary values.

   ▪ In the Summary Plots node, select Temperature. The graph for the two scenarios displays as shown in the following image. Note that your graph may vary slightly depending on the point locations that you chose to plot.

   ▪ Note the higher temperatures for the 36 fin model, compared to the 24 fin model.

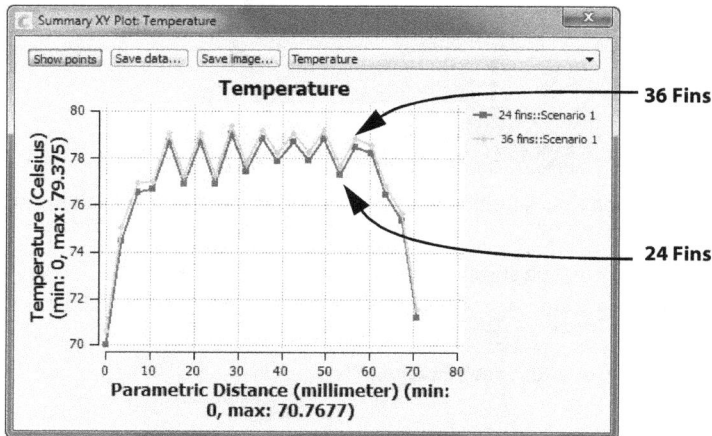

9. Close the two XY Plot dialog boxes.

Apply a Parts Results.

In this task, you will apply a parts result to verify the maximum temperature reached by the PCB and the LEDs.

1. Select the Results tab, and in the Results Task panel, click ⬛ (Parts). The Parts panel and Parts dialog box displays as shown in the following image.

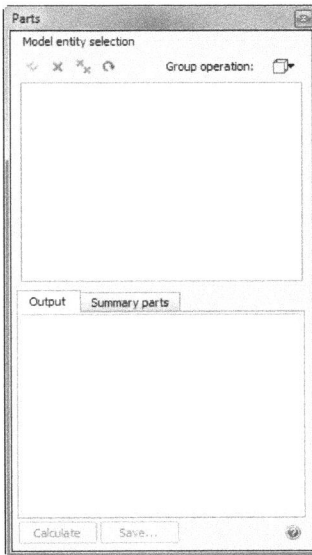

2. In the Group operation drop-down list, select LED and then select the checkbox next to each LED, as shown in the following image.

   - This group was previously created and provides an easy way to select a group of components instead of selecting them individually.

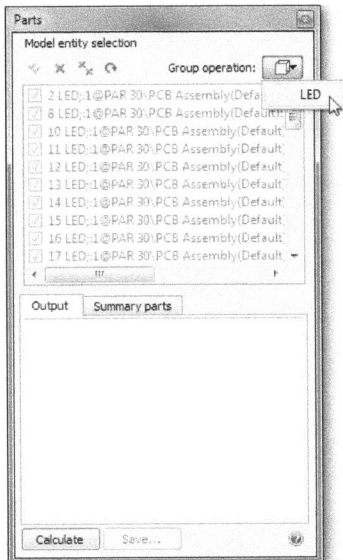

3. In the Parts dialog box, click Calculate.

   ▪ The temperatures for the LEDs are calculated, as shown in the following image.

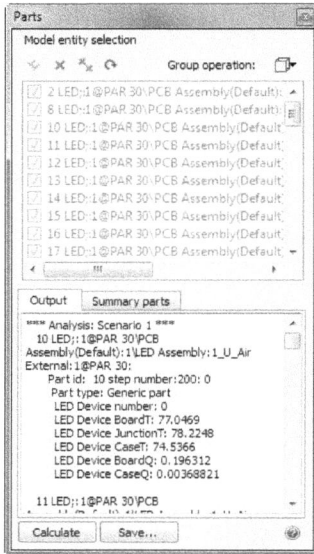

4. In the Planes panel, click Σ (Make Summary).

5. Select the Decision Center tab, right-click on the Summary Values node, and select Update summary values.

   ▪ The values for all LEDs display in the Parts table, as shown in the following image.
   ▪ Note the higher temperatures for the 36 fin model, compared to the 24 fin model.

Result Quantity	24 fins Scenario 1	36 fins Scenario 1	Reference	Units
Summary Part 2				
Board heat flux	0.195347	0.19536	N/A	W
Board temperature	80.588	80.8383	N/A	Celsius
Case heat flux	0.00465268	0.00464015	N/A	W
Case temperature	77.1074	77.3703	N/A	Celsius
Junction temperature	81.7601	82.0105	N/A	Celsius
Summary Part 8				
Board heat flux	0.196627	0.196634	N/A	W
Board temperature	76.1776	76.5108	N/A	Celsius
Case heat flux	0.00337265	0.00336617	N/A	W
Case temperature	73.9847	74.3245	N/A	Celsius
Junction temperature	77.3574	77.6906	N/A	Celsius
Summary Part 10				
Board heat flux	0.196312	0.196342	N/A	W
Board temperature	77.0469	77.4584	N/A	Celsius
Case heat flux	0.00368821	0.0036583	N/A	W
Case temperature	74.5366	74.9782	N/A	Celsius
Junction temperature	78.2248	78.6365	N/A	Celsius
Summary Part 11				
Board heat flux	0.196417	0.196393	N/A	W
Board temperature	76.8122	77.1279	N/A	Celsius
Case heat flux	0.00358289	0.00360659	N/A	W
Case temperature	74.4079	74.6996	N/A	Celsius
Junction temperature	77.9907	78.3062	N/A	Celsius
Summary Part 12				
Board heat flux	0.195519	0.19544	N/A	W
Board temperature	80.1027	80.4039	N/A	Celsius
Case heat flux	0.00448083	0.00455053	N/A	W
Case temperature	76.7949	77.017	N/A	Celsius
Junction temperature	81.2758	81.5765	N/A	Celsius
Summary Part 1				
Avg temperature	67.7224	68.1489	N/A	Celsius
Max temperature	69.0288	69.3767	N/A	Celsius

6. Select the Results tab, and in the Results Task panel, click (Parts).

7. In the Design Study Bar, select 1_Layer to add the PCB to the Parts dialog box.

- Select the checkbox next to 9 PCB2.
- Click Calculate to see the calculated results, as shown in the following image.

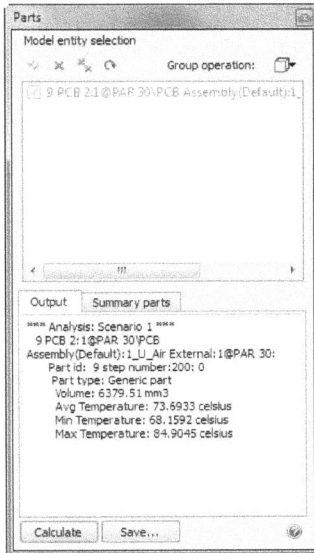

8. In the Parts panel, click $\Sigma^{\ast}$ (Make Summary).

9. Select the Decision Center tab, right-click on the Summary Part 9 in the Summary Values node, and select Update summary values.

- Scroll to the bottom of the parts list and note that the PCB results are added, as shown in the following image.
- Note the higher temperatures for the 36 fin model, compared to the 24 fin model.

Case heat flux	0.00500091	0.00550695	N/A	W
Case temperature	79.5052	79.8537	N/A	Celsius
Junction temperature	85.1062	85.4506	N/A	Celsius
Summary Part 40				
Board heat flux	0.195158	0.195148	N/A	W
Board temperature	80.8746	81.3277	N/A	Celsius
Case heat flux	0.00484202	0.00485168	N/A	W
Case temperature	77.2035	77.6469	N/A	Celsius
Junction temperature	82.0455	82.4986	N/A	Celsius
Summary Part 27				
Board heat flux	0.194433	0.194501	N/A	W
Board temperature	84.6142	84.984	N/A	Celsius
Case heat flux	0.00556701	0.00549864	N/A	W
Case temperature	80.2138	80.6524	N/A	Celsius
Junction temperature	85.7808	86.1511	N/A	Celsius
Summary Part 9				
Avg temperature	73.6933	74.041	N/A	Celsius
Max temperature	84.9045	85.2734	N/A	Celsius
Min temperature	68.1592	68.4948	N/A	Celsius
Volume	6379.51	6379.69	N/A	mm3

10. In analyzing the results, it appears that the temperatures for the 36 fin heat sink are higher than those for the 24 fin heat sink. This is likely due to the decrease in space between fins that occurs when adding additional fins to the model, thereby choking the flow and reducing the convective heat transfer.

This exercise shows the true value of Autodesk CFD. If the 36 fin heat sink was a new design, this analysis saved the cost of prototyping to find out the design, which, although it intuitively seems like it should have been better, is in fact less effective. We have better efficiency with less material, so the cheaper design is thermally better as well.

11. In the Quick Access toolbar, click ▣ (Save) to save the study, model orientations, etc.

Exercise: Analyze the AEC Results Set

In this exercise, you will open an existing design study for a small office lobby. The office has windows and walls that are subject to external conditions, while the interior has air conditioning. The objective in this exercise is to:

- Analyze the scenario using Global and Iso Surface results to assess the temperature.

Open a design study in the Autodesk CFD Environment.

In this task, you will open a design study and review the current setup.

1. Launch Autodesk CFD, if not already running.

2. In the Home tab, click ⬜ (Open). If prompted to save an open design study, click Yes.

3. In the Open dialog box, browse to the *C:\Autodesk CFD 2017 Essentials Exercise Files\Results\Office_Results* folder. Select and open *Office_Results.cfdst*.

4. Select the View tab and click ⬐ ˙ (Axes).
   - Ensure that all axis types are toggled off, as shown in the following image.

Reviewing the Global results.

In this task, you will review the global Temperature and Thermal Comfort Temperature.

1. Select the Results tab.

2. In the Quick Access Toolbar, expand ⬜ ˙ (Visual Style) and select Transparent. Note that the model color reflects the last iteration of the analysis and it displays the Velocity Magnitude result, as shown in the following image.

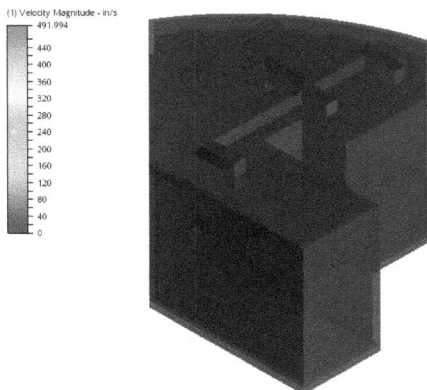

3. Select the View tab and in the View Settings panel, click Apply View. In the *Office_Results* folder, select and open the *Orientation.xvs* file. This loads a saved view orientation.

4. In the Results tab, in the Global panel, in the Global Result drop-down list, select Temperature and in the Global Vector drop-down list, select Velocity Vector.

    ▪ In the Design Study Bar, expand the Wall (solar) and Window (solar) nodes and remove the check mark next to all of the parts to remove them from display.

    ▪ Note the hot spots on the floor that result from the light passing through the windows.

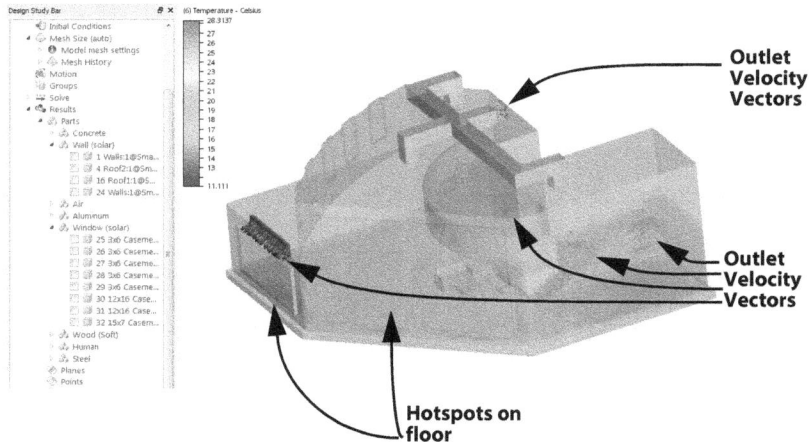

Outlet Velocity Vectors

Outlet Velocity Vectors

Hotspots on floor

5. In the Global panel, in the Global Result drop-down list, select Comfort Temperature and in the Global Vector drop-down list, select Velocity Vector.

    ▪ As you might expect, the comfort temperature gradient shows slightly cooler temperatures in the lower level, relative to the top.

    ▪ Also, near the back of the office where two inlet diffusers are located, the temperature appears at its lowest.

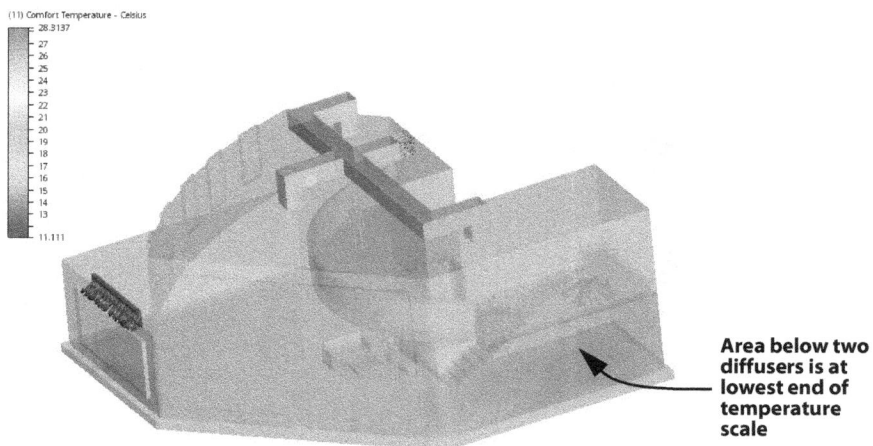

Area below two diffusers is at lowest end of temperature scale

Analyze the Planes Results.

In this task, you will use Planes results to investigate the temperature around the occupants.

1. Select the Results tab and click [icon] (Planes) to activate the Planes panel.

    - In the Planes panel, click [icon] (Add).
    - In the Quick Access Toolbar, expand [icon] (Visual Style) and select Outline.
    - Left-click on the plane and select [icon] (Align to Y Axis) in the mini-toolbar to change the default orientation.
    - Drag the arrow shown in the following image, until the plane intersects the occupant.

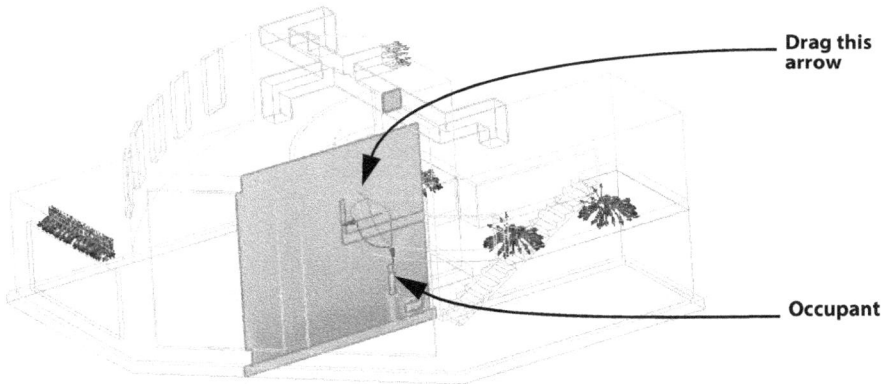

Drag this arrow

Occupant

2. In the ViewCube, select FRONT.

3. Left-click on the plane and click (XY Plot) in the mini-toolbar to open the XY Plot dialog box.

   - In the Title field, type **Lower Level**.
   - Edit the Divisions per segment from 20 to **80**. This will increase the number of data points between the two points you select.
   - Click Add points and select the two points shown in the following image. The two points should be 2-3 feet above the occupant's head. This is the upper bound of the occupied zone.

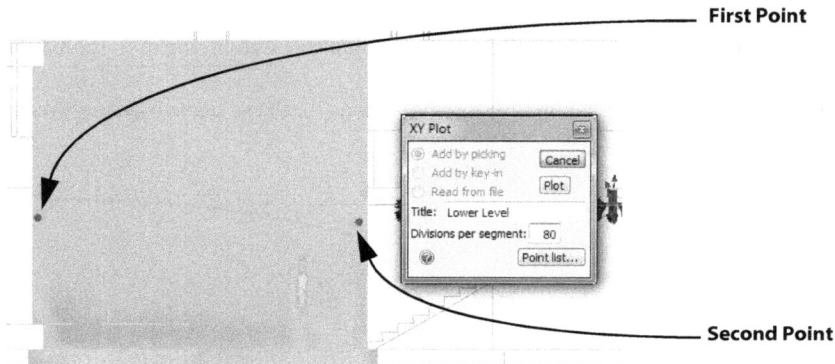

First Point

Second Point

4. In the XY Plot dialog box, click Plot and review the graph of the temperature, as shown in the following image. Your graph may differ depending on exactly where the plane is located and points were selected.

   - Note that the spike is likely due to the occupant's body temperature.
   - Close both XY Plot dialog boxes.

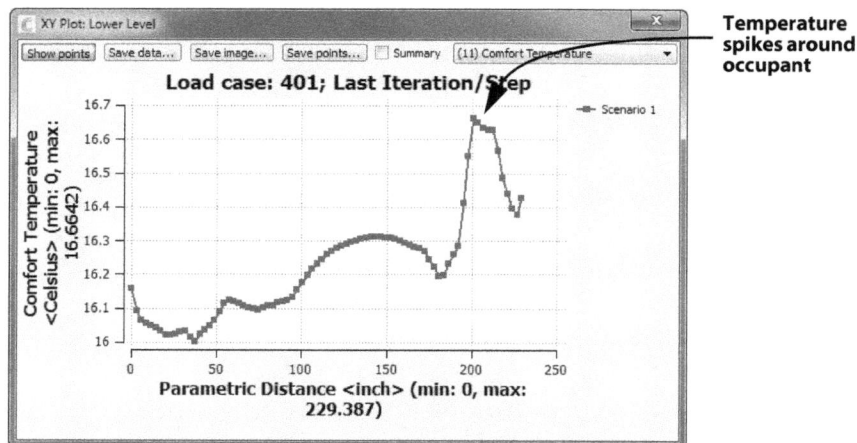

Temperature spikes around occupant

5. In the Design Study Bar, in the Planes node, remove the check mark next to Plane 1 to toggle off its display.

6. In the View Cube, click (Home).

7. In the Planes panel, click ✚ (Add) to add another plane.

- Left-click on the plane and select ⊙ (Align to Y Axis) in the mini-toolbar to change the default orientation.
- Drag the arrow shown in the following image, until the plane intersects the second level occupant.

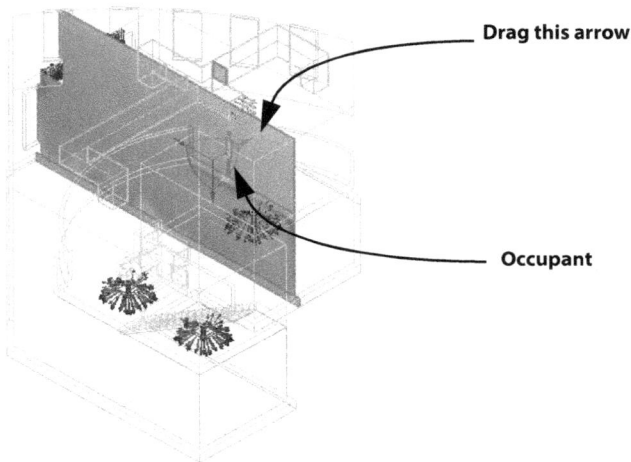

Drag this arrow

Occupant

8. In the ViewCube, select FRONT.

9. Left-click on the plane and click ⬙ (XY Plot) in the mini-toolbar to open the XY Plot dialog box.

- In the Title field, type **Upper Level**.
- The Divisions per segment should still be set to **80** from the previous step.
- Click Add points and select the points shown in the following image.

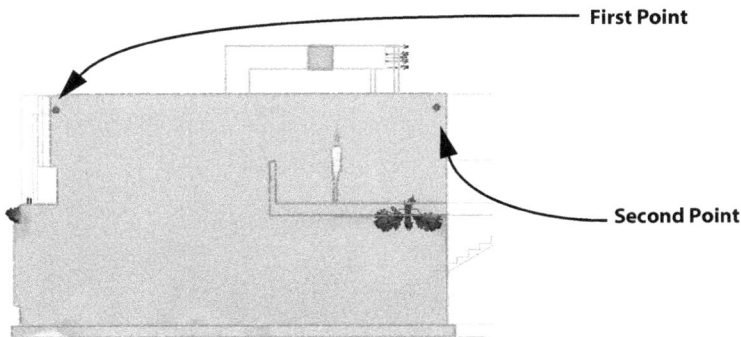

First Point

Second Point

10. In the XY Plot dialog box, click Plot and review the graph of the temperature, as shown in the following image. Your graph may be different depending on exactly where the plane is located and points were selected.

- As you would expect, the temperature in the upper level is higher than the lower level.

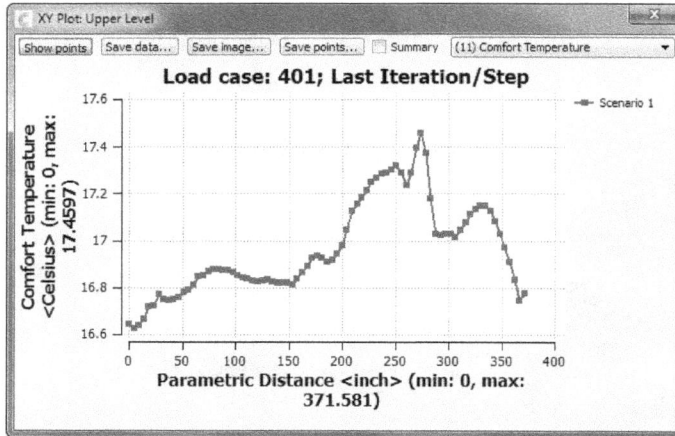

11. Close both XY Plot dialog boxes.

12. In the Design Study Bar, in the Planes node, remove the check mark next to Plane 2 to toggle off its display.

13. In the Quick Access Toolbar, expand ⬜ (Visual Style) and select Transparent.

Analyze the Iso Surfaces Results.

In this task, you will analyze the Iso Volume results, to observe the airflow in the room.

1. In the Results Tasks panel, click ▱ (Iso Surfaces).

2. In the Design Study Bar, in the Parts node, expand the Air and Wood (Soft) nodes and remove the check mark for 33 Volume under Air and all parts under Wood (Soft), to remove them from display.

   ■ Reorient the model as shown in the following image.

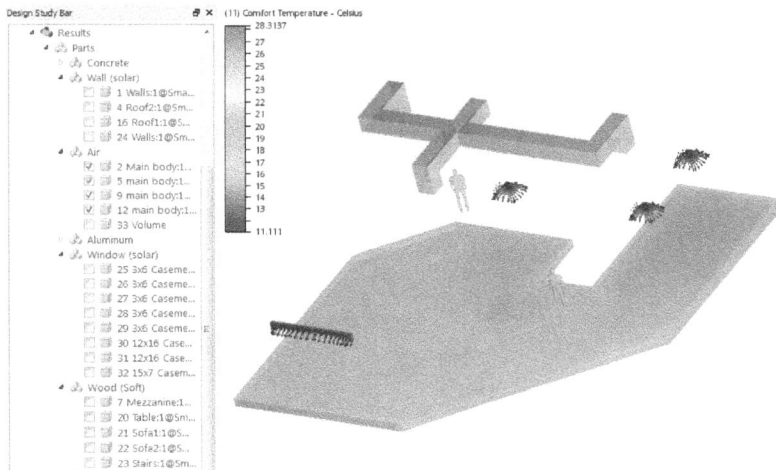

3. In the Iso Surface panel, click ✛ (Add). In the Iso Surface panel, make the following edits:

   ■ In the Quantity drop-down list, select Temperature.
   ■ In the Color By drop-down list, select Temperature.
   ■ In the Vector drop-down list, select Velocity Vector.

4. In the Iso Surface panel, click ✎ (Edit) to open the Iso Surface dialog box, as shown in the following image.

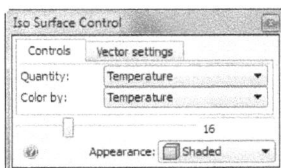

5. In the Iso Surface Control dialog box, in the Appearance drop-down list, select Transparent.

6. In the Iso Surface Control dialog box, select the Vector settings tab and edit the Same Lengths value to **0.25** and the temperature value to **14.5**, as shown in the following image.

   - This creates an iso surface that shows every location where the temperature in the model is 16 degrees Celsius.

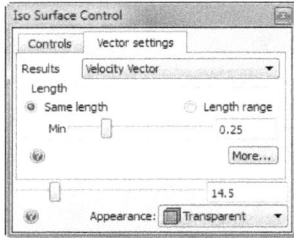

7. The iso surface updates as shown in the following image, indicating locations where the temperature is 14.5 degrees Celsius. As expected, the air closest to the air conditioning diffusers is lower than anywhere else on the model.

8. Edit the temperature to **15** and note that the iso surface updates as shown in the following image.

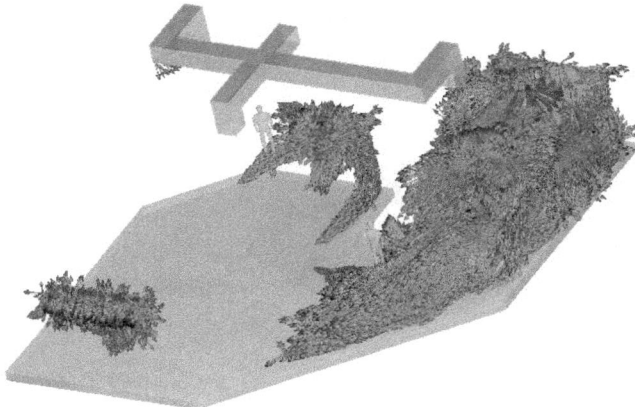

9.   Edit the temperature to **16** and note that the iso surface updates as shown in the following image.

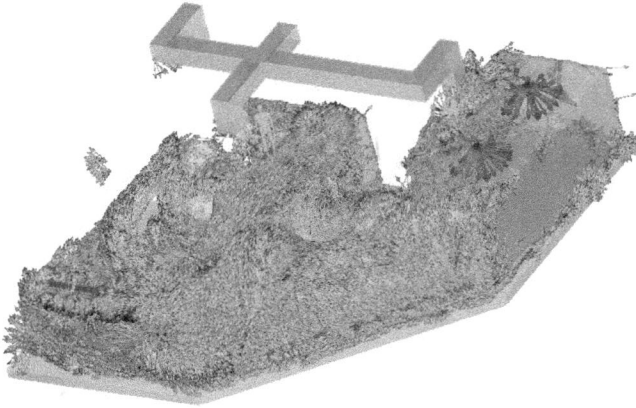

10. In the Quick Access toolbar, click ⊟ (Save) to save the study, model orientations, etc.

Validation Checklist

A simulation is only useful when the results can be trusted. A highly recommended final step in the Autodesk® CFD workflow is to validate the results to ensure that they are realistic. This chapter identifies several checks that you should consider before accepting results in Autodesk CFD.

Objectives

After completing this chapter, you will be able to:

- Identify the checks required to validate your Autodesk CFD simulation results.

Lesson: Validating Your Simulation

To ensure you have acceptable results, you should validate your simulation results with some fundamental checks.

Objectives

After completing this lesson, you will be able to:

- Identify the checks required to validate your Autodesk CFD simulation results.

Verifying Your Simulation

Before drawing final conclusions from any results in Autodesk CFD, you must first validate them. Even if physical test results are not available for benchmarking, the following checklist of validation considerations will provide increased confidence in the solution.

Check Inputs

A common issue with simulations is that, even for experienced users, a missed decimal point, wrong units or a mistake in assigning materials, will produce poor results. Input items to check include:

- CAD Geometry
- Material assignments
- Boundary conditions
- Solver settings

In the Autodesk CFD Setup tab, the Design Study Bar is useful in quickly scanning all of the materials and boundary conditions.

The Design Study Bar, as shown in the following image, provides a convenient format to check material assignments along with the units and values used for the boundary conditions.

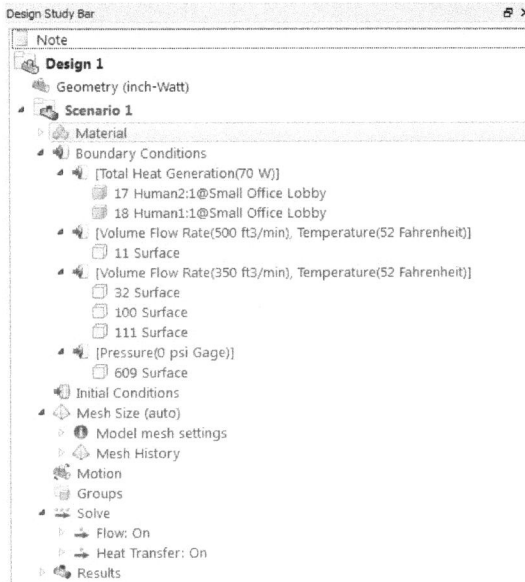

Another technique for validating correct inputs is checking the results to ensure that the solver has interpreted your intentions correctly. Two examples are described as follows:

- External flow simulated for a building at an altitude of 5,000 feet and ambient temperature of 32F should result in a density of 1.073 Kg/m^3 according to published air tables. In Results, set the Global Results to Density to verify that the air density is correct.

- Flow rates are specified for an HVAC system at 100 CFM at each duct inlet to a large factory. You can add a Plane oriented normal with the flow path and use the Bulk Calculator to verify the assigned flow rate.

> **Tip**
>
> The Summary File is very useful in spotting potential issues as it provides a very concise listing of the operating conditions of the model. An example is shown in the following image.
>

Mesh

A poor quality mesh can provide misleading results. If there are any doubts about the mesh, clone the scenario, add mesh refinement, and run the analysis again to verify that the results do not change considerably.

Convergence

During the early stages of convergence, the results change substantially while the solution is being completed. Interpreting results too early and terminating the solution prematurely can lead to incorrect conclusions. Check the convergence monitor in the Output bar to ensure that the results are not changing more than 3% over the last 10-20% of the iteration steps. If any doubt persists, restart the simulation and run for another 100 or 200 steps and then check again. Simulations with poor convergence behavior usually indicate poor mesh quality, incorrect boundary conditions, or less than ideal solver settings.

Hand Calculations

Although closed form solutions are typically limited by underlying assumptions, they are still a very useful means of validating overall simulation results. It is highly recommended to have fluid flow and heat transfer references available, such as Fluid Mechanics by Frank White, as a benchmark.

Test Models

At times, correct simulation results may not seem intuitive at first. Even after going through the previous checks, the results may not be fully explained. In these cases, separate test models may prove beneficial. For example, a sub-model isolating the area in question, can be quickly simulated to confirm the results.

Consider the model shown in the following image. A sub-model (as shown on the right) can be used to quickly validate results in an isolated area of the overall design model (as shown on the left).

Overall Design Model   **Isolated Sub-Model**

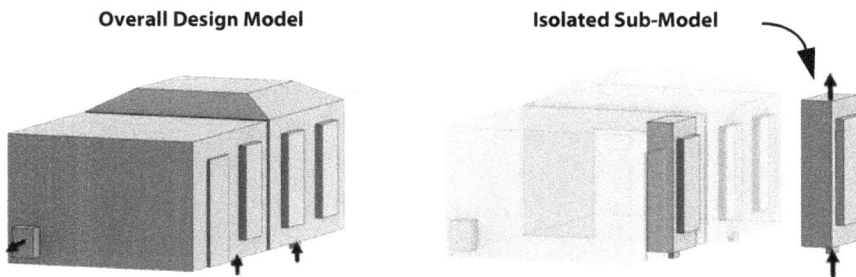

Additional Resources

Use the following additional resources to find more information on Autodesk CFD:

- Access help:
    - http://help.autodesk.com/view/SCDSE/2017/ENU/
- Access the Autodesk Knowledge Network:
    - https://knowledge.autodesk.com/support/cfd/troubleshooting#?sort=score
- Contact Autodesk through the accounts page:
    - https://accounts.autodesk.com/

Now that you have completed this course, you have all of the required skills to set up, solve, interpret and validate an analysis. Proceed with caution but also with confidence as you incorporate your new skills into your design and analysis practice.

www.ingramcontent.com/pod-product-compliance
Lightning Source LLC
Chambersburg PA
CBHW080659220326
41598CB00033B/5265